Discourse Anal

This introductory textbook presents a variety of approaches and perspectives that can be employed to analyze any sample of discourse. The perspectives come from multiple disciplines, including linguistics, sociolinguistics, and linguistic anthropology, all of which shed light on meaning and the interactional construction of meaning through language use. Students without prior experience in discourse analysis will appreciate and understand the micro-macro relationship of language use in everyday contexts, in professional and academic settings, in languages other than English, and in a wide variety of media outlets.

Each chapter is supported by examples of spoken and written discourse from various types of data sources, including conversations, commercials, university lectures, textbooks, print ads, and blogs, and concludes with hands-on opportunities for readers to actually do discourse analysis on their own. Students and instructors can also utilize the book's comprehensive companion website, with flash cards for key terms, slides, additional data samples, for in-class activities and self-study.

With its accessible multi-disciplinary approach and comprehensive data samples from a variety of sources, *Discourse Analysis* is the ideal core text for the discourse analysis course in applied linguistics, English, education, and communication programs.

Susan Strauss is Associate Professor of Applied Linguistics at Penn State University.

Parastou Feiz is Associate Professor in the Department of English at California State University—San Bernardino.

IMAGE CREDITS FOR THE PAPERBACK COVER

"Minneapolis, Minnesota. Ruth and Caren Brink telephone a friend to talk about a party to which they are all going." Jack Delano, March 1942. (Credit: Library of Congress, Prints & Photographs Division, FSA/OWI Collection, [LC-USW3-000987-D])

"Bill Tatnall, half-length portrait, seated, facing left, playing guitar, Frederica, Georgia." Alan Lomax, June 1935. (Credit: Library of Congress, Prints & Photographs Division, Lomax Collection, [LC-DIG-ppmsc-00364])

"On board the fishing boat Alden out of Gloucester, Massachusetts. Frank Mineo, owner and skipper, shouting orders to his crew." Gordon Parks, June 1943. (Credit: Library of Congress, Prints & Photographs Division, FSA/OWI Collection, [LC-USW3-031269-E]).

"Tom Collins, manager of Kern migrant camp, talking with one of the members. California." Dorothea Lange, November 1936. (Credit: Library of Congress, Prints & Photographs Division, FSA/OWI Collection, [LC-USF34-009876-C]).

"Oregon, Klamath County, Merrill. Young woman from a South Dakota farm, where her family still lives." She and her husband are migratory laborers and live in a shack in Klamath County waiting for potato harvest to open. "My husband just day labors." Dorothea Lange, August 1939. (Credit: Library of Congress, Prints & Photographs Division, FSA/OWI Collection, [LC-USF34-020721-E]).

"Children at Sunday school class, Manzanar Relocation Center, California." Ansel Adams, 1943. (Credit: Library of Congress Prints and Photographs Division, Ansel Adams's Photographs of Japanese-American Internment at Manzanar, [LC-DIG-ppprs-00347])

"African American boy selling The Washington Daily News—sign on his hat reads, 'Have you read The News? One cent'—headline reads 'Millionaire tax rends G.O.P.'" (Credit: Library of Congress Prints and Photographs Division, National Photo Company Collection [LC-USZ62-69050]).

Discourse Analysis
Putting our Worlds into Words

Susan Strauss and Parastou Feiz

Penn State University and California State University San Bernardino

Routledge
Taylor & Francis Group

NEW YORK AND LONDON

First published 2014
by Routledge
711 Third Avenue, New York, NY 10017

and by Routledge
2 Park Square, Milton Park, Abingdon, Oxon OX14 4RN

Routledge is an imprint of the Taylor & Francis Group, an informa business

© 2014 Taylor & Francis

The right of Susan Strauss and Parastou Feiz to be identified as authors of this work has been asserted by them in accordance with sections 77 and 78 of the Copyright, Designs and Patents Act 1988.

Library of Congress Cataloging-in-Publication Data

Strauss, Susan G.
  Discourse analysis : putting our worlds into words / Susan Strauss, Penn State University and Parastou Feiz, California State University — San Bernadino.
    pages cm.
  1. Discourse analysis—Textbooks.   2. Discourse analysis—Problems, exercises, etc.   I. Feiz, Parastou, author.   II. Title.
  P302.S733   2013
  401'.41—dc23   2013024239

ISBN: 978-0-415-52218-2 (hbk)
ISBN: 978-0-415-52219-9 (pbk)
ISBN: 978-0-203-12155-9 (ebk)

Typeset in Helvetica Neue and Optima
by Apex CoVantage, LLC

Printed and bound in the United States of America
by Edwards Brothers Malloy, Inc.

Contents

Preface and Acknowledgments

This is a book on discourse. It is a book that introduces a number of approaches to the analysis of discourse. It reflects the ways in which the two of us teach courses on discourse analysis in our respective universities. Our courses are populated with students whose areas of specialization have ranged from English and applied linguistics to business; communication; media studies; anthropology; recreation, park, and tourism management; Asian studies; Russian; French; German; Spanish, Italian, and Portuguese; science education; math education; literature; composition studies; creative writing; and early childhood education. We provide a collection of perspectives and tools that users of this book might employ in their own work involving the analysis of discourse. We subscribe to no one individual theory about discourse. We address various theories in the individual chapters, and leave open the application of other theories from multiple disciplines that most adequately account for the discursive phenomena under investigation.

We have chosen the title *Discourse Analysis: Putting our Worlds into Words* as the most succinct encapsulation of the processes of discourse and discourse analysis, where "worlds" refers to overlapping spheres of experience, perception, and communication and "words" refers to the multivariate ways in which we express those ideas, perspectives, and perceptions: both the said and the unsaid; the explicit and the implicit; the word, the gesture, or both.

As we hope to have shown throughout these chapters, words create worlds and worlds create words—and stances and identities are shaped and re-shaped, reflected and reified in the words and worlds of discourse.

We gratefully acknowledge the following individuals who helped us put this volume together: the students in our discourse analysis courses over the years at both of our universities; Derron Bishop, who read early versions of Chapters 2 through 6 and offered invaluable comments that we incorporated into the current version of the book; Xuehua Xiang, who read Chapters 2 and 3 and provided comments on those and who also provided us with sample discourse data for Chinese; Yumi Matsumoto, who gave us input on Japanese examples and provided one of her personal photographs taken in Japan, and Jongoh Eun for supplying us with some of the Korean examples. We thank Brian Goldfarb, our friend and colleague, who gave us the best support friends and colleagues could ever ask for, including his creative suggestions for the book cover. As for data excerpts, a small number of examples and some data presented in this book were written and collected for projects conducted by the Center for Advanced Language Proficiency Education and Research (CALPER) at the Pennsylvania State University under grants from the U.S. Department of Education. And we thank the staff at Routledge/Taylor and Francis for their support and input at every stage of this process, especially Ivy Ip, Leah Babb-Rosenfeld, Elysse Preposi, Denise File, and the production team.

Susan thanks her children Tenaye, Mihret, Adanech, Biniyam, Bereket, and Terefech for their patience and enthusiasm and infinite curiosity about words and worlds and meanings. Their love kept this process moving, from the first word we put on paper until the very last. She also thanks Noriko Akatsuka for introducing her to the field of linguistics, and now for being an adoring adoptive grandma to her six children. This book is dedicated to them and to the memory of Susan's loving mother, Beatrice Eleanor Strauss, who courageously fought brain cancer during the early days of her professional academic career. Susan also thanks her father, David Strauss, and her sister, Beryl Strauss, for being there when she needed them.

Parastou thanks her husband, Brian Goldfarb, for his unbending support, the inspiring conversations, and invaluable input throughout the process of writing this book. She is also grateful to her mother, Jaleh, for her love and consistent encouragement, and to her aunt Monir and brother, Ali, for always being there. This book is also dedicated to Parastou's father, Bahram Feiz, who was the first person who inspired her to think about the power of words.

CHAPTER ONE

Introduction

Discourse, Words, and the World

> Through language we shape our own relation to a socially organized lifeworld, one where the verbal calibration of diverse perceptions becomes part of the negotiation of ongoing social life . . . The word disrupts the world: Nothing in the lifeworld remains the same once language is invoked. (Du Bois 2011b).

LANGUAGE AND DISCOURSE

It is not an overstatement to assert that some form of language occupies nearly every moment of our waking lives: letters, words, sentences, signs, symbols, and thoughts—printed, spoken, computer-generated, flashed on screen, finger-spelled, imagined, and recalled. By and through language, we

---

DISCOURSE is the social and cognitive process of putting the world into words, of transforming our perceptions, experiences, emotions, understandings, and desires into a common medium for expression and communication, through language and other semiotic resources. Such semiotic resources include gestures, eye gaze, vocal intonations, and interactional gaps of silence; they include color and shape and imagery; and all elements of expression and communication that accompany our words and ideas—or that replace them, complement them, contrast them, or situate them in contexts. **Discourse** is the **social and cognitive process** that reflects, creates, shapes, re-creates, and reifies meaning in the lifeworld.

---

connect with some people, and put others off. We praise and complain, argue, agree, exaggerate, and downplay. By using language and *not* using language, we empathize and we ignore. We can be exuberant or caring or impassive.

We are constantly surrounded by and immersed in language. Our lives are jam-packed with language in its multiple forms, accompanied by the myriad semiotic resources that combine to shape language into discourse. (Coulthard, 1985).

Language is the very stuff that our daily communications are made of. It so completely fills our lives that we typically pay little attention to it; we may even take it for granted. On the surface, everyday language is commonsensical; it is there and we use it—to exchange ideas, to express desires, to take stands, to imagine, to create, and to understand. It is the very essence of what makes us human.

When some aspect of a communicative activity goes wonderfully right or woefully wrong, we find ourselves reviewing language, rewinding and playing back what we've heard or rereading what we've read, just to see why.

However, it's not the *language* that we're attending to when we notice words and phrases and tones of voice and attitudes. It is not the language itself that moves us or angers us or inspires us to act (or react). It is the *discourse.*

Discourse is the social and cognitive process of putting the world into words, of transforming our perceptions, experiences, emotions, understandings, and desires into a common medium for expression and communication, through language and other semiotic media. Discourse is more than letters and words, appearing one at a time or strung together, reflecting bits of thought and bits of meaning. Discourse is the composite process whereby elements of language combine with other elements of semiosis, like gestures, eye gaze, fluctuations in voice—rhythm, intonation, rate of speech, and spates of silence. It includes color and shape and imagery. Discourse is visual and aural; it is creative and musical—an entire system of social semiotics with its own patterns similar to the patterns of grammar in language (e.g., Hodge and Kress,1988, 1993, 2010; Kress and van Leeuwen, 2001, 2006).

Discourse includes "all forms of meaningful semiotic human activity, seen in connection with social, cultural and historical patterns and development of use." (Blommaert, 2005: 3). Discourse "reaches out further than language itself in the forms as well as meanings that can be the focus of analysis" (Jaworski and Coupland, 2006: 6). Discourse is language "recruited 'on site' to enact specific social activities and social identities" (Gee, 2005: 1). "Discourses[1] are ideas as well as ways of talking that influence and are influenced by the ideas" (Johnstone, 2008: 3).

It is no wonder that the study of discourse has become key to a range of disciplines across the social sciences (communication, anthropology, sociology, political science, psychology, education, ethnic studies), humanities (gender studies, literature, history, composition, languages, media studies, arts and architecture), and sciences (geography, medicine, engineering).

Discourse: Putting the World Into Words

Expressing an emotion, depicting an event, labeling an object, locating a point in space—all involve choice. We choose words from among other possible words, or we invent one if our bank of existing words is insufficient. We use our limited repertoire of words, expressions, and symbols, and our even more limited patterns of grammar to "verbally calibrate" (Du Bois, 2011b), to express what we *mean*, in explicit terms or through gesture or drawing or implicature. And each and every time we do, we reveal something about how we perceive the world, we understand something about how others perceive it, and we guide others to see the world in various ways.

As Harris (1983: ix) notes in the introduction to his translation of Saussure's *Cours de linguistique générale*, "[w]ords are not vocal labels which have come to be attached to things and qualities already given in advance by Nature, or to ideas already grasped independently by the human mind. On the contrary languages themselves, collective products of social interaction, supply the essential conceptual frameworks for men's analysis of reality and, simultaneously, the verbal equipment for their description of it. The concepts we use are creations of the language we speak."

* * *

Nothing in discourse is neutral. Each and every instance of discourse is imbued with some element of stance; it is motivated by a perspective.

Stance in discourse is one primary area of focus in this book. We define stance in the following way.

This book is about discourse. It is about the reflection, creation, shaping, re-creation, and reification of meaning in situated contexts. It is about locating and understanding meaning through various analytic lenses and using a variety of units of analysis: grammar and grammatical units, genre and generic structure, register, reference, deixis, information structure and intonation units, conversation analysis, conversational implicature, speech acts, politeness, face threatening acts, indexicality, identity, and the social construction of ideology and power.

> **STANCE** is the **speaker's or writer's feeling, attitude, perspective, or position as enacted in discourse.** *Stance-taking* is an inevitable consequence of participating in and producing discourse, of putting the world into words. Stance emerges in a speaker's or writer's choice of one linguistic form over another, the coloring of utterances with prosodic contours or punctuation, the sequential ordering of utterances; it emerges in gestures, silences, hesitations, hedges, and in overlapping stretches of talk. In all of these instances of discourse (and others), a speaker's or writer's stance is enacted and created; it is negotiated and re-negotiated.

* * *

We provide a number of theoretical and methodological approaches to the analysis of discourse and texts,[2] where micro-level instances of language and discourse combine to create, reflect, and shape the broader, macro-levels of meaning. The chapters in this book are systematically organized, with many common threads running through them. Each presents a theoretical and methodological overview of a number of approaches commonly used in discourse analytic research. Each includes excerpts of actual discourse, culled from face-to-face interactions, television (talk shows, dramas, sitcoms, weather, commercials), film, textbooks, cookbooks, magazines, print ads, and websites, to illustrate the concepts and methodologies presented. Each chapter includes sample analyses of these and other data excerpts, together with exercises and follow-up questions to encourage readers to probe well beyond the information provided. Each chapter also includes data excerpts from other languages, for readers interested in applying concepts from the English-based examples to other languages.

The chapters are organized as follows:

Chapter 2: The Building Blocks of Language: The Stuff That Discourse Is Made Of

Chapter 2 takes a basic cognitive approach to *grammar*, presenting it as a fluid and dynamic system of essential structure—a structure that is driven by conceptual imagery and choice. Nouns, or ways of naming entities and ideas, reflect conceptual schemas in terms of individuation or agglomeration, singularity or plurality, degrees of concreteness or abstractness. The noun *snow* typically denotes a mass of frozen precipitation, as it falls or as it has covered the ground. Pluralized, *snows* refers to repeated *cycles of snowfall.* In grammar and in discourse, a simple *-s* at the end of the word makes a conceptual difference. It reflects perception. It reflects *stance. Verbs* like *suffer* verses *experience* or *undergo* convey differing points of views of events and the entities involved in them. Adjectives like *classic* and *signature* and adverbs like *now* or *more than ever* underscore qualities of things and time frames for events, drawing attention to some elements in the discourse and eclipsing others. Grammar and discourse and stance are inextricably related. One cannot be analyzed without the other.

Chapter 3: Genre, Modality, Register, and Participation Framework

The chapter introduces genre as social practice, as a metaphorical, socioculturally shaped frame of discourse that provides basic structure with permeable boundaries to communicate essential content within a context and for a particular purpose. Recipes are discursive genres, as are narratives, sermons, lectures, and comedic monologues. Genres vary. Modalities (spoken, written, electronic, and hybrid) vary. Registers of discourse range from the everyday to the technical. Participation frameworks provide perspectives for participant roles like speakers, hearers, overhearers, and audiences. And with each variation and with each shift, the discourse changes—at times in blatantly obvious ways, and at times only subtly. The chapter provides these and other frames of reference that are crucial to the analysis of discourse.

Chapter 4: Reference, Deixis, and Stance

Reference involves designating things, ideas, entities, and people by picking them out with words and sometimes gestures. How we "refer" to things involves choice: How important is the entity to the speaker or writer? How specifically does it need to be designated? Is quantity relevant to referential choice? Is specificity? How much attention is the hearer or reader guided to pay to this referent? Such linguistic choices (with occasional gestures) pervade all of discourse. The chapter provides detailed discussion concerning how instances of reference pattern within discourse. We discuss socio-cognitive motivations underlying the range of meanings of possible markers of referential choice.

Chapter 5: Information Structure, Cohesion, and Intonation Units

The frameworks of information structure, cohesion, and intonation units provide insights into the ways in which topics, persons, ideas, memories, and events are introduced into the discourse and then developed. The chapter discusses the notion of "consciousness" from the point of view of givenness and newness of information—essentially, assumptions that producers of discourse make concerning the ability of discourse recipients to follow and process. The chapter shines light on the various ways in which language-in-interaction converts an individual's personal experience and perception into a common communicative medium.

Chapter 6: Conversation

The analytic focus of discourse in this chapter shifts to talk-in-interaction, the mutually achieved understanding between and among participants in naturally occurring conversation. The chapter provides a detailed overview of Conversation Analysis (CA), pointing out mechanisms underlying turns-at-talk, including the mechanisms of turn construction, turn organization, turn sequencing, and speaker change. What is of prime importance in a CA-based analysis is the micro-second by micro-second orientations of conversational participants to talk as it emerges in interaction, rather than the general notion of "context" (e.g., where the talk takes place, who the interactants are, their relationship histories, etc.).

Chapter 7: Pragmatics—Implicature, Speech Act Theory, and Politeness

In contrast with Conversation Analysis, context is key to the study of pragmatics and to all fields related to it. Pragmatics is the area of linguistic and socio-linguistic study that is concerned with the ways in which speakers/hearers and writers/readers create and derive meaning from non-literal interpretations of spoken, written, electronic, and hybrid discourse. From this perspective, implicature and inference drive meaning making and interaction. The chapter presents various approaches to and applications of conversational implicature, speech act theory, and politeness, with some discussion of pragmatics across cultures.

Chapter 8: Indexicality, Stance, Identity, and Agency

Chapter 8 examines pragmatic meaning from the perspective of indexicality. Rooted in semiotics, where meaning derives from the combined elements of signs, symbols, and context, an indexicality-centered approach to discourse analysis provides keen insights into the cognitive and social construction of stance (e.g., affective, epistemic, moral, elitist). The chapter presents an overview of indexicality, from a deictic and referential perspective, followed by in-depth discussion of indexicality as the patterned, context-dependent connections of linguistic forms to meanings evoking abstract concepts of personal and social identity, gender, agency, power, authority, entitlement, emotion, elitism, resistance, aesthetics, morality, responsibility, imagination, freedom, and so forth—all elements of communication and interaction that pervade our daily lives and existence.

Chapter 9: Critical Discourse Analysis

Chapter 9 presents the broad, interdisciplinary methodological approach to language and society with the central view of *discourse as social practice*. The chapter presents CDA and its goal of uncovering patterns of discourse through which ideologies are shaped, communicated, and propagated—ideologies that involve hidden dimensions of power, control, injustice, and inequity. These are "hidden" because they are normalized and naturalized, often packaged in discourse as common-sense assumptions of social reality and the "truth." The chapter presents basic approaches to analysis by three foundational scholars (Fairclough, van Dijk, and Wodak) and concludes with data excerpts for readers to analyze on the basis of these three (and other) approaches.

In short, no instance of discourse is value-free or stance neutral. Speakers and writers make choices—sometimes consciously, yet more often not: Choices of words, grammatical constructions, prosodic fluctuations, gestures, grimaces, head nods, eye gaze, colors and images—all combine to form the social and cognitive processes and products of discourse.

* * *

This book represents our views on discourse and the ways in which we teach Discourse Analysis in our own classes. The book is informed by work in multiple disciplines by scholars and discourse analysts who have influenced our ways of thinking and have forever changed our ways of seeing. Most of these scholars are cited here. We owe a debt of thanks to them and to our former teachers who first ignited our interests in language and discourse. Those interests are now never-ending passions.

The book is designed for the non-linguist in fields such as business and marketing, communication, psychology, health and human development, sociology, history, education, literature, medicine, and law. It may prove useful to the linguistics specialists in all related fields of study, e.g., applied linguistics, psycholinguistics, sociolinguistics, and communicative disorders. We hope, too, that it will be of interest to anyone in any field who is curious about language and discourse and how discourse both shapes the world and is shaped by it.

In thinking about language, cognition, and social interaction, we must strive for the analytic over the superficially descriptive. For in language and discourse, as in life, what is on the surface typically reflects a mere fragment of what lies below. An utterance is not an utterance on its own; its meaning derives from a systematic, contextually situated whole. We hope to provide some guidance to readers of this book to uncover those systems, to make sense of the parts that comprise the wholes, and to "see" the world in new and compelling ways.

NOTES

1. See Gee (2010) and Johnstone (2008) for discussions and underlying meanings of *discourse* as a "mass noun" and its use in the plural form, i.e., *discourses*, as a "count noun." In this book, we use the term *discourse* to refer to processes, as discussed above, as well as the outcomes and products of such processes.
2. We use the term *text* in the sense of representation of discourse for the purpose of analysis. This may mean spoken discourse (transcribed or not), written discourse, visuals, graphics, and so forth. See Blommaert (2005); Chafe (1992); Fairclough (1995a, 1995b, 2003); Widdowson (2004); and others for more perspectives on "text."

CHAPTER TWO

The Building Blocks of Language

The Stuff That Discourse Is Made Of

> Views of grammar are critically dependent on assumptions made about semantics. In particular, the autonomy of grammar appears self-evident given the prevalent assumption that meanings consist of truth conditions. The meaningfulness of grammatical elements becomes apparent only by adopting a conceptualist semantics that properly accommodates our ability to conceive and portray the same objective situation in alternate ways. The term *conceptualization* (emphasis original) is interpreted broadly as embracing any kind of mental experience. It subsumes (a) both established and novel conceptions, (b) not only abstract or intellectual "concepts" but also sensory, motor, and emotive experience, (c) conceptions that are not instantaneous but change or unfold through processing time; and (d) full apprehension of the physical, social, cultural, and linguistic context. Thus, far from being either static or solipsistic, conceptualization is viewed as the dynamic activity of embodied minds interacting with their environment. (Langacker, 1998: 3)

LANGUAGE, DISCOURSE, AND MEANING

Discourse analysts need not be linguists. In fact, many are not. However, informed research on language, from communication studies to business, from science education to media studies, should be grounded in a fundamental understanding of language and the linguistic building blocks that combine to create meaningful expressions of experience and perception—all of which enable us to communicate ideas, establish positions, chat, tell stories, convince, dissuade, complain, wield power, exert domination, and rise up against it.

Every element of language that comprises discourse is imbued with *meaning* beyond what we know as "literal meaning."

In discourse, words don't exist as individual, discrete entities. They are not simply labels for us to identify and name things or to describe actions. Discourse necessarily involves words and grammar and other features of language[1] whose meanings are inextricably linked to our experiences, our cultures, our situated contexts and conventions of practice, and, by definition, to some form of prior discourse. In discourse, words combine with other words and parts of words, such that all elements of language express *meaning* well beyond literal meaning and well beyond structure-based meaning.

LANGUAGE AND GRAMMAR: THE CREATION OF MEANING

In the sections that follow, we will elaborate on this discussion of words, meaning, and structure. We'll use the term *grammar* to introduce some of the more basic categories of language and to introduce a repertoire of elementary terms that will aid us in our work in analyzing discourse. We begin the discussion with a brief look at how some linguists view *grammar as structure*, governed in whole or in part by rules of syntax. We will then move to a more pliable view of grammar as a socio-cultural-cognitive system of language — an approach to grammar that is essential to the analysis of how people use language in everyday life to communicate, invent, solve problems, and daydream.

Formalist Approaches to Grammar: Form Is Independent of Meaning

For some linguists, grammar and grammatical rules exist independently of the meaning and function of utterances. In this paradigm, grammar consists of an autonomous system of abstract, mathematical rules that generate acceptable or grammatical strings of words that can account for syntactic constructions of all languages of the world. Such rules allow humans to compose an infinite number of sentences from a severely limited number of possible linguistic categories. The purpose of linguistic analysis here is to uncover abstract syntactic rules in a systematic and scientific way. What constitutes linguistic *data* is the syntactically "correct" example. Sample sentences are invented by linguistics to illustrate target grammatical phenomena.

The Primacy of Syntax

Let's analyze two classic example sentences that permeate the early literature embracing the primacy-of-syntax view of grammar. The focus here is on structure, essentially concerning how subjects, verbs, and objects (if required), combine in English to express a coherent thought:

(1) <u>The farmer</u> **kills** the duckling. (Sapir, 1921/2011: 86)
(2) <u>Colorless green ideas</u> **sleep** furiously. (Chomsky, 1957)

With just a cursory reading, one can immediately identify the part of each sentence commonly known as the verb. The verbs in (1) and (2) have been highlighted with boldface type to help them stand out (*kills, sleep*). One can also identify the subject of each sentence (*The farmer, Colorless green ideas*); these sentential subjects have been underlined in the sentences, also to help them stand out. Beyond the subject and verb, one might sense that the syntax in (1) would not be complete without knowing whose or what type of life is taken by the farmer.[2] Thus, the words, "the duckling," functioning here as the direct object, completes both the grammar and the thought, serving to answer the question: *What or whom does the farmer kill?*

Because of the type of verb used in (2), "sleep," there is no further information necessary to process the syntax. Instead, what follows the verb in this sentence is an adverb, the function of which is to add detail to the action expressed by the verb, thus answering the question: *How do colorless green ideas sleep?* Furiously.

Now, it is well known that there is little (if any) discernible literal meaning to the sentence in (2). In fact, it was initially composed for this very reason, i.e., to illustrate that a sentence can be grammatically acceptable in form, independent of meaning (Chomsky, 1957). The two adjectives, colorless and green, are designedly contradictory. And ideas cannot sleep—furiously, soundly, or otherwise. Yet, the syntax doesn't jar us. It doesn't make us think twice or shake our heads in confusion.

To carry the notion of the primacy of syntax one step further, have a look at example (3), from Pinker (1994: 208).[3] Yes, this *is* a sentence. It has a subject and a verb and even a direct object of that verb.

(3) <u>Buffalo buffalo</u> **buffalo** Buffalo buffalo.

As we did with examples (1) and (2), we have again highlighted the verb using boldface type and underlined the words that comprise the subject of the sentence. Where a version of the word appears with an initial upper case B

(Buffalo), it refers to a city in New York State. Thus, the first two words, "Buffalo buffalo," as the sentential subject, designate some indeterminate group of bison from Buffalo, New York, just as Buffalo museums would refer to the museums of the city of Buffalo. The third word is the verb "buffalo," meaning "to bewilder, baffle, or bully." And finally, the last two instances, identical in form as the initial two, Buffalo buffalo, serve as the direct object of the verb "to buffalo." Q: *What or whom do Buffalo buffalo **buffalo?*** A: Buffalo buffalo. There is a certain degree of reflexivity[4] here. That is, the subject and object have the same form and designate members of all one group—the Buffalo buffalo do something to their own kind (in other words, Buffalo [adj.] buffalo [noun] bully [verb] themselves [direct object—reflexive]). These additional examples work much in the same way:

(4) <u>Bear</u> **bear** bear.   (Ursae tolerate ursae.)
(5) <u>Fox</u> **fox** fox.   (Vulpae deceive vulpae.)

While the meanings of (3), (4), and (5) border on the nonsensical, it is still possible to extract the intent of each complete string of words. As we attempt to process the whole of the message, we find ourselves breaking down the words into grammatical categories or word classes, striving to locate the verb, to identify the subject, to determine whether a direct object might be needed, and if so, to find it.

Such formalist approaches to language and linguistic analysis (including Generative Grammar[5]) are grounded in structure and specific sets of universal rules that allow for certain word combinations (grammatical utterances) and disallow others (ungrammatical utterances). Form takes precedence. Meaning rests at the level of each individual word filling a particular slot for a particular category of grammar (e.g., Noun Phrase (NP) subject + Verb Phrase (VP)). In primacy-of-syntax views of grammar, form and structure remain uninfluenced by conceptual meaning, farmers kill ducklings, ideas sleep, and foxes outfox their own kind. Formalist approaches to language and linguistic structure are concerned with the sets of rules for how humans create grammatically possible utterances. Syntax (i.e. focusing on structure and how words string together in language) and semantics (i.e., focusing on individual word meaning) are independent domains of inquiry.

Other Approaches to Grammar: Form and Meaning Are Inextricably Connected

Other views of language consider grammar as an integral part of any communicative process, from the ever-silent realm of an individual's inner speech and self-directed private speech (Vygotsky, 1968), to all forms of socially grounded communication in any modality—be it spoken or written; mediated graphically, digitally, or electronically; or any one of the possible hybridized combinations thereof. Though varied and diverse in their approaches and foci of analysis, these linguists share the belief that grammar is not an autonomous aspect of the human mind that works independently from meaning and function. Tomasello (1998) refers to this group of linguists as "cognitive-functional linguists" (p. xi) and describes their general approach to linguistics as follows:

> Indeed, because they take a more psychological approach to human linguistic competence, cognitive and functional linguists do not accept the distinction between syntax and semantics as it is characterized by Generative Grammar. To these linguists [i.e., cognitive-functional], all language structures are symbolic instruments that serve to convey meaning, from the smallest morpheme to the most complex structures. (p. xi)

Another major difference between cognitive-functional approaches to language, grammar, and discourse, and the more formalist ones, concerns the notion of *choice*. That is, speakers and writers and texters and bloggers *do* follow rules of syntax. Of course they do. But when we speak and write or text and blog, we are making choices. Choice pervades all of the ways we use language, at every level, from the word or lexical level to all levels of grammar and beyond.[6] When we use language to think and to communicate, choice is ever-present.

Sometimes those choices are consciously driven. We may have searched for just the right word, trying this one, scratching it out (or backspacing over it to make it disappear), and then typing another, until the precise image of what we were hoping to convey takes its intended shape. We may have similar experiences in the online production of speech, stopping mid-word or pausing to select our very best candidate from the list of possible other words spinning through our head at the same time—all in the course of seconds, or microseconds. We may actually utter a word, stop ourselves, and then change it, explaining that the prior choice wasn't what we really meant.

Sometimes, though, choice is less intentional, less conscious. Such less-transparent linguistic choices tend to occur more often at the level of grammar, as we will see later in this chapter.

We'll use two very basic examples to introduce the interrelated notions of choice and meaning as they relate to discourse and grammar. Here are two sets of sentences. We've left blank spots to be filled in. Each possible answer would yield a grammatically correct utterance. How does the image of the scene change for you with each possible choice? Does your image of the writer or speaker change depending upon which word is used in the blank spaces? If so, how? If not, why not? What other words could you think of that might complete the A and B blanks and spark a new array of images?

Choice—An Introduction

1. Here is the report that you _____. I hope that it is _____.
                                      A   B

   A: asked for, need, were looking for, noted, requested
   B: okay, to your liking, satisfactory, what you want, not too short

2. We had _____ time at your _____.
                       A   B

   A: such a good, a marvelous, a great, a pretty good, an okay
   B: party, barbecue, bash, celebration, get-together, soirée, partay

---

GRAMMAR AND MEANING

The process of analyzing discourse requires an understanding of the components of language and how these components fit together to express meaning. In contrast with formalist ways of thinking, our view of grammar considers linguistic meaning not as something that is given, static, or objectified. That is, grammatical meaning cannot be predicted *a priori* by pre-determined rules, nor can it be reduced to the domain of the literal, however *literal meaning* may be defined. Rather, meaning requires context. It is fluid and emergent. Meaning expressed through discourse and grammar reflects conceptual understandings and perceptions, socio-cultural expectations, and both collective and individual stances and viewpoints. Meaning is dialogically built through discourse and grammar in concert with lived experiences and in response to other current and prior discourse.

Yes, words fill the slots within traditionally understood categories of grammar, such as parts of speech (e.g., nouns, verbs, adjectives, adverbs, and prepositions) and parts of structure (e.g., phrase, clause, sentence). However, words used in discourse *mean* something. Each word conjures up an array of concepts and images, as we saw with the case of words like *party, bash, soirée,* and *partay.* Other words conjure up more powerful images, like *kill, soothe, die, survive, struggle, destroy, reconstruct,* or *furiously.* When we hear or read words like these, we want to know more. What happened? Why? How? Who is involved?

Let's take Sapir's invented example of English syntax to illustrate the first steps toward developing these ideas:

The farmer kills the duckling.

The sentence contains two nouns and a verb in the present tense. There is a basic conceptual structure presented here, as we outline:

Who is involved?	One farmer and one duckling.
What is happening?	He (or she?) kills it.
Why?	No idea. No clues are provided here.

The sentence is categorically grammatical. We can immediately identify its subject, verb, and object. It is a perfect example of language. But it is not discourse. And it is unlikely that such a sentence was or ever will be uttered verbatim in an actual context, unless it is in response to a question posed by an interlocutor hearing an ongoing narrative: Q: "And then what <u>happens</u>?" A: The farmer <u>kills</u> the duckling. As represented here and as cited elsewhere in the literature, this sentence is responsive to nothing.

When we view grammar from perspectives other than formalist ones, our views of structure change; our views of linguistic and discursive meaning expand exponentially. We have within our grammars of language an array of choices, multiple alternatives right there for us to transform experiences and perceptions and understandings into words. Grammar provides us with infinite ways of perceiving and relating events as they occur in our lives. The same event can be represented in myriad ways by individuals who have witnessed that event and lived it, or who have only heard about it or read it in a book. The grammar of any language provides linguistic resources for speakers to express what they have experienced, directly or indirectly, reacting with an acute intensity or a detached impassiveness. Each rendition of one event by multiple witnesses or experiencers will contain linguistic details pointing to each individual's own particular vantage point. We illustrate this next, taking the instance of the farmer and the duckling as a neat and simple example for English.

ALTERNATE NPS AND VPS FOR "THE FARMER KILLS THE DUCKLING"

If, hypothetically, someone chose to recount this event (either having witnessed it directly or having found out about it in another way), the details of the event would take on an altogether different meaning. The event would become an instance of discourse, and the words used would move beyond simple language and structure.

In which *genre* would such a sentence occur? Is the genre a narrative, ordinary conversation, a news story, an essay, a religious sermon, a political debate? As you will read in Chapter 3, genres constitute larger units of discourse, setting the frame for the conventions and expectations surrounding how language and discourse are used and organized at a broader level.

Essentially, there are two characters involved, a farmer and a duckling, and one action, killing. The larger, more powerful entity is the one who performs the action on the smaller, less powerful one. Why the original noun phrase *The farmer*? Why the original verb *kill* (and why is it in the present tense?)? Why the original noun phrase *the duckling* as the direct object?

Since this would hypothetically be a discursive use of language, the teller would have a long list of options, minimally including inventories of nouns and verbs from which to choose that would enable that teller to verbally match his or her perspective of the event. The following below contains some candidate samples.

Does the farmer have a name? Is his or her name in any way relevant to the story? Should it be mentioned? (If so, will our story recipient know who it is?) Is the farmer kind or cruel? Is the duckling so badly injured that the act of killing it is actually an act of beneficence? Was the farmer or the farmer's family hungry?

the farmer:	the farmer, Jake, Martha, the ranch hand, the owner, the grower, he, she, the guy, the gal, a creep, an euthanasist, the monster, the saint, a passerby, the boss, an underling, a hick, our friend, the picker, Mr. Green Jeans, Ms. Haymaker, the benevolent man, the kind woman . . .
the duckling:	the baby duck, the duck, the gosling, the chick, the bird, it, a creature, an animal, a hatchling, the poor innocent thing . . .
kills:	mutilates, smothers, puts out of misery, finishes off, slaughters, butchers, ends a life, sends to heaven, snuffs out, relieved of suffering, says good-bye to, sends off to greener pastures, bids adieu to . . .

ADJECTIVES AND ADVERBS THAT MAY FIT THE STORY

One could add yet more choices by expanding the parts of speech inventory and including categories of words like adjectives (we have added a handful to the previous box) and adverbs, as in the following box.

adjectives:	kind, cruel, enraged, insane, benevolent, incensed, thoughtful, fluffy, soft
adverbs:	accidentally, unfortunately, intentionally, with ether, with a machete, for a prize, in the silo, behind the barn, in front of its mother, last night, early Sunday morning, to end its suffering, just one hour ago

As should be evident from the previous activity, grammar clearly does serve as a communicative mechanism for structure, concept, and choice. It provides resources for speakers and hearers to make visible to their recipients (and to themselves) how it is they conceptualize an event, how they evaluate the participants, how they understand and express causes and effects, how and where they attribute blame or gratitude or empathy, how and through what means speakers and writers attempt to sound objective and value-free, and how hearers and readers are positioned to interpret the discourse. We do all of this and more with the words we use—the words that fill each slot for each grammatical category, traditionally referred to as "parts of speech."

Other perspectives of this event might well use altogether different syntax, as in *The duckling dies* (or *died*), whereby the act of killing fades into the background, now drawing our attention directly to the outcome, *the duckling's death*.

At issue here, and throughout the foregoing discussion, are language, grammar, conceptualization, and perspective-taking or *stance*. Which contextual elements of the story are salient in the event retelling? Which remain backgrounded? Which are not even mentioned? Why?

Grammar, Conceptualization, Stance, and Discourse

Words express concepts and ideas. How we choose our words and how we string them together to say what we mean, in speech or writing, reveals much about who we are, how we feel about things, what we think about things, how strongly things matter to us. Some processes involved in word selection are deliberate and painstakingly planned. Some are much less obvious, even to ourselves.

And regardless of how it is that we produce discourse, nothing in it is neutral. Just as words and language are imbued with meaning, discourse is imbued with *stance*. Each and every instance of discourse is produced from a perspective, a position, a stance. It could be a stance of authority and regulation, as in a one-word sign that says "STOP" or "YIELD." It could be one of elation or sadness or seemingly neutral objectivity. It could be one of certainty or doubt. Discourse emerges from and is built on stance and perspectives. We begin our discussion of perspective-taking with an introduction to grammar as a conceptual mechanism linking language and thought.

GRAMMAR AND CONCEPTUALIZATION

Grammar is essentially conceptual. It is the very mechanism through which we organize our thinking and express thoughts and ideas in words, phrases, and sentences—emphasizing here, downplaying there. Speakers and writers choose words and phrases and structures to construe reality, to represent detail in explicit granularity or in broad outlines of shapes and shadow, to demonstrate empathy, to imply blame or innocence, and to underscore fortuitousness or intentionality—and virtually anything in between or beyond the range of possibilities just noted for construing the world using the symbolic system of language.

Grammar is inextricably tied to human cognition and functions in concert with "other cognitive facilities, especially with perception, attention, and memory" (Radden and Dirven, 2007: xi). As noted by Langacker (2008: 3–4): "The elements of grammar—like vocabulary items—have meanings in their own right . . . [Grammar] is thus an essential aspect of the conceptual apparatus through which we apprehend and engage the world." It is tied to human feelings and emotions, to logic and planning, to our past and present, and to future experiences. Grammatical categories are conceptual categories.

In the sections that follow, we will introduce some of the basic parts of speech (i.e., nouns, verbs, adjectives, and adverbs) and discuss their conceptual meanings and contextual functions in discourse.

Conceptualizing Things—Nouns

Nouns name things. We use nouns to identify things and people. We use nouns to name locations and ideas. Some nouns are concrete. They name things that are visible or tangible, like "tree," "telephone," "water," or "apparition." Some exist as concepts, emotions, and beliefs, like "idea," "gratitude," "independence," and "fatalism." And some are somewhere in between, like "atmosphere" or "universe." All of these word types are nouns. Sometimes the same word can refer to a concrete thing, like "school" (i.e., the building) and "school" (i.e., education, the institution of schooling). The distinction between **concrete nouns** and **abstract nouns** is a conceptual one. Depending upon the context and the communicative intent of the speaker or writer, the same noun might be used to express a concrete thing or an abstract idea.

Another important distinction that grammarians make concerning nouns involves the very basic categories **count** and **non-count (or mass)**. Some nouns fit squarely into one category type and rigidly resist the other type. Most nouns, though, can be construed as count or non-count/mass types, depending on usage and context, and not just the word itself. Let's take *peach* as an example:

peach	an individual piece of fruit (a *peach* / six *peaches*)	COUNT TYPE
peach	a flavor or main ingredient (pie, jellies, jams, yogurt), a color (*peach* peignoir), a substance ("The baby even had *peach* in his ears.")	MASS TYPE

In fact, *fruit* in general is often construed as a mass/non-count type of noun (just as we mention it right here in this sentence) when the image we have of it or would like to convey of it is more of an amorphous substance, or when discrete individuation of an item is not relevant.

This flexibility in object construal, specifically in the case of fruit (as concrete nouns), becomes all the more clear when we write up shopping lists for the produce department. Here is a hypothetical example:

Shopping List (Fruits)

apples	oranges
grapes	watermelon
strawberries	grapefruit
cantaloupe	peaches

Some nouns appear in the plural form and are thus used as *count nouns* (apples, oranges, grapes, strawberries, peaches). Others are in the singular form and used here as *mass or non-count* nouns (watermelon, cantaloupe, grapefruit), but each of these words could easily be pluralized and used as count nouns as well (e.g., two watermelons, three cantaloupes, six grapefruits). Why do you think this is so? Just by virtue of the presence or absence of the English plural marker -*s*, how does your construal of these items change? What seems to influence your use of singular vs. plural in conceptualizing the previously listed fruits? The mental processes of conceptualizing everyday items is so conditioned by our grammars[7] that most of us are not consciously aware of this very tight concept-language connection.

Let's take another example of a noun that may be used variably in English, both as a mass noun and as a count noun: snow.

More often than not, we consider *snow* as a non-count/mass type of noun, as in the following examples:

> They rarely see <u>snow</u> in Southern California.
> Send over some <u>snow</u> to us in Meckenbeuren. Ours is already gone.
> They're predicting <u>snow</u> for the entire Northwest this weekend.

But, the word (or more precisely the concept) can also be used with contextual features that are more consistent with a count-type usage:

> **One** <u>snow,</u> in particular, was remarkable. (referring to one snowfall, from among others)

Here is a discourse-based example from the children's book, *The Pilgrims' First Thanksgiving* (Mcgovern, 1993: 8–12):

> **Winter**
>
> . . . The first winter in Plymouth was terrible for the Pilgrims. They could not finish building their homes before <u>the snow</u> fell. They could not find enough food in the forests . . . That winter, many of the Pilgrims got sick. Many of the Pilgrims died.
>
> **Spring**
>
> At last <u>the snows</u> began to melt. Spring was coming . . .

THE BUILDING BLOCKS OF LANGUAGE

Just by virtue of a single -s at the end of the word *snow* in the Spring description of the weather, the focal point of this image shifts from the occurrence of frozen precipitation that covers the ground, tree limbs, and rooftops to a *regularity of snowfall events*—one snowfall and then more, which contributed to the harshness of that first winter. Both versions of the clause in question are perfectly grammatical—what shifts is the conceptual representation (and hence perspective) of the weather condition in question:

At last the <u>snows</u> began to melt.

(Original version: **plural, count type**—drawing attention to the mass of snow surrounding the Pilgrims *and* to the many times that snow fell that winter.)

At last the <u>snow</u> began to melt.

(Variation: **singular, non-count/mass** type—drawing attention to the mass of snow surrounding the Pilgrims.)

Grammar is so much more than mere structure. Grammar does have meaning in its own right. One -s at the end of a word can change the conceptual imagery.

Practice with Mass Nouns and Count Nouns

Count	Non-count (mass)
desk	wood
can	aluminum
lamp	electricity
moon	moonlight
panda	bamboo
train	railroad

How do you know that the words in the **left-hand column** are count nouns? Can you naturally add an -s to make them plural?

What about the nouns in the **right-hand column?** Can you naturally add an -s to make them plural?

What, conceptually, is at play with regard to singularity and plurality? Name some other typical **count nouns**:

_____, _____, _____, _____

Name some other typical **non-count (mass) nouns:**

_____, _____, _____, _____

Can you think of some non-count (mass) nouns that can be used like count nouns?

    Here is one example: water → waters

What sort of conceptual changes occur when *water* becomes *waters*?

    Here is another example: cheese → cheeses

Now what sort of conceptual change occurs when *cheese* becomes *cheeses*?

Nouns: Unified Wholes vs. Individuated Members

We find similar conceptual patterns in English grammar that reflect discrete individuation on the one hand and circumscribed sets of collectives on the other.

These individual vs. collective patterns become especially salient with so-called **collective nouns** that refer to various types of membership sets. Collective nouns designating human groups include words like: *faculty, staff, family, team, the House, the Senate, police, jury, congregation, company, board, force, band, orchestra, committee, the IRS, college,* where individual members belong to a common group with common ties of various types and sources. Collective nouns referring to animals include *flock, litter, herd, gaggle, pod, pride, cry,* and *cete.*

When reference is made to collective entities in discourse using collective nouns, we find an interesting variability in the co-occurring verb forms, at times exhibiting the **third-person present tense singular -s** (or other irregularly transparent third-person singular present tense forms like *is, has, does*), at times the non-singular form. Note how such choice of verb form affects

Tenure-line <u>faculty</u> **are** invited to apply for seed grants through P&G.

(plural verb *are*—conceptually pointing to multiple individual faculty members who may be interested)

The <u>faculty</u> **expresses** its dissatisfaction with Hill's most recent action.

(singular verb *expresses*—conceptually pointing to the group as a whole) the conceptual realizations of the group or individuals in question, as in the examples on the previous page.

Now, of course it is not "grammatically" possible for each and every collective noun in English to occur at *any* time with *either* a singular verb form *or* a plural verb form in the present tense, but the general variability is indeed possible. And the variability is meaningful from the dual points of view of concept and perspective.

Some variations are dialectal. In British English, for example, we might find the word *couple* co-occurring with plural verb morphology, while in

---

British English: *couple* + plural morphology, pointing to each of the two individual members:

"A couple **have** had three foster children removed from their care because they belong to the UK Independence Party." (BBC News, November 2012).

American English: *couple* + singular morphology, pointing to the unit as a whole:

"The New Jersey couple **has** no idea how the new law [concerning international adoption from Russia] will affect them." (Gringberg, 2012).

American English, we tend to find the word occurring more often with singular morphology, as in the above examples.

Similarly, British English tends to use plural verb forms with seemingly singular collective nouns, such as sports team names designated by the countries, cities, counties, towns, or other institutions to which the teams belong, thus underscoring a focus on the group composed of individual members, rather than the group as a unified circumscribed whole. In contrast, American English uses singular verb forms.

Here are a few examples:

British English: "singular" team names with plural (non-singular) verbs

Euro 2012 final: Spain v Italy as it happened (football/soccer)

All the action and analysis as Spain **retain** their European Championship trophy in style. (cf. singular: . . . *as Spain retains its European* . . .) (BBC News, July 2012)

American English: "singular" team names with singular verbs

Anytime Cleveland **Wins** it is a Favorite NFL Moment (Gissiner, 2012)

Some of these dialectal differences in collective noun usage may be predictable. However, by virtue of the grammatical patterns, it becomes clear how team membership and participation are both grammatically referred to and conventionally accepted by speakers of the dialects in question.

In the noun patterns that we address next, the referents are non-human, and the distinctions rest between pointing out abstract wholes or sets, on the one hand, and concretely specific individuated parts that comprise those sets, on the other—often with the abstract concept being a mass type noun and the concrete specific members, count type.

Examples of this type of noun include:

Abstract, unified set	Concrete, specific types of members
cutlery	knives (and the different types)
flatware	spoons, forks, knives, utensils
aircraft	planes, dirigibles, hot air balloons, helicopters
produce	fruits and vegetables (and the various types)
ammunition	bullets, BBs, missiles, grenades
weaponry	guns, missiles, grenades, knives, blunt objects

Words conjure up images and images conjure up words. Some nouns denote abstract, amorphous concepts. Others denote concrete entities with sharply detailed shapes, sizes, and features. All pattern meaningfully within our discourse to illustrate, explain, relate news—to communicate our ideas, findings, and feelings. And all contribute in varying degrees to our ways of seeing and to our ways of having others see what we see.

Next, you will find excerpts from a news story reporting the discovery of a large number of World War I relics. These "relics" are bullets, variably referred to in this article and the photo captions as: *ammunition, pieces of ammunition, pieces of bullet, bullets,* and *explosives*.

First World War ammunition frozen in time for nearly a century has been found as glacier melts (excerpts), by Alex Gore. 9/2/2012

First World War <u>ammunition</u> frozen in time for nearly a century has been discovered in northern Italy.

<u>More than 200 pieces of the ammunition</u> were revealed at an altitude of 3,200 metres by a melting glacier on the Ago de Nardis peak in Trentino.

photo caption 1: Frozen in time: <u>The ammunition</u> was discovered as a glacier melted in Trentino

photo caption 2: <u>Explosives: More than 200 pieces</u> of the 85–100mm caliber <u>bullets</u> were found

photo caption 3: Conflict: <u>The bullets</u> were spread over a 100-square-metre area between 1915 and 1918

photo caption 4: Discovery: <u>The ammunition</u> was revealed at an altitude of 3,200 metres on the Ago de Nardis peak.

(Gore, 2012)

SINGULAR AND PLURAL NOUNS IN DISCOURSE

How do these images appear in your mind as you read through the excerpts? Do the plural versions take on different imageries than the singular version, *ammunition?* If so, how? If not, why do you think this is the case?

Discourse is inherently driven by choice, which is inherently driven by perspective and purpose. We have isolated the grammatical category of nouns as our initial entry point into the domain of analyzing discourse to illustrate these ideas.

We'll now have a quick look at verbs, adjectives, and adverbs as they appear in actual discourse.

CONCEPTUALIZING ACTIONS, MOVEMENT, STATES, PERCEPTION, COGNITIVE PROCESSES—VERBS[8]

We review verbs here, very generally, to give an idea of how verbs reflect and create meaning in discourse. Verbs express actions, movement, states, perception, and cognitive processes. One major quality of verbs that will come into play in the analysis of discourse is **transitivity**. Verbs are often categorized as **transitive** or **intransitive**. Simply put, transitive verbs take direct objects and intransitive verbs *cannot* take any type of object at all.

Transitivity is then obviously related to grammatical structure. However, in discourse, the concept that underlies transitivity is potentially very powerful. In certain contexts, the use of transitive verbs expresses *power, strength, agency, will, intentionality,* and *deliberateness,* while the use of intransitive verbs expresses *spontaneity, automaticity,* and *occurrences that might be beyond our control.* Naturally, the key word in the grammar-concept link is *context*. Where do these types of constructions appear? Who or what are the subjects of the transitive or intransitive verbs? Who or what are the objects of the transitive verbs? Are subjects animate? Are they human? What about the objects?

Even working just at the word level, look at the following word lists. Compare the potential imagery that a single transitive verb can conjure up. Who or what might the subject be? Who or what might the object be? To what extent does the object of the verb change as a result of the action of that verb performed by the subject? Try this with a variety of potential subjects (human, non-human, animate, inanimate) and a variety of potential objects.

Transitive Verbs:

> *blemish, stain, ruin, destroy, demolish*
> *nibble, nosh, snack on, eat, devour, inhale, scarf down*
> *hit, pound, tap, strike, beat, pummel*

Who or what do you imagine the subject(s) to be?

Who or what do you imagine the object(s) to be?

How much "power" does the subject seem to have over the object?

To what extent does the object undergo a change as a result of the subject and verb?

Practice with Transitive and Intransitive Verbs

Typical transitive verbs: (take a direct object)	Typical intransitive verbs: (cannot take a direct object)
eat	sleep
drink	remain
write	happen
read	revolve
tease	laugh
discover	arrive
throw	live
spend	descend
absorb	complain
make	be (am, is, are)
cover	disappear
show	appear
drop	fall

---

raise	rise
lay	lie
grow (hair, tomatoes)	grow (to increase in size)
run (a business)	run (to move faster than walking)
walk (a dog)	walk (to ambulate)
climb (a tree)	climb (to move upward)
fly (a plane, a kite)	fly (to move in the air)

Locate the transitive and intransitive verbs in the following paragraph that describes how to hold a golf club. For transitive verbs, be sure to indicate what the direct object is.

How to Hold a Golf Club:

Hold the club in your left hand. Place your right-hand pinky ("little finger") between the index finger and middle finger of your left hand. Align both thumbs so that they follow the line of the club shaft. Both thumbs should point downward and be parallel to the line of the club shaft.

(Hint: These are the verbs you should identify: *hold*, *place*, *align*, *follow*, *point*, and *be*. Which are transitive? intransitive?)

Now, write your own "how to" description about how to fold and fly a paper airplane.

In the first paragraph, describe *how to fold the paper*. In the second paragraph, describe *how to fly the plane*.

Be sure to use both transitive and intransitive verbs. (Feel free to use some of the verbs from the previous lists, in addition to your own.)

How do transitive and intransitive verbs appear to differ in terms of how they express both control and movement?

VERBS IN DISCOURSE

Carrying the grammar-concept link further, we need to examine the **tense and aspect** involved in the spate of discourse under investigation. What is being discussed? Is it an event, an action, or a state? Is it past, over and done with, or is it still happening? Is the consequence of the event relevant to anything else in the discourse? Is the consequence depicted as temporary or permanent? All of these features, and more, are expressed through **tense and aspect marking** on verbs.

The following excerpt is from a web-based article about a winter storm on Prince Edward Island (an island province of Canada just north of Halifax and east of Quebec City). The first line shown in the figure is in bold. It is the headline of the news story.

As you read the excerpt, pay attention to five things:

- What or who are the subjects? (animate, inanimate, human?)
- What types of verbs occur with the subjects? (transitive, intransitive?)
- What or who are the direct objects? (animate, inanimate, human?).
- Which tense and aspect markers are used? (**present, past, perfect, progressive?**)
- How do grammar and conceptualization intersect with the overall image of this news excerpt?

Winter blast causes <u>outages, traffic restrictions</u> **on Prince Edward Island (excerpt)**

<u>A blast of winter weather</u> **has left** Maritime Electric crews working to restore power . . . to . . . customers affected by power outages.

A spokesperson for the company said <u>three areas</u> **are suffering** <u>outages</u> caused by the weather.

<u>The Maritime provinces</u> **are grappling with** <u>heavy snowfall, blowing snow and rain</u> today.

(***The Guardian***, 2012)

You might want to organize your findings using tables or other graphic devices, such as this one, to help you isolate some of the variables.

SUBJECT	VERB	DIRECT OBJECT
Winter blast	causes	outages, traffic restrictions
A blast of winter weather	has left	Maritime Electric crews working
Three areas	are suffering	outages
The Maritime provinces	are grappling with	heavy snowfall, blowing snow, and rain

NOTES about tense and aspect:

- Winter blast *causes* outages, traffic restrictions on P.E.I.—"causes" is in the present tense. It is in a *news headline*.
- A spokesperson for the company *said* . . . (The verb "say" is in the past tense. The event is over and done with. There is an anonymous entity responsible for the details provided here.)
- Three areas **are suffering** outages (The verb is in the present progressive, the action is immediate and ongoing, and it involves a negative consequence for human **experiencers**. Here, "people" are conceptualized through a geographic location—"three areas.")
- The Maritime provinces are grappling with heavy snowfall, blowing snow, and rain. (The verb is in the present progressive, the action is immediate and ongoing, and again, it involves a negative consequence for human **experiencers**. Here again, "people" are conceptualized through a geographic location—"The Maritime provinces.")

ANALYZING THE VERBS IN DISCOURSE

Which entities in the previous discourse are framed as particularly powerful? Which are framed more as victims? What, in the discourse, creates such a contrast of forces?

Let's now move to adjectives for a brief view of how they pattern in discourse.

CONCEPTUALIZING QUALITIES AND ATTRIBUTES OF PEOPLE, THINGS, EXPERIENCES, AND EVENTS—ADJECTIVES

The function of adjectives is to provide detail concerning the quality, color, size, shape, scale, physical characteristics, and personality traits of nominal entities (i.e., nouns or **noun phrases [NPs]**). Adjectives express speakers' and writers' perceptions, evaluations, and judgments about people, things, experiences, and events.

In linguistics, adjectives are often discussed on the basis of the categorical distinction of **attributive** and **predicative** adjectives. This distinction, too, like transitivity in verbs, relates to syntactic structure. That is, **attributive adjectives** precede the noun and **predicative adjectives** follow a copular element or linking verb in the utterance, e.g., verbs like *be, become, seem, feel, taste*.

Some adjectives *must* precede the nouns (i.e., they must be attributive) and conversely, some adjectives *must* follow a copula or linking verb (i.e., they must be predicative), or the expressions will not make sense:

---

obligatorily attributive adjectives (must precede the noun)

"Magenta is George's favorite color."
              adjective noun

***His color   is   favorite.**
    noun   [copula] adjective

Fugues begin with a main   theme.
              adjective   noun

***The fugue's theme   is   main.**
    noun   [copula]   adjective

obligatorily predicative adjectives (must follow a copula)

Her sister did not   feel   appreciated.
noun   [copula] adjective

***Her appreciated sister.**
    adjective   noun
The children were asleep when we came home.
    noun [copula] adjective

***The asleep   children.**
    adjective noun

So, while sentence structure is clearly a factor in the placement of adjectives relative to the nouns and noun phrases they modify, the effect that such adjective and noun placement has in discourse can be remarkable—especially with respect to such conceptual features as the permanence or temporariness of such quality, the seemingly inherent nature of that quality to the nominal referent, and so forth.

To illustrate:

Attributive: The **Handsome** Boy Modeling School.
Predicative: Seventeen Ways to Look **Handsome**.
                        [copula]

Attributive: Meryl Streep wore a **gorgeous** gown.
Predicative: Meryl Streep's gown <u>was</u> **gorgeous**.

[copula]

The following excerpt contains a number of adjectives, some attributive and some predicative. It is a commentary, purportedly by Chef Wolfgang Puck, that accompanies a "Featured Recipe" on the Wolfgang Puck website. This recipe is for one of the more well-known Puck pizzas. The adjectives are in boldface font and we have underlined them to help them stand out more.

With this rather narrow focus on adjectives, attend to the following issues:

- What is the adjective type? (Attributive or predicative?) How many attributive adjectives did you locate? How many predicative adjectives? List them together with the nouns that they occur with.
- Do you find any adjective strings, i.e., with more than one attributive adjective in a row? Would it be grammatically possible to do this with predicative adjectives? Why or why not?
- How do the predicative adjectives differ from the attributive adjectives in this excerpt with respect to permanence of the quality associated with the nouns they describe? How does this affect your read of the excerpt? How does this affect your conceptualization of the noun and its descriptor?

Featured Recipe

Pizza with <u>smoked</u> salmon and caviar

When I opened the **<u>original</u>** Spago in 1982, this quickly became its **<u>signature</u>** pizza. If you feel **<u>decadent</u>**, you can top the pizza with Sevruga, Beluga, or Osetra caviar; less **<u>expensive</u>** salmon roe or just **<u>chopped fresh</u>** chives are also **<u>elegant</u>**.

(Puck, n.d.)

ADJECTIVES IN DISCOURSE

With just these few lines, we can see how crucial adjectives are to discourse. In this excerpt, they present qualitative information about the larger item in question (a special pizza) and elements relating to its historical origins, in

31

addition to a handful of ingredients (both from the original recipe and suggested alternatives). Moreover, these adjectives set a descriptive tone in the discourse that positions the author, the pizza, and the reader squarely within a domain of exclusivity, taste, and culinary style.

Which adjectives are obligatorily attributive?

<u>**signature**</u> pizza → *the pizza is signature
<u>**original**</u> recipe → the recipe is original (a very different meaning)

Now, compare adjective placement and the consequent meaning changes that occur as a result of such alternation:

<u>Attributive</u>
Smoked salmon → Predicative: The salmon is smoked.
<u>Attributive</u>
Chopped, fresh chives → Predicative: The chives are **chopped**.
                                   The chives are **fresh**.
<u>Predicative</u>
If you feel **decadent** → Attributive: The **decadent** you.
[variation: The dessert looks **decadent**. vs. A **decadent** dessert.]
<u>Predicative</u>
Chives are **elegant** → Attributive: The **elegant** chives.

How does adjective placement affect your reaction to the text as a reader? How does it change the "attributes" and their relationships to the nouns and noun phrases in question?

CONCEPTUALIZING MANNER, LOCATION, TIME, DURATION, INTENSITY, DIRECTION, AND MORE—ADVERBS

In grammar, adverbs may be among the least understood "parts of speech" and at the same time one of the most powerful grammatical categories in terms of stance marking. Put simply, adverbs modify verbs. But how? And what does it really mean to "modify a verb"?

Adverbs are not well understood because they appear in a wide variety of forms and structures. The simplest way to recognize an adverb is by noticing the traditional -ly at the end of a word. *Slyly, shyly, readily, consequently, appropriately, immunoelectrophoretically,* and *otorhinolaryngologically* are all adverbs. However, *unlikely, earthly,* and *fatherly* are not. (They are adjectives.)

Beyond the nearly telltale *-ly* adverbial morpheme, though, there are countless other ways of grammatically modifying a verb. In English, time reference words like *today, yesterday* and *tomorrow* are adverbs—as are time reference phrases like *at 2:32 p.m., before the bell rang, right in the middle of my daydream*, and *just before the farmer kills the duckling* are also adverbs.

Adverbs "modify verbs," typically by answering such questions as: *How?, When?, Where?* and *Why?:*

How:	*with his bare hands, painstakingly, without looking, in red ink, instead, by pushing it uphill, from top to bottom, very quickly* (there are two adverbs here), *so carefully* (two adverbs here, too)
When:	*at 4:30, before the sun came up, while the boys were sleeping, last month, every six hours, yesterday*
Where:	*in the bedroom, at the bank, behind the desk, on Mars, outside, here*
Why:	*for his own pleasure, for a better tan, so he'd win, because she was the better candidate, so investors would have more faith*

An adverb can also be a full subordinate clause, i.e., clauses beginning with words like *because, if, when, while, provided that*, as in <u>*Just as I was about to send you a message*</u> ← [ADV], *you logged off*. And an adverb can be a single word that modifies a full sentence that precedes it: *If you read everything that's on the syllabus then you'll do fine in Smith's class*, **maybe**.

From the points of view of both syntax and conceptual meaning, adverbs are often optional. They provide specific details of time, place, location, manner, and direction.

One example of a grammatically (or pragmatically) obligatory adverb are the words, *too* or *also*. (See Chapter 5, Information Structure, for additional discussion of cohesion).

Hydrogen is an element.
*Oxygen is **also** an element. / Oxygen is an element, **too**.*

THE BUILDING BLOCKS OF LANGUAGE

Adverbs provide additional details that the speaker or writer chooses for such purposes as:

- clarification (*in other words, at the very least, in rare cases*)
- evaluation (*rightly so, unethically, for better or worse*)
- precision (*exactly, on the dot, within nanoseconds*)
- certainty (*of course, probably, certainly, without a doubt*)
- uncertainty (*maybe, perhaps, if we're lucky, weather permitting*)

Just as we have done with nouns, verbs, and adjectives, we next present two brief excerpts to illustrate how adverbs function in discourse and to provide a glimpse into the variety of multiple grammatical shapes adverbs can take. The first excerpt is from the U.S. Marines' recruitment website. The second is from a "Dear Abby" letter from a concerned educator.

The U.S. Marines segment was culled from the page that introduces a plan for prospective recruits to initiate their physical training program. The adverbs have been underlined and marked in boldface type. You'll note the typical *–ly* forms, but also pay attention to the more complex grammatical structures that function as adverbs.

As you read through the segment, pay attention to the following areas to guide your analytic observations:

- How many adverbs or adverbial constructions do you find in the excerpt?
- What portion of the discourse in question is actually adverbial in function? (Bear in mind that this is an abridged excerpt).
- Do some adverbs appear to be more necessary to the content of the message than others? That is, within this spate of discourse, do some adverbs appear obligatory, while others might be optional? If so, which seem to be obligatory in order to express the content of the message and which appear to be optional? When adverbs are not obligatory, what sort of information do they provide?
- What conclusions can you draw concerning adverbs in general and adverbs in discourse?

Physical Prep 365-DAY PLAN

The intensity of your training will depend on how long you have **before attending OCS**. **If you are one year out**, you should start **slowly** and build your endurance and strength **throughout the year** . . .

> If you have a year to get **physically** and **mentally** prepared, speak to your OSO and track your workouts **in your Officer Training Guide** . . . Your year should progress **as follows:**
>
> > Start slowly . . .
> > **Progress evenly . . .**
> > **Taper your last week . . .**
>
> **(U.S. Marine Corps, n.d. a)**

ADVERBS IN DISCOURSE

Now, let's have a look at the Dear Abby excerpt. None of the adverbs in these few paragraphs is marked with the *–ly* morpheme, but there are many adverb tokens in the excerpt. Comparing the Dear Abby excerpt to the U.S. Marine Corps excerpt, what differences do you find concerning the *position* or *stance* of the respective pieces? In the Dear Abby piece, do you note more tokens of grammatically "optional" adverbs? That is, are they crucial to the actual content? What do these constructions add to the discourse?

> DEAR ABBY: I have worked in the field of education **for more than 40 years, with the last 25 years serving in adult education**, helping students complete their high school equivalency diploma.
>
> *Big* changes are impending **worldwide in this very important educational service. Starting in 2014**, the cost may go up. **Up until two years ago**, the classes in our community were free. The testing cost $7.50, which paid for a printed diploma. **Since then**, the cost has gone up—**first to $25** and **then to $35**.
>
> **Now** the GED program has been bought by a for-profit organization and the costs will go **higher than ever.**
>
> **(Van Buren, 2013)**

MORE ADVERBS IN DISCOURSE—STANCE MARKERS

Adverbs are often regarded as *stance markers* par excellence. Biber and Finegan (1988, 1989) and Conrad and Biber (2001) address adverbs and adverbial constructions as methods for "speakers and writers to convey their personal feelings and assessments in addition to propositional content" (Conrad and Biber, 2001: 57).

Adverbs often mark attitudes, perceptions, viewpoints, and epistemic positions vis à vis persons, ideas, concepts, events, objects, and the like, and they do so in lexically transparent ways. In fact, the basic function of an adverb seems to do just that—mark stance.

Grammar requires some degree of basic structure, but within that structure, we make choices—of nouns or pronouns, count nouns or mass nouns. We might use mass nouns as count nouns and vice versa. We choose to describe nouns by using adjectives, and these may be predicative or attributive, they may denote color or texture or taste. Verbs express actions and motions and states. They specify (*peruse, pore over, glance at, examine*) and they generalize (*read*). They might signal power or agency or dominance or submission (See Chapter 8, Indexicality, and Chapter 9, Critical Discourse Analysis). With adverbs, we provide details about events and actions and states—the *how* or the *when* or the *where*. Discourse involves a constant stream of choices, each of which conveys varying degrees of granularity in meaning with regard to fluidity and abstractness or tangibility and concreteness, estimation or precision, control or spontaneity, and so forth.

To understand grammar and its intricacies is a first step in the understanding and analysis of discourse.

REVIEW AND REFLECTION: GRAMMAR—COUNT NOUNS, MASS NOUNS, VERBS (AND TRANSITIVITY), ADJECTIVES, AND ADVERBS

1. Nouns in English and nouns in other languages:

We discussed count nouns and mass nouns in English from a conceptual viewpoint, noting that, in the case of fruits, for example, the actual distinction between the *count* type and the *non-count* or *mass* type depends upon the conceptual imagery of the item.

An example was our shopping list:

apples and oranges	commonly occur in the PLURAL form for a shopping list
BUT	
watermelon and cantaloupe	are more common in the SINGULAR for a shopping list

We can posit that this is because the larger fruits are less often conceptualized as a group of many.

Here is a list of fruits from a shopping list in Chinese:

苹果	apples
葡萄	grapes
草莓	strawberries
哈密瓜	cantaloupe
橙子	oranges
西瓜	watermelon
葡萄柚	grapefruit
桃子	peaches

There is no plural marker at all in Chinese for such fruits on a list. There is no distinction necessary on a shopping list for plural or singular entities, unless a number of items were specified, in which case, the form would also change.

Here is a partial shopping list in French. (Rivière, 2010). Note the use of singular and plural marking for certain food items:

oeufs	eggs
huile d'olive	olive oil
beurre	butter (same in English; not plural for a shopping list)
yaourts	?yogurts (**plural in a French shopping list**, but not English)

Why do you think *yaourts* 'yogurts' appears in the plural form here?

How about other nouns as shopping list items in English (grocery, clothing, school supplies, sporting goods)? Are some used alternatively in the singular (as if mass nouns) and some in the plural? How does this distinction change the conceptual imagery of the nouns? How about similar lists in other languages that you know? What sorts of conceptual distinctions regarding nouns seem to be at play in those languages?

2. We introduced the notion of transitivity when we discussed verbs and two major categories of verbs, transitive and intransitive. Transitive verbs take direct objects. Intransitive verbs do not.

   Here is a short passage from *National Geographic Kids* magazine (2013, p. 27), pointing to a spoof website and internet hoax of 1998. The piece appears within a larger article "Real or Fake? Can You Believe Every-thing You Read?" and is intended to have readers of this magazine decide whether selected entries are actual or made up. (In this case, the Tree Octo-pus is a made-up phenomenon, but many people believed it was real.)

We want to focus on two areas here: nouns and verbs.

A. Identify **the subjects** (nouns) of the sentences as well as the **verb type**: transitive or intransitive. In the case of transitive verbs, also locate the direct objects (nouns).

Scientists have discovered a rare land octopus that lives in the rain forests of Washington State. The Pacific Northwest tree octopus, or *octopus paxarbolis,* spends its first few months in the ocean before moving onto land to mate, absorbing the moisture it needs from the damp rain forests. Logging and suburban growth are threatening the rare cephalopod's habitat, so activists are trying to lend an arm—er, hand—to place the animal on the endangered species list.

Which verb type is more frequent? Transitive or Intransitive
Why do you think this is so?
B. How many different ways is the "rare land octopus" referred to? Make a list of the different ways the author mentions it.
What does this tell you about language and discourse? How general or how specific can we be—through grammar and linguistic choice?

3. This is an excerpt from the website of U.S. shipping company, FedEx. Identify the subjects of each sentence and the verbs that go with those subjects. Can you then identify the transitive verbs? What are they? What are the direct objects? Are there any intransitive verb(s)?

Things you can do on the FedEx website: menu items

Create a shipment
Get rates and Transit Times
Schedule a Pickup
Customize your Delivery
Order Shipping Supplies
Pay your Bills Online
Update your Address Book
File a Claim on a Package

All of the verbs are in the imperative mood. That is, they all look like directives or commands. Are they really directives or are they *choices*?

What category of verbs are they (i.e., transitive or intransitive)? Are there any direct objects? Do you think that this type of verb usage is typical for menu items on a website? Why or why not? What supporting examples can you provide that help you make this argument? (To support or refute, it's probably a good idea to locate other websites with menu lists.)

4. Adjectives and Adverbs: Read the following excerpt. It is taken from a review for the 2011 Mitsubishi Endeavor (Edmunds, n.d.). How does the combined use of adjectives and adverbs reflect the author's stance regarding this vehicle? Do you note other ways of describing nouns in addition to adjectives? Try to articulate the various ways in which nouns are described here.

    Identify as many adverbs as you can. Look for one-word adverbs (e.g., *once* or *since*) in addition to multiple-word adverbs. What is the predominant type of imagery used here? How is that imagery established and then built upon?

    > Like most everything in your refrigerator, some cars are best used before their expiration date. The 2011 Mitsubishi Endeavor is like that forgotten leftover container in the back of the fridge: It was once an appetizing selection of ingredients, but now is best discarded in favor of fresher fare.
    >
    > When the Endeavor debuted in 2004, it was good enough to take the top spot in an Edmunds comparison test that pitted it against the Honda Pilot, Nissan Murano and Toyota Highlander. In the intervening years, however, the Mitsubishi has remained relatively unchanged, and has since been overshadowed by newer and redesigned models. The Endeavor's strength—a pleasing blend of performance, handling and comfort—has since faded with time.

PRACTICE WITH DATA ANALYSIS— PUTTING IT ALL TOGETHER

I. Parts of Speech in Advertising

Data excerpts A and B are from website descriptions of fragrances for women. The first is for Coach Signature Eau de Toilette. The second is for Jean Naté™

After-Bath Splash Mist. The products are similar in many respects. They also differ.

Read through each excerpt and conduct a preliminary analysis guided by a focus on nouns, verbs, adjectives, and adverbs.

Mark the nouns in one color. Mark the adjectives in another color. (You may want to use different shades or different colors for the various types of adjectives that you find.) Mark the verbs in another color. Be sure to note: (a) the subjects of the verbs and (b) the objects (when the verbs are transitive). What types of adverbials do you find?

After conducting this preliminary analysis, try to take it at least one step further.

What seems to be the primary selling point for the Coach product? What seems to be the primary selling point for the Jean Naté™ product? That is, what types of features are underscored in each "dataset"?

Given that, who do you imagine the target consumer audience to be for the Coach product? Who do you imagine as the target audience for the Jean Naté™ product? Explain using excerpts from the data to support your points.

In doing this work, did you discover anything about grammar, language, or discourse that you had been unaware of before? Please elaborate.

What sorts of implications can you draw with regard to discourse and everyday life, discourse and marketing, discourse and language teaching, discourse and communication—discourse and virtually all fields of study?

A. Fragrance—Coach Signature Eau de Toilette (Sephora, n.d.).

> Inspired by the COACH Signature collection, this fragrance evokes a sense of classic luxury. At once understated and flirty, its fresh florals are set against a beautiful sense of coziness and warmth.
>
> The fragrance opens playfully: it sparkles with mandarin, guava, and the exclusive scent of Gant Waterlily, a rare note captured through the advanced Nature Print® process. The heart notes present a feminine bouquet of jasmine, mimosa, and tuberose. As the scent dries down, its base lingers on the skin with warm and luscious notes of vanilla, amberwood, and orris.

B. Fragrance—Jean Naté™ After-Bath Splash Mist (Revlon, n.d.)

> Refresh, renew and revitalize your senses. The light citrus scent you love—all over. Clean Naté . . . Clean never felt so fresh!™ Go one step beyond any clean you've ever known with Jean Naté™. The light clean scent refreshes your senses all day long.

II. Analyze the following excerpt from the "First to Fight" page of the U.S. Marines website

Before you start, read the passage. What is your overall impression of this excerpt? Are you moved in any way—either positively or negatively? Do you have absolutely no reaction whatsoever? (Hopefully, not.)

You can use your preliminary skills at analyzing discourse to uncover some of the linguistic features that work together to create initial impressions. Conducting a micro-level analysis of discourse helps us to understand better why certain discourse moves us in the way that it does. It even helps us to gauge and re-think some of our initial reactions and later change our opinions regarding the discourse, once we see it in a more systematically analytic light.

Use your knowledge of the four basic categories of grammar that we covered in this chapter, i.e., nouns, verbs, adjectives, and adverbs, as a foundation for your analysis. Again, and as always, begin your analysis first by marking the nouns and verbs, the subjects and objects, the various types of adjectives, and the multiple types of adverbials.

How would you describe this type of discourse? Is it informational? Is it persuasive? Who do you think is the target audience?

How does this website compare to the websites for the U.S. Army, the U.S. Navy, and the armed forces of other nations in the world? Base your responses on an analysis of the discourse.

U.S. Marines FIRST TO FIGHT

No one knows where the next conflict or crisis will emerge. Ridding the world of these threats requires a lightweight, nimble force that not only can respond rapidly, but also take control when it gets there. When unexpected threats arise, it is the Marine Corps that is best prepared to face them down.

Marines are first to fight because of their culture and because they maintain a forward-deployed presence near various global hotspots. The Marine Corps' forward presence consists of multiple Marine Expeditionary Units, or MEUs. MEUs spend at least six months training for a variety of amphibious operations before they are deployed. Then, for six months at a time, Marine Expeditionary Units embark upon United States Navy warships and prepare to launch a range of missions—from humanitarian and peacekeeping missions to full-scale combat engagements, on extremely short notice. Few have what it takes to become Marines, but now many have the opportunity to delve into the training and mindset of these elite, prepared warriors. This behind-the-scenes glimpse of an actual MEU training exercise reveals what it takes to maintain this constant state of readiness. You've heard of their "First to Fight" reputation. Now see them earn it.

(U.S. Marine Corps, n.d. b)

III. Discourse Analysis in English and Other Languages— Newspaper Discourse on Natural Disaster in Japan: English, Chinese, French, Spanish

Here, we present some examples of discourse in other languages: Chinese, French, and Spanish.

Use what you have learned in this chapter concerning English and analyze the discourse in these languages in a similar manner.

Focus on:

* Nouns (count / non-count or mass; concrete, abstract)
* Verbs (transitive or intransitive)
* Adjectives (attributive: placed before the noun or predicative: placed after the copular verb)
* Adverbs (identify the various types of adverbial constructions in the languages that you know)

The texts are from the first few paragraphs of major news outlets on the March 11, 2011 earthquake and tsunami in Northern Japan.

A. English

Powerful Quake and Tsunami Devastate Northern Japan

By MARTIN FACKLER

TOKYO—Rescuers struggled to reach survivors on Saturday morning as Japan reeled after an earthquake and a tsunami struck in deadly tandem. The 8.9-magnitude earthquake set off a devastating tsunami that sent walls of water washing over coastal cities in the north.

Concerns mounted over possible radiation leaks from two nuclear plants near the earthquake zone. The death toll from the tsunami and earthquake, the strongest ever recorded in Japan, was in the hundreds, but Japanese news media quoted government officials as saying that it would almost certainly rise to more than 1,000. About 200 to 300 bodies were found along the waterline in Sendai, a port city in northeastern Japan and the closest major city to the epicenter.

Thousands of homes were destroyed, many roads were impassable, trains and buses were not running, and power and cellphones remained down. On Saturday morning, the JR rail company said that there were three trains missing in parts of two northern prefectures.

(Fackler, 2011)

B. Chinese

"日本媒体昨日报道，日本宫城县仙台市观测到高达10米的巨浪。电视画面显示，仙台机场的跑道<u>被淹没</u>，数十人爬上了机场大楼的房顶。海啸抵达仙台市河口时，造成了严重灾害，水墙一般的宽阔巨浪<u>冲向</u>陆地，<u>卷裹了</u>汽车、房屋等陆地上几乎所有的东西<u>不断推进</u>，多栋房屋着火，农田<u>被海啸吞噬</u>。巨浪将一艘大船<u>高高卷起</u>，<u>撞向</u>防浪堤。"

(Sina, n.d.)

C. French

Le 11 mars 2011, 14h46: un séisme et un tsunami dévastateurs frappent le Japon.

PHOTO APPEARS IN ORIGINAL TEXT (not shown here)

La vague emporte des voitures dans les rues de la ville de Kesennuma, dans la préfecture de Miyagi, au Nord du Japon. (photo caption)

Le Japon a été frappé vendredi par le séisme le plus puissant de son histoire. La secousse de magnitude de 8,9 s'est produite à 14h46 (6h46 heure française) au large des côtes nord-est du pays près de la ville de Sendaï. Elle a été suivie par un tsunami dévastateur et meurtrier. Le dernier bilan—encore très provisoire—établi dans la nuit par les autorités japonaises fait état de plus de mille morts et disparus.

(*Le Parisien*, 2011)

Hints:

Transitive verbs: frapper, emporter, suivre, (se) produire,
Adjectives: dévastateur, le plus puissant dans son histoire, de magnitude 8,9
Voice: Active: <u>un séisme et un tsunami</u> dévastateurs frappent
    Passive: Le Japon a été frappe / Elle (la secousse) a été suivie par un tsunami

What are the subjects of these verbs? What discursive effect does this create?

La vague (photo caption)
La secousse
Le dernier bilan

D. Spanish

Un terremoto de magnitud 8.9 arrasa Japón y deja miles de muertos

Un terremoto destructivo de magnitud 8,8 ha sacudido la costa noreste de Japón y ha provocado un tsunami con olas de hasta diez metros que ha alcanzado la ciudad de Sendai, donde el agua ha arrasado todo a su paso, incluyendo casas, coches, barcos y granjas y ha llegado a los edificios. También en el noreste del país, las autoridades niponas han declarado la emergencia nuclear después de que la central nuclear de Fukushima Daiichi se viese dañada por el seísmo. En la sala de control de su reactor número 1, se registraba esta noche un nivel de radiactividad 1.000 veces superior a lo normal.

(Reuters, 2011)

Hints: transitive verbs: arrasar, dejar, sacudir, provocar, alcanzar, arrasar
intransitive verbs: llegar
reflexives: verse, registrarse
tense/aspect: present tense: terremoto arrasa . . . y deja; present perfect: ha sacudido, ha provocado, ha arrasado, etc.
adjectives: terremoto destructivo, terremoto de magnitud 8.9, dañada.

What are the subjects of these verbs? What discursive effect does this create?

SUGGESTIONS FOR FURTHER READING

Boyle, R. (2011). Patterns of change in English as a lingua franca in the UAE. *International Journal of Applied Linguistics*, 21,2: 143–161.

Breeze, R. (2011). Disciplinary values in legal discourse: a corpus study. *Iberica,* 21,Spring: 93–116.

Caballero, R. (2007). Manner-of-motion verbs in wine description. *Journal of Pragmatics,* 39: 2095–2114.

DeWall, C. N., Buffardi, L. E., Bonser, I., and Campbell, W. K. (2011). Narcissism and implicit attention seeking: Evidence from linguistic analyses of social networking and online presentation. *Personality and Individual Differences*, 51: 57–62.

Francesconi, S. (2011). Images and writing in tourist brochures. *Journal of Tourism and Cultural Change*, 9,4: 341–356.

Grünloh, T., Lieven, E., and Tomasello, M. (2011). German children use prosody to identify participant roles in transitive sentences. *Cognitive Linguistics,* 22,2: 393–419.

Hopp, H. (2013). Grammatical gender in adult L2 acquisition: Relations between lexical and syntactic variability. *Second Language Research*, 29,1: 33–56.

Kua, S. (2003). Involvement vs attachment: Gender differences in the use of personal pronouns in televised sports in Taiwan. *Discourse Studies,* 5,4: 479–494.

Macauley, R. (2002). Extremely interesting, very interesting, or only quite interesting? Adverbs and Social Class. *Journal of Sociolinguistics.* 6,3: 398–417.

Segel, E. and Boroditsky, L. (2010). Grammar and art. *Frontiers in Psychology,* doi:10.3389/fpsyg.2010.00244.

Sharifian, F. and Lotfi, A. (2007). "When stones falls": A conceptual-functional account of subject-verb agreement in Persian. *Language Sciences*, 29: 787–803.

Luzon, M. J. (2012). "Your argument is wrong": A contribution to the study of evaluation in academic weblogs. *Text and Talk*, 32,2: 145–165.

Tse, P. and Hyland, K. (2010). Claiming a territory: Relative clauses in journal descriptions. *Journal of Pragmatics*, 42, 7: 1880–1899.

Verspoor, M. and de Bie-Kerekjarto, A. (2006). Colorful bits of experience: From bluestocking to blue movie. *English Studies*, 87,1: 78–98.

Wierzbicka, A. (2007). Shape and color in language and thought. In A. Schalley and K. Drew (Eds.), *Mental States: Language and Cognitive Structure*, Vol. 2. Amsterdam: John Benjamins.

Xiang, X. (2003). Multiplicity of self in public discourse: A comparative analysis of the use of personal references in two sports radio shows in the U.S. and China. *Language Sciences*, 25: 489–514.

LINKS

BBC News. (2012, November 24). *UKIP couple have foster children removed from care.* Retrieved from: http://www.bbc.co.uk/news/uk-20474120. Accessed December 20, 2012.

Gringberg, E. (2012, December 29). Families 'in limbo' after Russian adoption ban. *CNN*. Retrieved from: http://www.cnn.com/2012/12/28/living/russian-adoptions-limbo/index.html. Accessed December 20, 2012.

BBC News. (2012, July 1). *Euro 2012 final: Spain v Italy as it happened*. Retrieved from: http://www.bbc.co.uk/sport/0/football/17875873. Accessed December 24, 2012.

Gissiner, B. (December 3, 2012). Any time Cleveland wins it is a favorite NFL moment. In *Yahoo Voices*. Retrieved from: http://voices.yahoo.com/anytime-cleveland-wins-favorite-nfl-moment-11919530.html?cat=14. Accessed December 29, 2012.

Gore, A. (2012, September 2). First World War ammunition frozen in time for nearly a century has been found as glacier melts. *The Daily Mail*. Retrieved from: http://www.dailymail.co.uk/news/article-2197174/First-World-War-ammunition-frozen-time-nearly-century-glacier-melts.html#ixzz2GdOt5Y2B. Accessed December 31, 2012.

The Guardian. (2012, December 30). Winter blast causes outages, traffic restrictions on P.E.I. Retrieved from: http://www.theguardian.pe.ca/News/Local/2012-12-30/article-3148620/Winter-blast-causes-outages,-traffic-restrictions-on-P.E.I./1. Accessed December 31, 2012.

Puck, W. (n.d.). Recipes. In *Wolfgang Puck* website. Retrieved from: http://www.wolfgangpuck.com/recipes/search/results/Pizza. Accessed December 31, 2012.

U.S. Marine Corps. (n.d. a). *Physical prep*. Retrieved from: http://www.marines.com/becoming-a-marine/ocs-physical-prep. Accessed December 31, 2012.

Van Buren, A. (2013, May 20). GED hopefuls should get diploma before costs go up. In *Yahoo News*. Retrieved from: http://news.yahoo.com/g-e-d-hopefuls-diploma-costs-050115801.html. Accessed May 20, 2013.

FedEx. (n.d.) Retrieved from: http://www.fedex.com/us/. Accessed December 30, 2012.

Edmunds. (n.d.). 2011 *Mitsubishi Endeavor review*. Retrieved from: http://www.edmunds.com/mitsubishi/endeavor/2011/?sub=suv&ps=used#fullreview. Accessed May 21, 2013.

Sephora. (n.d.). *Coach Signature*. Retrieved from: http://www.sephora.com/signature-P259929. Accessed May 23, 2013.

Revlon. (n.d.). *Jean Naté.* Retrieved from: http://www.revlon.com/Revlon-Home/Products/Fragrance/Jean-Nate/Jean-Nat%C3%A9-After-Bath-Splash-Mist-15-flpt-ozpt-443-mL.aspx. Accessed May 30, 2013.

U.S. Marine Corps. (n.d. b). *First to fight.* Retrieved from: http://www.marines.com/operating-forces/first-to-fight/. Accessed May, 21, 2012.

Fackler, M. (2011, March 11). Powerful quake and tsunami devastate northern Japan. *The New York Times.* Retrieved from: http://www.nytimes.com/2011/03/12/world/asia/12japan.html. Accessed May 23, 2013.

Sina. (n.d.). 《仙台沉没.》 Retrieved from: http://news.sina.com.cn/c/2011-03-12/053222099634.shtml. Accessed May 23, 2013.

Le Parisien. (2011, March 3). Le 11 Mars 2011, 14h46: Un séisme et un tsunami dévastateurs frappent le Japon. Retrieved from: http://www.leparisien.fr/tsunami-pacifique/le-11-mars-2011-14h46-un-seisme-et-un-tsunami-devastateurs-frappent-le-japon-11-03-2011-1352998.php. Accessed May 21, 2013.

Reuters. (2011, March 3). Un terremoto de magnitud 8.9 arrasa Japón y deja miles de muertos. In *El Mundo.* Retrieved from: http://www.elmundo.es/elmundo/2011/03/11/internacional/1299824643.html. Accessed May 22, 2013.

NOTES

1. These "other features of language" include prosodic and graphic variations for spoken and written discourse, respectively. For SPOKEN discourse: examples include tone of voice, volume, intonation (e.g., rising, falling), extended and audible in-breaths or exhalations, and such phonological elements as emphasis ("Did you say '*you ca'n*' or '*you can'T* "?), vocalic alternations (e.g., *hey* vs. *hi*), and consonantal alternations (e.g., *goin'* vs. *going*). For WRITTEN discourse, examples include graphic or symbolic variations, such as punctuation marks, typeface alternations (e.g., bold, italic), UPPER and lower case alternations (*WHY NOT*?, or *i think he looks like einstein.*), abbreviated expressions (*ru ok*?), using numbers to express symbolic meaning beyond quantity or measure, emoticons, the overall visual representation of text-based discourse on a page or screen, and the like.

2. Some may argue that the word string "The farmer killed" is grammatical in and of itself, suggesting that a direct object of the verb is still assumed, though not overt. Similar examples are: "We've already **eaten** [e.g., lunch]"

or "Jennifer still **smokes** [e.g., cigarettes]" where objects of transitive verbs (see this chapter and the Appendix) are understood but not realized at the surface.

3. This is an abridged version of the original, invented by Pinker's student Annie Senghas, which contains eight instances of the word *buffalo*: "Buffalo buffalo Buffalo buffalo buffalo buffalo Buffalo buffalo," including one relative clause construction (Pinker, 1994: 208).

4. A reflexive construction in language means that the subject of the sentence and the direct object of the sentence are the same. Reflexive pronouns, e.g., *myself, himself, herself, yourself*, express this: *Pick yourself up and brush yourself off . . . He nominated himself for the job.* Reflexive pronouns in Spanish include *me, se, te, nos: Berta se mira mucho al espejo* ('Berta looks at herself a lot in the mirror'). For French, reflexive pronouns include *me, te, se, nous, vous: Le capitaine s'est cassé le bras avant le match.* ('The [team] captain broke his arm before the game,' literally 'broke himself the arm . . .'). Note how *reflexive* pronouns are expressed in other languages like: Japanese (自分), Korean (자기), and Chinese (自己 or 自身), each denoting a different type of self-reference or reflexive personhood reference.

5. Noam Chomsky defines Generative Grammar as ". . . simply a system of rules that in some explicit and well-defined way assigns structural descriptions to sentences. . . . Perhaps the issue can be clarified by an analogy to a part of chemical theory concerned with the structurally possible compounds. This theory might be said to generate all physically possible compounds just as a grammar generates all grammatically 'possible' utterances" (cited in Harris, 1993: 39).

6. By "all levels of grammar and beyond," we refer to all systems of language, including phonetics (the study of human speech sounds), phonology (the study of the speech sound inventories and patterns of a particular language), morphology (the study of meaning at the level of the word and smaller), semantics (the study of meaning at the level of the word and greater), pragmatics (the study of meaning beyond the literal or beyond what is expressed overtly), as well as the broader domains in which we use language to create meaning, including elaborating, re-phrasing, revising, editing, and so forth. Choice is possible and it is ever-present.

7. "Grammar" is used more frequently in English as a mass or non-count noun. Here, we use it as a count noun (and pluralize it) to refer to the various languages of the world, each with its own grammatical system—e.g., the grammars of Japanese, Korean, Chinese, and Persian do not distinguish nouns as mass and count nouns in the same way as the grammars of other languages, including English, do.

8. The category of "verb" in this section refers to **lexical verbs**, e.g., *run, hide, play, think, say, become, scurry, compete*, etc. as opposed to **auxiliary verbs** used in tense and aspect constructions (e.g., *have, be*) and **modals** (e.g., *could, may, should*). See Appendix for more examples.

Genre, Register, Modality, and Participation Framework

> Genres are not just forms. Genres are forms of life, ways of being. They are frames for social action. They are environments for learning. They are locations within which meaning is constructed. Genres shape the thoughts we form and the communications by which we interact. Genres are the familiar places we go to create intelligible communicative action with each other and the guideposts we use to explore the unfamiliar. (Bazerman, 1997: 19)

INTRODUCTION

As we have discussed preliminarily in Chapter 1, discourse is not reducible to language and how it is used in texts. Certainly, the topic of how language is used by speakers or writers to converse, narrate, theorize, and rhetoricize enjoys a good bit of attention by scholars in academic disciplines that are speech- and language-central—disciplines like applied linguistics, communication, media studies, education, anthropology, English, foreign languages, marketing, business, and philosophy. But a focus solely on language does not provide a complete picture of any discursive event. To this, one must add perspectives concerning the myriad other semiotic features of discourse, from paralanguage and voice quality to gestures and punctuation, from clothing style and posture to font size and type style, colors, lighting, artwork, and music—all as relevant to and concomitant with the messages conveyed through linguistic means.

And as we have discussed in depth in Chapter 2, language is not necessarily discourse. Discourse is linked to context. Discourse requires participants. Discourse is built on responsivity. And discourse is bounded by structure.

This chapter introduces the major components involved in discursive structure. We introduce *genre* as a metaphorical frame that refers to the culturally shaped (and ever-transforming) sets of conventions that establish broad boundaries for the constitution of various discourse types. Within this invisible frame emerge conventionally driven patterns of language and discourse. These patterns center on the basic content of the discourse, on how information related to that content is organized and sequenced, and on the relevant lexico-grammatical features, all of which combine to shape discourse into one genre or another. We will also see how extralinguistic meaning-filled elements of context serve in the constitution and molding of genres.

With *genre* established as a broad and basic analytic unit of discourse, we can then examine *modality. Modality,* also called the "channel" in some of the communication-based literature, refers to the medium in which discourse is produced. Typically (and overly simply), *modality* involves three very basic modes of communicating: oral or spoken, written, and e-discourse. Intuitively, we can sense how our own use of language changes from one modality to the next. We don't usually speak like we text. We don't usually write like we speak. And we don't usually text like we write. How true are these statements? You can test them on your own. Say your phone-generated texts aloud to the person you were contacting instead of using your keyboard. Handwrite your conversations with your best friend onto a piece of paper, instead of speaking them. Call up that same friend and speak your most recent research paper, instead of asking her or him to read it. More than likely, none of these endeavors will last very long or yield particularly fruitful communicative results.

Genre and *modality* are inextricably linked to *register*—a concept that addresses the linguistic and contextual components that constitute genres. *Register* refers to the range of multiple possibilities concerning lexical and grammatical choice within genre: What specific words are used in the communication? How formal and technical and field specific might they be (compare the terms: *drinks* and *libations,* or *tree octopus* and *octopus paxarbolis*)? How do the various grammatical constructions fit the genre? Are there contractions used? Is first person singular subject pronoun "I" used often (compare: *I then performed the experiment* to *The researcher then performed the experiment*)? Is "I" used at all? How about second-person singular pronoun "you?" If "you" is intended to express a plural meaning, how is that accomplished?

And, as we will observe, *register*-based language choice serves to both maintain generic boundaries and also expand them, often blurring some of the metaphorical lines between one specific genre and others. (See also Chapter 9, Critical Discourse Analysis.)

Context enters into the study of *register* by providing additional detail about the communication: Are color photographs included in "how to" discourse, or is the text composed simply of words and line diagrams? Are participants who might be engaged in "small talk" actually total strangers, brought together fortuitously through seat assignments on an airplane, in a theatre, or sharing a ski lift chair? How do participants establish common ground to first initiate a conversation? What, in the discourse, signals that they are strangers? Again, context is key to both *genre* and *register.*

To illustrate one complex and robust area of *register*, we introduce the category of *institutional discourse*. In *institutional discourse*, varieties of genre and register combine to *define, create,* and *recreate* those institutions. We provide examples of what constitutes institutional discourse in general, together with the various genres and registers that are associated with them and that help define them. We revisit the topic of institutional discourse again in Chapter 6 (Conversation).

Finally, also related to genre, register, and discourse, is the concept of *participation framework* (Goffman, 1981). We cannot truly understand the complexity of discourse unless we are aware of the various participants involved in it. We assume the existence of certain categorical understandings of "speaker" and "hearer," "addressee" or "interlocutor," but sometimes these categories are more complicated. Here is one example: A diner complains to his server about what seems like a massive amount of butter on his baked potato. The comment is heard by a fellow customer, a complete stranger, at the next table who exclaims, "It's not even real butter!" Not previously included in the initial discourse, this second individual deemed his own talk topically and contextually relevant, entitling him to chime in as a commiserating overhearer. Likewise, the category of "audience" becomes more conceptually and interactionally dynamic than a body of viewers or listeners, shifting their status between intended overhearers of talk and actual addressees. The analytic lens of *participation framework* will provide us with novel ways of "seeing" discursive events and making new sense of them.

Genre, modality, register, and participation framework go hand-in-hand in how we produce and understand discourse.

GENRE AS METAPHORICAL FRAME OF DISCOURSE

If discourse is the stuff of human communication, thinking, problem solving, and interaction, genre constitutes the sets of frames that delimit discourse

GENRES are metaphorical frames of discourse that are both shaped and constrained by socio-cultural conventions of practice, and reshaped and recreated through discourse and social practice. Genres exhibit culturally recognizable discursive patterns for the conveyance of essential propositional content to some form of audience or hearer (imagined or real), within a particular context, with a view to accomplish a particular communicative purpose.

into categories or units. Genre enables us to classify discourse, to identify its general purpose, to understand discursive messages and how they work, and reciprocally, to create and recreate meaning both within the familiar, conventional generic boundaries and beyond.

Genre essentially is a metaphorical frame that provides structure for discourse (Bakhtin, 1981, 1986: 103; Bazerman, 1997; Swales, 2004). With structure comes consistency and recognizability (Bakhtin 1981, 1986; Eggins and Martin, 1997; Martin, 2008a; Swales, 1990, 2004). Genre provides us with ways of naming how we use and understand discourse — prose, conversation, narrative, oratory, poetry, novel, novella. It associates discourse with function and purpose and practice. It establishes limits and recognizable boundaries, allowing us to identify a particular instance of discourse as belonging to the genre of instruction or advertisement, stand-up comedy, or magic show. Likewise, discourse involves mixing of genres, where generic lines may blur. A prime example is the hybrid genre of the "infomercial." These are essentially advertisements, but structured as if something else — an in-studio demonstration, with personal testimonies by individuals who have used a product and whose lives have changed as a result. And these performances double as promotional discourse to sell appliances or cosmetics or medications.

The English words "Once upon a time . . ." signal the opening of a particular type of story. "Knock Knock!," said in just the right tone within just the right context and followed by silence, elicits its generic response of "Who's there?" and we anticipate yet one more formulaic sequence, followed by the unfolding of a specific and predictable type of play on words. The words "Dearly Beloved, we are gathered here today . . ." signal the opening of a funeral or a wedding. Each set of formulaic expressions occurs at the beginning of a specific and recognizable genre: a fairy tale, a knock-knock joke, an invocation. The genre-initial word clusters signal that a specific type of discourse will soon be underway.

Other genres are even more rigidly codified, such that the text of the message must remain entirely intact, if the exemplar is to be considered valid and a true instance of a specific genre type. This is the case with many religious prayers and rituals, like *The Lord's Prayer* in Christianity, the *Kaddish* in Judaism, and *Salah* (daily prayers) in Islam. Codified expressions of national loyalty like "The Pledge of Allegiance," must be uttered with a verbatim fidelity to its original text and in a contextually appropriate manner and place. Barack Obama's 2009 inauguration oath actually required a re-administration by Chief Justice John Roberts, due to Roberts's inadvertent transposition of the adverb "faithfully," and Obama's responsive repetition of Roberts's inaccurate line. The following excerpt contains this line, and it has been amended to reflect only the words spoken by Obama:

> ". . . I, Barack Hussein Obama, do solemnly swear . . . that <u>I will execute</u> the office of president to the United States <u>faithfully</u> . . ."

The oath, as written for verbatim recitation, contains this line: ". . . that <u>I will faithfully execute</u> the office of the president . . ." (Mears, 2009). The oath, as initially taken by President Obama, did not conform to the official wording of the Oath of Office of the President of the United States.

Most genres, however, are less strictly bound to code and rote repetition. Yet they maintain elements of essential content and structure that help to classify the discourse into one genre or another.

THE GENRE OF THE COOKBOOK RECIPE

Take the common cookbook recipe, for example. The genre of the recipe exists for the triple purpose of sharing cooking methods with others, verbally and pictorially illustrating those cooking methods as a means of verbatim instruction or suggestions for approximate replications, and applying those cooking methods in an attempt to replicate the dish (or modify it according to one's own tastes).

Following, you'll see two recipes for oven-fried chicken, each from classic "American" cookbooks. One, *The Good Housekeeping Illustrated Cookbook* (1989) and the other, Rombauer and Becker's *The Joy of Cooking* (1931/1997). If words or phrases appear in boldface type in the original, boldface type also appears here. *The Joy of Cooking* recipes use boldface type to lead readers elsewhere for additional clarification or explanation, if necessary.

Recipe 1—Oven-Fried Chicken: *Good Housekeeping*

Oven-fried Chicken

Color index
page **45**
Begin 1 ¼ hrs
ahead
4 servings
315 cals per serving
Good source
of Vitamin A,
niacin

¼ cup butter or margarine
¾ cup cracker meal
1 teaspoon salt

⅛ teaspoon pepper

1 2 ½ - to 3-pound broiler fryer, cut up

1. In 13″ by 9″ baking dish, melt butter or margarine in 400°F oven. On waxed paper, mix cracker meal, salt and pepper. Remove dish from oven.
2. With tongs, roll chicken in melted butter or margarine, then coat with crumbs on all sides; place in dish. Bake 40 to 50 minutes.

(Good Housekeeping, 1989: 263)

Recipe 2—Oven-Fried Chicken: *The Joy of Cooking*

OVEN-FRIED CHICKEN 2 servings
Preheat oven to 350°.
   Disjoint:
      A broiler, 422
   Wipe dry. Dredge it in:
      seasoned flour
   Heat to the point of fragrance in a heavy skillet:
      ¼ cup butter
Sauté the chicken lightly. Remove from the skillet to a rack in a shallow pan. Baste with the skillet pan drippings. Bake uncovered until tender, 30 to 40 minutes, basting with added fat if necessary and turning occasionally. Serve with: **Poultry Pan Gravy, 341; or Sauce Périgueux, 347, or Quick Canned Soup Sauce I, 348.**

(Rombauer and Becker, 1997: 424)

Recipes, as a genre in U.S. American culture, have the same basic structure. They typically provide: the name of the dish, the number of servings, the ingredients list in various formats, and directions for cooking. The list of ingredients, in addition to itemizing the foods, condiments, and spices themselves, also often designates required amounts of such ingredients—measured in cups, teaspoons, tablespoons, ounces, pounds, drops (for liquids like extracts and colorings), and an array of food-specific quantifiers like head (cabbage, lettuce), clove (garlic), slice (bread, dried meat, cheese), and sprig (parsley).

Cooking directions typically reflect a basic chronological order—designating steps that need to be taken first, second, next, and so forth, sometimes numbered and sometimes not. They often provide guidelines for cooking times and desired outcomes (e.g., "simmer 20 minutes or until tender," "bake 15 minutes longer, until done"). Some recipes suggest sauces or other dishes for accompaniments. Some suggest arrangements of the food on the serving dish, together with garnishes for color or balance.

However, while the form and essential contents of a recipe are rather "standard" in a culture, much variation exists from cookbook to cookbook, and from chef to chef, with regard to actual directions and additional commentary. And it is essentially within such variation that we find differences in the stances of recipe authors vis à vis food in general, cooking and preparation styles, aesthetic presentation, author expertise, and assumed expertise on the part of the recipe user—stances that encapsulate the following orientations toward food: Food is art. Food is nutrition. Food is filling or light, fancy or simple. Food unites family. Food is expensive. Food is inexpensive. Food connects couples. Food transcends the sensory perception of taste. Preparation takes time, or it is quick. Cooks need detailed instruction, or just basic guidelines. Cooks share authors' views of food and family and culinary art, or not.

These stances, and more, become visible as we examine discourse from the points of view of language as conceptually and interactionally meaningful, and genre as frame for social action (Bakhtin, 1986; Bazerman, 1997; Fairclough, 2003; Miller, 1984; among others). That is, the way each recipe is organized and presented—through words and graphics—reveals much about the presenter's stances.

Let's compare the two recipe samples. At first glance, they look similar. The dish name is identical. Ingredients are similar, but not identical. Cooking times and suggested oven temperatures are similar, but again, not identical. *Good*

Housekeeping suggests in a side column how many hours in advance to start preparation; it indicates nutritional content, including calories and vitamins. It provides the step-by-step cooking directions in the format of a numbered list. And it includes a side column reference to page 45, containing nine 1 ½" x 2 ½" glossy color photos (i.e., three rows and three columns) of various chicken dishes, from Moo Goo Gai Pan (the photo at the top left) to Chicken à La King (the photo at the bottom right). The photo for Oven-Fried Chicken appears in the bottom row, center, showing about eight different pieces of oven-fried chicken piled asymmetrically on a blue dinner plate and garnished with a small number of fresh, dark green spinach leaves, on one edge of the plate sprinkled atop the meat. There are no color photos available anywhere in *The Joy of Cooking*.

These two recipes differ in some less obvious ways as well. We can characterize the differences preliminarily from the point of view of *expectations of presenter* vis à vis *the cook's level of experience and general familiarity with cooking*. Based on a number of discursive patterns in these recipes, we could posit preliminarily that *The Joy of Cooking* approach is more specific in terms of ingredients designations and more technical in terms of directives.

The following table illustrates some of these patterns. What appears here in boldface type in the *Joy of Cooking* columns also appeared in boldface in the original.

Joy of Cooking	*Good Housekeeping*
disjoint broiler and wipe dry	1 2 ½-to 3-pound **broiler** fryer, cut up
¼ cup butter	¼ cup butter or margarine
shallow pan	13" x 9" baking dish
Dredge it in **seasoned flour**	use tongs to roll chicken, coat with crumbs on all sides
Heat (¼ cup butter) *to the point of fragrance* in a heavy skillet [emphasis added].	Melt butter *or margarine* in 400°F oven

From the outset, *The Joy of Cooking* frames the reader as both agentive and knowledgeable. The initial word is a verb, a technical directive to render the fowl into parts: "disjoint broiler." There is an underlying assumption that the reader understands the meaning of the directive "disjoint," and knows how to do it. *Good Housekeeping* refers to the action as already accomplished, either at the store, the butcher shop, or at home, using a more everyday term, with "cut up" functioning here as an adjective—not a verb. From a *GH* perspective, the individual who actually performs this action appears inconsequential to the actual preparation. The chicken itself is specified as a **broiler** in the *Joy of Cooking*, with a brief explanation found on page 422, as follows: "Young chickens of either sex are called **broilers** if they weigh about 2 ½ pounds and **fryers** if they weigh 2 ½ pounds to 3 ½ pounds . . . " The fact that a terminology list, like a glossary, is included, makes it look more like a technical and professional book. In *Good Housekeeping,* the designation of which particular type of chicken to be used is ambiguous, and thus seemingly immaterial, with the recipe calling for a "2 ½-to 3-pound broiler fryer."

The *Joy of Cooking* presents its recipe such that if cooks do not know how to prepare **seasoned flour**, for example, they can look it up elsewhere (and find the recipe on page 552, in an entirely different section)—almost like a textbook, with an academic approach. *Good Housekeeping* (GH) simply lists the individual ingredients for this one recipe: cracker meal, salt, and pepper. "Seasoned flour" is a term that will recur in the *Joy of Cooking* (Joy) and will be used in other main dish recipes. Further, while *Good Housekeeping* suggests either butter or margarine for its recipe, butter is the only option in *The Joy of Cooking*.

With regard to actual cooking instructions, *GH* provides information at minute levels of detail for the seemingly less experienced cook, while *Joy's* assumption of the cook's prior knowledge continues to emerge and solidify. This is reflected in three ways in the *Joy of Cooking* recipe: 1) The cook is free to select his or her own cooking vessel as a shallow pan; its specific size is unimportant. 2) The verb *dredge* appears with no explanation, no reference to other pages in the book, and no simplification of its meaning. Compare this directive with the parallel one in *GH*: "use tongs to roll chicken" (*in other words, not your fingers*), "coat with crumbs on all sides" (*in other words, not just the top or not just the bottom, but everywhere*). 3) The cook is positioned as expertly able to gauge the proper consistency of the butter, discernible not through an explicitly visual recognition, but an olfactory one: "Heat (¼ cup butter) to the point of fragrance in a heavy skillet." *GH* relies only on the cook's eyes and logic of following directions.

Same genre. Same dish. Two recipes. Each different from the other in terms of stances toward food and toward the preparer of food. *GH,* with its numbered list of steps, color photos of dishes, and simplified means of describing food preparation activities, appears to address cooks with less experience who are in need of explanations and visual presentation ideas, while *Joy*, with its black-and-white lettering and line drawings and more technical directives, seems to target cooks with greater experience and expertise in the kitchen. As you will note later in this chapter, such discursive differences between the *GH* recipe and the *Joy* recipe can be accounted for as differences in *register.*

Genre: Content and Purpose of Discourse

What shapes discourse into genres, then, are *essential content* and *purpose.* Content or informational substance is at the core of any genre. At the level of informational substance or "propositional content," (Halliday,1994) genres serve as rhetorical vehicles to communicate facts, to present ideas, to question reality, all within culturally influenced sets of conventions. As frames of discourse, genres *instruct, entertain, inform, invite, move, impel,* or *impassion.* And genres succeed in doing all of this and more, because they reflect our individual experiences within our social and cultural situations through recurring conventionalized forms and structures (Bakhtin, 1986; Bazerman, 1997; Bhatia, 2004; Devitt, 2004; Hyon, 1996; Miller, 1984; Swales, 2004).

Think about any genre you know: online dating profiles, wedding invitations (sometimes a happy result of the former!), movie trailers, chemistry experiments, textbook prefaces, investors' meetings, auctions, documentary films, educational standards documents, bio statements, political speeches, interviews, rock concerts, cookbooks, radio announcing, and music videos, just to name a handful. What makes each category cohere into just that—a category—is essentially the content and the purpose of the discourse. As you will see, content and purpose influence overall structure, organization, lexicogrammatical choices, paralinguistic features, and extralinguistic elements of the context in which the discourse unfolds, all of which are bounded by convention and culture.

To illustrate, let's take a look at one of the most pervasive genres of discourse, **narrative**.

THE GENRE OF THE NARRATIVE

Narrative is a common discursive genre that crosscuts other genres. Narrative commonly occurs in ordinary conversation and throughout genres of institutional discourse. Narratives occur during mealtimes and in board meetings. Narratives are stories with a purpose, stories built in discourse to elicit emotion, to portray a viewpoint, to convey a moral lesson, to judge and seek likemindedness, to persuade, to (consciously or subconsciously) construct one's or others' identities (Bamberg, 2010; Baquedano-Lopez, 2001, 2008; Bauman, 1986; Cohen, 2010; Linde, 1993; Schiffrin, 1996). "Personal narrative is a way of using language or another symbolic system to imbue life events with a temporal and logical order, to demystify them and establish coherence across past, present and yet unrealized experience" (Ochs and Capps, 2001: 2). In addition, narrative "gives form to what we imagine, to our sense of what is possible" (Bruner, 2010: 45).

Following you'll find a sample narrative—a brief story about an experience someone had while alone in a foreign country. Think about the following guiding questions as you work with the data sample (and genre sample) for the first time:

- What elements of the speaker's identity are revealed in the narrative? (gender, age, education, profession)
- What sorts of feelings is the speaker expressing? How? Does s/he actually name the feelings?
- How are the details of place represented?
- How are the details of time represented?
- How do the details of place and time work together to depict this speaker's feelings during the event?

This is an oral narrative of a past personal experience. The speaker is telling a story about an event that occurred in a small village in China. There are no particular linguistic markers here that explicitly signal any of the features of

Data Sample: Narrative

This summer, I was—I spent six weeks teaching in southern China, and I was teaching in a village. So during the week, while I was teaching, I lived with a host family in that village. So I think it was maybe less than a week into this process . . . I had a room to myself. It was kind of a big living room, with not much in it. But there was a couch in one corner and that's where I slept . . . So one night I had gone to bed, probably around eleven o'clock, and had been asleep I guess about an hour when all of a sudden I was woken up because the light in my room had turned on and . . . there was a strange man standing in the room, ((laughter)) and he was sort of—he had turned the light on, his back was to me. So I don't know if he even saw me, but he was kind of looking around, and I didn't have any idea what to do with this you know random man who had just walked into my room and turned the light on. I thought "Oh no!" And so I didn't say anything. And in a few seconds he turned off the light and left . . .

the speaker's identity that we asked you to notice, i.e., gender, age, education, profession. But you may have formulated your own hypotheses about this as you read the story, based on sentence structure, grammatical constructions (including the past perfect, e.g., *I **had gone** to bed, I **had been** asleep, the light in my room **had turned on**, . . . who **had** just **walked** into my room and **turned** the light **on**.*), and other aspects of word choice (e.g., *a strange man, this random man*). The speaker's very discursively **deliberate use of the past perfect** may serve as an **index**[1] of the speaker's educational level and/or a highly developed sensitivity to English grammar concerning time reference and event depictions (building tension and contrast in the narrative), in that many of these instances could have easily been expressed using the simple past. The speaker's reference to the intruder as "a man," may **index** the speaker's gender identity as "a woman," with the "man-woman" contrast underscoring her feeling of being threatened as a woman by a male intruder. (See Chapter 8, Indexicality). None of these implicit clues to the speaker's identity is expressed literally or overtly.

Likewise, there are no explicit language tokens that label any of this speaker's emotions, though here, you could likely identify those with more certainty than the linguistic features that point to the speaker's identity. What *are* the emotions expressed in this narrative? How does the gradual depiction of emotions contribute to the development and delivery of this oral narrative? (See Chapter 8, Indexicality and *affective stance*).

In fact, the speaker of this narrative, Heidi, is a graduate student specializing in teaching English to Speakers of Other Languages (ESOL). The basic story line is clear: Heidi had spent part of her most recent summer teaching English in southern China and something happened that made her feel both uncomfortable and scared while she was alone in this new environment in a small village of a foreign country.

Just using this small narrative sample, we will identify some of the basic patterns of language use that combine to shape the structure of a narrative (Bruner, 1986, 1990, 2010; Capps, Ochs, and Bruner, 1996; Labov and Waletzky, 1968; Labov, 1972a, 1972b, 2010; Linde, 1993; Ochs and Capps, 1996, 1999, 2001).

1. *Narratives are "tellable"* (Ochs and Capps, 2002) or *"reportable"* (Labov, 2010)
2. *Narratives contain settings and "orientations" that provide backgrounds for the stories to develop.* (Labov and Waletzky, 1967; Labov, 1972a, 1972b, 1997; Linde, 1993; Ochs and Capps, 1996, 2002)

Background details of time and place—orientation:
This summer
six weeks teaching in southern China
in a village
I lived with a host family in that village
a room to myself
kind of a big living room
a couch in one corner, where I slept

3. *Personal narratives are most often stories of past time experiences con-structed with <u>subjectively ordered memories</u> to link past to present (and to link past and present to future). These memories emerge through sub-jective, <u>experiencer vantage points</u> and <u>temporal descriptions</u> (Goffman, 1974; Ochs and Capps, 2001).*

Experiencer vantage points—explicit and implicit commentary by nar-rators that reflects their internal states of feeling and thinking—both as experiencers of the event in the past and experiencer-narrator of the story in the present as it is being retold:
So <u>I think</u> it was <u>maybe</u> less than a week into this process.
So one night I had gone to bed, <u>probably</u> around eleven o'clock.
So, <u>I don't know</u> if he even saw me . . .
and <u>I didn't have any idea what to do</u> with this you know random man . . .
I <u>thought</u> "Oh no!"

Temporal descriptions—situate the events within a recognizable tem-poral space, using time adverbials, shifts in tense, and aspects; to depict ongoing events and states, clarify background details, enhance contrasts between personal expectations and reality, link remote past to recent past, link past to present, relive and recreate experiences in collabora-tion with a present-time interlocutor (or reader):
I <u>spent</u> six weeks teaching. [simple past]
I <u>was teaching</u> in a village . . . [past progressive]
So, during the week, <u>while I was teaching</u> . . . [time adverbial w/past progressive]
. . . maybe <u>less than a week into this process</u> . . . [time adverbial]
I <u>had</u> a room to myself. [simple past]
So I **don't** know   [note this shift to *present tense*]

4. *Narratives are built around and driven by a <u>complicating action</u>* (Labov and Waletzky, 1967; Labov, 1997), *a <u>most reportable event</u>* (Labov, 2010) *or a <u>problematic event</u>* (Bruner, 1986; Capps, Ochs, and Bruner, 1996; Schiffrin, 1996). *A <u>complicating action</u> or <u>problematic event</u> or <u>most reportable event</u> is "the event that is the least common" of all elements in the narrative (Labov, 2010: 7) and often contains linguistic and paralinguistic cues concerning the reason the narrative is being told in the first place.*[2]

    <u>Complicating action, problematic event</u>—These actions or events are foreshadowed in the orientation of the narrative; details of time and place are gradually and systematically elaborated upon to allow for the sudden, unexpected, or otherwise problematic issue to be highlighted in the retelling.

    Note now the orientation, temporal descriptions, and the experiencer vantage points that highlight the problematic event:
    I had gone to bed around eleven o'clock . . . had been asleep about an hour,
        when <u>all of a sudden I was woken up</u> because the light in my room
        had turned on <u>and . . . there was a strange man standing in the room.</u>

5. *Narratives often express a <u>resolution</u> of the problem or a <u>calming down</u> of the intensity related in the story.*

    And in a few seconds he turned off the light and left.
    Note also Heidi's shift in reference terms concerning the intruder:
    First mention (heightened surprise—part of problematic event):
    There was a strange man in the room.
    Second mention (calmer perspective):
     . . . this you know random man who had just walked into my room.

6. *Narratives always express a viewpoint. In so doing, explicit labeling of feelings, emotions, impressions, judgments of self or other, and other aspects of such viewpoints may or may not be present. Often, narratives establish contrasts* (e.g., between expectations and reality, present and past, negative and positive, known and known) *as discursive means of systematically building such viewpoints.*

    We find no explicit labeling of emotions in Heidi's narrative—her feelings and reactions are depicted entirely through a **series of contrasts** (built discursively through the following images, including her use of past perfect, as noted):

    Heidi is alone in a foreign country
    she is living with a host family

thus: she had specific expectations of safety, comfort, and privacy
But these expectations were jolted:

sleeping soundly	→	awakened (suddenly)
darkness	→	("the light had turned on"—as if spontaneously)
alone	→	someone else is there ("there was a strange man")
safety, comfort, and privacy	→	upended by intruder
fear, suspense, uncertainty	→	relief (the man left)

Narratives are genres that typically occur within other genres of oral, written, or e-discourse. They emerge in the midst of ordinary conversation. They occur in news stories, in academic research, in political speeches, in confessions (both religious and criminal), and in late-night talk show interviews (e.g., Bamberg, 2010). They appear in religious practices (Baquedano-López, 2001, 2008; Benor, 2012) and all throughout business and industry (Breeze, 2012; Williams, 2012). Narratives can provide two diametrically opposing viewpoints in plaintiff-defendant opening statements, with one narrative portraying one "truth," and the other, a markedly different "truth" (Cooke, 1996; Harris, 2001; Matoesian, 1999). Narratives function reciprocally to express viewpoints on the teller's side and to affect viewpoints on the recipients' side. Minimally, a narrative might serve to entertain or to seek alignment and empathy from its addressees, as we observed in Heidi's sample. Maximally, narratives seek to persuade, alter opinions, and effect change (Bauman, 2001: 183; Fairclough, 2003: 84).

So far, we have examined two types of discursive genres: the recipe and the narrative. One is brief and visually systematic—lists, ordered steps leading to a finished product, imperative verb forms (e.g., *melt, mix, roll, sauté*), and a limited range of linguistic content. The recipe is, by nature, formulaic and conventionalized, for ease of use and replication. The second, the narrative, is unlimited in length. It takes shape and develops through the interplay of past memory and on-site current interaction. Unlike the recipe, the narrative, by nature, exhibits a richness of linguistic form, a complexity of language use to depict sights and sounds, experiences and feelings—and all the while, maintaining elements of structure and of convention that make a narrative a narrative.

MODALITY AND REGISTER

Modality: Oral, Written, and E-Discourse

Modality refers to the medium through which communication takes place, typically oral modalities (face-to-face, telephonic, audio/video), written modalities (discourse produced on paper with writing or drawing implements, or discourse produced using a word processor), and electronic modalities (online discourse, including texting, gaming, social media, online retail). Discourse often reflects combinations of modalities, or **multimodal discourse** (Kress and van Leeuwen, 2001), where elements of semiotic modes of oral, written, electronic, digital, aural, and graphic communication combine in the creation of discursive meaning in texts.

Genre and modality go hand in hand. Modality refers to the communicative medium through which discourse is produced, i.e., through oral communicative means, written communicative means, and electronic means or "electronic language" (Collot and Belmore, 1996), which includes both text messaging (Crystal, 2009; Hutchby and Tanna, 2008; Soffer, 2012) and online communication (Crystal, 2011; Georgakopoulou, 2011; Herring, 1996, 2012, 2013; Herring, Stein, and Virtanen, 2013; Hutchby, 2001).

We outline next some basic distinctions and relevant features of discourse in each broad type of discourse modality.

Oral discourse is most often associated with face-to-face and telephonic interactions.

- Oral discourse lends itself to immediate responsiveness on the part of other co-present participants.
- While private speech (Vygotsky, 1986) and self-talk (Larrain and Haye, 2012; Tovares, 2010) are typically self-directed, oral discourse is primarily other-directed.
- Oral discourse is evanescent (Chafe, 1994: 42). Once something is said, unless it is recorded on tape, through a digital recording device, or by a human transcriber or reporter, the utterance becomes merely a memory. Words and phrases and utterances cannot be revised—only repeated and re-done and, once said, retracted.
- The organizational and syntactic features of oral discourse can be quite distinct from the syntax and content organization in written discourse and in e-discourse.
- Oral discourse exhibits personal displays of affect, empathy, and stance through vocal characteristics such as volume, rate of speech, verbal and non-verbal response tokens, in addition to facial expressions, head shakes and head nods, eye gaze, and gesture.
- Oral discourse can be entirely spontaneous and unplanned, evolving and changing on a second-by-second basis, as speakers interact, re-think, and re-formulate, while engaged in conversation, interviews, and oral personal narrative.

- It can be planned, (not scripted), organized by a pre-determined set of topics or informational bits intended to be addressed, as in the genres of lectures, sermons, police interrogations, and legal proceedings.
- It can be scripted and delivered through oral modalities, intended to sound as if it is non-scripted oral interaction, e.g., theatre, campaign speeches, award speeches, lectures, and sermons.
- It can be scripted and delivered through and contain many organizational and syntactic features of written discourse, e.g., news broadcasts, documentary film narration—both live and audio-video-recorded.

Written discourse is typically associated with paper, pencil, word processor, and print media.

- Written discourse does not lend itself to immediate responsiveness by others—responses, if produced at all, are inherently delayed. Written discourse is permanent (Chafe, 1994: 42), and will last as long as the life of the medium on which it is produced.
- Written discourse can be spontaneous or unplanned, or painstakingly composed, edited, revised, withheld, and even destroyed in advance of communication.
- It can be used for private self-reflection and rehearsal with no reader intended.
- The organizational and syntactic features of written discourse can be quite distinct from the syntax and content organization in oral discourse and e-discourse.

Electronic discourse is typically associated with screen-based media, like texting, email, and other online practices, such as social media (e.g., Facebook, LinkedIn, Twitter, E-Harmony), specialized information (e.g., Trip Advisor, AllRecipes), general information (e.g., corporate websites, university websites, online news), retail sales (e.g., Amazon.com) and gaming.

- Electronic discourse is often referred to as a hybrid type of discourse (Biber and Conrad, 2009)—exhibiting features of oral discourse on the one hand and written on the other.
- Like oral discourse, e-discourse lends itself to immediate responsiveness by other participants currently online, though not inherently.
- Like in written discourse, responsiveness may also be delayed, if no online participants are present, or if none chooses to respond.

- Like written discourse, e-discourse may be permanent, lasting as long as the screen or site maintains the discourse.
- And, like written discourse, e-discourse can also be edited and revised.
- Unlike both oral and written communication, e-discourse is almost exclusively other-directed.
- E-discourse can exhibit personal displays of affect, empathy, and stance through graphic and symbolic conventions, e.g., emoticons, reduplicated exclamation points and other specialized uses of punctuation, specialized uses of typewriter key symbols, specialized uses of digits (e.g., 143, 'I love you': 1432, 'I love you, too'; 9, 'my mom's watching'), and abbreviations (lol, @TEOTD 'at the end of the day') (Crystal, 2009; Ling and Baron, 2007).

In the following section, you'll find two data samples from a similar genre: job applications for a teaching position. Both are applications to teach English in the United Arab Emirates. One discourse sample is an oral, audio- and video-taped monologue that responds to the question: "Why do you want to teach English in the UAE?" The second is an application letter by a prospective candidate addressed to the personnel director of an American English language school in Abu Dhabi. Both applicants are female and both have some previous experience teaching English as a Second Language.

Read the transcribed text of the next oral application. This is clearly a "hybrid" modality, exhibiting some features of oral discourse and some of written. Try to identify which features tend to be more associated with oral discourse and which with written. You can use the characteristics that we listed previously for each. (In the next section, will discuss features of oral *registers* and written *registers* in more detail.)

After working with this data sample, you should also be able to discover additional commonalities and additional differences between the modalities as you work with actual discourse data.

- Which features of **oral** discourse do you note?
- Which features of **written** discourse do you note?
- Which linguistic features of discourse emerge in the text only because this is a video-recorded, oral medium of communication? NOTE: Please don't use this clause as support: "<u>and I'm making this video</u> so you . . . " Try to locate instances of discourse that are less obvious to answer this question.

DATA SAMPLE: Oral Job Application (Supplementary Materials) 1—Teaching English in the UAE

Hi, my name is Jennifer Newcomb. Thank you for taking the time to watch this video and learn a little bit more about me. I am making this video to give you a better idea of who I am and to answer your question, "Why do you want to teach English in the UAE?"

I want to teach in the UAE because I have a lot of experience in dealing with people from other countries. I uhm grew up in New York City, and there's a lot of people there from all over the world. Along with that, when I was in high school, I had a part-time job tutoring some children who just arrived from Tunisia. The kids were brothers, and one didn't know any English at all, actually. The older brother knew a little and he could even write a few words, too. So I taught them the basic words in English and both of them learned so quickly. And so it was really amazing to see them improve and to understand more in school. I was happy, because they even started to make some American friends at their school.

When I was in college, I taught classes in English as a Second Language. It's a class that they offer in some of the nearby high schools for adults who have just arrived in this country. My students were all beginners, and they actually didn't speak any English at all. But it was really exciting. It was also challenging, but very exciting to see them begin to understand the grammar of English and put it all together, like words and phrases and sentences. They all wanted to learn grammar more than anything else and it was fun to see how much progress they made.

I hope I'll have the chance to work in Abu Dhabi and have the same kinds of experiences.

Who is the applicant? What are her qualifications? How are the applicant's identity and qualifications represented in the discourse?

Now, read through the data sample for Job Application 2, which is a letter of application. As you did with the oral text, think about the following guiding questions:

- Which features of **oral** discourse do you note?
- Which features of **written** discourse do you note?
- Do you note any hybridized discourse features, e.g., a mixture between what sounds like oral discourse and what sounds like written discourse?

DATA SAMPLE: Job Application (Supplementary Materials) 2—Teach English in Abu Dhabi (Letter)

September, 23, 2012

Mr. George Bunche, Director
American Education Center
P.O. Box 2590
Abu Dhabi, UAE

Dear Mr. Bunche,

This letter is a supplement to the attached application form. I have experience teaching English to a small group of international students who came to the Amarillo area as high school exchange students. The students came from China, Korea, Iraq, Egypt, Saudi Arabia, and Brazil. We watched videos in English and read American newspapers. I had the students practice reading, writing, listening, and speaking in English.

I feel that I am highly qualified to teach for you. I am a native speaker of English. I studied Spanish in high school and I studied French for two years in college, so I know what it means to have to learn a language. I know how hard it is to learn spelling in French, so I can imagine what students feel like when they have to try and learn the spelling of English words.

I am an organized teacher. I have experience in making lesson plans and materials. My students say that I am outgoing and they like my personality as a teacher. I do not mind spending extra time after class explaining grammar to students if they have questions. I am happy to share my culture with my students.

I have attached a resumé that includes my other work experience and also the names and addresses of three references.

I look forward to hearing back from you soon.

Thank you for considering my application.

Sincerely,
Samantha Weigler
457 Hillside Avenue
Amarillo, Texas 79101
USA
sam.weigler443@noprovider.com
(817) 888–8888

What types of *obvious* similarities and differences do you notice between oral and written modalities of discourse? For example, the visual format of the letter is based on a set of formal conventions for the genre of the "business letter," with date, greeting, heading, body, closing, and the signer's contact information. The transcript represents spoken words documented on paper, with "paragraph breaks" arbitrarily assigned according to content or topic shifts. We don't really think in paragraph format, nor do we process oral discourse in paragraphs. But, when language is graphically represented through a written modality, we chunk it, we break it up in an organized fashion, so that we can more easily process the content, keeping related ideas together logically and finding ways and places to draw lines between the discourse.

Both versions contain an explicit reason for the submission of the materials: (a) in the oral application supplement, ". . . I am making this video to give you a better idea of who I am and to answer your question," and (b) in the business letter, "This letter is a supplement to the attached application form." Both indicate that other materials have also been submitted to accompany the application itself ("*to give you a better idea of who I am* and *to answer your question*" [emphasis added] and "This letter *is a supplement to* the attached application form" [emphasis added]).

Presentation of Self: Speaker/Writer and Addressee

These obvious points of comparison serve as basic foundations on which to analyze each data sample more deeply. As one difference, we'd consider the place in which the applicant states her own name. In the letter, the applicant's name appears at the end. In the video recording, it is in the very first line. Why do you think this is so? And why is this tidbit of information important?

Each document, in its own way, is a **presentation of self** (Goffman, 1959/1990; Schiffrin, 2006; Tannen, 2009). In the case of the video recording, providing a name at the opening of the discourse is both natural and expected. The initial line of this sample resembles a mini self-introduction, not unlike one that would be delivered in a room full of strangers, where each member rises, says his or her own name, and includes a line or two connected to his or her presence at the meeting or gathering (e.g., small seminars, sales meetings with new employees, group therapy sessions, 12-step meetings, and so forth). There is a perceived immediate need to match the person and the person's face with a name. In contrast, in the case of the letter, an initial self-introduction is neither relevant nor expected. The discursive interaction is not with a human face, but a piece (or bundle) of paper. The name of the writer does not appear until the very end, at the signature line, both conventionally and in this exemplar.

The writer of the letter provides information about herself in a sequence and style that differ significantly from those of the on-screen recording. Self-presentation in the formal, written version is accomplished with a personal distance between writer and reader. The order in which information is provided and the level of detail associated with the information help to maintain that distance. From a receptive point of view, the reader of the letter can choose to scan quickly down to the signature line before reading, peek at the sender's name at the return address on the envelope, flip through the sheets to peruse the application form first, or simply just read the letter and ascertain the writer's identity at the end. The addressee in the video format is an explicit reference to the viewer as "you" ("so you can learn a little bit more about me"). The addressee in the letter is a titled individual, formally and conventionally greeted as, "Dear Mr. Bunche."

Presentation of self: organization of information, presentation style

- With regard to the organization and presentation of self and information in each modality, note the following crucial distinctions:

  o **ORAL modality**, as exhibited in the <u>video recording</u>: The propositional content contained in each clause or sentence is almost always linked to the next clause or sentence by explicit logical connection markers, expressing:

additives	"And," "Along with that"
cause or consequentiality	"so," "and so," "because"
contrast	"but"

  o **WRITTEN modality**, as seen in the <u>letter</u>: typically *implies* the logical connections between clauses and sentences and paragraphs, leaving it up to the reader to *infer the logic* — as either additive, consequential, contrastive, and so forth.

- With regard to the content and delivery of the self-presentation in each, note how the video-based oral version differs from the written version:

  o **ORAL modality**, The speaker is appealing to ***narrative*** as a means of underscoring her teaching experience and abilities. The speaker's presentation of self revolves around a general narrative with two related stories highlighting the *success of others*, all brought about by her work and dedication and excitement.

o   The oral narrative is itself built on contrasts, notably in a **before and after** format of cause and consequentiality, with the "before" condition relating to a "pre-teaching" situation and the "after" condition relating to a "post-teaching" situation. That is, students' abilities are framed *as if starting at zero* in both cases, e.g., "and **one didn't know any English <u>at all</u>**, actually," and "they actually didn't speak any English at all." The successes of the teacher and her students becomes evident in the resulting in "improve[ment] and to understand[ing] more in school," "begin[ning] to understand the grammar of English," and "how much progress they made," with the process being "challenging" ("but very exciting").

o   By focusing on adjectives, we can observe even more distinctly how this speaker narrates about her own teaching experiences, almost exclusively represented through her witnessing the growth of her students:

" . . . and so it was really *amazing* to see them improve"
"It was also *challenging*, but very *exciting*."

o   **WRITTEN modality**, A presentation of self that explicitly mentions the writer's qualifications (and not implied through narrative or through the perspective of *the other*): "I feel that I am highly qualified to teach for you," "I am an organized teacher," "I have experience . . . (mentioned in two places) (in) doing *x*."

In fact, note how the writer uses the first person pronoun "I" throughout:

I am writing to apply . . .
I have experience teaching English . . .
I had the students practice reading . . .
I feel that I am highly qualified . . .
I am a native speaker of English . . .
I studied Spanish . . .
I studied French . . .
I know how hard it is to learn spelling in French . . .
I can imagine what students feel like . . .
(and so forth)

71

This format, then, is a **presentation of self** through self-definition, essentially providing answers to the questions: *Who am I? What can I do for you? Why/how do I match your job description?*

Essentially, we have two instances of the same genre, a supplementary job application document, each representing a different discourse modality, **oral discourse** and **written discourse.** This genre of job application discourse inherently revolves around the activity of ***presentation of self***. In the one exemplar, the applicant frames herself as qualified by virtue of the success of others. She reflects her expertise and ability to relate to and empathize with students through a narrative of "excitement"-filled experiences as tutor and teacher. The video-based modality complexifies the genre: It is now also a **performance,** not just a job application. (Tseng, 2010). In the second exemplar, the applicant frames herself as qualified by virtue of a long list of personal accounts and experiences that position her simultaneously as expert, agent, authority, advance planner, and as an empathetic superior.

REGISTER

> **REGISTER** refers to the sets of grammatical, lexical, and prosodic features of discourse within genres that together signal or index membership within a specific group, such as social class, age group, generation, profession, national culture, school culture, etc. As such, *registers* also index ideologies and identities.

If *genre* is the WHAT of discourse, *modality* and *register* are the HOWS. We have just examined two samples to provide a brief illustration of some of the HOWS as they relate to *modality* and the means through which discourse is produced. In this section, we will continue the HOW discussion, by introducing the concept of *register* and thereby focusing on the individual grammatical and lexical items that combine to help shape genres into their respective categories.

As we noted in Chapter 2, discourse is imbued with linguistic choice, whereby language users select (consciously or not) words and constructions and tones of voice and rates of speech. They do this to interact, to think and problem solve, to write and converse, to represent their views and to comment on views of others. The expression of self and social belonging (or isolation), the indexing[3] of personhood, identity, and ideology, becomes evident and identifiable in discourse through *register*. (Agha, 2004, 2005, 2007; Biber, 1994; Biber and Finegan, 1988, 1989; Duranti, 2011; Ferguson, 1982, 1994; Halliday 1978, 1977/2002; Hymes, 1974; Irvine, 1979). "A register is a linguistic *repertoire* that is associated, culture-internally, with particular social practices and persons who engage in such practices" [emphasis original] (Agha, 2004: 24). That is, *register* is not simply a single word or a specialized expression, it constitutes an entire array of linguistic, paralinguistic, and metalinguistic practices that combine to index the ways in which we engage in social interaction—in speech, in writing, and through technological mediation (Agha, 2004, 2005).

As we have observed in the previous section on modality, features of the interaction greatly affect how discourse is produced and communicated: Interaction that takes place via an oral means (e.g., face-to-face, telephonically, video-mediated) exhibits grammatical and lexical characteristics that written discourse may not. This became especially salient in the discussion concerning sentence structure and logical connectors in the job application video, e.g., *and, because, so, and so, and along with that*). Further, as we observed in the two oven-fried chicken recipes, the discourse can differ solely on the basis of *register*, when the genre is identical and the modality is identical. Moreover, we probably would not have even noticed the *register* differences in the first place, had we not compared the one exemplar to the other, and vice versa. We may have simply been satisfied having understood both the genre and the very general *register* of the recipe for an everyday meal.

Here are just a few common examples of register:

1. **Colloquialisms**—found in ordinary conversation between peers, oral narrative, e-discourse (e.g., social media posts, emails between peers), some genres of written discourse:
    1. Grammatical reductions of forms, e.g., "I want to" → *I wanna*, "Are you going to?" → *Are you gonna*? ; "don't you?" → *Doncha*?
    2. Informal words, lexical reductions, and phrases in place of unmarked or formal counterparts:
        1. "yes" → *yeah, uh-huh*
        2. "no" → *naw, nope, uh-uh*
        3. "can" → *c'n*
        4. "because" → *'cause, cuz, cos*
        5. "I am so happy to be here" → *I'm so happy ta be here.*
        6. "et cetera," "and so on" → *and stuff like that*

       7.   men, boys, males (and females) → (you) *guys*

       8.   information → *info*

       9.   very → *way, really, rill, totally*

3. Colloquial fillers and hesitation markers, e.g., *like, uhm, you know*

4. Profanity, near profanity, exclamations, e.g., *Sh—! What the—?*

5. Slang, in-group expressions

       1.   *Don't be* **chicken**.   (unmarked: "afraid")

       2.   *That's* **cool**.   (unmarked: "okay, good.")

       3.   *skird*   (unmarked: "scared")

       4.   *wasted*   (unmarked: "drunk, on drugs")

6. Verbs expressing extreme degrees of subjective, personal emotion:

       1.   I *love* raw eggs over hot steamed rice.

       2.   I *hate* black socks with sneakers on guys.

2.   **Formalisms**—in ordinary conversation where some degree of deference is expected (e.g., asymmetries involving age, profession, social status); in e-discourse where some degree of deference is expected; in written discourse, especially business correspondences, academic research, laws and legal contexts, policy documents, and contracts.

•   Formal words or expressions in place of unmarked or colloquial expressions:

    o   *Please be advised that . . . in the matter of . . . You are hereby notified that . . . In response to your first question . . . It has come to my attention that . . .*

    o   need → *require*

    o   if → *should you, in the event of*

    o   men, women → *males, females*

    o   because of → *due to*

    o   adverbials: *herewith, heretofore, in spite of, notwithstanding*

    o   adjectives: *foremost, utmost*

    o   show → *indicate*

    o   more → *supplement, supplementary*

    o   person → *party, individual, the "Lessee"*

    o   rain, snow, drizzle → *precipitation*

•   The use of subjunctive mood in non-formulaic expressions (e.g., *If I were to make the decision, I'd . . .*)

o   With two sentential subjects and a verb of obligation, permission, suggestion, or requirement—visible only in third-person singular:

<u>The student absence policy</u> [subject 1] *requires that each student* [subject 2] **submit** [subjunctive mood] *a note to the attendance office in the event of a partial or full day absence.*

3. **Technical lexicons**: Note that some lexical items are also used in everyday conversational registers (e.g., *clipper, appearance, reaction, factor, slab, difference, wait*) or cross-cut more than one technical register (e.g., *downgrade, solution, fraction, fragrance, faction, bid*). The meanings of words are linked to genres and contexts in which they are used, and may change dramatically from genre to genre and from context to context.

weather:	clipper, trough, high pressure, landfall, tropical storm, downgrade, arctic
legal:	bailiff, deposition, *in camera*, juror, appearance, Certified Shorthand Reporter
chemistry:	chloride, distillation, reaction kinetics, ions, molecules, solutions
math:	ratio, multiplication, factor, divisor, sum, difference, square root, fraction
culinary:	dredge, fragrance, baste, dice, knead, bouillon, consommé, potage
food service:	bus, menu, gratuity, wait, hold the mayo, beverage, short order
architecture:	cantilever, blue lines, balustrade, soffit, elevation, cornice, façade
construction:	plans and specs, change order, slab, finish, rebar, HVAC, culvert
gaming (face-to-face):	bid, raise, Texas Hold 'em, flush, La Partage, street bet, Baccarat, Keno
gaming (online):	Pandaria, Azeroth, faction, Ponyville, The Yellow Angry Bird, Poppit

INSTITUTIONAL DISCOURSE AND REGISTERS

In this section, we introduce institutional discourse as representative of specific types of registers, and as related to the technical lexicons as listed in the previous section. We consider as *institutional* any discourse produced for and by members of specialized sectors of society, organized through specific types of social order, who act in accordance with designated specific purposes, all of which is beyond the discursive scope of everyday life. Mayr (2006: 4) cites Agar's (1985: 6) definition of institution as "a socially legitimized expertise together with those persons authorized to implement it," and expands the concept by qualifying that "institutions are not restricted to physical settings and can refer to any powerful group, such as government or the media."

The power that institutional discourse may create emerges from the overall organization of discourse, including aspects of expertise, authority, and rights to participation (as speakers, writers, artists, musicians) and the institution-specific way of using language and other semiotic media, including genres and register.

Institutional discourse is a ripe area for the study of registers of all kinds, especially with regard to the specialized lexicons and the concomitant characteristic and routinized features of grammar. Lexico-grammatical and pragmatic conventions that are associated with institutional discourse can include:

- À priori designations of participatory roles: who, when, where, and how

  o patterns of personal reference:
  o avoidance of first person "I," such as *The Court, the researcher* (cf. "I")
  o consistent use of first person "I," for self-presentational purposes such as

    o *I am writing to apply, I feel that I am highly qualified, I have experience teaching English.*

  o second person "you" replaced in direct address by titles such as *Senator Cartwright, Mr. Mayor, Your Honor, If it pleases The Court*

- Non-technical, commonly occurring nouns, adjectives, and verbs typically associated with that register, as in weather reporting: *churn, push through, widespread, swath, high, low, dump*

Different from ordinary conversation (See Chapter 6, Conversation), which occurs literally anywhere from homes and shopping malls to waiting rooms, commuter trains, restaurants, and elevators, institutional discourse is anchored to designated places and specific contexts. Further, unlike in ordinary conversation, participant roles involve varying degrees of pre-determined expectations concerning the overall conduct of the participants, including speakership rights and turn-taking patterns, lexico-grammatical choices, vocal characteristics (e.g. volume, rate of speech, intonation), and personal appearance (e.g., attire, hair style, facial expressions and affect displays, eye contact). See Drew and Heritage (1992), Levinson (1992), and Mayr (2008, 2012) for work on institutional discourse and Kress and van Leeuwen (2001) for related treatments of multimodal discourse.

The following is a partial list of genres and sub-genres of institutional discourse. As you review the list, think about the relevance of place, modality, context, and participatory roles for each discourse type. Also, think about the genres (and sub-genres) of discourse that may be produced in each type of institutional discourse, from the points of view of *content* and *purpose*.

- classroom interaction
  (Cazden, 2001; Mehan, 1979, 1985; Sinclair, 1987; van Lier, 1996; Strauss and Feiz, 2012; Waring, 2008).
- mathematics education, science experiments, written scientific argumentation
  (Gerofsky, 2004; Hundt et al., 2012; Kelly et al. 2001).
- medical encounters, clinician notes, surgical narratives, laboratory reports
  (Ainsworth-Vaughn, 1998; Antaki and Jahoda, 2010; Cordella, 2004; Denvir and Pomerantz, 2009; Gill et al., 2010; Heritage and Maynard, 2006; Heritage and Robinson, 2011; Labov and Fanshell, 1977; Peräkylä, 1995; Robinson, 2008, 2011; Pomerantz et al., 2007; Stivers, 2012).
- legal proceedings, courtroom discourse, police reports, depositions (oral and transcribed), affidavits, laws, court orders
  (Agar, 1985; Bhatia et al., 2012; Harris, 1995; Hashim and Hassan, 2011; Lakoff, 1989; Philips, 1984; Sidnell, 2008, 2010a).
- service encounters
  (Bailey, 1997; Codo, 2011; Coupland, 1983; Kevoe-Feldman and Robinson, 2012; Merritt, 1976).
- business practices, contracts and contract negotiations, floor trading
  (Bargiela-Chiappini, 2009; Bargiela-Chiappini and Harris, 1997; Pomerantz and Denvir, 2007)
- media discourse: TV (talk shows, interviews, reality shows), radio (music, talk, advice), internet based (websites, web-based audio, web-based

video, YouTube, news outlets), print media (newspapers, magazines, newsletters, letters to the editor, print ads)

(van Dijk, 1988, 1991; [inst. sp.] Fairclough, 1995a, 1995b; Bell and Garrett, 1998; Clayman and Heritage, 2002; O'Keefe, 2006; Greatbatch, 1986, 1988; Heritage, 1985; Heritage and Clayman, 2002; Clayman, 2010, 2013a, 2013b).

- sports discourse
(Glenwright, 2012; Halone and Meân, 2010; Meân and Halone, 2010; Tavakoli and Ghadiri, 2011; Tovares, 2010).
- discourse of religion
(El-Sharif, 2012; Singh et al., 2011; Vigouroux, 2010; Wharry, 2003).
- weather reports
(Lee, 2006; Spillner, 1997; Vannini and McCright, 2007).

Institutional Discourse—AccuWeather ("Breaking Weather") Storms Across New England

In keeping with our discussion of genre, modality, and register, we introduce the genre of the on-camera video recorded *weather report*. As we have been emphasizing, genre is characterized by both content and purpose. In the case of the weather report, both should be self-evident. Content: weather. Purpose: to broadcast weather predictions and attach weather-related circumstances to multiple facets of our daily lives.

AccuWeather (www.accuweather.com), established in 1962, provides meteorological forecasts online to news outlets and businesses in the United States and throughout the world. Twenty years later, The Weather Channel (www.weather.com) emerged as a 24-hour weather-only television network. Its website provides meteorological data for nearly 100,000 locations throughout the world. Other websites include Weather Underground (www.wunderground.com) and Weather.gov/NOAA, by the National Weather Service—National Oceanic and Atmospheric Association (www.weather.gov).

These meteorological sites provide similar content information for similar purposes. All provide data in the forms of forecasts, reports, advisories, warnings, maps, graphics, and videos—all with relevance to our professional lives, our personal lives, our leisure, and our business. Should we take a sweater or ear muffs? An umbrella or snow boots? Will they close the Wimbledon roof for the Men's Finals? Are we ordered to "evacuate" or "hunker down"? Will insurers pay more in claims settlements with Sandy classified as a post-tropical storm or a hurricane ? Will our premium rates rise? Will stocks fall? (Fox on Stocks, 2012)

Let's have a look at two seemingly similar exemplars of the video-based weather report (see Strauss, 2013, for a similar discussion of this genre). The first is from the AccuWeather.com website, accessed and transcribed on Friday, June 8, 2012. The second is from the weather segment of a web-based broadcast of the NBC New York News, aired on Thursday evening, June 7, 2012. The weather issues at hand involve Atlantic summer thunderstorms—no hurricanes, no Nor'easters, no warnings, no advisories—just typical summer weather on the east coast of the United States. See Strauss (2013) for more discussion of both datasets.

Essentially, we have two instances of the same genre, presented through the same modality, culled from the same type of institutional discourse, and reporting on similar weather conditions within hours (not days) of each other. Yet, the discourse between the two involves some strikingly different patterns—patterns which can be accounted for in terms of *register* differences.

Here are a few points to consider as you read through the text:

- Do you find that the presentation style contains more features of oral discourse or written discourse? What types of register elements do you notice (i.e., colloquial, conversational, formal, technical?)
- Which geographic locations are covered by this report?
- Underline (or highlight) the *technical, weather-related terms.*
- Underline (or highlight) common, everyday terms that are associated with the weather conditions being reported.

DATA SAMPLE: Weather Report 1—AccuWeather

Breaking Weather—6/8/12 Florida Stays Wet

Spotty but gusty storms now firing up across New England, most of which are staying away from the major cities. We have a line of storms pushing from northern Wisconsin across the U-P of Michigan, but it looks like the heaviest downpours are impacting much of the Deep South. This is all due to an old stationary boundary right around the Gulf Coast that's interacting with a lot of tropical moisture across the Gulf of Mexico. Notice this big blob over the northeast coast of Mexico ((pointing to the weather map showing precipitation in green)), well, that's going to continue to push off to the North and East—very slowly, and we may see some heavy heavy rainfall along I-75 from Tallahassee to Tampa. Right now, most of the storms are staying north of Tampa. But it's been quite unsettled north of Miami. Storms hit north of Fort Myers and Naples earlier. Those are continuing to push across Lake Okeechobee and West Palm Beach. In the last two hours or so, West Palm Beach has already picked up over an inch of rain. It's going to stay wet here, right on into the weekend. Storm systems in North Texas will continue to move East along that old boundary and we are going to see some slow-moving storms dumping a lot of rainfall. Watch out along I-10 and in the darkest green, which includes New Orleans, we're talking anywhere from four to six inches of rain. I'm Jeannette Calle.

(Accuweather, 2012)

This probably looks like any on-camera weather report we've seen in the United States. Probably nothing stands out as remarkable.

In our guiding questions, we asked you to attend to features of modality and instances of register in simple terms and determine whether this is closer to oral or written style. Just base your observations on the text.[4]

What is your answer to our first question, and why? Note: There is no single correct answer to start with—but whichever style you choose, you need to present a detailed argument, with examples from the data to support your findings. For example:

- Oral discourse features / everyday or conversational register—notes for supporting evidence: a) Some imperative usage: "Notice this big blob," "Watch out along I-10"; b) a few colloquialisms: "this big blob," "well," "we're talking anywhere from four to six inches of rain"; c) contractions: "that's," "it's"
- Written discourse features / formal register; technical register—notes for supporting evidence: a) complex sentence structures: "We have a line of storms, pushing from northern Wisconsin across the U-P of Michigan, but it looks like the heaviest downpours are impacting the deep south"; b) only a few explicit conjunctions, e.g., "but"—most of the sentences involve *implied* connections—as additive, causal, consequential, and so forth; c) more formal and technical registers: "due to," "stationary boundary," "unsettled"

Based on these observations (and others that you have made), do you stand by your initial impression concerning modality features or register, or have you adjusted that view to some extent? Why? Which elements in the discourse have contributed to your position?

As for the geographic region(s) covered by the report, we have nearly the entire Atlantic Seaboard, and parts of Gulf Coast.

How about our questions concerning technical, weather-related terms, on the one hand, and common, everyday terms naturally associated with weather, on the other?

Nouns and noun phrases: *spotty but gusty storms, a line of storms, the heaviest downpours, an old stationary boundary, tropical moisture, most of the storms, storms, over an inch of rain, storm systems, slow moving storms, rainfall, four to six inches of rain*

Verbs: *firing up, staying away, impacting, interacting, push off, staying north, hit, push across, picked up, move, dumping*

Just by analyzing the nouns and verbs (and how they combine), we can put forth a few preliminary ideas leading toward an analysis of this discourse.

Before we do, however, let's have a look at the second exemplar from the NBC New York News weather segment.

We'll ask you to attend to the same set of guiding questions that we posted for the AccuWeather excerpt as you read through the NBC text the first few times:

DATA SAMPLE: Weather Report 2—NBC New York News

NBC New York, Evening Weather for Thursday, June 7, Janice Huff @4nyweather

((addressing in-studio co-anchors Tom Llamas and Shiba Russell, though eye gaze is directly at camera)) . . . Alright, hey, wha- lookit you guys, behind you, that beautiful shot there from the Top of the Rock.

((shift to reporting of weather)): There are clouds rolling overhead and there's a shower moving over the City right now. Little tiny shower. There it is. ((photo of NYC)) And the temperature is 71 degrees in mid-town. Well, before we had that shower move over the park in midtown, we

---

saw temperatures up to 78. That was the high for the day in the Park. Warmed up about five degrees as we anticipated. Bridgeport with a high of 73. Ya hit 80 in Newark this afternoon. And close ta that at LaGuardia at 79. Here's our headlines: Watch out for that pop up shower or possibly a gusty thunderstorm with small hail. Most of us won't see anything this evening, but they're randomly out there. Warmer weather still tomorrow and into the weekend. Saturday's high 84. Sunday not quite as hot. And there may be a spot shower or thunderstorm popping up each afternoon as well. But, during the daytime, most of the day will be nice and sunny and warm. 70s right now to the North, Newburgh, Poughkeepsie, Danbury 75. Even out over Long Island, Islip and West Hampton both at 71. There's that shower moving over Midtown down towards the Village right now. ((map shows green precip moving over Greenwich Village), now extending into Queens and eventually maybe even Brooklyn might get touched by it, too. To the south of the city, there are some heavier thunderstorms—heavy rain and maybe some hail and quite a bit of lightning in Howell and Manchester. That's moving to the south and east. That's the general direction today. The past couple of days, they were moving from north to south. Now northwest to southeast. That big upper level low is slowly moving out but the air is still unstable so the afternoon showers are still popping up, but they're gone by 9:00 pm in most locations. Seventy one at 7:00 o'clock this evening and we still may have a spotty thunderstorm here and there, but the rest of the evening should be nice and dry. Seven-Day Forecast: Well, no major changes except the temperatures warm up. Eight-three on Friday, 84 Saturday, and close to 80 on Sunday, so each day there could be a storm or shower that pops up in the late afternoon, say between 3:00 pm and 6:00 pm. On Monday, it's nice and dry, 82. A little muggier on Tuesday but the 80s stay with us all through next week, so pretty nice weather coming up for all outdoor plans. Back to you guys.

(NBC Universal Media, 2012)

Once again, this probably looks like or sounds like the hundreds or maybe even thousands of other news-based weather segments you've seen.

Now, let's explore more deeply.

Does this segment reflect more features of oral discourse or written discourse, according to what you see in the transcript? Which oral discourse features can you identify? Which written discourse features can you identify? How do these features relate to the overall discourse in terms of genre, content, purpose, and register variations?

Compare and contrast how you might feel as a viewer of this weather report and of the AccuWeather report. In what ways are your reactions to the two discourse samples similar, and in what ways are they different? And, most importantly, why do such impressions and realities created by discourse matter in our everyday lives?

The weather anchor's delivery of the report opens with a bit of conversation with her two in-studio co-anchors. In fact, prior to the start of this transcript, all three had been conversing about a topic entirely unrelated to weather. The actual segue into the weather portion is achieved by virtue of the cam shot of New York City, visible to the weather anchor, but at the backs of her co-anchors. The conversational tone (and its concomitant style and register features) continues throughout the broadcast. In fact, as viewers, we feel that we, too, are being addressed as if we were her conversational partners, or at least silent addressees—and this, especially so, if we are living in or near the same viewing area that she is reporting about: *"Well, before **we** had that shower move over the park in midtown, **we** saw temperatures up to 78,"* and *"**Ya** hit 80 in Newark this afternoon."* The first person plural pronoun "we" is ambiguously inclusive, referring at once to Ms. Huff and her co-present colleagues as well as to the viewers in the area. Similarly, the second person pronoun "you," reduced to *"ya" in "Ya hit 80 in Newark . . ."* "sounds as if she is addressing that area directly, too. (Also: *"Most of us won't see anything this evening,"* and *". . . the 80s stay with us all through next week . . ."*). The scope of her addressed audience is nicely circumscribed, grammatically and thus conceptually, as if to include viewers targeted in the broadcast area as addressees, and everyone else, as ratified overhearers (see Participation Framework that follows). This is all accomplished seamlessly. Viewers likely don't mind the apparent informality of her discourse. Viewers are framed as included within her scope of address on the one hand, or excluded and simply overhearing these reports of local weather and daily temperatures, on the other.

Now would be a good time to compare and contrast the two datasets. As you do this, you should attend to the following types of discursive features (and others that you discover on your own):

1. What technical or genre-specific weather related nouns are used in each? (For starters, note how many times and in what contexts the word *storm* [or *storms*] occurs in the AccuWeather report. Compare that type of reference practice with weather-related terms in the NBC News segment).

2. What common, everyday weather-related nouns are used in each?
3. In what way might the geographic focus of the weather reports be relevant to their overall tones and registers?
4. What types of verbs are used in each? How do the nouns and verbs combine to create meaning related to weather? Is the weather itself portrayed in any way as "agentive" or "powerful?" In both reports? Why do you think this is so?
5. Regarding the use of personal pronouns: Does the word "we" mean the same thing in both the AccuWeather report and in the NBC New York News report? That is, who does "we" refer to in the one report? Who does "we" refer to in the other?
6. How is the audience positioned in each broadcast? What are the discursive features that work together to create the respective types of audience positioning?

As we have seen so far with the oven-fried chicken recipe, identical genres expressed through identical modalities may differ in terms of register and consequently in terms of discursive framing of stance on the part of the author or producer or speaker vis à vis readers and hearers and audiences. Speakers may be authoritative or dispassionate. Authors may frame themselves as exclusively expert or inclusively collaborative. Weather report producers may portray rain and thunder and storms as powerfully moving (even animate) forces of nature, or simply as facts of life or facts of weather, made accessible to us via science, mathematical equations, and technology. Each instance of weather reporting has its own effect. The AccuWeather broadcast serves a different purpose than the television news-based broadcast—the register differences from one to the other clearly illustrate this.

Genres do indeed constitute and create the general WHAT of discourse. And modality and register do combine to constitute the HOW in multiply complex and robust ways.

Before we conclude this chapter, we introduce one additional concept related to the discussion of *genre* as WHAT and the complexity of the HOWS that make discourse and genre come to life.

Participation Framework

Recall that the Weather Report Sample 2, from NBC New York News, opened with a conversation between a meteorologist and her two co-anchors. From a very simple perspective, we can construe such interactional exchange on the basis of *speaker* and *hearer,* with each role being fulfilled by the person (or persons) *doing the speaking* on the one hand, i.e., the speaker, and the person (or persons) *doing the hearing* (or *being addressed*) on the other, i.e., the hearer or addressee. Naturally, roles shift easily and frequently in and out, back and forth. Speakers become hearers and hearers become speakers, and so continues the exchange.

But this model of seemingly linear, bi-directional, or even cyclical communicative exchange does not match how interaction takes place in reality. In Chapter 6 (Conversation) we will address turns and turn-taking practices in depth. For now, though, we'll keep the discussion on the non-technical side, and will illustrate how the speaker-hearer-speaker model is insufficient to account for discursively built oral interaction, using the notion of *participation framework* (Bell, 1984, 2001; Clark and Carlson, 1982; Clayman and Heritage, 2002; Duranti, 1986; Goffman, 1979/1981; Goodwin, 1999; Larson, 1997; Levinson, 1988; Marcoccia, 2004; Rae, 2001).

In terms of participant roles, it is easy to imagine a dyadic relationship between a speaker and a hearer, with their respective roles changing depending upon who is doing what, speaking or listening. The framework might work fine when two persons, and only two persons, are involved in an interaction. But once more individuals participate, such dyadic frameworks crumble. Social interaction is precisely that—social. The likelihood of only two parties being constantly present during a conversation or any other situated oral communicative practice is slim. Other parties may be present. There may be additional addressees. There may be additional listeners. There may be additional speakers. And there may be overhearers. That is, ongoing talk that is not addressed to a specified individual may be overheard by someone else. It happens all the time. And that someone else might be an entire audience or a single member. Audiences can be framed in discourse as direct addressees or as ratified overhearers, i.e., participants in oral interaction who are not the direct addressees of a talk show host or celebrated pastry chef, but intended indirect recipients of the discourse nonetheless. A non-ratified overhearing person may be co-present at a communicative event, or just outside a door, but where a speaker is not aware of that person's presence. Or, even eavesdropping—with a glass to a wall, an ear tipped deliberately in one direction, earbuds hooked up to specialized recording devices disguised as flowers or a fountain pen, or simply customers at a restaurant catching wind of other customers' complaints or raves.

Participation frameworks, then, help us to more accurately analyze discourse by virtue of who is involved beyond the rigid and linear model of a single speaker and a single addressee. Concepts such as *overhearers* and *overhearing audiences* are key to understanding discourse in general, and media discourse in particular (Bell, 1984, 1991; Bubel, 2008; Clark and Schaefer, 1992; Dynel, 2011; Heritage, 1985; Katayama, 2009; Kozloff, 2000).

As we observed briefly with the NBC News weather report, viewing audiences can be discursively framed as addressees (i.e., the persons living in the New York and New Jersey viewing area *and* the co-anchors during some parts of the segment) or overhearers (i.e., all other viewers of the broadcast) as "ratified overhearers," with the discourse intentionally designed for their ears and eyes. Bell (1984), in his work on audience design, refers to such recipients of discourse as **auditors**. Non-ratified participants who hear discourse that is not intended for them but whose presence is known by the speaker(s) are referred to by Bell (1984) as **overhearers**. And folks who catch wind of oral discourse not intended for them and whose presence is not known by the speaking party or parties are referred to in the literature as **eavesdroppers**.

In the case of the video-based job application that we examined earlier (Jennifer Newcomb), the discourse was designed expressly for a specific addressee (or group of addressees)—certainly not us and not the other random viewers of the video. The content is responsive to the general original application instructions and specifically to the question "Why do you want to teach English in the UAE?"

In the case of the weather reports, the viewers are clearly the targeted audience, but by virtue of the two distinct ways of framing both the deliverers of the news and the audience, we can sense the sometimes subtle and sometimes direct shifts in our own participatory roles in this discourse.

Returning to the restaurant scenario at the beginning of this chapter, the complaining customer is naturally the speaker and the waiter is naturally the addressee. As for the overhearing client, he would be considered a non-ratified overhearer, or even an eavesdropper, in Bell's terms.

How many times in the past month have you been an overhearer—both in the ratified and unratified senses? How many different ways have you been framed as an audience member, whether in a lecture hall, a theater, a place of worship, or while watching TV, movies, and Internet broadcasts? In what contexts have you become an eavesdropper or an auditor?

Party-line telephone service, in which users shared the same telephonic loop, was once popular in the United States (1940s and 1950s) and was a prime locus for occurrences of such phenomena on a daily basis. Waiting in line for concert tickets, on buses and trains, in restaurants and rest-rooms—we are all subject to discourse that may not have been meant for our ears (and eyes). We hear it, and take it in, and react—spontaneously or not, and somehow, such discourse, too, grows and evolves and makes its way into other discourse, and so goes the cycle of how we speak and write and interact, producing and responding to discourse at every step along the way.

REVIEW AND REFLECTION: GENRE, MODALITY, REGISTER, AND PARTICIPATION FRAMEWORK

1. In addition to "Knock-knock," (to open "knock-knock jokes") and "Dearly Beloved," (to open a wedding ceremony or other religious rite), what genres in English and other languages that you know are signaled by specific genre-opening discourse? (e.g., "Once upon a time," *il était une fois* or *il y a bien longtemps* (French), *había una vez* (Spanish), むかしむかし あるところに。。。(Japanese)).

    What do such generic formulas say about the interrelationships between language, genre, and culture in terms of predictability and rec-ognizability? Can you locate instances of variation where certain generic formulas are used to create new and hybrid genres of discourse (in Eng-lish or other languages)?

2. In what ways are genres of discourse predictable and recogniz-able? What makes them so? Identify five examples of discursive genres that you are familiar with. Do they follow any particular patterns of overall organization and structure? Describe those. What are the features of register that are associated with each genre?

    If at all possible, compare one genre in English to a seemingly similar genre in another language. In what way are socio-cultural perspectives reflected in genre? That is, what elements of social practice and cultural practice do you find reflected in particular genres of discourse? These will become salient by comparing multiple exemplars. Discuss the notion of "genre as social practice" by comparing multiple instances of the "same" genre—you might want to compare English and *other varieties of English*, such as "Academic English" across multiple disciplines (e.g., education and engineering), or U.S. recipes and Canadian recipes (or French and Belgian recipes, Salvadoran and Peruvian recipes, and so forth).

3. Following you'll find an excerpt from *The Everything Kids' Science Experiments Book* (Robinson, 2001: 36–7).

Try this: Seesaw

Materials:

Pencil
Ruler with inch markings
10 pennies, minted after 1982 (because you need them to have the same metals inside)
Procedure:

1. Place the pencil on a hard surface such as a table.
2. Place the ruler on the pencil so that it balances at the 6-inch mark.
3. Place five pennies at one end of the ruler.
4. Take five more pennies and find the location on the other side of the ruler that will make the ruler balance.
5. Clear the ruler off.
6. Place six pennies at the 2-inch mark on the ruler.
7. Find the location on the other side of the ruler at which only three pennies will balance the original six.

What other genre(s) of discourse does this remind you of?

Are there any similarities that you notice between the genre of the (*kids'*) *science experiment* and the *recipe*?

What are those similarities? That is, what features of lexicon, grammar, and structural organization do these two genres share? In what ways are they different?

In other words, how do the two instances of *genre* compare and contrast from the point of view of both *genre* and *register*?

4. In Question 3, we asked you to compare and contrast the genre of the *recipe* with that of the kids' *science experiment*. The most visually obvious basis of comparison would be structure. From there, we'd need to look at purpose and register. What other elements would we need to consider to compare and contrast discourse in various genres?

Here, compare and contrast two genres related to "problem solving discourse."[5]

The first two examples in A are math word problems. The example in B is a riddle.

A. Math word problems (Math Stories, n.d.):

1. Once upon a time, there were three little pigs—ages 2, 4, and 6. *What was their average age?*
2. Each little pig wanted to build a house. Pig #1 wanted to build a house of straw. Straw costs $4 a bundle. He needs 9 bundles. *How much will he spend?*

B. Riddle: (Craig, n.d.)

Farmer Higgs owns three pink pigs, four brown pigs, and one black pig. *How many of Higgs's pigs can say that it is the same color as another pig on Higgs's farm?*
Answer: None because pigs cannot talk.

The exemplars of the math problem and the riddle set the scene with introductory background information. The math problem is a mixed genre, based on a "fairy tale" (note the "Once upon a time" opening line).

The discourse in both A and B involves numbers. One of the genres requires numerical calculation. The second requires a different sort of logic.

The expected answers to both types of discourse reveal much about the purpose of the discourse.

How are these two instances similar to each other and how are they different? Explain your answer in detail and support your argument using excerpts and patterns from the "data."

5. Along these same lines, how are the following pairs of genres similar to and different from each other?

Think about features of: structure, organization, content, purpose, modality, register, and participation framework, in addition to linguistic forms and other relevant semiotic media for each. What discursive features does each pair share? That is, what precisely do they have in common? In what ways do they differ?

university lecture	and	religious sermon
university lecture	and	TED talk
TED talk	and	magic show
board game rules	and	traffic laws

Can you think of other potentially parallel genres of discourse that can be compared and contrasted in the same way that you have thought about these genre pairs?

6. Provide some examples (English and other languages) of how genres change and transform over time, particularly through the combinations of multiple modalities (see Kress and van Leeuwen, 2001) and the intermixing of generic features and related features of register. We provided one example of data, using a video-based job application. What other instances of hybridized, multimodal genres can you think of?

List at least five examples from various fields (e.g., social media [Facebook, YouTube performances, cries for help, social awareness], local advertising, corporate advertising, pharmaceuticals, mathematics education, media-based advice-giving programs, infomercials, medical or dental training, matchmaking services—for starters). Examples of hybridized discourse like these abound in our everyday lives.

Analyze the discourse (linguistic features, visual elements, and audio elements [if relevant]) in each exemplar. Which genres of discourse and which types of social practices are actually being mixed? What are the purposes of each of the five hybrid genres that you have identified? How is such purpose enhanced as a result of this very instance of multimodalities and generic mixing?

PRACTICE WITH DATA ANALYSIS—PUTTING IT ALL TOGETHER

I. Narratives

Next, you'll find two data excerpts. Both include narratives. One is from a face-to-face conversation between friends. The person telling the narrative is male. The topic of talk is a frightening event where the interlocutors thought they were going to die, at least for a moment during which the event took place. The second narrative is from the for-profit petition-hosting site, Change.org. The topic of that narrative, also produced by a male, concerns the clothing line carried and promoted by Abercrombie & Fitch.

As you read through the narratives, you should attend to the following:

The genre is narrative. That has been established.
In each case, who is telling the story? For what purpose?
Can you identify any of the characteristic elements of narrative in either or both?
How are these elements similar? How are they different?
How does each teller of the narrative present himself?
How do the components of modality and register figure into each?

Face-to-face conversation between friends:

Jenna: Yesterday, on the way to the lab this guy cut me off and I had to slam on my brakes. I skidded out of control and I thought I was gonna die in that split second. Did anything I like that ever happen to you?

Ted: Yeah. Once.

Jenna: What happened?

Ted: I was uh I'm rafting, white water rafting in Banff uh with some family members en I was in the back of the raft. It was a class three rapids. Not terribly dangerous but they were pret-pretty big rapids. And it was the first big rapid of the day, and we went down to the- It- was a hole- in the river - that's why it was kind of a dangerous rapid. Ya shoot down, you don't see it. It's called a surprise rapid. We didn't see it until we got out there. So we go in there and the whole raft goes up, and I thought the whole raft'd be gone, but it was really just me who'd been fallin' out of the raft. ((laughter)) and apparently my uncle fell out from the front at the same time, and uh, which is scary enough, of course, just falling out. But then I came out underneath the raft. So I was in this raging water en I didn't know what to do in the process. I just panicked for- I don't know- maybe a second or two, at the most, but then I slowly made my way to the side, but the—the thought of dying. It was the only time in my life the thought of well "I'll be dying" crossed my mind.

Jenna: Oh Jeez, that was scary!

Online petition posted to Change.org:

Abercrombie & Fitch CEO Mike Jeffries: Stop telling teens they aren't beautiful; make clothes for teens of all sizes!

Petition by Benjamin O'Keefe, Orlando, Florida

> "A lot of people don't belong [in our clothes], and they can't belong. Are we exclusionary? Absolutely." —Mike Jeffries, Abercrombie & Fitch CEO

As a young adult who suffered from an eating disorder, through much of middle and high school, I remember looking at the ads for Abercrombie & Fitch or combing the racks and not seeing anything that fit me. As silly as it seems, as a kid, it made me feel worthless to not be able to wear the "it" styling that everyone else was wearing. For the 30.54 percent of teens that struggle through weight problems they know my sentiment. But now I know that I am not worthless; in fact I am FULL of worth and it's time we show young people across the world that they are too! Instead of inspiring young people to make healthy choices and better themselves, Mike Jeffries and his company have told them they will never be good enough. Well he is wrong.

Mr. Jeffries owes young people an apology, because contrary to what he may believe, whether you can fit into Abercrombie or not, you are beautiful . . .

(O'Keefe, n.d.)

Write up an analysis in which you compare and contrast these two data segments using the concepts that you worked with in Chapter 2—lexico-grammatical structure, including nouns and pronouns, verbs (transitive / intransitive), tense and aspect (see Appendix), adjectives, and adverbs. Using these concepts in conjunction with what we have studied in this chapter, compare and contrast the two narratives from the point of view of: What is the purpose of the story-telling in each? What do you know about the writer from the point of view of his own perspective? (Provide as many examples of this as possible.) How does the language, i.e., discourse, of each reveal the author's point of view and underscore his purpose in telling the story?

II. Discourse Analysis in English and Other Languages:
The Genre of the Recipe: English, Japanese, and French

We've provided three recipes here, all for a steamed or boiled spinach dish. The recipe in English, from epicurious.com, provides cooking instructions for a Japanese dish called *ohitashi,* "seasoned boiled spinach." The Japanese recipe for *ohitashi* (from Kikkoman.com) follows. The recipe in French is for *épinards à la vapeur,* "steamed spinach."

To the extent that you can, compare and contrast the following contents:

- Verbal descriptions of the dish that may accompany the recipe.
- Directives: How are these presented grammatically? Imperatives? Other forms?
- Testing for doneness. Is there an end point designated that indicates when the cooking is complete?
- What common elements do the recipes share? (Think of structure, organization, lexico-grammatical items.) Where and how do they differ?
- In what ways is genre an instance of social practice? How is "culture" reflected in these examplars? Explain in detail and support your argument using excerpts and patterns from the following data and/or from other exemplars that you have chosen.

IMPORTANT QUESTION: We are asking you to compare and contrast these three exemplars. Once you've completed this work (in detail), think about what actually constitutes *comparability*. That is, in some respects, these three recipes are absolutely comparable. In other respects, and depending upon the purpose of the research, these three may not be comparable at all. Think about these issues carefully and discuss with your class.

English Recipe

Japanese Ohitashi Spinach Salad

This is an easy traditional Japanese dish frequently served as a side dish with sushi or as part of a rice bowl meal.
servings: 4 servings

Ingredients

1 lb spinach leaves (You can substitute mustard or any other form of bitter greens)
½ cup Dashi (Fish stock)
1 ½ T soy sauce
1 T sesame oil
Dried Bonito flakes (this is a dried, flaked, white fish which can be found in most Asian markets)
Toasted sesame seeds

Preparation

1. Parboil spinach in lightly salted water until just tender (about 1 minute), place in colander and rinse with cold water. (Yes, you can use frozen spinach provided you don't over-steam it.)
2. Squeeze out any remaining water by pressing leaves against the bottom of the colander until the lump of spinach takes the shape of the colander.
3. Remove spinach from colander and cut length-wise and width-wise into approximately 1 inch squares.
4. Make Dashi by adding ½ tsp of dashi granules to ½ cup of boiling water. Or add ⅛ cup of the bonito flakes to ½ cup boiling water
5. Mix the Dashi, sesame oil, and soy sauce together in a small bowl to complete the dressing.
6. Pour dressing over the spinach and mix thoroughly.
7. Sprinkle with bonito flakes and/or toasted sesame seeds.

(Epicurious, 2012)

Japanese Recipe

Recipe: ほうれん草のお浸し **(horenso no ohitashi 'seasoned boiled spinach')**

(PHOTO in original, but not reproduced here.)
みずみずしい青菜をゆでた、おなじみの小鉢です。鮮やかなグリーンとしょうゆの香りに誘われます。
caption below photo

ほうれん草　　　　　　　　　　　　160g
キッコーマン特選丸大豆しょうゆ　　小さじ2
だし汁（かつおだし）　　　　　　　小さじ2
かつお節　　　　　　　　　　　　　少々

作り方

<u>下ごしらえ</u>
　ほうれん草は塩少々（分量外）を加えた、たっぷりの湯でゆでる。
何度かに分け、固い根元から入れゆでるとよい。ゆで時間は約20秒
が目安。
　冷水にとって急激に温度を下げると、鮮やかな色が保てる。
　水気をしっかりとしぼり、まな板に向きをそろえておき、根元を
切ってから**3cm**長さに切る
<u>浸す</u>
　ほうれん草に半量のだし汁としょうゆを加えて和え、味を含ませる。
　器に移し、残りのだし汁としょうゆをかけて、かつお節をふる。

(Kikkoman, n.d.)

French Recipe

Épinards à la vapeur

Donne 4 portions
Catégories: <u>Plats d'accompagnement</u>, <u>Plats végétariens</u> et <u>Plats de légumes</u>

Ingrédients

- 2 sachets de 300 g d'épinards, parés
- Beurre
- Huile d'olive

Préparations

Cuire les épinards salés à la vapeur le temps qu'ils tombent.
Les essorer à la main et les hacher grossièrement.
Au moment de servir, faire sauter les épinards dans un peu d'huile
d'olive et de beurre.

(Di Stasio, n.d.)

SUGGESTIONS FOR FURTHER READING

Cargill, M. and O'Connor, P. (2006). Developing Chinese scientists' skills for publishing in English: Evaluating collaborating-colleague workshops based on genre analysis. *Journal of English for Academic Purposes*, 5,3: 207–21.

Coupland, N., Garret, P., and Williams, A. (2005) Narrative demands, cultural performance and evaluation. In J. Thornborrow and J. Coates (Eds.), *The sociolinguistics of narrative.* Amsterdam: John Benjamins. Pp. 67–88.

Dafouz-Milne, E. (2008). The pragmatic role of textual and interpersonal metadiscourse markers in the construction and attainment of persuasion: A cross-linguistic study of newspaper discourse. *Journal of Pragmatics*, 40,1: 95–113.

Derks, D., Fischer, A., and Bos, A.E.R. (2008). The role of emotion in computer-mediated communication: A review. *Computers in Human Behavior*, 24,3: 766–85.

Duranti, A. (2003). The voice of the audience in contemporary American political discourse. In D. Tannen and J. Alatis (Eds.) Linguistics, Language, and the Real World: Discourse and Beyond: Georgetown University Roundtable in Languages and Linguistics, 2001. Pp. 114–34. Washington, DC: Georgetown University Press.

Flowerdew, J. and Peacock, M. (2006). Genre analysis of tax computation letters: How and why tax accountants write the way they do. *English for Specific Purposes*, 25: 133–53.

Gerofsky, S. (2004). *A Man Left Albuquerque Heading East: Word Problems as Genre in Mathematics Education*. New York: Peter Lang Publishing Co.

Herring, S., Scheidt, L., Bonus, S., and Wright, E. (2004). Bridging the gap: A genre analysis of weblogs. *Proceedings of the 37th Hawaii International Conference on System Sciences.*

King, K. and Punti, G. (2012) On the margins: Undocumented students' narrated experiences of (il)legality. *Linguistics and Education* 23,3: 235–49.

Newman, M. (2005). Rap as literacy: A genre analysis of hip-hop ciphers. *Text*, 25,3: 399–436.

Niederdeppe, J., Shapiro, M.A., and Porticella, N. (2011) Attributions of Responsibility for Obesity: Narrative Communication Reduces Reactive Counterarguing Among Liberals. *Human Communication Research*, 37: 295–323.

Pisnski Peterlin, A. (2005). Text-organizing metatext in research articles: An English-Slovene contrastive analysis. *English for Specific Purposes*, 24,3: 307–19.

Quaglio, P. (2009). *Television Dialogue: The Sitcom* Friends *vs. Natural Conversation*. Amsterdam: John Benjamins.

Rundbald, G. (2007). Impersonal, general, and social. The use of metonymy versus passive voice in medical discourse. *Written Communication,* 24,3: 250–77.

Salager-Meyer, Alcalaz Ariz, M., and Zambrano, N. (2003). The scimatar, the dagger and the glove: Intercultural differences in the rhetoric of criticism in Spanish, French, and English medical discourse (1930–1995). *English for Specific Purposes,* 22: 223–47.

Shuck, A. and Ward, J. (2008). Dealing with the inevitable: Strategies of self-presentation and meaning construction in the final statements of inmates on Texas death row. *Discourse & Society*, 19,1: 43–62.

Sznnycer, K. (2010). Strategies of powerful self-presentations in the discourse of female tennis players. *Discourse & Society.* 21,4: 458–79.

van Mulken, M. and van der Meer, W. (2005). Are you being served? A genre analysis of American and Dutch company replies to customer inquiries. *English for Specific Purposes,* 24: 93–109.

Vasquez, C. (2007). Moral stance in workplace narratives of novices. *Discourse Studies*, 9,5: 653–75.

LINKS

Mears, B. (2009). Obama re-takes oath of office at the White House. In *CNN Politics.* Retrieved from: http://politicalticker.blogs.cnn.com/2009/01/21/obama-re-takes-oath-of-office-at-the-white-house/. Accessed September 8, 2013.

AccuWeather. http://www.accuweather.com.

The Weather Channel. http://www.weather.com.

Weather Underground. http://www.wunderground.com.

Weather.gov/National Weather Service—National Oceanic and Atmospheric Association (NOAA). http://www.weather.gov.

Fox on Stocks. (2012, November 8). *Hurricane Sandy or post-tropical storm Sandy?* Retrieved from: http://foxonstocks.com/how-does-hurricane-sandy-or-post-tropical-storm-pts-sandy-affect-the-stock-market/. Accessed June 2, 2013.

AccuWeather (2012). Retrieved from: http://www.accuweather.com/en/weather-video/breaking-weather-snow-cancels-flights-in-denver/1670024770. Accessed June 8, 2012.

NBC Universal Media. (2012, June 7). Weather. In *NBC New York* website. Retrieved from: http://www.nbcnewyork.com/video/#!/weather/stories/Evening-Weather-for-Thursday--June-7/157929735. Accessed June 30, 2012.

Math Stories. (n.d.). *House of math word problems for children*. Retrieved from: http://www.mathstories.com/. Accessed May 23, 2013.

Craig, J. (n.d.). Riddles. In *Jack Craig's Home Page*. Retrieved from: http://www.angelfire.com/fl/JackCraig/HUMOR-RIDDLES.html. Accessed May 23, 2013.

O'Keefe, B. (n.d.). Abercrombie & Fitch CEO Mike Jeffries: Stop telling teens they aren't beautiful; make clothes for teens of all sizes. In *Change.org* website. Retrieved from: http://www.change.org/petitions/abercrombie-fitch-ceo-mike-jeffries-stop-telling-teens-they-aren-t-beautiful-make-clothes-for-teens-of-all-sizes. Accessed May 12, 2013.

Epicurious. (2012, April 27). *Japanese ohitashi spinach salad.* Retrieved from: http://www.epicurious.com/recipes/member/views/JAPANESE-OHITASHI-SPINACH-SALAD-50181150#ixzz2UOxIdnG6. Accessed May 25, 2013.

Kikkoman. (n.d.). ほうれん草のおひたし. Retrieved from: http://www.kikkoman.co.jp/homecook/college/sub/ohitashi.html. Accessed May 25, 2013.

Di Stasio, J. (n.d.). Épinards à la vapeur. In *à la di Stasio*. Retrieved from: http://aladistasio.telequebec.tv/recettes/recette.aspx?id=134. Accessed May 23, 2013.

NOTES

1. See Chapter 8 (Indexicality) for a full discussion of how contextually based linguistic forms evoke abstract concepts such as personal and social identity.
2. If a narrative is not deemed "reportable" or "newsworthy," it may be dismissed by interlocutors through response tokens like "so what?" or "et puis?" ("and then?") or "y qué" ("and what?") (Labov, 2010: 8), or through other (implicitly or explicitly) demonstrable expressions of disinterest.
3. Chapter 8 (Indexicality) discusses this area of pragmatics in detail.
4. Audio and video of this broadcast may no longer be available, and we simplified the transcript to avoid including specialized diacritics for prosody, rate of speech, and pauses, so as not to encumber the visual representations of the text with unfamiliar markings at this point in the book. See Chapters 5 (Information Structure and Intonation Units) and Chapter 6 (Conversation) for a more detailed discussion on the relationships of prosody, rate of speech, and pausing to oral discourse.
5. See Gerofsky (2004) for a detailed comparison between math word problems and riddles.

CHAPTER FOUR

Reference, Deixis, and Stance

It is a condition of successful reference that the speaker should select a referring expression—typically a proper name, a definite noun-phrase or a pronoun—which, when it is employed in accordance with the rules of the language-system, will enable the hearer, in the context in which the utterance is made, to pick out the actual referent from the class of potential referents. If the expression is a definite noun-phrase operating as a definite description, its descriptive content will be more or less detailed according to the circumstances; and the manner of description will often depend upon the speaker's assumption that the hearer is in position of quite specific information about the referent. (Lyons, 1977b: 180)

INTRODUCTION

> **REFERENCE** involves the relationship between words and the things, ideas, entities, states, and people that such words designate. Reference can be divided into two broad types: <u>highly specific</u>, where the referent is easily identifiable and specific (e.g., *Prince William and his wife, Catherine*) and <u>generic</u>, where the referent itself is not actually identifiable (e.g., ***A prince** must be **a man** of courage*).

In this chapter, we explore how meaning is created and expressed in oral and written discourse through an approach that extends beyond the grammatical categories introduced and discussed in Chapter 2 and beyond the generic categories discussed in Chapter 3. Most importantly, in this chapter and in every chapter that follows, we systematically illustrate the points we made in Chapter 1: that nothing in discourse is neutral and that every instance of discourse is motivated by a perspective.

We appeal to the interrelated concepts of *reference* and *deixis* as the first set of lenses through which to view discourse from a meaning-based perspective. These categories of meaning form the foundation on which we can build our understanding of discourse in general and *stance* in particular.

To explain the concept of *reference* and its importance to the analysis of discourse, we begin with a brief news story adapted from CNN World online about Prince William and his then recent bride, Catherine:

Prince William, Catherine Visit Prince Edward Island in Canadian Tour

1. Prince Edward Island, Canada (CNN)—**Prince William and his wife Catherine** will tour Prince Edward Island on Monday, the fifth day of their Canadian tour.

2. **The Duke and Duchess of Cambridge** will start the day with a visit to Province House, the second oldest active legislature building in Canada.

3. Later, **Prince William** will emphasize the Canadian military's contributions to the training of search-and-rescue pilots by taking part in a "waterbird" emergency landing exercise in a helicopter at Dalvay-by-the-Sea.

4. On Monday evening, **the royal couple** will travel to Yellowknife, in the Northwest Territories, for the next phase of their trip.

5. **William and Catherine** are expected to visit four provinces during their nine-day tour—their first official foreign trip **as a married couple**. After the Northwest Territories, **they** are scheduled to visit Alberta.

(CNN News, 2011)

You may be able to imagine the faces of the two people in the story. If not, you could always find photos of both individuals in newspapers, magazines, and online. "Prince William" in the news story refers to a single, identifiable celebrity. "Catherine" refers to a single and identifiable person, who is now a celebrity through marriage. Yet, the two are mentioned in the news story using seven different terms of reference: 1) *Prince William and his wife Catherine*, 2) *The Duke and Duchess of Cambridge*, 3) *Prince William*, 4) *the royal couple*, 5) *William and Catherine*, 6) *a married couple*, and 7) *they*.

These reference terms involve the following types of noun phrases (see Chapter 2 and the Appendix):

- proper nouns
    with and without titles (specific): *William, Catherine, Prince William, the Duke and Duchess of Cambridge*
- relationship term (specific): *his wife*
- collective noun (specific): *the royal couple*
- collective noun (generic): *a married couple*
- subject pronoun (specific): *they*

The types of reference terms in this brief extract make different aspects of each individual's identity prominent, including their names, titles, and their relationship to each other. These types of word choices also point to the individuals' gender, nationality, and royal family membership.

Reference is one of the most basic categories of language use. *Reference* involves the relationship between words and the things, ideas, entities, states, and people that such words designate (based on Finch, 2005: 167). *Reference* can be divided into two broad types: **highly specific**, where the person or thing mentioned (the referent) can be identified through the use of proper nouns (e.g., Prince William, William Faulkner, Bill Clinton) or with definite noun phrases that enable a listener or reader to actually identify the thing or person (e.g., the royal couple, the first book I ever read, the president, a gaping hole in the wall) or **generic**, where the person or thing mentioned (the referent) is a member of a class (e.g., apples are good for your health, a duke is a member of royalty, the baboon's greatest enemy is the leopard), and not identifiable on its own. That is, with **generic** reference, there isn't a particular *apple*, or *duke*, or *baboon* that is being discussed—rather, reference is being made to that thing or person or entity *in general*. (See Brown and Yule, 1983; Enfield and Stivers, 2007; Evans, 1982; Halliday, 1994; Halliday and Matthiessen, 2004; Lyons, 1977a, 1977b, 1995).

The second category of meaning that we will explore in this chapter is called *deixis*. *Deixis* is from the Greek word *deiktikos* meaning 'to point, to show.' It signals the 'demonstration' of an entity, in the sense of *pointing to something*. A deictic expression is one that requires context in order for the speaker or hearer to know what is being referred to. For more detailed discussions of deixis and deictic expressions, see Duchan et al. (1995); Enfield (2003a); Fillmore (1982, 1971/1997); Hanks (1992, 2005, 2009); and Levinson (1983), among others. (See Chapter 8 for further discussion of *deixis* from the point of view of indexicality).

Let's use the following cartoon as an example:

As we can see, the salesperson here points out two distinct lights on a cell phone: one that indicates that the battery is dying, and the other that (jokingly) indicates that the conversation is dying. In both cases, the salesman points to one light or the other using the identical expression, "this light," to designate each. The word choice, "this light," is the same, but the actual thing that he is referring to (i.e., the referent) changes as his finger designates which light accomplishes which function. If the salesperson did not point to each light, it would be impossible to understand which one he was talking about. This example illustrates how context is crucial to the understanding of deixis and deictic expressions.

"This light warns you that your battery may be critically low. And *this* light warns you that your conversation may be critically dull."

Deictic expressions include personal pronouns, especially *I* and *you*, adverbs of time and place, especially *here, there, then* and *now,* and demonstratives like *this* and *that*. Without knowing the time, the place, and/or details relating to the participants in the communication, it is impossible to know, for example, when *now* is, or where *here* refers to. The actual referents for *I* and *you* change depending upon who is speaking or writing and who is listening or hearing. The deictic term *now* typically means "the moment of speaking or writing," but the reference point for that time is not fixed.

As we examine discourse through the lenses of reference and deixis, we begin to understand the speaker's or writer's attitudes with respect to the

---

STANCE is the **speaker's or writer's feeling, attitude, perspective, or position as enacted in discourse.** *Stance taking* is an inevitable consequence of participating in and producing discourse, of putting the world into words. Stance emerges in a speaker's or writer's choice of one linguistic form over another, the coloring of utterances with prosodic contours or punctuation, the sequential ordering of utterances; it emerges in gestures, silences, hesitations, hedges, and in overlapping stretches of talk. In all of these instances of discourse (and others), a speaker's or writer's stance is enacted and created, it is negotiated and re-negotiated. *Stance taking* is one of the very outcomes of putting the world into words.

---

people, things, and ideas that they are speaking or writing about. We refer to the attitude of the speaker or writer as *stance.* We define stance as follows:

Sometimes, these discursively expressed attitudes sound very strong; sometimes they are weak and seemingly much more subtle. Sometimes, too, the words themselves may sound subtle or neutral. But through the analytic lens of *reference* and *deixis* we can discern much more about meaning and stance than what meets the eye.

Using these two interrelated approaches to the analysis of discourse, we can observe clearly, concretely, and with precision, the notion that language use is not a one-way endeavor, but that speakers and writers make certain linguistic choices on the basis of assumed knowledge and experiences of their hearers and readers. And, we will observe that these choices are reflective of various types of *stances* that the speaker or writer might be taking.

REFERENCE

The process of reference in language involves the ways in which language users speak *about* something or someone, the ways in which they introduce an entity into the discourse, and the ways in which they elaborate discussion of that entity, person, concept, or idea. The verb "refer" is evident in the word and this may help to make the sense of reference all the more clear. The process might seem commonsensical: If one wants to refer to a particular thing or a particular person, all one need do is simply label it, just call it by name. An apple, after all, is an apple. Or is it? (See Chapter 5 for more on reference and cohesion.)

Here is a simple scenario that might better illustrate how reference works. You've just entered your friend's house and you see on the coffee table a large glass bowl filled with shiny, Red Delicious apples. After you've settled into the armchair and made yourself comfortable, your friend notices that you are still eying the bowl on the table and its contents. She extends an offer for you to take one. Here are some possible ways this might be done:

Would you like <u>an apple</u>?
Would you like <u>that apple?</u>
Would you like <u>a Red Delicious?</u>
Would you like <u>some fruit?</u>
Would you like <u>a piece of fruit?</u>
Would you like <u>one of those from my grandfather's orchard?</u>
Would you like <u>one?</u>
Would you like <u>it?</u>

Now, there are many alternative ways for your friend to have expressed the offer, instead of "would you like . . . " (e.g., "take one," "have some," "help yourself," "want one?," "care for an apple?," gestural offer of an open palm with fingers pointing toward bowl, and so forth).

But how many different choices would she have to *refer* to the item(s)?

Each instance of reference in the previous list denotes the identical object, i.e., one or more of the apples in the bowl. However, each word choice makes salient something different about the item(s) as it relates to the offer. Sometimes the salient feature is related to quantity (e.g., one entire piece of fruit, more than one, or part of one). Sometimes the salient feature is related to whether the hearer and speaker both recognize the object in the same way— For example, if your friend says, "would you like *that* apple?," would you know which very specific one she was talking about? And sometimes the salience is related to degrees of specificity of the referent itself. That is, how does the speaker label the object? Does she use the common term, *apple,* the variety-specific name *Red Delicious*, the generic category marker *fruit*?" (This would work especially well as a referent choice if there were Granny Smiths and Galas in the bowl as well.) Does she intend to mark a contrast in the available choices for the hearer ("Would you like one of **those** from my grandfather's orchard? [. . . or one of **these** from the farmer's market?"])?, Or, does she just use a pronoun, such as "it" or "one"? In the latter case, there is a combination of the salient features of both quantity and identifiability.

The pronouns *one* and *it* each designate a singular object—in the case of *it* the assumption is that the speaker and hearer both know exactly which item is being referred to. If not, the sentence might sound ungrammatical or at least grammatically awkward, and the oddness here comes from the need for context—the speaker would need the context to determine which individual apple the hearer was looking at. In the case of *one*, there is no such assumption and the features of specificity and identifiability do not come into play; there is no indication which particular item is being presented in the offer—it's just one member among a group.

We summarize these various word choices according to the following: 1) nouns and their determiners and pronouns, and 2) the salient characteristics that might be designated by each choice, all of which reflect meaning beyond the surface, objective level of each individual word.

TABLE 4.1: Summary of NP Referents and Salient Characteristics Designated Through NP Choice

Determiner + noun, pronoun	salient characteristics designated through NP choice
an apple	quantity (1), generic name of fruit
the apple	identifiable member in the group of apples
that apple	very specific member in the group of apples
a Red Delicious	quantity (1), specific name of the variety of fruit
some fruit	partial, mass quantity of generic category of food

(continued)

TABLE 4.1 (*continued*)	
Determiner + noun, pronoun	**salient characteristics designated through NP choice**
a piece of fruit	specific, individuated quantity generic category of food
one of those from my grandfather's orchard	quantity (1), member of group from specified source
one	quantity and food type, combined into a pronoun of singularity, with the assumption that the item is known by both hearer and speaker
it	specific item is known and identifiable by hearer and speaker

As we can see, each type of reference makes salient a slightly different feature of the context—typically concerning the degree of identifiability, the number, and/or the specificity of the object. The choice of which determiner and which noun or which simple pronoun is used is very much dependent upon the speaker's perspective relative to the referent and to the hearer/reader within each context of communication.

Thus, every instance of discourse is indeed motivated by a perspective.

Reference in Actual Discourse

What we observed in this example is just the tip of the iceberg when it comes to language and reference. And, as the example shows, reference and stance go hand in hand. See also Chapter 5 (on reference) and Chapter 8 (on indexicality).

Reference: The Basics—Nouns, Determiners, Pronouns

In discourse, referents shift and change all the time. These changes typically concern three categories: nouns, determiners, and pronouns. Sometimes speakers and writers make the choices consciously. Other times not.

In this chapter, we will further develop the notions of determiners and pronouns (introduced in Chapter 2), since these categories of language carry the bulk of interactional weight with respect to the speaker-hearer-referent, writer-reader-referent relationship.

Determiners

Recall that determiners are a closed set of words that precede nouns in a noun phrase and indicate such features as definiteness, indefiniteness, number, and possession. Every determiner serves as a means of "picking out" a referent in some specific way, and each determiner "picks out" that referent differently.

The following is a list of common determiners, using illustrations from movie titles, considered as either classic, among the best of all time, or both:

Articles

Definite: the   *The Lord of the Rings*
Indefinite: a(n), ø   *A Clockwork Orange, (ø) City of God*

Demonstratives

this, these, that, those   *Catch That Kid!!*

Possessives

my, your, his, her, its,   *His Girl Friday*
our, your

Quantifiers

each, every, all, any, some,
several, both, no   *No Country for (ø) Old Men, Some Like it Hot*

Now, try it yourself: Locate the determiners in the following movie title list.

How to Train Your Dragon
Back to the Future
Jaws
Something Wicked This Way Comes
Strangers on a Train
My Neighbor Totoro
In the Heat of the Night
To Kill a Mockingbird
That Thing You Do

Just from these few examples, do you begin to get sense of how even such a small part of speech as a determiner creates meaning within discourse? Let's experiment. If we take an original title and then change the determiner, in what ways does the meaning of the referent *mockingbird* shift?

To Kill a Mockingbird →   *To Kill the Mockingbird*
To Kill My Mockingbird
To Kill That Mockingbird
How to Train Your Dragon →   *How to Train That Dragon*
How to Train My Dragon
How to Train Some Dragon
How to Train Any Dragon

As soon as we see the range of possibilities concerning how to designate the noun in each title (*mockingbird* and *dragon*), we also begin to see the range of ways that each referent becomes relevant in a communicative context: Is the referent identifiable? Is it framed as belonging to someone? Is quantity or number reflected in the designation? These are questions that come into play any time we make reference to any item or any entity, great and small.

Pronouns

As we noted in Chapter 2, pronouns are a closed class of words that replace a full noun referent. Pronouns can designate entities in the immediate discourse, e.g., *I, you, this, that,* or they can designate entities mentioned previously in the discourse, e.g., *he, she, they, them, it.*

Because pronouns, like determiners, reflect varying degrees of sharedness of information (See Chapters 2 and 5) between the speaker-hearer and the reader-writer with respect to the referent in question, pronouns are also key factors in discursive reference.

In English, pronouns can be classified very basically as subject pronouns, object pronouns, possessive pronouns, and reflexive pronouns. Representative examples are listed here, together with a number of song titles (all Beatles titles) to help illustrate their functions and meanings within these very limited spates of discourse:

subject pronouns: I, you, he, she, it, one, we, you, they

> *<u>I</u> Am the Walrus*
> *Ain't <u>She</u> Sweet*
> *<u>You</u>'ve Got to Hide Your Love Away*

object pronouns: me, you, him, her, it, one, us, you, them

> *Ask <u>Me</u> Why*
> *And I Love <u>Her</u>*
> *Anna (Go to <u>Him</u>)*
> *Please Please <u>Me</u>*

possessive pronouns: mine, yours, his, hers, ours, theirs

> *You'll Be <u>Mine</u>*

reflexive pronouns: myself, yourself, himself, herself, ourselves, yourselves, themselves

> *Think for <u>Yourself</u>*

In keeping with the Beatles' song title theme, have a look at the following list and identify the pronouns in each title.

> *All You Need Is Love*
> *You Can't Do That*
> *To Know Her Is to Love Her*
> *Tell Me Why*
> *Baby, It's You*
> *I Me Mine*
> *P.S. I Love You*
> *One After 909*

Regarding this small set of pronouns and their relationship to reference, some of them seem straightforwardly clear. For example, in *To Know Her Is to Love Her,* the third person object pronoun *her* refers to one specific and identifiable female. Similarly, all first person pronominal referents, i.e. *I* (subject pronoun), me (object pronoun), and *mine* (possessive pronoun) seem to refer simply to the person who is singing or who wrote the song. And the same may hold true for the second person pronominal referent *you* (both subject and object pronouns) as simply designating the person for whom the song was written or to whom it is being sung, especially in the title *P.S. I Love You.*

However, does the second person subject pronoun *you*, in *All You Need Is Love,* presuppose a particular individual who is hearing the song? Is there one specific person who is "picked out" by this pronoun? On the contrary, this instance of *you* is often referred to as "generic you," in that the message carried by the utterance that includes this pronoun is intended for all hearers, listeners, and readers, as individuals and as a group.

So, when we hear words like *I* and *you* in discourse, we don't always know who is being referred to by those pronouns. In the next section, we introduce the notion of *deixis*—a key concept in the study of pragmatics in general, and in the discursive construction of meaning, in particular.

DEIXIS

As we noted in the introductory section for this chapter, *deixis* means "pointing to something," from Greek *deiktikos* 'to point, to show.' The cell phone cartoon introduced earlier illustrates precisely how *deixis* works in communicative contexts.

The reason *deixis* is so important in communication is that the meaning of the deictically marked referent can only be discerned through the context in which the communication takes place. This underscores the statements that we made earlier that any linguistic expression carries multiple layers of meaning beyond objective word meaning.

Let's illustrate with a few telling examples. The first is from a Season 4 episode of *Friends*. In this excerpt, Ross has decided to learn how to play rugby as a means of impressing his British girlfriend. He and Joey are watching a rugby match on TV, and Joey is explaining some of the rules.

Friends Excerpt—"The One with All the Rugby"

Joey: ((**pointing to the TV**)): Okay, Ross, look-look-look-look, look **right here**.
That's called a *scrum*, okay? It's kinda like a huddle.
Ross: And is a *hum* kinda like a *scruddle?*

(Cohen et al., 1998)

Beyond the clever linguistic humor or Ross's response (meshing 'scrum' and 'huddle' into 'hum' and 'scruddle'), what is crucial here is the co-occurrence of Joey's pointing to the TV and his direction to Ross to look "right here." Without the added feature of physical pointing within the context of this interaction, the directive to "look right here" would be meaningless. An interlocutor, hearing this type of instruction without any added contextual direction, would likely respond "look where?"

The second example is from the (1939) film *The Wizard of Oz*. Dorothy has begun her journey down the yellow brick road. She and Toto pause at a crossroad, in front of a scarecrow. They both soon learn that the scarecrow can talk.

Wizard of Oz Excerpt—Dorothy and Scarecrow

Dorothy: Now which way do we go?

Scarecrow: **That way** is a very nice way ((pointing right with his whole right arm))

Dorothy: Who said that?
                     ((Toto, her dog, barks at the scarecrow, indicating that he was the one who'd spoken))

Dorothy: Don't be silly, Toto. Scarecrows . . . don't talk.

Scarecrow: It's pleasant down **that way**, too ((pointing left with his whole left arm))

Dorothy: That's funny, wasn't he pointing the other way?

Scarecrow: Of course, people do . . . go **both ways**! ((crossing arms in front of him and pointing in both directions))

(Baum and Fleming, 1939)

Once again, without the added gesture of pointing, the expressions "that way" meaning "to the right" and "that way" meaning "to the left," would sound identical, possibly nothing but verbatim repetition, one of the other. Instead, however, as we see here, the intended meaning of each utterance is diametrically opposite.

Deixis and Shifters

As we have observed, from the viewpoint of meaning, it is difficult to restrict certain types of word meanings to just one denotational meaning (e.g., dictionary definition) or another. Word meaning occurs at multiple levels—and this becomes especially apparent with deictic expressions. In fact, these types of expressions are also commonly referred to as "shifters," precisely because the referents that they point to necessarily shift within discursive contexts. (For original work on shifters, see Jakobson, 1957, and Jakobson, Waugh, and Monville-Burston, 1995.)

The following provides a short list of common deictic expressions:

---

pronouns: I, me, mine, we, us, ours, you, yours, one, it
demonstratives (as pronouns OR determiners): this, these, that, those
adverbs: OF TIME: now, then, later, soon, today, tomorrow
               OF SPACE: here, there

In the two sections that follow, we explain in detail how the meaning of the referents in deictic expressions can change according to the context: *I* and *you* and *this* and *that.*

I and *You*

With regard to person deixis, the concept of "shifters" becomes especially visible in first and second person reference. That is, *I* is the default subject reference term for *any* speaking or writing subject. *I* is one of the two tiniest words in the English language, and yet its application is infinite—anyone, anywhere on the planet, choosing to speak or write about him or herself in English must use *I* (as well as its object variant *me* and its possessive variants *my* and *mine*).[1] In terms of meaning, *I* shifts according to who it is that is invoking reference; its meaning then, is infinite, in terms of actual reference.

We can extend the application of infinite reference potential to the pronoun *you* (as subject or object as well as its possessive variants *your* and *yours*). For example, *you* in a song refers to the person for whom it was written, the person to whom it is, was, has been, and can and will be sung. Its meaning shifts such that *you* can refer to any person to whom such an utterance has ever been or will ever be said.

As we have seen, *you* carries an even more complex meaning than that. Using the song title *All You Need Is Love*, to illustrate, it also becomes clear that *you* might, in fact, designate the very person for whom the song was written or a particular individual to whom the song is sung, or to a particular addressee of the corresponding declarative utterance, i.e., someone who hears this sentence in a conversation rather than in song. However, as we also noted, *you* used in a more *generic* sense could also refer to an unspecified person or group of people. Also, *you* used generically contrasts significantly in terms of meaning and contextual feature salience with other seemingly similar terms as *one, we, everyone,* etc. Thus, by virtue of its "shifter" use, *you* designates a different range of potential referents than does *I*.

This *and* that— *"near to speaker" and "far from speaker": One way of looking at it*
  The demonstratives *this* and *that* are also shifters, as we observed in the *Wizard of Oz* example. *That way* meant "to the right" in the Scarecrow's first utterance and its exact opposite, "to the left," in the second. What is crucial in this scenario is the gesture of pointing that renders meaning to the choices that Dorothy faces in her journey along the yellow brick road.
  Now, how do you think the meaning might change had the Scarecrow said instead, "this way" to designate a right turn and "this way" to designate a left turn (similar to the double use of "this light" in the cartoon illustration)? Or even, "this way" for one direction and "that way" for another?
  In traditional explanations about demonstrative reference, linguists often explain that *this* is the reference term that points to something "close to the speaker," and *that* is the reference term that points to something "far from the speaker." We first imagine closeness or proximity in terms of physical space, so *this* would refer to an item in space that is near, and *that,* an item that is far. To some degree, the explanation works.
  Illustrating the "near speaker" vs. "far from speaker" interpretation, let's examine a pair of seemingly contrastive examples: One from Episode 074 of *Seinfeld* ("The Cigar Store Indian"), and one from Episode 6 of *Monty Python's Flying Circus* ("20th-Century Vole"). Both examples involve multiple participants interacting within a room. Each involves reference to a piece of furniture. In the *Seinfeld* excerpt, George and his friends are on their way out the door, when suddenly George turns and sees something that shouldn't be on the table:

Seinfeld Excerpt—Episode 074, "The Cigar Store Indian"

George: ((yelling)) Wow! Who put **this cup** right on the new table!
Jerry: ((picking up the cup)) I was having coffee; I put it on the coffee table.
George: But you didn't use a coaster, Jerry, you left a stain! ((George then runs to the kitchen))
Kramer: Whoa boy! There's always one at every party, huh?

(Gammill et al., 1993)

In the *Monty Python* example, Larry Saltzburg has just finished systematically firing three of his six scriptwriters. The remaining three are now scooting under a table to hide.

Monty Python's Flying Circus Excerpt—Episode 6, "20th Century Vole"

Saltzburg:	((really threatening)) Are you being indecisive?
Fourth Writer:	Yo. Nes. Perhaps. ((runs out))
Saltzburg:	I hope you three gentlemen aren't going to be indecisive! ((they try to hide under the table)) What the hell are you doing under **that table?**
First Writer:	We dropped our pencils.
Saltzburg:	Pencil droppers, eh?

(Chapman et al., 1969)

In each excerpt, the interactants are co-present in the room with the speaker of the *this-* or *that*-marked utterance. And, while some aspect of physical proximity may indeed be at play here, it is likely that there are other contextual features that are influencing the choice of referent—features such as importance of the referent to the immediate context and to the speaker or identifiability of the referent on the part of the hearers. In other words, the speaker of each demonstrative-marked utterance is making salient some features of the context that have to do with how easily the hearer is expected to recognize the thing being pointed out. There is a qualitative difference in stance between "Who left **this cup** right on the new table?" (strong complaint, with the immediate concern that the cup has damaged his mother's brand new furniture) and "What the hell are you doing under **that table?**" (affront to the three remaining writers who seem to have no backbone).

Let's have a quick look at an excerpt from the Laurel and Hardy (1932) film, *Helpmates*. In the excerpt, Hardy's wife has been out of town, and she is now coming home, unexpectedly early. Hardy phones his friend Laurel to come over and help him clean the house before his wife arrives. Laurel only knows his friend, Hardy. He has not met Hardy's wife.

Helpmates Excerpt—Laurel and Hardy

Hardy: I'm in a slight predicament . . . My wife's coming
        home today at noon unexpectedly, and look at
        this house.

Laurel: What's the matter with it?

Hardy: What's the matter with it? You never met my wife, did you?

Laurel: Yes, I never did.

Hardy: Whaddayou mean, "Yes I never did?"

Hardy: ((holding up a photo of his wife's scowling face and pressing
        it to his chest with the photo facing outward toward Laurel;
        he points at her face)). **That's** my wife.

(Roach and Parrott, 1932)

The elements of humor in this excerpt are linguistically driven: Laurel answering a negative question with an affirmative response to actually intend a negative response ("Yes, I never did"), and Hardy disdainfully designating the horribly mean-looking woman in the photo as his wife: "That's my wife."

The excerpt actually contains two instances of demonstrative reference: "Look at this house," and "That's my wife." In the first case, Hardy's use of *this* could indeed reflect the "near speaker" interpretation. Both Hardy and Laurel are co-present; they are IN the house, and the speaker and referent could not conceivably be any nearer to each other; moreover, *that* would be impossible here in designating the speaker's intended referent.

In contrast, the second case, involving Hardy's use of "That's my wife" actually goes squarely against the traditional interpretation. He is holding the framed photo directly in front of him. In fact, it is pressed to his chest; it is literally ON his body—conceivably, the speaker and referent could not be any nearer. Yet, the demonstrative choice is *that*. Further, the utterance sounds completely natural. It does not sound as if Hardy is breaking any particular rule of "grammar."

Also, if we revisit the cartoon that opened our discussion on *deixis* (Figure 4.1), we find the salesman using the expression "this light," while pointing to the phone buttons on the phone that the *customer,* i.e., the hearer, is holding, not the speaker himself. Clearly, the traditional "near speaker" approach, typically associated with English *this*, also breaks down to some degree in this comic.

A more useful and discursively revealing way of looking at instances of *reference, deixis* and *stance* is provided here. We introduce the notion of *focus of attention* as a way to account for a number of referential shifts in discourse.

DEIXIS AND STANCE—FOCUS OF ATTENTION FOR HEARER, RELATIVE IMPORTANCE OF THE REFERENT TO THE SPEAKER

As we noted, when speakers and writers choose their forms of *reference*, sometimes they make very conscious choices and sometimes such choices are below the level of consciousness. The analysis of discourse reveals much about these types of choices, whether language users are aware of what they are selecting or not.

We'll begin with demonstrative reference, since we've seen some indication that the traditional view of "proximity to speaker" may or may not be at play when speakers and writers refer to things. First, relative closeness or distance is not easy to measure. Second, even in just the few examples that we've reviewed so far, ("this cup" in the *Seinfeld* clip, "that table" from *Monty Python*, "this house" and "that's my wife" from *Helpmates*), there is more at play than simply physical "nearness" or "distance." That element at play is *stance,* the inevitable skew that language adds to communicative meaning.

In the previous instances of reference, it's not just *any* cup that George is referring to, it's not just *any* table that Larry Salzburg is mentioning, and certainly not just *any* woman that Hardy is pointing out in the photo. These are not objective, neutral means of picking out references. In all cases, the instances of reference are tinged with some element of the speaker's attitude or feeling or perspective.

What's more, there is a high degree of systematicity in how *stance* is created and expressed through reference and deixis in discourse. That systematicity can be gradually discerned as we begin to understand the various ways in which meaning is constructed through contextually situated language use.

Using *reference* as a lens through which to analyze discourse, we examined a number of possible features of the interactional context that become salient through a wide range of varieties of referential choice, first in the CNN newswire excerpt about the royal couple and then in the "apple(s) on the coffee table" examples. As we summarized in Table 4.1 for the apples on the table, there are a number of potential ways in which referential meaning is discursively constructed between speakers/listeners and writers/readers related to such systematic notions as specificity, identifiability, and quantity/number, in addition to what the listener/hearer is expected to already know or understand about the referent.

With regard to *deictic expressions,* particularly the demonstratives *this* and *that,* used both as determiners and pronouns, meaning is similarly constructed in interaction. Additionally, *stance*, or the speaker's/writer's attitudes, is also systematically expressed through the various choices of these terms.

Let's revisit the demonstrative system of reference in English for a moment.

This and *these* are traditionally viewed as designating a referent that is "near speaker." *That* and *those* are traditionally viewed as designating a referent that is "far from speaker." Yet, we found, in the analysis of just a few sets of data excerpts, that this distinction may not work so well.

Here is another possibility (Strauss, 1993, 2002):

- When using demonstratives *this* and *these* (as determiners or pronouns), the speaker is doing at least two things: 1) *drawing the hearer's attention most strongly to the item being referred to with a **high degree of focus,*** and 2) *designating the referent as "new" or "as if it is new"*—as if the referent is <u>actually</u> *not shared* or <u>framed</u> as *not shared*. **THE REFERENT IS OF HIGH IMPORTANCE TO SPEAKER.**
- When using demonstratives *that* and *those* (as determiners or pronouns), the speaker is 1) *drawing the hearer's attention to the item being referred to with a **medium degree of focus,*** and 2) *designating the referent as "shared" or "as if it is shared"*—as if the referent is <u>actually</u> *shared* or <u>framed</u> as *shared*.

Since the pronoun *it* can also be used in may interactional contexts where *this* and *that* are used as pronouns, it would help us to better understand *reference* in general, and *deictic stance marking* in particular, by including *it* as part of the system of demonstrative reference.

- When using pronoun *it*, the speaker is 1) *drawing the hearer's attention to the item being referred to with a **very low degree of focus,*** and 2) *designating the referent as "unquestionably shared" or "as if unquestionably shared"*

With these basic criteria in place, let's first review some of the instances of *this* and *that* that we have already examined—both verbatim and with a few variations. We apply the framework in Examples A, B, C, and D as follows:

117

A. <u>Apples on the table</u>:

Would you like **that** apple?

Hearer is expected to share knowledge of the referent.

Would you like **this** apple?

Hearer considers the referent new. Hearer will need more from speaker (e.g., gesture).

Would you like **it**?

Hearer is expected to unquestionably share knowledge of the referent.

B. <u>Wizard of Oz</u>:

That way is a very nice way.

Hearer is expected to share the direction referred to; hearer may need more information from speaker (e.g., gesture, pointing).

This way is a very nice way.

Hearer should attend with HIGH FOCUS. Hearer may need more information from speaker (e.g., gesture).

It's a very nice way.

Hearer is expected to unquestionably share knowledge of the referent. No additional information should be needed.

C. <u>Seinfeld</u>:

Who put **this cup** on the table?

Hearer should attend with high focus. Referent is important to the speaker and framed as "new."

Variant:

Who put **that cup** on the table?

Hearer should attend with medium focus. Referent is important to the speaker and framed as "shared."

Who put **it** on the table?

Hearer is expected to unquestionably share knowledge of the referent.

D. *Monty Python:*

What the hell are you doing under **that table?**

Hearers should attend with medium focus. Referent is framed as "shared."

Variant:

What the hell are you doing under **this table?**

Hearers should attend with high focus. Referent is important to speaker and framed as "new."

With regard to pronoun *it* as signaling *unquestionably shared information*, the following television commercial for Staples Office Products serves as a perfect illustration, since the expectation is that all parties involved unquestionably assume that they can locate the speaker's intended referent, just by virtue of pronoun *it*.

Television Commercial for Staples Office Products

Setting:	A small office, with a printer off to the side. A young employee is standing in front of the printer. Behind him is a group of 3–4 other office workers in a small huddle at a table.
Guy at printer:	((turning around to address other workers, as he removes the printer cartridge)) Hey guys. Sorry. I think the printer's out of ink.
Other worker:	Just shake **it**.

((The guy at the printer picks up the ENTIRE PRINTER, and SHAKES IT.))

(Staples, n.d.)

Clearly, the confusion here has to do with the extremely low referential function of "it." While the office worker intended the "it" to refer back to "the printer cartridge" that was currently in the guy at the printer's hand, the guy at the printer interpreted "it" as referring back to "the printer." No elaboration concerning the referent appeared necessary at the time of the initial utterance—it only becomes clear that a problem exists once we see how meaning has been constructed by the intended recipient of the message.

Now, let's put everything together and observe how both *reference* and *deixis* work in discourse to serve a multiplicity of communicative purposes (e.g., presenting factual information [and how we view such information as "factual"], expressing opinions, persuading others to accept our viewpoints, and many others).

At the end of this chapter, you'll find the full text of an essay entitled, "The Fatal Promise of Cloning" by Charles Krauthammer (*Time*, 2002). This essay was written on the heels of the Human Cloning Prohibition Act, submitted to the Senate in May, 2002. The essay is especially and unusually rich in tokens of deictic references *this, these, that,* and *it*. While the stir surrounding the issue has settled, it is interesting to observe how opinions on such a volatile and controversial topic were expressed in discourse.

Following are the first four paragraphs of the essay. We have highlighted instances of our target forms *this*, *these*, *that*, and *it*. (Demonstrative *those* would clearly have been relevant here, but there are no tokens in this excerpt).

1. As the cloning debate rages in Washington, there is news from the scientific frontier. **It** involves cows, but tomorrow **it** could easily involve humans.

2. Scientists at Advanced Cell Technology in Worcester, Mass., took a skin cell from Cow A, cloned **it** (by injecting the nucleus into a cow egg whose nucleus had been removed), then implanted the embryo in the uterus of Cow B. **That embryo clone** grew into a fetus, which, had **it** been born, would have been Cow C. But **it** was not born. The fetus was removed from the uterus and harvested for **its** tissues. **These tissues** from the clone were then put back into the original Cow A. Lo and behold, **it** worked. **These cells** from the clone were not rejected by Cow A and even organized themselves into functioning tissue (such as a kidney).

3. An amazing success. **This** is precisely what the advocates of research cloning are promising. Clone, grow **it** and then use the cloned tissue to create near identical replacement parts for the original animal and thus presumably put us on the road to curing such human scourges as Alzheimer's disease, Parkinson's, spinal-cord injuries and the like.

4. Do **this** in humans, and we might have thousands cured, millions relieved of suffering. Who could possibly stand in the way of **this research**?

As you read through these introductory paragraphs, can you begin to predict where the author is taking you with his line of argumentation? At first blush, if it's not clear, don't worry. It will become clear as you gradually analyze the essay as a piece of discourse data.

From the point of view of *reference*, let's first identify the topic: Cloning. This is evident in the title and in the first line of the essay. In the first line, it is referred to not simply as "cloning," but as the "cloning debate." From the outset, we know that it is a debate and that there will be two strongly opposing sides to the issue: Those who advocate cloning and those who oppose it. Moreover, the debate is "raging"—our first clue that the essay will be chock full of stance markers. And, to discern that stance, we will appeal to our lenses of *reference* and *deixis*.

What is being referred to:	cloning, elements in the schema CLONING
How are those elements referred to:	news, a skin cell, the nucleus, a cow egg, the embryo, the uterus, that embryo clone, a fetus, it, the fetus, its tissues, these tissues from the clone, it worked, IT worked, these cells, functioning tissue, an amazing success, THIS

This list of referents, while not exhaustive, points to the *step-by-step process* that the author has simplified here to reflect a layperson's understanding of how cloning takes place: what is involved, how it's done, what results (a fetus, that is not born), leading to amazing success, and finally, the entire process itself, all encapsulated simply by pronoun "this." The author's position, though we still cannot pinpoint it exactly, is adumbrated through these multiple choices of words and expressions.

Let's move to how the participants are referred to, through nouns (and noun phrases) and pronouns.

Who are the participants:	scientists
How are they referred to:	Scientists at Advanced Cell Technology, advocates of research cloning, *this* research

These individuals as they appear in the first four paragraphs of the essay represent one side of this "raging" debate. Still, we are unsure about the author's position vis à vis the issue. We have clear access to his stance marking strategies, but where he will take us in the argument is yet to be seen.

Next, we are presented with an impressive list of the benefits of such scientific research on cloning. Again, we have isolated the instances of nominal reference and provide them here:

How are the benefits referred to:	near identical replacement parts, curing human scourges, Alzheimer's disease, Parkinson's, spinal-cord injuries, the like, thousands cured, millions relieved of suffering

Through a careful read, we can begin to discursively follow the author's logic, as we come to the fourth paragraph—which contains two tokens of the **high focus** "this" marker, one in each of the sentences that comprise the paragraph, repeated here:

> Do **this** in humans, and we might have thousands cured, millions relieved of suffering. Who could possibly stand in the way of **this research**?

The reader's attention is directed strongly, first, to pronoun *this*, which refers back to the simple, step-by-step process that has the capacity to produce potentially amazing results, benefitting millions of ailing people. The second instance of *this* functions as a determiner and occurs as part of the full noun phrase *this research*—urging the readers to *attend strongly* to the referent. And the referent is located at the tail end of a rhetorical question: "Who could possibly stand in the way **of this research**?" The answer here, we predict, is "no one," or more fully, "No one, and no one should."

Surprisingly, though, that is not the answer.

The remainder of the essay is built around how the author represents the response to the foregoing question—who could (and should) stand in the way? It appears immediately, in the opening line of paragraph 5:

> **Opening to paragraph 5:**
>
> **We** do, say cloning advocates [highlighting added].

From this paragraph until the end of the essay, (i.e., eight additional paragraphs), the author builds his argument, with multiple tokens of **high focus** "this," all of which point to his opposition to the very people and ideologies and research that he now argues so strongly against.

In addition, the remainder of the essay is also peppered with instances of "we," "us," and "you" with meanings that shift and change. Most notable perhaps is his use of "we," which points variably to and echoes both camps: his opposition, as we note in paragraph 5, and his own network of support that he is now attempting to build via the essay.

Such variability of such reference through "we" is evident in the final two paragraphs, shown here:

> 13 **We** will never go there, **the research-cloning advocates assure us**. Promise. Cross my heart and hope to die. But what are such promises

worth? At some point, **we** **need to muster the courage to say no**. At some point, **we** **need to say**: **We** **too care about human suffering,** but we also care about what **this research** **is doing to our humanity**.

14 **We** need to say **that** today, before it is too late. The time to stop human cloning is now.

The author's position has now been made crystal clear. Discursively, what we find here is a systematic building up of an argument using familiar reference terms, including demonstratives that modulate between **high focus** ("this") [information important, framed as unshared and "new"], **medium focus** ("that") [referent framed as within sphere of shared knowledge with reader], and **low focus** ("it") [referent framed as unquestionably shared knowledge with reader].

Initially, the establishment of the author's position feels somehow labyrinthine. We might have assumed that his preponderant use of "this" was being associated with the side that he is on and not the side that he is arguing against. Clearly, a "near speaker" interpretation of the deictic term would have led to such an assumption. In the same vein, we also find his use of "shifter" "we" functioning in much the same way—where "we" refers at times to his opponents and at times to himself and his supporters. Note, however, Krauthammer's final use of first person plural reference in the last clause of the penultimate paragraph: ". . . what this research is doing to **our** humanity." The author could have easily written "what is this research doing to (ø) humanity?" However, by virtue his choice of possessive determiner "our" with the abstract noun "humanity," he bypasses the generic reference term "(ø) humanity" in favor of a referring expression that now, all the more strongly establishes a bold line division between himself/his supporters and the scientists/researchers that he so adamantly opposes. Moreover, because of this determiner choice, the noun becomes an instance of specific reference—it is no longer generic. The author and his supporters are now collectively represented as the defenders of humanity, of everyone's humanity—including that of the researchers who have been framed throughout the essay as responsible for placing all of humanity at risk. The use of *our* now includes the author and everyone opposed to cloning and it *excludes* the researchers and scientists who argue in favor of it.

This is merely a brief demonstration on how isolating only reference terms (including deixis) can serve as a departure point for a fuller study of language and discourse. It is designed to underscore the necessity of taking into account micro-level instances of discourse in the overall, macro-level construction of meaning.

We will revisit the Krauthammer essay in more detail in the final section of this chapter, entitled "More Practice Analyzing Discourse."

* * *

We have examined discourse through the lenses of *reference* and *deixis* and have discovered how powerful word choice can be, at all levels of communication.

We began with the news story about Prince William and Catherine, and then moved to an invented scenario about apples in a bowl. We observed in detail the connections between words and the people and things that such words designate—from highly specific referential terms: *Prince William, the Duke and Duchess of Cambridge, the royal couple, that apple, Red Delicious*, to generic terms of reference: *a married couple, fruit*. We also observed how referential choice serves to pick out various features that point to the speaker-hearer-referent relationship (e.g., that apple, one, it).

We then reviewed some technical terminology to develop not only the proper metalanguage to use when discussing reference, but also to shape how it is we analyze discourse. These terms include:

- Determiners: articles, demonstratives, possessives, quantifiers
- Pronouns: subject, object, possessive, and reflexive

In the section on *deixis*, we discussed the necessity of context in the creation of meaning and introduced the concept of "shifters" (e.g., I, me, mine, this, that, now, then, later, there) and their importance in discourse. Here, we provided extended discussion on *I* and *you*, as well as *this*, *that*, and *it*.

The entire chapter on reference and deixis serves as a departure point for further discussion of stance. These notions of reference and deixis comprise the foundation for any analysis of discourse.

We have observed that the speaker's/writer's selection of one tiny term over another, be it a conscious choice or not, absolutely works to shift features of meaning within discourse. At times, such meaning distinctions can be minor (e.g., "it's pleasant that way, too" vs. "it's pleasant this way, too") or major (e.g., "what this research is doing to our humanity" vs. "what this research is doing to humanity"), or anything in between. All the time, though, as we have seen, any type of linguistic choice is clearly and unequivocally an indicator of the speaker or writer's attitude vis à vis features within the context of the communication; it is clearly and unequivocally an indicator of *stance*.

We often take language for granted—especially in the simple ways that we label things and people and events. Now, more than likely, as you listen and read and write and interact, you'll have gained a much stronger sense of language, a much keener awareness of what language can do.

REVIEW AND REFLECTION: REFERENCE, DEIXIS, AND STANCE

1. Reference: The meaning and salient contextual features that emerge in discourse.

Read the following conversation excerpted and adapted from Norris (2000: 127) involving a mother (Patricia) who is telling a story at the dinner table about an incident that happened to her daughter (Amy) when Amy was a little girl. Amy is now a college student and is home for Thanksgiving break. Patricia has just commented to the family that she has told this story at a recent party.

THE CHIPMUNK STORY

Patricia: and I told the story
about you and the little chipmunk
out in the garage . . .

Amy: that thing scared the heck out of me.
it was twice
and the first time
"there's a rat in there
there's a big mouse in there
I saw it."

QUESTIONS FOR THE CHIPMUNK STORY

1a. First, identify all of the referents in the narrative excerpt. Do you find both nouns and pronouns? As for the nouns, how do these appear? For example, are they *just* the noun or do they also appear with DETERMINERS and/or ADJECTIVES?

1b. How are the humans referred to?

1c. What are the various ways in which the *animal* in the story is referred to?

1d. Is there ever a repeated use of a particular reference term for the animal? Why do you think this might be the case?

1e. How does "event time" and understanding of the situation affect forms of reference, especially with regard to features of salience in the discourse, including the way in which the narrative is begun by Patricia?

2. Read the following two transcripts from the film *Dreamer: Inspired by a True Story* (Robbins et al., 2005). The story is about the Crane family, who live on a "horseless horse ranch" in Kentucky. The two principal characters are Ben Crane, the father, who is expert at training and managing race horses, but not so expert in business or family matters, and Cale Crane, Ben's daughter—a preteen with a dream of her own. As a result of a risky business move by Ben, the family comes to own an injured thoroughbred, Soñador ("Dreamer" in Spanish), thus rendering the horse ranch no longer horseless. With lots of care, training, hope, and belief in the power of dreams, the Crane family and their team of trainers nurse Soñador back to health.

    A. In the first excerpt, Cale has written a story in her class about a king, his castle, and a magic horse. Ben Crane has visited Cale's school for a meeting, and while there, he read her story.

DREAMER—EXCERPT A

Ben: I read your story tonight at school.
Cale: The stupid one about the king?
Ben: Yeah, the stupid king.
Ben: ((sighing)) I make mistakes Cale, I'm sorry.
Cale: So you like the stupid king?
Ben: Yeah. I like the stupid king.
Cale: I love the stupid king.
Ben: He loves you too.

QUESTIONS FOR *DREAMER*, EXCERPT A:

2a. First, identify all of the noun phrases (determiners + (adj) + noun) and pronouns. You might want to organize these according to human/person referents and inanimate referents.

    HUMAN/PERSON REFERENTS   INANIMATE REFERENTS

2b. What can you say about pronoun "I" as a "shifter" and the scope of who it refers to?

2c. What other words or parts of speech might be necessary to look at in order to fully understand this excerpt? Why? How would a systematic examination of other linguistic markers enhance your analysis?

2d. What are the multiple ways in which "the king" is referred to? How does this excerpt help us to more fully understand the concept of "shifter?"

B. In the second excerpt of the film, Ben and Cale are in the midst of an argument. Cale's horse, Soñador (Sonya, for short), has just run her first race since her accident. It was a "claiming race," i.e., a race in which all entered horses are technically "for sale," and may be "claimed" for a price. Ben had been confident that since Soñador had sustained such a serious injury in the past (an injury which had been no secret in the horse racing world), no one would even want her—but entering the race seemed clearly to be to everyone's advantage.

DREAMER—EXCERPT B

Ben: She was a good horse, Cale. I'm gonna miss her, too.
Cale: Oh, please don't treat me like a little kid. You should try to get some of your money back. I get it. It's business.
Ben: That's right. It is. But I wasn't trying to sell Sonya, okay?
Cale: You lied to me. You said I'd always have Soñador. You stood right there and said it. But you raced her and she got claimed.
Ben: Well, welcome to the world of horse racing, Cale! Where everything doesn't end up the way you want it to.
Cale: She wasn't for sale!
Ben: Every race horse, everywhere in the world, right now, is for sale! Get that!
Cale: She wasn't just some race horse. She was *our* horse.

QUESTIONS FOR *DREAMER*, EXCERPT B:

2e. In this example, identify all of the ways that the horse, Soñador, is referred to. Make a list of these. How many different types of expressions are used to refer to her? What do these multiple ways of referring seem to mean to the people involved in the interaction?
2f. How might you characterize the *stances* of each character in the story? What types of *patterns* of language use create these stances?
2g. Create your own table of meaning using references to Soñador in parallel with Table 4.1 in the Reference section of this chapter (i.e.,

the "apple" examples). That is, list the actual forms of reference on the left and the salient contextual features underscored by each on the right.

2h. In addition to the individual reference terms (both full noun phrases and pronouns), do you notice any other expressions, any other type of language use that might be relevant to your analysis of speaker stance? Explain.

2i. Do you find any uses of "this" or "that"? Where and how are they used?

PRACTICE WITH DATA ANALYSIS— PUTTING IT ALL TOGETHER

I. Demonstratives in Argumentative Discourse

First, let's re-visit Charles Krauthammer's (2002) *Time Magazine* essay, "The Fatal Promise of Cloning." We have some guiding questions for you. Then, we'll ask you to briefly compare the use of demonstratives in argumentative discourse in other languages. We have provided two excerpts for you—one in Korean and the other in Spanish. Both are on the same controversial topic of cloning.

II. Exercises for "The Fatal Promise of Cloning"

1. Read the full essay once. Summarize the various positions reflected in the essay: that of the author and that of his opponents.

2. Locate all instances of demonstrative usage "this/these" and "that/those," as both determiners and pronouns. (NOTE: For "that," be sure not to include uses of "that" as in 'the book **that** I read yesterday, or 'She said **that** she'd be here.' See Appendix for a brief discussion of this grammatical use of "that," i.e., as a complementizer and as a relative pronoun for a relative clause.)

3. How many tokens of "this" (and "these") and "that (and "those") do you find?

4. Do "this" and "that" systematically signal "close to speaker" vs. "far from speaker?" How about "new information" vs. "shared information?" Is

there anything else that the author's use of these constructions seems to be signaling? Explain your findings in detail.

5. Focusing only on demonstrative reference choice, how does the author formulate his opinion on the issue? Specifically, which uses of demonstratives express the opinions and positions of those criticized by Krauthammer? Which uses of demonstratives reflect his own opinion?

6. Are there other instances of **reference** or any other types of language use that help to express the author's stance? What are they? Make a list of how these tokens pattern within the essay.

Examples: personal pronouns, coordinating conjunctions (especially "but") , adverbs, and so forth.

Now, have a look at how writers of strongly argumentative discourse use demonstratives to express their own stances vis à vis the issues, their opponents, their supporters, and so forth.

III. Discourse Analysis in English and Other Natural Languages—Demonstratives in Korean and Spanish Articles on Cloning

KOREAN

[사설] 인간복제, 보고만 있을 건가

Source: 국민일보, Date: 12/28/2002

인간의 오만과 맹신이 끝내 재앙을 초래하고 말 것인가. 미국 유사종교 집단인 라엘리언의 비밀조직 클로네이드가 예고한 바대로 최초의 복제인간이 탄생했다는 외신이 들어왔다. 클로네이드 소속의 프랑스 과학자 부아셀리 박사는 26일 한 대리모가 복제된 여자 아기를 출산했다고 밝혔다. (. . . Dr. Boisselier, a French scientist revealed that a surrogate gave birth to a cloned female baby.) 이 아기가 진짜 복제인간인지 여부는 아직 확인되지 않았지만 (It has not been confirmed whether **this baby** was a real human clone, but . . .) 클로네이드는 지난 11월 5명의 여성이 복제인간을 임신해 첫 복제아기가 12월 중 태어날 것이라고 예고했었다. 부아셀리 박사는 이 아기가 복제인간이라는 것을 증명하기 위해 다른 과학자들에게 세포검사를 허용할 방침이라고 공언했다. (Dr. Boisselier declared that the cell test would be allowed by other scientists to prove that **this baby** is a human clone.)

클로네이드의 한국지사는 지난 7월 한국인 20대 여성이 복제수정란을 임신했다고 밝혀 국내에서도 복제인간 출생이 임박했다는 우려를 자아냈다. 또 이탈리아의 복제전문가 팀도 내년 1월초 복제인간이 세르비아에서 출생할 것이라고 밝혀 복제인간의 탄생이 지구촌 여러 나라로 확산될 조짐 마저 보이고 있다.

　　인간복제는 생명창조의 섭리에 도전하는 인간의 오만과 호기심,그리고 과학기술로 영생을 얻겠다는 집단적 맹신에 의해 저질러지고 있다. 이러한 행위는 유전자 손상에 의한 기형인간의 출생과 유전질환의 확산을 불러오 고 (**This kind of action** may bring about birth of deformed human caused by genetic damage and spread of genetic diseases . . .)유전자 조작까지 이어져 인류에 대재앙을 초래할 위험이 크다. 인간복제를 통해 아기를 얻고 과학적 호기심을 충족시키겠다는 허황된 욕심이 결국 파멸을 가져온다는 경고다.

　　인간복제에 관여해온 추종자들은 무책임한 행위를 즉각 중단해야 한다. 아울러 이들이 법제의 미비를 틈타 인간복제를 확산시키지 못하도록 엄격한 복제금지 관련법을 서둘러 제정해야 한다. (Furthermore, we should enact a strict law on human cloning prohibition hurriedly so that **these (people)** cannot spread human cloning while taking advantage of inadequate legal system.)

SPANISH

MITALIPOV: "NO DEBEMOS CLONAR HUMANOS PORQUE SABEMOS QUE NO ES SEGURO"

Sábado, 1 de junio de 2013 Teknautas, *El Confidencial*

　　El año pasado, diez días antes de Navidad, un embriólogo japonés que trabaja en EEUU hizo el descubrimiento de su carrera. En un plato de cultivo de su laboratorio había una comunidad de células sanas, creciendo y dividiéndose totalmente ajenas a la importancia de ese hecho. El embriólogo, llamado Masahito Tachibana, hizo una foto y se la mandó apresuradamente a todo su equipo, incluido su jefe, un genetista nacido en la Unión Soviética en 1961 llamado Shoukhrat Mitalipov.

　　Pasaron varios días en silencio, cruzando los dedos para que **esas células** no,

　　se muriesen, como tantas veces había pasado durante los últimos años . . . .

　　Trece años después de **aquello,** Mitalipov asegura haberlo conseguido y todo,

　　apunta a que tiene razón . . .

　　. . . ¿Cómo ha conseguido hacer algo que muchos investigadores pensaban

　　que era imposible hacer? . . .

　　. . . Después del fracaso de Hwang Woo Suk seguimos intentándolo porque **este** era nuestro área de trabajo . . . . Así es como empieza la vida y nosotros queremos saber cuál es la molécula responsable de activar la vida. **Este** es un proceso muy complicado y artificial . . .

. . . ¿En qué enfermedades va a aplicar ahora el uso de <u>estas células</u> madre?

Ahora que ya hemos descubierto que se pueden generar **estas células** a partir de material de pacientes, queremos usar **estas células** en tratamientos. Queremos volver a los estudios con monos y ensayar tratamientos, generando neuronas, células beta para tratar la diabetes y otros tipos celulares. Primero haremos las células en el laboratorio, luego las trasplantaremos en el momento adecuado y veremos si son eficaces. **Eso** será muy importante para después volver a los ensayos con humanos.

¿Es eso malo para España?

No. La ciencia que hacemos es internacional, puede aplicarse en cualquier lugar.

Por supuesto hay países que apoyan más la ciencia, pero estas técnicas se usarán en cualquier lugar. Los resultados son internacionales y si logramos llevar las células madre a tratamientos para nosotros solo habrá pacientes, no nacionalidades.

. . . El estudio con monos sí estaba financiado por el Gobierno, pero al ir a humanos tuvimos que continuar con donaciones privadas. Probablemente nuestro trabajo reavive el interés en **este campo** y espero que España vuelva a él con más financiación. Si lo hace, los científicos puedan volver a España.

* * *

What kinds of patterns (even very preliminary ones based on just these excerpts) do you note? Do we find a similar way of using demonstratives to indicate FOCUS in other languages? If so, how? If not, why not?

Based on your reading and on looking at discourse data (that provided here and that which you have found elsewhere), think about the following:

A. How conscious are we about how we use demonstratives? What does this say about how we use language in general, both in speaking and in writing?

B. What do these patterns of demonstrative use reflect in terms of how we perceive and communicate information and feelings about issues, people, things—how we interact with others—in speech and in writing? (Think about demonstratives and other expressions/con-structions that co-occur with them in discourse.)

C. Why does the study of demonstratives provide such a solid founda-tion on which to build an analysis of stance in spoken and written discourse?

D. Look at demonstrative reference in advertisements, especially adver-tising slogans. For example:

- McDonald's: *I'm lovin' it.*
- Nike: Just do it.
- eBay: eBay's got it, whatever it is.
- Burger King: Have it your way.
- Aqua Velva: It just feels better with an Aqua Velva man.

Locate more of these types of slogans. What does the pronoun "it" refer to? Sometimes, the referent is specific and identifiable. Other times, it is not, and we need to fill the gap with our own imagination.

"It" can be extremely powerful from the perspective of meaning—at times, its meaning is limited and restricted; at times, it can mean almost any-thing we imagine it to mean.

Why does "it" work so effectively as a pronoun choice in advertising?

E. Analyze patterns of demonstrative use in discourse in other lan-guages (e.g., Japanese, Korean, Spanish, French, Persian, Arabic) where the systems of meaning might be slightly different from Eng-lish *this* and *that*. For example, Korean also has a three way system of demonstrative reference: 이, 그, and 저. So does Spanish: *esto, eso, aquél.* How do these deictic reference terms pattern within dis-course? Do you note similarities with English patterns? Differences? Explain.

F. Analyze patterns of demonstrative use (and other related forms) as markers of *stance* in other types of argumentative discourse—for example, political rhetoric (campaign speeches, nomination/accep-tance speeches) or op-ed columns in newspapers.

G. Analyze patterns of demonstrative use (and other related forms) as markers of *stance* in procedural discourse (e.g., instructional pro-grams like cooking or drawing). In some of these discourse genres, do you find typical "near speaker" vs. "far from speaker" uses of "this" and "that," respectively? How might these genres differ from other discourse genres in which demonstratives are also often used (e.g., extended weather reports).

Do this for programs (or instructional videos) in English and compare with similar programs (or instructional videos) in other languages. See how, for example, *esta, esto, eso, esa, aquél,* are used in Spanish. How is demonstrative reference used in French face-to-face or videotaped procedural discourse? How about Chinese, Japanese, Korean, Arabic, or Hebrew?

o   Compare how stance might be marked in each exemplar of discourse.
o   Does *genre* play any role in the distribution of demonstratives across discourse genres in other languages?

CRUCIAL QUESTION: How does the use of demonstrative reference or deictic reference terms (in English and other languages) shift in meaning from referring to entities in space and time (EXOPHORIC reference) to referring to entities and topics within a text (ENDOPHORIC reference)? See the discussion on cohesion in Chapter 5 for more detail.

Monday, Jun. 24, 2002

The Fatal Promise of Cloning

By Charles Krauthammer

As the cloning debate rages in Washington, there is news from the scientific frontier. It involves cows, but tomorrow it could easily involve humans.

Scientists at Advanced Cell Technology in Worcester, Mass., took a skin cell from Cow A, cloned it (by injecting the nucleus into a cow egg whose nucleus had been removed), then implanted the embryo in the uterus of Cow B. That embryo clone grew into a fetus, which, had it been born, would have been Cow C. But it was not born. The fetus was removed from the uterus and harvested for its tissues. These tissues from the clone were then put back into the original Cow A. Lo and behold, it worked. These cells from the clone were not rejected by Cow A and even organized themselves into functioning tissue (such as a kidney).

An amazing success. This is precisely what the advocates of research cloning are promising. Clone, grow it and then use the cloned tissue to create near identical replacement parts for the original animal and thus presumably put us on the road to curing such human scourges as Alzheimer's disease, Parkinson's, spinal-cord injuries and the like.

Do this in humans, and we might have thousands cured, millions relieved of suffering. Who could possibly stand in the way of this research?

We do, say cloning advocates. We would never countenance such work in humans, they say. Cows, yes, but we would never implant a cloned human embryo in the uterus of a woman and grow it to the stage of a fetus. We solemnly promise to grow human clones only to the blastocyst stage, a tiny 8-day-old cell mass no larger than the period at the end of this sentence, so that we can extract stem cells and cure diseases that way. Nothing more. No fetuses. No implantation. No brave new world of fetal farming.

This is all very nice. But curing with stem cells is extremely complicated. First, you have to tease out the stem cells from the blastocyst. Then you have to keep the stem cells alive, growing one generation after another while retaining their pluripotentiality (their ability to develop into all different kinds of cells). Then you have to take those stem cells and chemically tweak them in complex ways to make them grow into specialized tissue cells—say, neurons for a spinal-cord injury. Then you inject the neurons into the patient and get your cure.

The Advanced Cell Technology cow experiment suggests the obvious short circuit that circumvents this entire Rube Goldberg process: let the cloned embryo grow into a fetus. Nature will then create within the fetus the needed neurons, kidney cells, liver cells, etc., in far more usable, more perfect and more easily available form.

Tempting? No way, the cloning advocates assure us. We will never break that moral barrier. It is one thing to grow a cloned embryo, a tiny mass of cells not yet implanted. It is another thing to grow a cloned human fetus, with recognizable human features and carried in the womb of a woman.

I am skeptical of these assurances. Why? Because just a year or two ago, research advocates were assuring us that they only wanted to do stem-cell research on discarded embryos from fertility clinics but would not create a human embryo in the laboratory just for the purpose of taking it apart for its stem cells.

Well, that was then. Today these very same advocates are campaigning hard to permit research cloning—that is, the creation of human embryos for the purpose of taking them apart for their stem cells. They justify this reversal of position by invoking the suffering of millions. And they heap scorn on opponents for letting old promises and arbitrary moral barriers stand in the way of human betterment.

Well, the cow experiment shows the way to even more human betterment. Fetal tissue offers a far simpler and more promising way to produce replacement tissues—it skips all the complications of stem-cell biology and gives you tissue that you can implant right into the human patient. Millions are suffering, are they not?

Millions are suffering. This is precisely the argument that research-cloning advocates are deploying today to allow them to break the moral barrier of creating, for the first time, human embryos solely for their exploitation. What is to prevent "millions are suffering" from allowing them to break the next barrier tomorrow, growing cloned embryos into fetuses?

(continued)

We will never go there, the research-cloning advocates assure us. Promise. Cross my heart and hope to die. But what are such promises worth? At some point, we need to muster the courage to say no. At some point, we need to say: We too care about human suffering, but we also care about what this research is doing to our humanity.

We need to say that today, before it is too late. The time to stop human cloning is now.

SUGGESTIONS FOR FURTHER READING

Archard, M. (2010). Fields and settings. French *il* and *ça* impersonals in copular complement constructions. *Cognitive Linguistics,* 21,3: 443–500.

Brisard, F., Meeuwis, M., Vandenabeele, B., and Parret, H. (Eds.). (2004). *Seduction, Community, Speech: A Festschrift for Herman Parret.* Amsterdam: John Benjamins.

Enfield, N. (2003). Demonstratives in space and interaction: Data from Lao speakers and implications for semantic analysis. *Language*, 79,1: 82–117.

Gray, B. and Cortes, V. (2011). Perception vs. evidence: An analysis of this and these in academic prose. *English for Specific Purposes,* 30,1: 31–43.

Hanks, W. (2006). Spatial frames of reference in language and thought. *Language in Society*, 35,2: 285–96.

Hanks, W. (2009). Fieldwork on deixis. *Journal of Pragmatics*, 41,1: 10–24.

Jakobson, R. (1957/1995). Shifters and verbal categories. In L. Waugh and M. Monville-Burston (Eds.), *On language.* Cambridge, MA: Harvard University Press. Pp. 386–92.

Kay, P. and Fillmore, C. (1999). Grammatical constructions and linguistic generalizations: 'The What's X Doing Y?' *Language,* 75,1: 1–33.

Kuo, J. Y. (2008). A pragmatic approach to the interpretation of Mandarin bare nouns. *Journal of Pragmatics,* 40,6: 1082–1102.

Naruoka, K. (2006). The interactional functions of the Japanese demonstratives in conversation. *Pragmatics,* 16,4: 475–512.

Oh, S. (2001). A focus-based study of English demonstrative reference: With special reference to the genre of the written advertisement. *Journal of English Linguistics*, 29,2: 124–48.

Strauss, S. (2002). *This, that,* and *it* in spoken American English: A demonstrative system of gradient focus. *Language Sciences,* 24: 131–52.

Thiessen, A. (2008). The demonstrative noun phrase cette-fois (-ci/-la). *Journal of French Language Studies*, 18,2: 209–26.

Yoon, K. E. (2003). Demonstratives in Korean as interactional resources. *CLIC: Crossroads of Language, Interaction, and Culture,* 5: 67–91.

LINKS

CNN News. (2011, July 4). *Prince William crash-lands—on purpose—on Prince Edward Island.* Retrieved from*:* http://www.cnn.com/2011/WORLD/americas/07/04/canada.royal.visit/index.html. Accessed July 23, 2012.

Staples. (n.d.). Just shake it [TV commercial]. Retrieved from: http://www.youtube.com/watch?v=8qCthZz9sj0. Accessed September 23, 2013.

Kwukmin Ilbo (online news) 국민일보. (2002, December 28). [사설] 인간복제, 보고만 있을 건가 Retrieved from: http://cafe426.daum.net/_c21_/bbs_search_read?grpid=4yxQ&fldid=Gn8k&contentval=0004qzzzzzzzzzzzzzzzzzzzzzzzz&nenc=&fenc=&q=&nil_profile=cafetop&nil_menu=sch_updw. Accessed May 31, 2013.

El Confidencial (2013, June 1). Mitalipov: "No debemos clonar humanos porque sabemos que no es seguro." *Teknautas.* Retrieved from: http://www.elconfidencial.com/tecnologia/2013/05/20/mitalipov-no-debemos-clonar-humanos-porque-sabemos-que-no-es-seguro-4926/. Accessed May 31, 2013.

NOTE

1. Alternate ways to refer to oneself could include pronouns *one, we,* or even *you* and full noun phrases like *this reader* or *this researcher,* but these are far less common in discourse and they express different stances and different aspects of the speaker's or writer's identity than /.

CHAPTER FIVE

Information Structure, Cohesion, and Intonation Units

> The human mind is an endowment that allows the human organism to deal with its surroundings in ways that are more complex and effective than anything available to other living creatures. It combines at least three remarkable achievements that enable it to surpass the accomplishments of other nervous systems . . . One of them is language . . . Another is memory . . . The third is imagination. (Chafe, 1994: 9)

INFORMATION STRUCTURE is a discourse framework that pertains to the ways in which topics, persons, ideas, memories, and events are introduced into the discourse and referred to later in the discourse. **Information structure** is often divided into two basic categories: *new information* and *given information*, where the so-called *newness* or *givenness* of the "information" relates at once to propositional content as well as to stances of the discourse participants vis à vis such information and each other.

In this chapter, we will discover some of the ways in which language, memory, imagination, and intersubjectivity work together to create meaning in discourse. We will build on the concepts of both *reference* and *deixis* from Chapter 4, and incorporate elements from *genre* in Chapter 3 and a number of features of grammar discussed in Chapter 2. Here, we move beyond the scope of *reference* and *deixis* where things, people, ideas, and concepts enter into discourse as nouns plus the range of potentially co-occurring determiners (including no determiner at all) and pronouns, with the concomitant conceptual and interactional meanings expressed and created by those particular grammatical features.

This chapter offers a change of lens, now shifting focus to larger spates of discourse and texts and considering the notions of: *information structure, cohesion*, and *intonation units*. Essentially, *information structure* pertains to the ways in which topics, persons, ideas, memories, and events are introduced and referred to. The framework of information structure is often built on two basic categories: *new information* and *given information*, where the so-called *newness* or *givenness* of the "information" relates at once to propositional content as well as to stances of the discourse participants vis à vis such information and each other.

Cohesion pertains to the manifold ways in which the primary topics, events, entities, and ideas develop and progress into a culturally-shaped logical coalescence of discourse. That is: What are the primary topics or entities or ideas being discussed or written about? How are they introduced? How are they developed and expanded? What are the lexical, grammatical, conceptual, and metaphorical agents that work together to achieve such coalescence of words, ideas, and thoughts?

Intonation units are units of oral discourse that are analytically grounded in prosody, or the vocal fluctuations (e.g., rate of speech, volume, pitch, stress, and intonation) that color our spoken utterances, from vocalized wordless acknowledgments to propositionally complex instances of conversation and spoken narrative.

INFORMATION STRUCTURE

For decades, linguists have been intrigued by what Prince (1981: 224) calls "informational asymmetry"—a skewing in the grammatical and discursive expression of propositional content, where some bits of information are "newer" to the discourse and *less familiar to the recipient,* and some are "older" and hence *more easily predictable, recognizable, identifiable, or inferable*. Such informational skewing is evident at the level of single words, phrases, clauses, full sentences, and longer texts (e.g., written paragraphs, essays, narratives, and extended turns-at-talk). Alternations between *newness* and *givenness* are context-, participant-, and genre-dependent. Information structure points to the ways in which discourse participants "package information" (Chafe, 1976) based on how readily such information and bits of content may be understood by intended recipients. This interplay between language, discourse, and intersubjective cognition has been a focus of study among linguists for at least a half-century.[1]

> One presumably universal feature of natural language is that the objective information conveyed is not conveyed on a single plane. That is there is an INFORMATIONAL ASYMMETRY [emphasis original] in that some units seem to convey or represent "older" information than others . . . and perhaps this is not only universal, but also distinctive of human language—the crucial factor appears to be the tailoring of an utterance by a sender to meet the particular assumed needs of the intended receiver. That is, information-packaging in natural language reflects the sender's hypothesis about the receiver's assumptions and beliefs and strategies. (Prince, 1981: 224)

New information includes topics and references that the hearer or discourse recipient may not already be familiar with or may be unable to identify or recognize at all. *Given information* involves references to events, persons, and entities that the hearer is assumed to either already know or be able to understand, recognize, or infer.[2]

New (Unshared) Information in English

New information in English is often marked by *indefinite* reference markers, e.g., determiners: *a, an, some, any,* and *whichever.* Some cases of the *zero article*, e.g., with mass nouns and plural count nouns, also signal indefinite reference, as in:

Ø <u>Tomato slices</u> are dipped in Ø <u>egg</u> and   Ø <u>bread crumbs</u> and then baked.
  [plural count]   [mass/   [plural count]
                         non-count]

(See Appendix for more details.)

The concept of *new* indicates that the referent has not yet been introduced into the particular spate of discourse and establishes an interactional stance vis à vis the discourse recipient, such that inference, recognition, or identifiability is either not yet possible or not yet relevant. That is, the discourse recipient is presumed to not know the referent or to be unable to identify or recognize it.

We illustrated this briefly in Chapter 4 with the following examples from a book title and a film title.

Book Title:	To Kill a Mockingbird vs. ?To Kill <u>the</u> Mockingbird
Film Title:	Strangers on a Train vs. ?Strangers on <u>the</u> Train.

An indefinite determiner signals that the noun with which it co-occurs is both non-specific and non-identifiable. Indefinite articles *a* or *an* also signal the quantity "one." So, in the previous titles, designating which particular "mockingbird" or which particular "train" is irrelevant to the meaning of each title.

Some genres exhibit predictable patterns in the distribution of structures containing *new* information marked by indefinite determiners.

Fairy tales: *Once upon <u>a time</u>, there lived <u>an old fisherman</u> in <u>a village</u> near the shore . . .*

Jokes *<u>A man</u> walks into <u>a bar</u> with <u>a crow</u> on his shoulder . . .*

Q: What do <u>ducks</u> get after they see <u>a doctor</u>?

A: <u>A</u> bill.

Movie Synopses *<u>A small-time magician</u> with <u>questionable ethics</u> arrives in <u>a magical land</u> and must choose between becoming <u>a good man</u> or <u>a great on</u>e.* (Oz: The Great and Powerful)

Dorothy Gale is <u>an orphaned teenager</u> who lives with her Auntie Em and Uncle Henry on <u>a Kansas farm</u>. (The Wizard of Oz)

Aphorisms: *If <u>a man</u> speaks or acts with <u>a pure thought</u>, happiness follows him like <u>a shadow</u> that never leaves him.* (Buddha)

From <u>a drop of water</u>, <u>a logician</u> could predict <u>an Atlantic</u> or <u>a Niagara</u>. (Sir Arthur Conan Doyle)

<u>An honest man</u> is always <u>a child</u>. (Socrates)

As we can see in the examples, referents emerge initially as non-specific, non-identifiable entities. When we tell stories or narratives or jokes, we set the scene and we orient our readers or listeners to details of persons and times and places: Who is involved? Where does the story begin? What other details are essential to the plotline as it will develop? Do we assume that readers or hearers are already familiar with the persons and places in our story or might we introduce them as *new*? (See Chapter 3, Genre, Modality, Register, and Participation Framework for a detailed discussion of genre.)

If an inherently *given* reference term such as a proper noun is also used, e.g., Dorothy Gale (*The Wizard of Oz*), it is followed by a *new information-marked* construction, providing us with more background signaling an assumed informational nonsharedness with the audience: "*an* orphaned teenager who lives with her Auntie Em and Uncle Henry," not **"the** orphaned teenager," or simply "Dorothy Gale" with no further elaboration. Upon the mere mention of the protagonist's name, we are not expected here to know who Dorothy Gale is and how or why she is relevant to the plot as it develops.

For aphorisms such as the exemplars given, indefinite reference terms take the grammatical and discursive shape of *new information.* They mention entities that are not only non-specific, they are inherently not intended to pick out any entity as specific or identifiable, precisely because of their generic nature in terms of content and purpose: to portray an observation of life or character and to elevate that observation to the level (and extent possible) of universal generalizability.

Given (Shared) Information in English

Given information in English is often marked by the definite article *the* in a noun phrase or by a pronoun. *Given information* refers to entities that a discourse recipient is expected to recognize—either through everyday commonsense knowledge (e.g., "The *product of 0 x 1 is 0"),* through logical or inferential association with another referent (e.g., "there lived *an old fisherman* in a village near the shore"), through prior mention (e.g., "He [or the fisherman] returned home each night with an empty net") or through unique identifiability, i.e., in cases where there is one and only one instance of the named entity (e.g. "Everest, the tallest mountain in the world . . ." or "Does the sun always rise in the east and set in the west, even at the north pole?").

Other linguistic markers of definiteness include the determiners or pronouns *this, these, that,* and *those*, proper nouns designating an identifiable entity or individual[3] (e.g., Socrates, Spanky, Mick Jagger, Maroon 5, Denny's, Bubba Gump, Uranus), pronouns (e.g., *he, she, they, it, I, you, them*), and possessive determiners (e.g., *my, his, her, your*) (see Chapters 2, 4, and the Appendix).

As we have noted, first mention of an entity typically occurs with an indefinite reference term marking *new information*, and subsequent mention of that same entity is framed as *given, old,* or *shared* through markers of definiteness, e.g., definite determiners, proper nouns, or pronouns.

Have a look at the transcript excerpt from the Disney Pixar movie, *Finding Nemo* (Walters, Stanton, and Unkrich, 2003).

In the film, Nemo, who is a young and adventurous clown fish, heads into the open sea, despite his dad's warnings. He swims around a boat anchored nearby and gets "fishnapped" by one of the boat's divers. Nemo is gone— seemingly forever (but breathe a sigh of relief; he is found safe and sound later in the movie!). Marlin, Nemo's dad, puts two and two together—the boat, the divers, Nemo's disappearance. He swims out in the direction of the boat to find Nemo and Nemo's captors, and then loses sight of it. He runs into Dory, a female Blue Tang (a kind of fish) who, at first sight, appears quite absent-minded. We come to see, through Dory's words and actions, that she actually suffers from short-term memory loss.

Imagine the scenario, if you haven't seen the film, or try to recall it, if you have seen it. As you read through the transcript, attend to the following points:

- How are *new information* and *given information* encoded grammatically?
- Does *new information* ever evolve to *given* and back again to *new*? If so, how? And why?

Finding Nemo Excerpt

MARLIN:	**Has anybody seen <u>a boat</u>!?** Please! <u>A white boat</u>! They took my son! My son! Help me, please! . . .
DORY:	. . . Ohh. Oh, oh. Sorry! I didn't see you. Sir, are you okay?
MARLIN:	. . . No, no. They took him away. **I have to find <u>the boat.</u>**
DORY:	**Hey, I've seen <u>a boat</u>.**
MARLIN:	You have?
DORY:	Uh huh. **<u>It</u> passed by not too long ago.**
MARLIN:	**<u>A white one</u>?**
DORY:	Hi. I'm Dory.
MARLIN:	Where!? Which way!?
DORY:	Oh, oh, oh! **<u>It-it</u> went, um, this way!** And **<u>it</u> went this way!** Follow me!
MARLIN:	Thank you! Thank you, thank you so much!
DORY:	No problem . . .
MARLIN:	. . . Wait a minute . . .
DORY:	Stop following me, okay!? ((not recognizing Marlin now))
MARLIN:	**What? You're showing me which way <u>the boat</u> went!**

DORY:	<u>A boat</u>? Hey, I've seen <u>a boat</u>. <u>It</u> passed by not too long ago. <u>It</u> went this way. It went this way. Follow me!
MARLIN:	Wait a minute, wait a minute! What is going on? **You already told me which way <u>the boat</u> was going!**
DORY:	I did? Oh dear . . .

We find the patterns of information structure in language with first mention (new information) and subsequent mention (given information), referent identifiability (given), and a reversion back to non-identifiability (new). In spite of the fictionalized and comedic nature of this interaction, it nicely captures the very notion of informational asymmetry with which we opened the chapter, linking together language and memory and imagination. In this case, it is the speaker's perspective of information structure that is highlighted, i.e., the speaker's own ability to recognize or remember or identify the referent, which causes the alternations in grammatical and pragmatic marking for *new* and *given* information.

Locate the instances of *new* and *given* information in the following excerpt, taken from California's Walnut Valley Water District website.

Attend to the following points as you read through the data:

- How would you identify the *genre* of discourse?
- Identify the *new* and *given* entities and try to articulate a pattern for **where, how, and <u>why</u>** *new information* and *given information* is linguistically packaged in the way that it is.

How To Turn Off Your Water

Turn Off Procedure

Locate <u>your customer valve</u> . . . <u>The valve</u> is usually located on <u>a hose bib</u> where <u>the plumbing service line</u> enters <u>the house</u>. <u>A hose bib</u> is <u>an exterior water faucet</u> with <u>a threaded end </u>to connect <u>a lawn or garden hose</u>. Turn <u>the gate valve</u> clockwise . . .

Emergency Meter Valve

If <u>the operation</u> of <u>the customer valve</u> does not turn off <u>your water</u>, then locate <u>the meter valve</u> on <u>the street side</u> of <u>the meter assembly</u> and turn <u>the meter valve</u> a ¼ turn clockwise . . .

(Walnut Valley Water District, n.d.)

Based solely on an analysis guided by information structure, who do you assume to be the intended users of this website? Who do you assume would *not* appeal to the information provided here? Why? Homeowners would probably appreciate this way of delivering the information. Plumbers might feel annoyed. Or, perhaps they wouldn't search for the information online in the first place. They know what a hose bib is and they should be able to locate the gate valve and the meter valve.

We will conclude our introduction to information structure with one additional dataset. The example is extracted from an elementary level science website. You will note that it contains a preponderance of instances of definite reference, signaling shared or given or old information. As you read through the excerpt, attend to the following points:

- Note the underlined words and phrases—are all of the instances of reference definite?
- In what way is definiteness here related to *given information?*
- Do you note any instances of indefinite reference? If so, where?
- Do you note any instances of negation? (For example, the word "not," "no" or contracted "n't"). How might negation enter into an analysis of discourse from an information structural perspective?

---

11 <u>The Spinning Earth</u>: <u>Your World</u> is Tilted

By Ronen Plesser and John Heffernan

Having established how <u>Earth's</u> spinning causes <u>the alternation</u> of day and night, <u>this lesson</u> will introduce <u>the fact</u> that <u>Earth's</u> axis is not perpendicular to <u>the Sun</u>. <u>This</u> means <u>the Sun</u> does not lay always directly above <u>the equator</u> as students may have found in <u>the lesson</u> Spinning into Darkness and Light. In fact, <u>it</u> is sometimes to <u>the north</u> and sometimes to <u>the south</u> of <u>the equator</u>. <u>The alternation</u> of <u>these configurations</u> creates <u>the seasons</u> on <u>Earth</u>. Students will investigate <u>the effects the tilt</u> in <u>the axis</u> has on <u>the length of days and nights</u> at various latitudes in <u>the two hemispheres</u>.

(Plesser and Heffernan, n.d.)

We added the boldface type to the opening sentence for emphasis. How do you see the relationship of these opening words to the remainder of the discourse that follows? Here, we begin to gain a different perspective on the use of the word "information." That is, throughout this discussion and in much of the literature on "information structure," there is an emphasis on grammatical and discursive conventions used for the introduction of entities and topics into discourse, with centrally focused themes such as **new/first mention/ unidentifiable** on the one hand and **given/subsequent mention/identifiable** on the other. As you read through this lesson on science, you've likely noted the heavy skewing of definite reference markers. What makes these referents definite in the first place?

Another question that might come to mind is this: "Information" seems often to be discussed at the level of the word or the sentence or strings of contiguous sentences. How would you characterize the "information" presented here at a level beyond the word or sentence or strings of sentences? While most of the referents included in this discourse sample are definite, **is the information truly given or old or shared**? What sort of impression does this create as a sample of pedagogical materials for elementary school science? (For a more fine-grained analysis of information structure, see the section in this chapter on intonation units, with references to Chafe (1994), Prince (1981, 1992), Birner and Ward (2009) and other scholars that suggest concepts such as "assumed familiarity" and "accessible information" for entities that are new to the discourse but not new to the participants).

A micro-level focus on information structure within discourse can reveal much about genre in general, and about the author's or speaker's stance toward the information itself and toward the intended recipients of the discourse. Information structure as an analytic lens provides much insight into these areas, and more, and can aid the analyst in her or his discovery of deeper and non-literal meanings of discourse.

COHESION

COHESION is the process through which topics, events, and ideas coalesce into logical, culturally-shaped aggregates of discourse. *Cohesion* is related to how topics are introduced, developed, and maintained— monologically, or in collaboration; on paper; on screen; telephonically; or in the company of others.

Halliday (1994), Halliday and Hasan (1976), Halliday and Matthiessen (2004), and Martin (2008b) present four[4] categories of "cohesive resources" for English that serve to create cohesively textual meanings in discourse. These categories are essentially grammatical in form and they serve to create cohesive aggregation in language and discourse, from phrase to clause to sentence to larger texts—in all communicative modalities.

1. Reference
2. Ellipsis and substitution
3. Conjunction
4. Lexical cohesion

We will discuss each of these elements in more detail.

1. Reference (as defined in Chapter 4) involves the relationship between words and the things, ideas, entities, states, and people that such words designate. Halliday and Hasan (1976) propose two basic types of reference: ENDOPHORA and EXOPHORA.

Endophora is the act of reference to an item within the text itself (Strauss, 2002: 137). "Endo-" as a prefix means "inside, within."

Exophora is the act of reference to an item outside of the text itself (Strauss, 2002: 136). "Exo-" as a prefix means "outside of." Instances of exophoric reference require contextual features for the identification of the referent.

Endophoric reference is based on the actual words or ideas within the text or implied by it. Reference from within a text can either point backward **to a referent already introduced**, i.e., *anaphora*, or it can point forward **to a referent that has yet to be introduced**, i.e., *cataphora*.

Some of our discussion of information structure in the previous section actually involves *anaphoric* reference. Note the process from the *Finding Nemo* transcript:

Finding Nemo Excerpt

First mention: "Has anyone seen **a boat**?"
Subsequent mention: "I have to find the boat."
Subsequent mention: "It passed by not too long ago."
Referent: a boat ← the boat, it

Anaphora Is Backward Pointing

The referent "a boat" was introduced first, and later replaced by "the boat," and "it." Subsequent mention, through definite determiners and pronouns,[5] indicates a backward directionality of reference, specifying a presumably identifiable entity, idea, or person *already introduced into the discourse.*

Anaphoric reference is, without a doubt, the most basic, the most essential of all cohesive devices in language and discourse.

Cataphora is the instance of endophoric reference that *points forward. Cataphoric* reference, by its very syntactic and pragmatic nature, requires that the listener or reader attend more closely to the upcoming discourse, because a referent has just been introduced *as if* it were *already known or previously mentioned,* when in fact, it will not emerge until some time later in the discourse.

* * *

In *cataphoric* reference, identification of the entity or referent that it is picking out comes *after* the *cataphoric* item. We illustrate next using an example from lyrics of the song "Lincoln Portrait," by Aaron Copland. There are two instances of *cataphoric reference* in the excerpt: The first involves the pronoun *he,* used (twice) prior to the mention of the referent's name (*Abe Lincoln*). The second involves the demonstrative pronoun *this* (also used twice) to signal what will be coming as the words that Abe Lincoln said.

"Lincoln Portrait" Lyrics, by Aaron Copland

*He was born in Kentucky, raised in Indiana, and lived in Illinois. And **this** is what **he** said. **This** is what* <u>Abe Lincoln</u> *said: "*<u>The dogmas of the quiet past are inadequate to the stormy present</u> . . ."

Referent: He → Abe Lincoln

Referent: This is what Abe Lincoln said → "The dogmas of the quiet past are inadequate to the stormy present."

Cataphora Is Forward Pointing

Endophoric reference, then, involves backward pointing (anaphora) or forward pointing (cataphora) within the text itself

Exophoric reference, on the other hand, involves a pointing to the **referent that is *in the actual context* of the interaction**, but **not** yet mentioned **in the text**.

The following example is taken from the second class meeting of an Adult Education course at a large university in the northeastern United States. The instructor is taking care of administrative business, making sure that all participants in the class have the required materials.

Adult Ed Evening Class—Meeting #2

Instructor: Before we actually start the session, I wanted to ask, how many people are new?

((one student raises hand))

Instructor: So **you** need some- the syllabus: and s- Can **you** just pass **this** to **her**?

Referents: you: one individual in the class
you: a different individual in the class
this: course papers, including syllabus
her: the individual first addressed as "you"

Exophora Is Grounded In The Contextual Features Of Interaction

---

Without knowing the context, we would be unable to identify with any degree of specificity precisely who or what is being referred to by the pronouns *you, this,* or *her.* Who is the instructor addressing, with the first instance of *you?* And who, with the second instance? What, specifically is being passed from one student to the other? Context is crucial here in order for any of the discourse to make sense.[6]

Here is a summary of the basic components of reference:

ENDOPHORIC reference is **IN TEXT**. There are two types:

- **Anaphoric reference**, pointing **backwards** to an **already mentioned entity**.
- **Cataphoric reference**, pointing **forward** to an entity which will be **identified in the upcoming text** or discourse.

EXOPHORIC reference is **OUTSIDE OF TEXT**, and grounded in **CONTEXT**.

We will address the remaining cohesive resources now.

2. **Ellipsis** and **substitution**: Both processes are related at once to syntax and to lexico-grammatical meaning. **Ellipsis** involves the *deletion* of a word that is already recoverable from elsewhere in the discourse. **Substitution** involves the use of an *alternate word or alternate words* whose meaning is recoverable from elsewhere in the discourse.

149

> Ellipsis: *Keep* [this product] *out of* [the] *reach of children.*
> Substitution: *I wanted to open a checking account, and I* **did.** [I did = I opened a checking account]

3. **Conjunction**: This process relates to the grammatical and pragmatic linking of entities, events, ideas, and opinions, through such conventions as:

supplementation	and, as well, in addition, moreover
alternative	or, either, if not *x*
contrast	but, on the other hand, in contrast
concession	despite, nonetheless, even though
cause	since, because, due to
time	then, afterwards, suddenly, before
condition	provided that, if, unless

4. **Lexical Cohesion**: refers to the multiple ways of "saying the same thing" or almost the same thing, either explicitly or through associative means. Thus, the most simple and direct instance of lexical cohesion is repetition (Halliday, 1994: 330).

Please read **your contract** *carefully.* **This** *is* **a legal contract** *between you, the Owner, and us, Pacific Life Insurance Company.*
The first sentence is a request (actually, it is a directive) that specifies the addressee's "contract." The second sentence refers back to the "contract" in two ways: through the pronoun "this" and through the repetition of the word "contract," now qualified with the attributive adjective "legal," underscoring the importance of the document. *your* **contract** → **this** is a **legal contract**.
Other types of lexically achieved cohesion include:

> synonyms and antonyms—almost the same meaning or the diametrically opposite meanings; negation; parallel constructions:
>
> *Is the glass half* **empty** *or half* **full**?   [antonyms]
> Life of Pi *is* **not great**, *it's* **fantastic**!   [contrast—upgrade]

I don't need to **ace** *the final exam.*
I'm fine if I ***just pass.***   [contrast—downgrade]

metaphors, similes, and analogies—various ways of establishing comparison:

   it's a train wreck waiting to happen (in reference to a potential disastrous failure)

   it's like talking to a dead bear (in reference to someone who doesn't listen)

part—whole relationships—logical or inferential associations with other referents; associations with specific contexts, areas, disciplines, genres, etc.[7]

Restaurant Review:

Good **food, service** *just okay.* [associations with restaurant context: food, service, wait staff, maître d'hôtel, sommelier, ...]

Features of French press coffee maker:

beans, mesh, filter, stainless steel frame, aroma, dishwasher safe

Vincent van Gogh:

Starry Night, post impressionism, Zouave, Arles, Sunflowers

Wines:

bouquet, varietal, Jeroboam, appellation, nose

The category of lexical cohesion as described here, and as elaborated in Halliday and Hasan (1976), Halliday (1994), Martin (2008b), and elsewhere, is tightly connected to features of both genre and register (Chapter 3), where shared understandings of the conventions of structure, purpose, content, and lexical choice merge to create coherent discursive wholes.

Essentially, textual and discursive cohesion is achieved through, at the very least, the four (or five) categories of cohesive devices noted by Halliday and Hasan (1976) and Halliday (1994): reference, ellipsis and substitution, conjunction, and lexical cohesion. As you will come to see, all categories of these so-called "cohesive ties" (Halliday and Hasan, 1976) work together to achieve the meaningful coalescence of texts. You will also likely notice that it becomes difficult (and at times impossible) to discretely label one particular type of cohesive resource as separate and distinct from another type. Some of these categories cross-cut each other in multiple ways. All, however, do serve to create textual and discursive cohesion.[8]

As an exercise focusing only on cohesion and the cohesive resources just discussed, have a look at the following Wikipedia excerpt. It contains the introductory paragraphs to the entry for the game tic-tac-toe.

Attend to the following basic points so that you may gain a sense of how a reader's sensitivity to the types of cohesive devices just discussed (and others that you will discover) might enhance your understanding of discourse and texts:

- What genre or genres of discourse does this excerpt belong to?
- Which types of linguistic features appear to be relatively consistent to the genre (or combination of genres)?
- How are old and new information presented here?
- What are the patterns of cohesion that you can identify from the broad categories just discussed (reference, ellipsis and substitution, conjunction, and lexical cohesion)?
- Within those categories, do you note other instances of language, grammar, or discourse that also appear to enhance overall textual cohesion, but are not mentioned as categories of cohesion or are not mentioned within the sub-categories?
- Do you find yourself *forcing* a discovery of cohesion (between sentences and/or paragraphs), when, in fact something feels missing? Elaborate.

Tic-tac-toe

From Wikipedia, the free encyclopedia

Tic-tac-toe (or Noughts and crosses, Xs and Os) is a paper-and-pencil game for two players, *X* and *O*, who take turns marking the spaces in a 3×3 grid. The player who succeeds in placing three respective marks in a horizontal, vertical, or diagonal row wins the game.

Players soon discover that best play from both parties leads to a draw (often referred to as cat or cat's game). Hence, Tic-tac-toe is most often played by young children.

The friendliness of Tic-tac-toe games makes them ideal as a pedagogical tool for teaching the concepts of good sportsmanship and the branch of artificial intelligence that deals with the searching of game trees.

It is straightforward to write a computer program to play Tic-tac-toe perfectly, to enumerate the 765 essentially different positions (the state space complexity), or the 26,830 possible games up to rotations and reflections (the game tree complexity) on this space.

(Tic-tac-toe, n.d.)

We asked you to identify the genre or genres of discourse that this entry might belong to, and the linguistic features that are associated with the genre(s) in question. What is it (or what are they)? Identifying the genre and the related linguistic features is actually a bit tricky here. We know what the intended genre is: encyclopedic definition and elaboration of a term or concept. But, in view of how discourse is presented and organized, there appear to be multiple purposes at play here in the writing.

That is, using the propositional content contained in this excerpt, if you didn't already know about the game, what it looks like, or how it is played, would you be able to clearly envision the grid, how turn taking is achieved, what each player is supposed to do and when, how a player wins, or how the game ends in a draw, simply based on the excerpted text? Which elements of the game grid, turn-taking procedures, strategies for winning, and so forth, are clear to you from the data? Which are not? As we can glean from this excerpt, cohesion is not created solely through the devices enumerated by Halliday. We also rely a great deal on our background/life/socio-cultural knowledge to make connections within and with a text. The propositional content as presented here might suffice for certain readers. Other readers might find some detail lacking. Also, based on the structure and content of the last sentence in the excerpt, do you find that it is "cohesively tied," both linguistically and inferentially, to the prior text?

You might want to have a look at other websites that are intended to demonstrate the step-by-step procedures of "how to play tic-tac-toe." Any website will do.

How does the discourse in other sites targeting the rules and procedures of playing tic-tac-toe compare to the procedural discourse in the previous segment? Think about lexico-grammatical structures, visuals, graphics, accompanying videos. What changes from the perspectives of *information structure, cohesion,* and most importantly, *stance*? How do the notions of *genre as social action* and *discourse as social action* emerge in each dataset, i.e., the Wikipedia entry on tic-tac-toe and a website on how to actually play the game?

Throughout these chapters, we have been emphasizing the *social* element(s) of discourse, from the points of view of grammar, genre, reference, deixis, stance, information structure, and cohesion. We have noted how *meaning* is created discursively as speakers and writers, uploaders of videos, composers of songs, and authors of recipes produce discourse from the point of view of who will understand, grasp, or follow the information as presented, who might need elaboration and who might not, who belongs within the discursive sphere of interaction, who does not—and why. We have seen how tiny words like determiners can carry so much meaning—*the water* and *your water,* or *your contract, this,* and *a legal contract* might designate the identical referent, but not carry the same discursive meaning. Even the seemingly slight distinction between *a boat, the boat* and back to *a boat* again can reveal so much about participants and how they process, understand, and produce discourse in interaction—scripted or otherwise. Words like *beans, nose, bouquet,* and *pigeon chess*—when linked to context and situation and participants—illustrate the potential variations within so-called literal meaning, and the manifold ways in which literal meaning shifts and changes into discursive meaning within and across texts and genres.

In the next section, we will take a slightly different perspective on the structure of discourse and information flow. Rather than focusing only on lexico-grammatical elements, we will look at the prosodic units that constitute discourse and the relationship of these units to consciousness (i.e., lexico-grammatical elements AND the prosody through which they are delivered). By *consciousness* we will be discussing that of the speaker and that of the hearer in the process of contextually situated oral interaction.

INTONATION UNITS

Chafe (1972, 1974, 1976, 1987, 1994, 1998) explores the relationship between discourse and consciousness. "One way to think of consciousness is as a narrow spotlight that can at any one time be directed at only a small area of the available scene—but a spotlight that wanders constantly, sometimes with purpose and sometimes not" (Chafe, 1974: 111).

Exactly twenty years later, Chafe (1994: 53), compares consciousness to vision, using a similar analogy as the spotlight, where foveal vision and focal consciousness function much in the same way as the spotlight, and peripheral vision and peripheral consciousness constitute essentially everything else that might possibly enter into our fields of vision or fields of consciousness. And like a visual sensory organ, our consciousness scans input and stimuli, focusing in on one entity with varying degrees of precision and clarity, while other entities and peripheral matter recede into the distance, shifting from focal points of vision and consciousness to peripheral ones and back again. "Both vision and consciousness exist in a state of constant restlessness" (Chafe, 1994: 53).

The intonation unit (Chafe 1987, 1994), i.e., the short spate of speech bounded by prosodic features signaling both onset and completion, serves as a window into human consciousness, illuminating this very interplay between *foveal and peripheral consciousness*, and the flux between *immediate consciousness* (revealing the here and now of perception, thought, and opinion) and *displaced consciousness* (memory, imagination, recalled impressions, subjective distancing in time and space). The intonation unit reveals three basic states of consciousness: active, semi-active, or inactive. These consciousness states correlate largely with information status, as summarized:

consciousness state	information status
active	given
semi-active	accessible
inactive	new

Chafe (1994: 74) bases the concepts of givenness, accessibility, and newness on an orientation by the speaker with regard to the hearer's consciousness state, i.e., whether a referent, entity, idea, or topic is active, semi-active, or inactive in the listener's mind at the onset of an intonation unit. Note here the intermediary categories of both consciousness state (semi-active) and information status (accessible), designating referents and entities that are not new or given, but accessible within the minds of both speaker and hearer—a type of shared knowledge denoting "assumed familiarity," as in *He* [given] *just bought the new Hyundai Sonata* [accessible] or *Did you* [given] *see the moon* [accessible] *last night? It was full.* See also Birner and Ward, 2009; Gundel, 1985; Kuno, 1972; and Prince, 1981, 1992; among others.

Chafe (1994: 64–65) provides three functional categories of intonation units:

Substantive—carrying the propositional content of the intonation unit

Regulatory—typically in the form of discourse markers like *I see, no way!, and, but, m hmm, oh*

Fragmentary—typically truncated units, speech stopped in the middle

---

The following sample presents a portion of a narrative (from Chafe, 1998) that is transcribed in an intonation unit format. Different from the narrative samples that we have introduced elsewhere in this book, the details of this narrative are visually salient in that each unit of talk contains what Chafe refers to as a "focus of consciousness," with each instance of focus being expressed in one intonation unit.

You will note that the transcript contains prosodic notations as represented in this key (from Chafe, 1998: 98):

- . . . (number) indicates a pause measured *in seconds* signaling the onset of an intonation unit.
- . . indicates a shorter pause.
- Acute accent mark, e.g., *Móm,* indicates both high pitch and amplitude. It signals prosodic prominence.
- Grave accent mark, e.g., *Yòu knòw*, indicates relatively high pitch only. It signals prominence, but secondary to the acute accent mark.
- Square brackets around words in intonation units indicate that two speakers are speaking at the same time, or producing overlapping talk:

  Speaker 1: Shè ùsed to tell Vèrna to sàve [all the líght] bùlbs.
  Speaker 2: [*óh I knów it.*]

- A period at the end of a unit, e.g., . . *just líke a pìstol gòin' òff.* indicates falling pitch.
- A question mark at the end of a unit, e.g., . . *up in her béd róom?* indicates rising pitch.
- A comma at the end of a unit, e.g., *and if shé héard a nóise at níght*, indicates "other phrase-final pitch contours."

- Up or down arrows on each side of a segment indicate the left and right side boundaries of speech that are pronounced with higher pitch and amplitude (↑), or lower pitch and amplitude (↓).

This narrative was produced collaboratively between a brother and sister, now senior citizens themselves, recalling memories about their mother, who is framed here as "brave," as she lived alone and resorted to interesting behaviors that made her feel especially safe in her own home. In this excerpt, it is the sister who is telling most of the story. Her brother's turns are indicated in italics—as in the original text.

As you read through this brief excerpt, attend to the following points:

- What types of consciousness do you see revealed in the data? Specifically, where do you note focus and where do you note periphery?
- How are these marked linguistically? We know that it is the sister who is the primary speaker and the brother who is the recipient of the discourse—they share much of the family history expressed in this narrative.
- How are the referents introduced? That is, can you identify instances of new information, accessible information, and given information? How does reference to people and things change according to their status in the discourse (e.g., first mention, later mention, etc.)? What is your impression regarding the brother's ability to identify or recognize referents in the narrative?
- How do the turns appear to be managed? That is, we know that it is the sister who is the primary speaker and the brother, the addressee. At what point does the brother begin to speak? (NOTE: the sister's units appear in unmarked font; the brother's are marked in *italics*—lines 13, 14, and 17).

---

1. . . .   (2.6) Í can't believe,
2. . . .   (0.5) Yòu knòw Móm was prétty bráve.
3. . .   ↓When you come-
4. . .   when it comes right dówn tó it. ↓
5. . . .   (0.3) ↑ Did Í téll you what ↑ Vérna tóld me òne tìme-
6. . . .   (0.5) that when she líved thère alòne she kept-
7. . . .   (0.4) òld líght bùlbs
8. . .   up in her béd róom?
9. . . .   (0.4) and if shé héard a nóise at níght,
10. . . .   (0.6) she would táke a líght bùlb

> 11. . . . and thrów it on the cemènt wálk and it'd póp,
> 12. . .. just líke a pìstol gòin' òff.
> 13. . . . (0.2) *Whó.*
> 14. *Móm did?*
> 15. . . . (0.2) ↑ Yéah. ↑
> 16. . . . (0.6) Shè ùsed to tell Vèrna to sàve [all the líght] bùlbs.
> 17. [*óh I knów it.*]
>
> **(Adapted from Chafe, 1998: 98)**

The main speaker is the sister. The discourse is presented primarily from the point of view of her **displaced consciousness**, as she recalls specific details about their mother. The story is based on a memory of their shared past, some of the details of which are better known by the sister than by the brother. In fact, most of the details presented in this segment of the story were first made known to the sister through a third party, Verna. That is, the sister did not directly experience these events. Verna told her about them, and she is now telling her brother.

Elements of focus in the story are: "Móm" and "bráve" in line 1, for example, both of which are pronounced with prosodic prominence. In line 5, the words "Vérna" and "tóld" are in focus, since Verna represents the source of the information about their mother. The temporal adverbial "òne tìme-" is peripheral and serves to add to the background of the story.

As for the introduction of referents, "Mom" is introduced as an *accessible referent* in line 2, clearly known to both participants in this interaction. The speaker shifts to *given* "she" in line 6, as the re-telling of the anecdote first shared by Verna begins. The brother's contributions come in at lines 13 and 14, in response to details of a rather odd story, which point dually to the "bravery" their mother, and her utter creativity in making herself feel safe while alone in her house, and possibly frightened by unknown noises. *Who.* (line 13) and *Mom did?* (line 14) are uttered at the very end of this story segment that underscores the vividly eccentric behaviors of a woman with the ingenuity and inventiveness to find a way to frighten back a potential intruder. She'd created her own sort of wireless burglar alarm. The brother's contributions come at a point in the discourse where a signaling of "paying attention" is in order. His participation here demonstrates both his "understanding" and his "appreciation" (Chafe, 1998: 100).

This data excerpt belongs to the **genre of narrative**. How does this narrative representation differ from the other narrative samples that appear throughout this book? In other words, the development of the narrative is achieved using the graphic representation of intonation units, i.e., in a line-by-line format with fine-grained notations relating to prosodic contours. How does the content of the narrative, its structure and delivery, and how do the individual features of the story line itself differ from other instances of narrative that we examined in Chapter 3?

Do you note any of the other features of "narrative" that we introduced in Chapter 3? Did you observe any of the types of "cohesive ties" that we presented earlier in this chapter? Does a "cohesive tie" approach to a partial analysis of discourse appear to be compatible with an intonation unit approach? Why or why not? For each of these approaches to analysis, what types of discursive elements or features becomes salient? In other words, oral discourse can be represented in texts in multiple ways, e.g., in "paragraphs" designed and delineated on the basis of topic and content, in contiguous sentences with no paragraph breaks, in line-by-line representations where one full clause or one full sentence constitutes each line, or in the system presented here, using intonation units. Each system of graphically representing discourse foregrounds and makes salient particular elements of that discourse that other systems do not.

We have examined discourse from a number of different, but related, perspectives. We examined information structure and observed how the concepts of *givenness* and *newness* are framed in discourse. This given-new distinction focuses on assumptions that speakers and writers have concerning hearers' and readers' abilities to infer who or what is being talked about. Some of these assumptions could raise hackles if information that is clearly known to a listener or reader (i.e., given) is framed in the discourse as *new* (as in the "turning off your water" excerpt), or conversely, if the information is not well known to a reader and framed more as given (as in the tic-tac-toe excerpt).

In this chapter, we have examined a number of traditionally recognized resources for cohesion—from reference and repetition to lexical cohesion and logical or contextual or generic association, and considered how such cohesive devices combine to create meaning as well as to reflect stance.

We also briefly examined the role that prosody serves in reflecting elements of speakers' and writers'[9] consciousness, by viewing the framework of intonation units. According to (Chafe, 1994: 41), "[w]hen language is made overt, as in speaking and writing, it is able to provide a link between what would otherwise be independent nervous systems, acting as an imperfect substitute for the synapses that fail to bridge the gap between one mind and other. In short, language serves two basic functions. However it is used, it converts unique experience into something familiar and manageable, and overt language—speaking and writing—offers a way to narrow the chasm between independent minds." We will revisit this notion of *narrowing the chasm between independent minds* in the next chapter as we introduce Conversation Analysis.

REVIEW AND REFLECTION: INFORMATION STRUCTURE, COHESION, AND INTONATION UNITS

1. Information structure and cohesion

Some scholars of Pragmatics (See Chapter 7) note that given information is typically provided first, and then new information follows. This is referred to as the "given-before-new principle" (Gundel, 1988).

Have a look at the following excerpt from a children's website about dolphins.

Excerpt A: "Dolphins"

When <u>a calf</u> is born **it** is about 42 to 52 inches long and weighs about 44 pounds. **Its** dorsal fin and tail flukes are very flexible, but as **the calf** gets older both of these get stiffer . . .

 An <u>"auntie" dolphin</u> helps **the mother** with **the calf**.

(Think Quest, n.d.)

Which type of information seems to come first here?

Compare the previous segment of discourse to the following one, excerpted from a website on "The Enola Gay Controversy":

Excerpt B: "The Enola Gay Controversy"

The exhibit marking the 50th anniversary of the end of World War II featuring the refurbished B-29 Enola Gay proposed by the Smithsonian's National Air and Space Museum resulted in fierce controversy over how history should represent dropping an atom bomb on Japan. Experience the evolution of the Enola Gay controversy

---

> by reading through a chronological list of documents divided into five rounds. . .
>
> **(Gallagher, n.d.)**

What do you think constitutes *given information*? What constitutes *new information*?

What are the expectations of the writer concerning the readers' ability to identify what is being talked about? How do such expectations compare to those assumed by the writers of "Dolphins" in Excerpt A? How are the two excerpts similar? How are they different?

INFORMATION STRUCTURE, COHESION, GENRE—AS SOCIAL PRACTICE

2. As we noted in the chapter, *genre* may affect how information is organized in discourse, e.g., jokes often contain new information at the beginning:

> "A Frenchman walks into a bar. He has a parrot on his shoulder and the parrot is wearing a baseball cap. The bartender says, "Hey, that's neat—where did you get that?" And the parrot says, "France—they've got millions of them there."
>
> **(Keillor, 2009: 154)**

Where do you note *new information?* How is it packaged linguistically? Where do you note *given information?* Are there any linguistic elements that actually mark givenness? What are they? Which elements might be considered as signaling *accessible* information (e.g., "the bartender"). Why?

We also discussed *cohesion* and elements of cohesion. What types of cohesive ties do you note in the previous joke? What is the source of the humor here?

Much of the humor is based on:

- familiarity with the *genre* of the joke—"the bar narrative"
- exophoric reference item "that," signaling shared information between speaker and hearer (see also Chapter 4) as the source of the

misunderstanding and also the source of humor. There is more than a double entendre here: "That," as uttered by the bartender likely pointed to the parrot with the bartender addressing the man. It was responded to by the parrot, ambiguously referring to his baseball cap and to the man himself.

Try to identify the following:
* *new, accessible, given* information
* cohesive devices: reference, contrast, ellipsis, other devices

Regarding cohesion, as you read through this joke, bear in mind the **definition of cohesion** that we provided at the beginning of the section: as **the process through which topics, events, and ideas coalesce into logical, culturally-shaped aggregates of discourse**.

How are these aggregates of discourse culturally shaped in the following text? Do you sense the overall cohesion in the joke? If so, what creates it? If not, which parts of the text are unclear to you? Here is one more joke.

Chicken and Egg Joke:

It is morning. The rooster crows. The chicken and the egg are lying in bed. The chicken is smiling and lights up a cigarette, but the egg is upset. She mutters to herself, "Well, I guess we answered that question."

(Keillor, 2009: 68)

If you understood the joke, then you are familiar with a number of elements in the socio-cultural background of the story:

* The now cliché question concerning the dilemma of causality: "Which came first, the chicken or the egg?" See http://en.wikipedia.org/wiki/Chicken_or_the_egg for an overview of the philosophical dilemma and references to this question in popular culture.
* Are the referents *the chicken* and *the egg* instances of definite reference?

Do they pick out and identify a specific chicken and a specific egg? Is this given information? Accessible information? Explain.

162

- What is the relevance of the rooster with regard to morning?
- What is the relevance of *smile* and *cigarette*?
- What is the reference to "that question"?
- Are there any other instances of multiple-word meanings that contribute to the humor in this joke?

As we can see, grammar and language alone are not sufficient in order to understand discourse, especially humorous discourse, where references to socio-cultural elements require a good amount of background knowledge.

How does the progression of information, provided sentence by sentence, build up to create the humorous outcome of the story?

QUESTION: Based on the previous illustration, what implications can you draw connecting *information structure, reference, genre, and cohesion* to **literacy** in general?

That is, what sorts of background information or the so-called *given* and *accessible* types of information are necessary to understand written texts (in various disciplines like history or engineering or science), oral discourse (in everyday conversation, lectures, TV dramas, theatre), in genres such as jokes (like the previous one, and others)?

3. Intonation Units and Narrative

The following excerpt is adapted from the University of Santa Barbara Corpus. We refer to it as "the Lemon Story." Read through the transcript. You'll note that it appears in the format of intonation units. It is a narrative.

How does the narrative unfold? How does it take shape in this intonation unit format? That is, how does the information build up, unit by unit? What do those units reflect?

Do you find a predominance of units that reflect *immediate consciousness* or *displaced consciousness*? Identify elements of each and explain how these reflect the speaker's own consciousness. How does immediate consciousness add to the initiation of the narrative? How does the interplay between immediate and displaced consciousness affect the speaker's delivery of the narrative?

As you read through the transcript, see if you can identify some of the components of narrative that we pointed out in Chapter 3. What are those components?

163

Rewrite the story using a different format so that the narrative elements are more saliently represented. Does the shift in graphic representation create any shift in focus on the narrative elements? If so, how?

From the UCSB Corpus of Spoken English (Adapted)

MARILYN   . . . Oh look,
           a little lemon from the tree=
           ((skipped lines))
           we came back from a,
           . . . we had to go to . . the Ritz Carlton,
           out in Laguna,
           ((skipped lines))
           . . . And w- we're gone what.
           ((skipped lines))
           And uh,
           . . . we're pulling up.
           . . and I see this gir::l.
           Who I'd never seen before,
           Sort of d:art out of our driveway.
PETE: [uhhunh.]
MARILYN: [And]. . . stand there,
           And watch us pull in,
           And she goes like this.
           (TSK) . . Like,
           . .oh my God.
           I'm gonna-getting caught.
           And I said,
           Hi,
           Can I help you?
PETE: ((laughter))
MARILYN: you know.
           . . . And she goes,
           ((skipped lines))
           Oh,
           Um,
           I was just getting . . . some lemons.
PETE: ((laughter))

MARILYN:	And I said,
	Oh yeah?
	Who are you?
PETE:	((laughter))
MARILYN:	And she goes,
	Oh,
	. . I'm your next door neighbor.
PETE:	((laughter))
MARILYN:	No, she said,
	First she said,
	Kenneth said I could have some
	((skipped lines))
MARILYN:	Then he said,
	she said
	Oh! Kenneth said I could have some lemons.
PETE:	Right.
MARILYN:	I said,
	he did?
PETE:	((laughter))
MARILYN:	She goes,
	yeah.
	And I said
	Oh.
	And she goes,
	do y-
	you don't mind,
	do you?
	And I said,
	well yeah
	in fact I do mind.
	cause I thought the lemon tree was dying.
	I didn't see any lemons on it.
PETE:	unhun
MARILYN:	Cause she said,
	You wouldn't mind if I came back
	and got a whole bag full
	would you?
PETE:	Right.

> MARILYN: I said . . yeah
> PETE: ((laughter))
> MARILYN: There's like one lemon left on this tree that I can reach.

4. **Newspaper stories: Same topic. Different ways of presenting the story**

The following two newspaper stories are about Julia Pastrana, referred to in the media as the "ape woman" and "the ugliest woman in the world." As you will read, even her husband called her "bear woman." Julia suffered from a rare genetic disorder that caused extreme amounts of facial hair and a large, protruding jaw. One is from *The Guardian* (2013). The second, from *The New York Times* (Wilson, 2013). Julia died one hundred and fifty years ago. She was recently buried in February, 2013.

We've provided the opening lines of each story and the links to the entire pieces. Read through each excerpt and compare and contrast the two stories. Consider the following:

- Overall impressions created by the discourse—How is Julia referred to and descripted in each story? How are the details related to Julia's life represented and developed in each story?
- How are the readers positioned by the discourse in each? That is, think about information structure. Are details presented and/or packaged as *new*? as *given*? Does each story succeed in terms of creating "reader engagement" with the text? In what ways are the stories similar? In what ways are they different?
- Which story excerpt do you prefer? Why?

A. Mexican 'APE Woman' Buried 150 Years After Her Death

Julia Pastrana, who had genetic disorders that gave her a hairy face and protruding jaw, was exhibited at circuses around world (sub headline)

An indigenous Mexican woman once described as the "ugliest woman in the world" has been buried more than 150 years after her death . . .

Born in 1834, Julia Pastrana suffered from hypertrichosis and gingival hyperplasia . . .

(*The Guardian*, 2013)

B. An Artist Finds a Dignified Ending for an Ugly Story

By CHARLES WILSON
Published: February 11, 2013

Her own husband called her a "bear woman." An 1854 advertisement in *The New York Times* said she was the "link between mankind and the ourang-outang." She became known in the popular imagination during the mid-19th century as "the ugliest woman in the world." After she died from complications of childbirth, her body and the body of her baby appeared for decades in "freak" exhibitions throughout Europe.

On Tuesday, more than a century and a half after her death, in 1860, the woman, Julia Pastrana, will finally be given a proper burial near her birthplace in Sinaloa, Mexico.

(Wilson, 2013)

Can you draw any conclusions concerning general writing style, journalistic writing, and information structure? Expand these ideas by locating other parallel stories from different types of news outlets and analyzing them from the points of view of information structure and cohesion.

Now, look up five extended obituaries in your local newspaper(s). Compare the obituaries to the two excerpts, from the points of view of information structure, cohesion, and genre.

- How are these instances of discourse similar? (Compare and contrast the five obituaries to each other and also to the two excerpts).
- How are they different?
- What types of information are assumed to be "shared?" What types of information are assumed to be "new?"
- What roles do *genre* and *register* play in these instances of discourse?

PRACTICE WITH DISCOURSE ANALYSIS IN EXPOSITORY DISCOURSE: INFORMATION STRUCTURE AND COHESION IN ENGLISH, JAPANESE, AND KOREAN

Analyze the following samples of expository discourse in English, Japanese, and Korean. Pay attention to such issues as: information structure (new, accessible, and given), how "information" is presented in each, and cohesion (reference, ellipsis and substitution, conjunction, and lexical cohesion). Try to follow the "system" for each language. That is, what constitutes a "cohesive" paragraph in English? What constitutes a "cohesive" paragraph in Japanese? What constitutes a "cohesive" paragraph in Korean? How is *cohesion* achieved in each language? Are the systems parallel? Where and how do they differ?

After you've had a chance to closely analyze information structure, cohesion, and paragraph development in Japanese, Korean, and English, what sorts of implications can you draw with respect to academic writing in English? How might a writer's native language affect his/her expository writing in other languages, especially with respect to presentation of information as new, accessible, or given? How might cohesion differ—from the points of view of sentence structure, word choice, paragraph development, and the varying impressions of *logical continuity* expressed in each language? How might the concepts of *logical continuity* and *cohesion* be compared and contrasted in a discourse analytic study based on specific genre types?

Japanese

このプロジェクトは、日本語話者による会話形式、またはインタビュー形式のインタラクションをなるべく自然な形で録画し、そのビデオデータをもとに作ったデジタルビデオクリップを中上級の日本語教育での教材として提供することを目的としています。ビデオクリップは単に学習者の聴解能力を延ばすということにだけではなく、今まであまり語学教室内で体系的に紹介されることのなかった自然な話し言葉に触れる機会を増やし、それを細かく分析しながら見ていくことを通じて、社会言語的、語用論的、会話ストラテジー的な要素、また、非言語のコミュニケーションについて学習者の意

識を高めることにも活用していけるものと思われます。また、日本
語の授業でよく話題になるトピックに関しての生の日本語話者の声
を提示するこのビデオクリップ教材は、学習者の日本語力向上への
モチベーションを高めるのに役立てることもできるものと思われま
す

(Center for Advanced Language Proficiency Education and Research
[CALPER] at the Pennsylvania State University, "Learning through
listening towards advanced Japanese," n.d.)

English data sample

This project aims at providing digital video clips of speech samples, which can be incorporated into intermediate or advanced level
Japanese language courses. These video clips have been developed from
unscripted, spontaneous interview and conversations with various Japanese speakers. They can be used not only for improving learners' listening comprehension skills, but also for encouraging learners to explore
features of spontaneous speech, which have not been introduced systematically in the classroom. By doing so, we believe, we can increase
learners' awareness towards sociolinguistic, pragmatic, and strategic
factors as well as the significance of nonverbal means of communication. We also believe that these clips, which present Japanese speakers'
voices on topics frequently discussed in Japanese language classroom,
can provide strong motivation for the learners to increase their proficiency in Japanese.

(CALPER, "Learning through listening towards advanced Japanese,"
n.d.)

Korean data sample

한류 (韓流) 'The Korean Wave'

한류는 한국의 대중문화가 아시아를 중심으로 대중적인 인기을 얻
고 해외 사람들이 한국의 문화를 좋아하는 현상을 의미한다. 한류는 사
실상 여러 의미로 정의되고 있는데, 예를 들면 '한국 문화에 대한 열풍',
'한국대중 문화 바람', '한국 대중 문화 열기' 또는 '한국 대중 문화 붐'등
다양한 의미로 해석되고 있다.
'한류'라는 용어는 1999년 중국내에서의 한국 대중 문화의 열풍을 표현
하기 위해서 중국의 한 언론에서 사용한 이후 지금까지 널리 알려져 왔

다. 1996년 한국의 텔레비젼 드라마가 중국에 수출되는 것을 시작으로 1990년대 말에는 한국의 대중가요 또한 중국, 대만, 일본 등지에서 그 인기를 이어오고 있다. 당시 중국사회에서는 한국 드라마의 자유로운 생활배경과 표현 방식이 시청자들의 열렬한 호응을 얻었고 한국 댄스음악 또한 청소년들 사이에서 큰 인기를 얻어 한류를 생성하고 그 열풍이 지속되고 있다. 2000년도 부터 한국 드라마와 대중가요 뿐만 아니라 영화와 온라인 게임도 중국, 일본, 대만, 동남 아시아에서 큰 인기를 얻었고 특히 한국 드라마 열풍은 다양한 한국 문화를 알리는 데 긍정적인 영향을 미쳤다. 한류는 아시아에 그치지 않고 중앙아시아, 아프리카, 미국 등지로 확산 되어 2000년 대 중반 이후 현재까지 K-pop을 중심으로 유럽과 남아메리카에까지 그 영향이 미치고 있다. 이제는 한류의 영향으로 한국의 드라마나 대중가요에 뿐만 아니라 한국음식, 한국의류, 게임, 한글 등 한스타일과 같은 한국문화가 세계로 확대되고 있다.

(출처: 2011 국정정책 감사 자료집_한류
의 동향과 발전 방향_총괄 http://ko.wikipedia.org/
wiki/%ED%95%9C%EB%A5%98_(%EB%AC%B8%ED%99%94)

http://www.benhur.kr/board/cl_viewbody.php?code=bbs_
work&number=95&viewmode=clipcopy고정민 외 (2009), 한류, 아시아를 넘어 세계로, 한류문화산업교류재단

The Korean Wave refers to the phenomenon through which Korean popular culture has gained popularity, especially with regard to other Asian nations. Actually, The Korean Wave has taken on several meanings, such as 'the craze for popular Korean culture', 'the wind of popular Korean culture', 'the excitement of popular Korean culture', and 'the popular Korean cultural boom.'

The term, 'Korean Wave' was coined in China in 1999 by Chinese journalists to represent the early craze for popular Korean culture and its widespread following. This wave began with the first airing of Korean TV dramas in China in 1996. Korean pop music also spread to China, Taiwan and Japan in the late 1990s. Against a backdrop of a freer lifestyle and means of expression, the Korean drama received a fervent response by Chinese TV viewers. The word (and cultural impact) of 한류 (韓流) was created in China and continued to spread. Over time, it was not only the Korean drama and K-pop that propagated Korean culture, Korean movies and online games also gained popularity throughout China, Japan, Taiwan, and Southeast Asia. In particular, the Korean drama boom has had a positive effect on spreading Korean culture. The Korean Wave did not stop in East Asia. It also spread throughout Central Asia, the Middle East, Africa and America. Notably, the influence of K-pop has been felt in Europe and even South America since the mid-2000s. Now, the Korean Wave also reflects the spread of other aspects of Korean culture, including food, clothing, video games, and the Korean language.

(CALPER, "Discourse, genre, and the National Standards: The Korean Wave," n.d.)

SUGGESTIONS FOR FURTHER READING

Couper-Kuhlen, E. (2008). Intonation and Discourse: current views from within. In Schiffrin, D., Tannen, D., and Hamilton, H. *The Handbook of Discourse Analysis*. Blackwell, Malden, MA. pp. 34–54.

Du Bois, J. W. (1991). Transcription design principles for spoken discourse research. *Pragmatics* 1,1: 71–106.

Hickman, M. and Hendricks, H. (1999). Cohesion and anaphora in children's narratives: A comparison of English, French, German, and Mandarin Chinese. *Journal of Child Language*, 26,2: 419–52.

Iwasaki, S. and Horie, P. I. (1998). The 'Northridge Earthquake' Conversations: conversational patterns in Japanese and Thai and their cultural significance. *Discourse & Society* 9,4: 501–29.

Kendon, A. (1995). Gestures as illocutionary and discourse structure markers in Southern Italian conversation. *Journal of Pragmatics*, 23,3: 247–79.

Matsumoto, K. (2000). Japanese intonation units and syntactic structure. *Studies in Language,* 24,3: 515–64.

Minami, M. and McCabe, A. (1991). Haiku as a discourse regulation device: A stanza analysis of Japanese children's personal narratives. *Language in Society,* 20,4: 577–99.

Nevile, M. (2006). Making sequentiality salient: And-prefacing in the talk of airline pilots. *Discourse Studies*, 8,2: 279–302.

Pernis, P. (2007). Achieving spatial coherence in German sign language narratives: The use of classifiers and perspective. *Lingua*, 117,7: 1315–38.

171

Pickering, L. (2004). The structure and function of intonational paragraphs in native and nonnative speaker instructional discourse. *English for Specific Purposes*, 23,1: 19–43.

Ryshina-Pankova, M. (2006). Creating textual worlds in advanced learner writing: the role of complex theme. In H. Byrnes. (Ed.) *Advanced Language Learning: The contribution of Halliday and Vygotsky.* Continuum. New York, pp. 164–83.

Schleppegrell, M. J., Achugar, M., and Oteiza, T. (2004). The grammar of history: Enhancing content-based instruction through a functional focus on language. *TESOL Quarterly*, 38, 67–93.

Tomioka, S. (2009). *Why* questions, presuppositions, and interventions. *Journal of East Asian Linguistics,* 18: 253–71.

Vergaro, C. (2005). "Dear Sirs, I hope you find this information useful": Discourse strategies in Italian and English "For Your Information" (FYI) letters. *Discourse Studies*, 7,1: 109–35.

Wennerstrom, A. (1998). Intonation as cohesion in academic discourse: A study of Chinese speakers of English. *Studies in Second Language Acquisition,* 20,1: 1–25.

LINKS

Walnut Valley Water District. (n.d.). *How to turn off your water.* Retrieved from: http://www.wvwd.com/index.php?option=com_content&view=article&id=33&Itemid=28. Accessed February 20, 2013.

Plesser, R. and Heffernan, J. (n.d.). The spinning earth: Your world is tilted. In *Learn NC*. Retrieved from: http://www.learnnc.org/lp/editions/earth-sun/6572. Accessed February 3, 2013.

Tic-tac-toe. (n.d.). In *Wikipedia*. Retrieved from: http://en.wikipedia.org/wiki/Tic-tac-toe. Accessed February 23, 2013.

Think Quest. (n.d.). *Dolphins.* Retrieved from: http://library.thinkquest.org/3935/DOLPHINS.HTM. Accessed February 18, 2013.

Gallagher, E. J. (n.d.). The Enola Gay controversy. *Lehigh University Digital Library.* Retrieved from: http://digital.lib.lehigh.edu/trial/enola/about/. Accessed May 20, 2013.

The Guardian. (2013, February 13). Mexican 'ape woman' buried 150 years after her death. Retrieved from: http://www.guardian.co.uk/

world/2013/feb/13/mexican-ape-woman-buried. Accessed February 14, 2013.

Wilson, C. (2013, February 13). An artist finds a dignified ending for an ugly story. *The New York Times,* p. C1. Retrieved from: http://www.nytimes.com/2013/02/12/arts/design/julia-pastrana-who-died-in-1860-to-be-buried-in-mexico.html?pagewanted=all&_r=0. Accessed February 14, 2013.

Center for Advanced Language Proficiency and Research (CALPER) at the Pennsylvania State University. (n.d.). Learning through listening towards advanced Japanese. In *CALPER.* Retrieved from: http://calper.la.psu.edu/japanese.php. Accessed February 12, 2013.

Center for Advanced Language Proficiency and Research (CALPER) at the Pennsylvania State University. (n.d.). Discourse, genre, and the National Standards: The Korean Wave. In *CALPER.* Retrieved from: http://calper.la.psu.edu. Accessed February 12, 2013.

NOTES

1. Early work on the given-new distinctions in grammar included such dichotomous categories as old-new, shared-unshared, known-new, and so forth. For a variety of treatments of information structure in linguistics, cognitive linguistics, and pragmatics, see Birner, 1994, 2009; Birner and Ward, 1998, 2006, 2009; Bolinger, 1961, 1972, 1989; Chafe, 1970, 1974, 1994; Clark and Haviland, 1977; Dirven and Radden, 2007; Gundel, 1985; Halliday, 1967; Halliday and Hasan, 1976; Haviland and Clark, 1974; Kamio, 1997; Kuno, 1972, 1978; Prince, 1981, 1992; Ward and Birner, 1994, 2011.

2. In Systemic Functional Linguistics (Halliday and Matthiessen, 2004) information structure is discussed based on a distinction between Theme and Rheme, following the Prague school of linguists. In English, Theme (topic) is generally mentioned at the beginning and serves as the departure point of the message; it "functions to organize and carry forward the discourse" (Halliday and Matthiessen, 2004: 64). What accompanies the Theme—what comments on it and *develops* it—is the Rheme. Therefore, for example, in the sentence: "*The atmosphere outside* is beautiful . . ." (Halliday and Matthiessen, 2004: 65), the italicized section constitutes the Theme, followed by the Rheme, which is underlined. See work on topic-comment constructions and on languages that are topic-prominent, e.g., Chinese, Korean, Japanese.

3. Proper nouns preceded by an indefinite article are not definite, as in *There's a John Smith in my math class, too,* or *I'd marry any Jason any day.*

4. Halliday and Hasan (1976) and Martin (2008b) identify five discrete categories. Halliday (1994) maintains the same five categories, but addresses "substitution" as subsumed under the category of ellipsis.

5. Examples of anaphoric reference include definite determiners like *the, that*; pronouns like *he, hers, my, its;* adjectives that are inherently comparative or superlative, like *more, better, -er, -est;* adverbs that are inherently comparative like *equally, otherwise*; and appositives, like *Arthur,* <u>my next-door-neighbor</u> or *Jim Thorpe,* <u>the American athlete who lost his Olympic medals because of rule violations.</u>

6. Exophoric reference is related to *deixis* and *indexicality* in that without context, we are unable to identify the referents. See Chapters 4 and 8 for further elaboration of these topics.

7. See Halliday (1994) for discussion of metonymy, meronymy, and hyponymy.

8. Our ultimate goal as discourse analysts is not simply to be able to identify and label individual cohesive devices. Instead, by recognizing the cohesive devices that are used within given texts in conjunction with other discursive elements, our goal is to uncover patterns of discourse that not only hold texts together, but, more importantly, reflect the stances, ideas, and opinions of the speakers and writers, both at the surface of the discourse (explicitly) and beyond (implicitly).

9. Chafe (1988, 1992, 1994) indicates that written language has "covert prosody." The concept of intonation units can also be applied to written discourse: "writers and readers experience an auditory imagery of intonation, accents and hesitations" (Chafe 1988: 395) . . . The prosody of writing is captured by punctuation and other graphic signals. Chafe (1988: 395) terms "the punctuation unit" the "stretches of language between punctuation marks," and compares prosodic variations within such units to those within spoken intonation units.

CHAPTER SIX

Conversation

> . . . [W]hat is needed is not the cognitive science now available, but work which starts with empirically grounded observations about interaction, with practices of talk and other conduct in interaction which appear to underlie these observations, and with the organizations of practice which make for the recognizable features of interaction that constitute the distinctive sociality of humans. In other words, what is needed is not an analysis of interaction trimmed to meet the available cognitive science, but an account of how humans grasp the world and interact with it that takes account of the resources of interaction, on the one hand, and contributes to understanding its workings and capacities, on the other—a cognitive science whose ambition is to address observable, actual, ordinary human activity in a fashion at once answerable to the details of actual instances of talk and other conduct, on the one hand, and formulated to such general and formal terms as to embrace diverse exemplars of a phenomenon, on the other. (Schegloff, 2006: 142–43)

In Chapter 5, we observed units of meaning in discourse that point to aspects of the speaker-hearer or reader-writer relationship. In particular, we discussed how speakers and writers make discursive choices influenced by their own stances vis à vis the topic at hand and by their assumptions concerning the hearers' or readers' degree of familiarity with the topics and referents. We observed how memory and imagination are at work in the discursive constructions of events, with a narrow focus on information structure, expressing such concepts as newness, assumed familiarity, and givenness as they relate to reference and topic development. We examined traditional categories of cohesive resources, from reference to repetition, and from conjunction to logical or generic association, that shape topics, ideas, and genres into coherent texts. And we have observed the mechanism of the intonation unit as a reflection of consciousness, where sequenced bits of spoken discourse, each with a prosodically recognizable onset and a prosodically recognizable termination, provides a glimpse into the speaker's consciousness—foveal or peripheral.

In this chapter, the analytical focus shifts from assumed or projected sharedness and non-sharedness of concepts, entities, and information, situated within the minds of speakers and hearers or writers and readers, and from discursive coalescence constructed in texts through categories of cohesive ties, to the interaction-central, mutually achieved understanding between and among participants in naturally occurring conversational interaction.

Moving now to the methodology of Conversation Analysis (CA), we will examine how participants in talk-in-interaction collaboratively and intersubjectively monitor and respond to emerging speech on a microsecond-by-microsecond basis. We will observe the ways in which turns at talk are produced and organized; how turns may be held by speakers, expanded, cut short; how speakers change; how and when interlocutor responses emerge; and how participants make sense of the *actions* that constitute spoken turns. We will again visit the combined phenomena of grammar and prosody—this time, as they relate to the production and understanding of turns at talk. We will discuss these within the framework of Conversation Analysis.

CONVERSATION ANALYSIS

Conversation Analysis (CA) refers to the empirical study of naturally occurring situated interaction—from ordinary, everyday conversation among acquaintances and friends to institutional talk (e.g., medical encounters, business negotiations, government meetings, classroom discourse, service encounters, courtroom practices, 911 calls) (Antaki, 2011; Atkinson and Heritage, 1984; Cazden, 2001; Drew and Heritage, 1992; Gill et al., 2010; Goodwin, 1981, 2003; Goodwin and Heritage, 1990; Heritage, 2009; Heritage and Robinson, 2011; Mehan, 1979, 1985; Sacks, Schegloff, and Jefferson, 1974; Schegloff, 2007; Sidnell, 2010a; Sidnell and Stivers, 2013; among many others).[1]

The framework of CA is based upon talk and turn-taking as social action. That is, turns-at-talk, in addition to comprising the basic and essential units of conversation, are actually *doing* something: displaying agreement, allowing a primary speaker to continue by yielding a potential turn, expressing surprise or disbelief or exhilaration, aligning with one conversational partici- pant while creating distance from another, complimenting, requesting, deny- ing, disagreeing, downplaying, upgrading, etc. (Antaki, 2011, 2012; Clayman, 2010; Couper-Kuhlen and Thompson, 2008; Enfield et al., 2010; Ford, Fox, and Thompson, 2002; Fox and Thompson, 2007; Goodwin, 1995a, 1995b; Heath and Luff, 2013; Heritage, 1985, 2009; Heritage and Lindstrom, 2012; Levinson, 2013; Pomerantz, 1984; Pomerantz and Heritage, 2013; Sacks, Schegloff, and Jefferson, 1974; Schegloff, 1984, 2007; Sidnell, 2010a, 2010b; Stivers, 2012).

Such understanding of turn-taking and talk as social action emerges from the discipline-specific view of the analysis of interaction as both "con- text free and capable of extraordinary context-sensitivity" (Sacks, Schegloff, and Jefferson, 1974: 699). In this way, the analytical focus remains centered purely on the talk as it unfolds there and then in the interactions being studied. The focus is on how it is the participants in interaction parse and track, and monitor and project, emerging talk (not yet complete), and how they orient to the relevant facets of the interaction, i.e., the language, the body, eye gaze, and so forth (Schegloff, 2007). Central to the approach is talk-in-interaction that is both "situated" and "locally managed."

Conversation Analysis as a methodology and approach to the under- standing of human interaction has uncovered an extraordinary systematicity that underlies our interactional practices in conversation and in institutional talk—a systematicity to which participants in social interaction are keenly ori- ented, yet likely not explicitly aware of. The work of the conversation analyst is to discover how it is that the participants are hearing and reacting to turns at talk—what kinds of actions do they interpret them to be—discernible on the basis of the turn (a current turn, a prior turn, a next turn)—its shape, place- ment, timing, and organization vis à vis other relevant turns in the interaction.

Conversation analysts employ a set of conventions to regularize the transcription of recorded spoken discourse—conventions that capture, with utmost precision, the prosodic features of how each utterance is delivered. These conventions include orthographic modifications to capture sounds of reduced speech (e.g., *going to → gonna*; *would you → wouldja*; *have to → hafta*), variants in single word pronunciations (e.g., *the → thuh* or *thee, twenty → twenny, nuclear → nucular, actually → akshully*), and timing of pauses (in seconds and tenths of seconds) between turns and within turns. They also include a complex set of diacritics indicating such features as increased or decreased volume, relatively quicker-paced delivery of an utterance or part of an utterance (rush through), extended durations of vowel or consonant sounds (sound stretches), two speakers producing talk at the same time (overlapping speech), immediately contiguous utterances with no discernible pause in between (latching), in-breaths, outbreaths, laughter, and intonation contours (rising, slight rising, falling or terminal) as produced at turn beginnings, within turns, and at the ends of turns. We provide a list of the basic CA conventions at the end of this chapter (see Atkinson and Heritage, 1984; Jefferson, 2004; Ochs, Schegloff, and Thompson, 1996; Schegloff, 2007).

Turn Taking

The seminal article by Sacks, Schegloff, and Jefferson (1974) articulates with detailed precision the remarkable systematicity underlying the orderliness of talk-in-interaction. In this chapter, we outline the basic tenets of CA (Sacks, Schegloff, and Jefferson 1974; Schegloff, 2007) touching on how participants in conversation are oriented to the turn and its construction, organization, and sequencing; how turns are held; and how speakers change. We will examine issues of timing of next turns and the relevance of how overlapping talk, on the one hand, and gaps and pauses, on the other, both reflect and influence participants' affective involvement in conversation. A simple and basic point within the CA framework appears to be both commonsensical and obvious: "Overwhelmingly, one party talks at a time" (Sacks, Schegloff, and Jefferson, 1974: 699). However, what provides the most crucial insights into conversation and its related speech exchange phenomena are precisely those instances whereby *more than one* party talks at a time.

The following excerpt, from an original broadcast of a *Star Trek* episode, illustrates what a *one party talks at a time* transcript might look like. There is no overlapping talk whatsoever. Clearly, this is a script. It was written as a script. It looks like a script and it sounds like a script.

Star Trek Excerpt—Season 3, Episode 15, "Let That Be Your Last Battlefield"

((The scene opens as Kirk is pouring alcohol from a decanter into Commissioner Bele's liqueur glass.

Three men are seated around the table: Spock, Kirk, Commissioner Bele))

Commissioner Bele:	<u>Putt</u>ing the matter into the <u>hands</u> of your Starfleet Command is of course the <u>proper</u> procedure. = <u>How</u> long will it be before we <u>hear</u> from them, Captain.
Kirk:	<u>I</u> expect the answer is <u>a::l</u>ready on its way:::.
Commissioner Bele:	Well then <u>let</u> us <u>drink</u> to their <u>wi:se</u> solution to our <u>prob</u>lem. ((raising glass))
Kirk:	((nod)) Let's do.
	((glasses clink—Bele and Kirk))
Spock:	Com<u>miss</u>ioner, Starfleet <u>Comma::nd</u> may not arri::<u>ve</u> at the solution you an<u>tic</u>ipate. There <u>is</u> the matter of the <u>shuttle</u>craft. (0.2) which <u>Lo</u>kai ap<u>prop</u>riated, (0.2) Thee interro<u>ga</u>tion of that <u>matter</u> •h <u>may</u> be of <u>para</u>mount im<u>port</u>ance to Starfleet.
	(0.8)
Commissioner Bele:	•hhshm <u>Ge:</u>ntlemen. We are dis<u>cuss</u>ing a <u>que</u>stion of <u>degree:::</u>. (0.8) Surely, stealing a:: <u>shuttle</u>craft(h) uh cannot be >equa:<u>ted</u> with thee im<u>port</u>ance of (.) <u>murder</u>ing thousands of people<.(.)
Spock:	<u>We::</u> (0.2) do not <u>know^::</u> (0.2) that <u>Lo:kai</u> has <u>done</u> that.
	(1.2)
Commissioner Bele:	<u>One</u> thing we <u>are</u> agreed on is that <u>Lokai</u> i::<u>s</u> a criminal.
Kirk:	No:::: Com<u>miss</u>ioner. >The <u>o::</u>nly thing we a<u>greed</u> upon< is that Lokai [(.) <u>took</u> a <u>shuttle</u> craft.
	[((high pitched radio signal))]
Kirk:	Ex<u>cu::se</u> me. ((Kirk walks to intercom on wall))

(Coon et al., 1969)

Each turn has its own prosodic contours—complete with sound stretches, in-breaths, and rush-throughs (i.e., turns produced in a faster rate of speed than the surrounding talk, with the rushed talk appearing between two specific symbols: > *rushed talk* <.) But these vocal features, in and of themselves, are doing little if any interactional work. It is, after all, a script, and one that nicely illustrates one speaking party at a time, in what is artistically designed to be "situated interaction," involving "ordinary conversation," and taking what appear to be "conversational turns." But, it is not conversation—in fact, it is very far from it. The discussion that follows will provide more insight into the discipline of CA (Lerner, 2004c), its basic tenets, methodological practices, and analytical goals.

THE TURN: PARTICIPANTS' ORIENTATIONS TO TURNS, TURN CONSTRUCTION, TURN LENGTH AND SIZE, AND TURN CHANGE (FROM ONE SPEAKER TO ANOTHER)

The basic unit of analysis in conversation is the TCU: Turn Constructional Unit.

TCUs can be:

Lexical (one word) *Fabulous!*
Phrasal: *in the other room*
Clausal: *because someone was watching*
Sentential: *Gina's bringin' pizza an' beer.*

Turns can be composed of any one TCU type (i.e., a single unit turn) or any combination thereof (i.e., a multi-unit turn). Although "grammar" is a relevant issue in CA, as we have mentioned, and as we will see again, the traditional notion of the "sentence" is not. This is precisely because turns are often composed of **multiple TCUs**, some of which are indeed sentences and some of which are single words or phrases or clauses, and those that are "stand alone sentences" are more than a coherent syntactic string of words: Through turns, speakers *do* things in interaction.

The analytic advantage that the TCU carries as a primary unit of conversational interaction over the sentence is illustrated in the following excerpt, from Schegloff (1996: 62). The sentence, as a purely grammatical construct, carries little to no interactional force from a turn-taking perspective—in sharp contrast with the interactional strength of the TCU.

The excerpt is from a conversation involving three college students, Mark, Sherri, and Ruthie. Sherri, Ruthie, and Karen are roommates in a college dorm. Mark has come over to borrow notes from Ruthie for an upcoming exam in his Economics class.

> **College Dorm Conversation Excerpt—(SN-4: 02:23–33)**
>
> Sherri: [Look <u>o</u>nce a quarter et school is <u>enough</u>. = That's uh:: (.)
>   <u>f</u>inals.
> (??):   (<u>h</u>uh-)
> → Mark: I know whutcha mean. Me t[oo. <that's why I came here
>   d'<u>nig</u>ht. =
> (??)″   [°(Wha-)°]
> → Mark: = •hh I came tih talk tuh Ruthie about borrowing her: -
>   <u>n</u>otes.fer (.) <u>e</u>con.
>   (0.8)
> Ruthie: [Oh.
> Sherri: [You didn't come t' talk t' Kerin?
>   (0.4)
> Mark: No, Kerin: (.) Kerin 'n I 'r having a fight.
>
> **(Schegloff, 1996: 62)**

The lines in question involve Mark's turn, which actually contains four TCUs. Three are "sentences." One is a phrase.

I know whutcha mean	[sentence]
Me too.	[phrase]
That's why I came here d'night.	[sentence]
I came tih talk tuh Ruthie about borrowing her notes fer econ.	[sentence]

The first two are directly responsive to Sherri's prior turn—about final exams (that take place once a quarter[2]). Mark aligns with Sherri's opinion, and then produces his third TCU that projects the fourth, i.e., the one in which he provides his purported reason for visiting the girls' room in the first place. He does so using the demonstrative pronoun "that," a term referred to by Goodwin (1996) as a "prospective indexical," signaling that the reason is yet to be stated—it is coming up in the fourth TCU.[3] An analysis based solely on grammatical structures of sentences and phrases would not reveal the same interactional import. Participants in conversation are intuitively aware of how turns are constructed and delivered. Intuitively, we choose ways of interacting, of announcing, of aligning, ways of holding our turns, and ways of signaling their possible and actual completion. We track the words of others, monitor their stances and positions, and sense when a turn is complete or nearly complete. Clearly, Mark had more to say after his third turn, and his third turn is designed to indicate just that: there is more to come, and this turn is not yet over. Both Ruthie and Sherri understood that signal. They did not take a turn until Mark's was done, and interestingly, they both began speaking exactly at the same time, with their turns overlapping each other following a 0.8 second silence.

Let's examine in more detail how turn-taking is achieved in ordinary conversation, from the points of view of the size of turns, the organization of turns, and the allocations of turns, i.e., the mechanisms by which turns are produced and held by speakers, yielded by other potential speakers, and initiated by new speakers (adapted from Sacks, Schegloff, and Jefferson, 1974; Schegloff, 2007). For detailed discussion of turns and speaker selection, see Clayman, 2013b; Drew, 1984, 1998; 2013; Ford, Fox, and Thompson, 1996, 2002; Fox, 2001; Lerner, 2003, 2004a, 2004b; Sacks, 1987; Schegloff, 1980, 1988a.

- **Turn size and organization:** Turns can be long or short; their *size* or *length* or *distribution in terms of who speaks when* is not designated in advance. Rather, turn length, size, and distribution occur on a microsecond-by-microsecond basis, as ordinary talk unfolds and develops.
- **Turn allocation:** Turn change can come about by: 1) a speaker <u>overtly designating a next speaker</u> (e.g., *naming* the next speaker, *gesturing* to the next speaker that it is his or her turn to speak, *asking a question* and thereby designating a possible next speaker, for him or her to produce an answer), 2) <u>implying the relevance of a next speaker's turn</u>, 3) a <u>current speaker continues</u> speaking, 4) <u>a next speaker initiating a turn</u> at a point in the talk <u>where speaker transition or change would be relevant</u>, 5) <u>a next speaker initiating a turn where transition is not relevant,</u> in co-alignment with a current speaker, e.g., in displaying agreement, and 6) <u>a next speaker initiating a turn where transition is not relevant,</u> in competition with a current speaker, e.g., in displaying disagreement or interrupting, such that one speaker ultimately cedes the turn.

When one speaker continues the turn-at-talk, as in 3), mechanisms by which turn change occurs are all grounded in the concept of the TCU. That is, a current speaker's turn is constructed of TCUs—single words (lexical TCUs), phrases, clauses, and full sentences (doing more than just being words in a syntactically complete unit). When a TCU sounds complete, both grammatically and prosodically, a current speaker and an engaged listener recognize the potential space for speaker change. A new speaker might begin, the current speaker might continue, or there might be a silence—a gap—indicating that no speaker has opted for a turn at that particular moment in the talk.

Transition Relevance—The Potential for Turn Change Through Possible Completion of a TCU: Grammar and Prosody[4]

The concept of "grammatical completion" is dependent upon the interactants' sense of canonical structure of the language being spoken. A turn composed of an increment like:

What happened to that guy in

is obviously not grammatically complete. In no way does it sound complete. Turn transition, according to the mechanism surrounding the "transition relevance place," would not be canonically projected or expected. By adding minimally one more word, essentially any designation of "abstract or physical place" to complete the conceptual schema initiated by the preposition "in," (*Spain, physics, politics, line at the ticket counter*), the problem of grammatical structure is resolved. Possible speaker transition might now be projected, depending upon the prosody with which the utterance is delivered. A participant in conversation may deem that the TCU has been brought to completion, both grammatically and prosodically.

What happened to that guy in Yokohama.

Prosodic completion refers to the intonation contours of the TCUs, typically following three basic patterns: falling intonation, sharp rising intonation, and slight rising intonation. Both falling intonation and sharp rising intonation could (but do not necessarily) indicate completion of a TCU.

Falling intonation at the end of a grammatically complete TCU signals possible completion of that TCU. In CA transcription conventions, falling intonation is signaled by the diacritic mark resembling the period, regardless of the sentence type with which it occurs.

The Dow Jones industrial average rose 46.5 points yesterday.
Which brand of dish soap do you think I should use.

Sharp rising intonation is noted by a question mark following the TCU, again, regardless of the syntactic form of the utterance. This intonation contour typically occurs with certain types of questions[5] or expressions of disbelief or surprise.

Wouldja like more <u>coffee</u>?   *Wouldja like <u>more?</u> coffee?*
<u>She</u>? drives a <u>Mini</u> Cooper?   *She drives a <u>Mini</u> <u>Cooper</u>?*

Slight rising intonation, often referred to as "listing intonation," (Halliday, 1970; Schiffrin, 1994) typically signals that a speaker is intending to continue an utterance, or part of an utterance. With lists, interactants can hear that a speaker is in the midst of enumerating something, through the slight rise. This intonation is marked with a comma.

Your <u>coun</u>tertop choices would be <u>la</u>minate, <u>Cor</u>ian, <u>sile</u>stone, or granite.

Slight rising intonation **not** in the middle of a list (and still designated by a comma) indicates that the speaker may not be finished with a turn and/or that a speaker is eliciting some participation, however minimal, by an interlocutor (Auer, 2005; Clayman, 2013b; Ford, 2004; Ford and Thompson, 1996; Fox, 2001; Mondada, 2006).

Let's now have a brief look at the mechanism of the TCU in relation to the relevance of turn transitions. Next you'll find two turns excerpted from the larger data sample that you'll be working with on the next page. There are only two speakers involved here, Danny and Bob.

Earthquake Stories

Danny: and uh (.) go <u>ahead</u>. = uh (1.0) where were <u>you</u> on the- (0.2) >at four thirty in the morning<,

Bob: O(h)(h) I was uh- (1.8) <u>awake</u> actually. = he(h)((wheezing sounding laughter)) buhfore the earthquake <u>started</u>.

(Strauss, 1994)

Both Danny's turn and Bob's turn contain two TCUs each. In each case, the first TCU is sentential in type. Each is grammatically complete. Moreover, each also might be construed as *sounding* complete on the basis of prosody.

That is, there is a period at the end of each TCU, signaling not the end of a grammatical sentence, but *falling intonation.*

> Danny: *and uh (.) go <u>ahead</u>.*
> Bob: *O(h)(h) I was uh- (1.8) <u>awake</u> actually.*

In the case of the first TCUs uttered by each speaker, it might appear that transition to a next speaker would be relevant, but it is not. We'll have a closer look.

In the previous excerpt box, locate the transition between the two TCUs in Danny's turn and between the two TCUs in Bob's turn. In both cases, the potential transition relevance places are marked with an " = " sign, an indicator that the very next TCU is produced with no discernible pause whatsoever—in fact, the next TCU is directly contiguous, from a prosodic point of view, to the first. This mechanism is referred to as "latching." Participants in conversation, as current speakers or as current hearers, are keenly aware, at a subtly intuitive level, that turn transition may indeed be relevant upon completion of one TCU. One way of signaling to an interlocutor "this turn is not done yet," is by latching a first complete TCU with the very next TCU, with no pause, no hesitation in between. We also saw this mechanism in Mark's turn in the first example in this chapter, repeated here in a slightly different format, and showing how the third and fourth TCUs are latched together. Additionally, Mark draws an audible in-breath, marked here and in the conventions as •hh. An audible in-breath serves dually as a move by a current speaker to hold a turn and as an indicator to interlocutors that the current speaker is intending to continue:

> Mark: that's why I came here d'<u>night</u>. =   [third TCU]
> = •hh I came tih talk tuh Ruthie about borrowing   [fourth TCU]
> her:—<u>notes</u>.fer (.) <u>econ</u>.

Let's now look at a larger version of the earthquake data sample. The excerpt is from a two-party conversation, both audio- and video-recorded within a few weeks after the 1994 Northridge (California) earthquake. The earthquake hit Southern California in the pre-dawn hours of Monday, January 17. Danny and Bob are two university students who had met for the first time when this recording took place. Pairs of university students were invited to meet and discuss their experiences during these recording sessions. Some student pairs were total strangers (like Danny and Bob), some were acquaintances, and others were good friends or more than just acquaintances. The participants were asked to simply share their earthquake stories with each other: where they were, how they reacted, what they did, and so forth.[6]

As you read through the transcript, attend to the following points:

- Do you note any overlapping talk, where both people are speaking at the same time? If so, where? Are they long spates of talk or short? Are the instances of overlapping talk consistent throughout the excerpt? That is, do you find overlaps at nearly every turn or only some turns?
- Try to identify the TCUs within each turn. Note how grammar and prosody combine to signal that current speakers are either intending to continue their turns or getting ready to bring their turn to completion. You should make a list of these mechanisms: Which features of grammar are used here to extend Bob's turn? Which features of prosody (including in-breaths)?
- Try to determine how speakership changes in this excerpt. Indicate the turns where you find evidence of:
  - A current speaker overtly designating a next speaker.
  - A current speaker implying the relevance of a next speaker's turn.
  - A current speaker continuing to speak, with no speaker change.
  - A next speaker opting to speak, where change is relevant.
  - Silence—where no speaker produces a turn, but where change was indeed relevant, i.e., a transition relevance place where the TCU sounded complete both grammatically and prosodically.

Earthquake Stories

Bob: H[i.
Danny: [Da::nny,
Bob: [he he ((laughter)) Bo(h)b.
Danny: [again,
          (0.1)
Danny: and uh (.) go ahead. = uh (1.0) where were you on the- (0.2)
          >four thirty in the morning<,
Bob: O(h)(h) I was uh- (1.8) awake actually = he(h)((wheezing
          sounding laughter)) buhfore the earthquake started.
          (2.0)

> Bob: •hh Uhm (2.0) I ws <u>stayin</u> with my <u>girlfriend,</u> (.) at <u>her</u> place, (2.0) •h and uh (0.1) I couldn't <u>sleep.</u>
> (2.0)
> Bob: >It w's<- (2.0) about four fif<u>tee::n</u> in the morning, (0.4) an' (1.0) I was <u>awake,</u> an jus' <u>lyin'</u> there, an I (1.0) <u>felt</u> the first <u>tremor</u>s come <u>i::n</u> an' (1.0) •hh just (.) reached over a(h)nd EARTHQUA(h)::K(h)E (1.0) <u>grabbed</u> her an uh (0.4) <u>ra:n</u> out inta the <u>hallway.</u> =
> Danny: = oh you <u>di:d,</u> =
> Bob: = [yeah
> Danny: [°yeah°
> (0.8)

(Strauss, 1994)

Participants engaged in everyday conversation are oriented to such interactional resources, even at the most basic level of turn taking—the predictable and systematic mechanisms by which turns are produced, how they are organized, how they are held and maintained, how and where speakers change. Such orientations are visible in the participants' interactional behaviors—the most minute elements of vocalization (slight rising intonation, sound stretches, latching two turns together); "prospective indexicals" pointing to as yet unstated bits of information (***that's*** *why I came here d'night*); pauses within a turn at grammatically odd places, e.g., separating the subject from its verb and deploying grammatical conjunctions within long spates of talk (e.g., *I was jus' lyin' there, an **I** (1.0) **felt** the first tremors come i::n an'* (1.0)); taking audible in-breaths (•hh), and other grammatical and prosodic resources at points in an extended conversational turn where speaker change may be anticipated, but unwanted.

Speakers and listeners are indeed oriented to these and other conversational mechanisms, the "normative and habituated practices associated with TCU boundaries" (Clayman, 2013b: 160), though not at the same level as the analysts who study talk-in-interaction. Researchers of conversation have uncovered these systematic, consistent, regular, and predictable patterns of interaction whereby talking with others involves much more than just *conversing, shooting the breeze, chatting, discussing,* and *exchanging ideas.* There is more going on below the surface of our words and our grammar and our vocal contours—much that has already been explicated by researchers in this discipline, and so much more that has yet to be discovered and documented.

Mutual orientations between current speakers and co-partici-pants: transitions, forfeiting transition, assessments, collaborative turn constructions, adjacency pairs, and repair

We have examined some of the mechanisms by which turns at talk are built and maintained. We have examined the construct of the TCU, in which content, grammar, and prosody combine to form turns at talk. In the remainder of this chapter, we will briefly address conversational behaviors as they relate to speakers and co-participants. Specifically, we will examine some of the places where **turn transition** may begin (and why), co-participant **behaviors designed to forfeit a possible turn transition**, co-participant behaviors in **expressing and withholding evaluation (assessments)**, and **collaborative construction of turns** by more than one speaker. We will also briefly discuss the concept of **adjacency pairs** and their function within conversation from the point of view of both relevance and expectations. Finally, we will examine **repair** as a phenomenon **for resolving actual mishearings and misunderstandings** and for projecting conversational "trouble" before it materializes in talk.

Projecting Possible Completion: New Speaker Takes a New Turn

Co-participants in conversation continually monitor and project the precise places in ongoing talk where speaker change might be possible, often in overlap with another speaker, as in the following examples from three different datasets, all adapted from Sacks, Schegloff, and Jefferson (1974: 707):

Example 1: [Crandall: 2–15–68:93]

A: Well, if you knew my argument why did you bother
    to a:s[k,
B: [Because I'd like to defend <u>my</u> argument.
    (Note the contrasting intonation between "my argument" spoken by
    A and "<u>my</u> argument" with audible, emphatic stress spoken by B)

Example 2: [Civil Defense HQ: 2:88]

B: Well it wasn't me [::
A: [No, but you know who it was.

Example 3: [NB:I:6:7]

A; Sixty two feet is pretty good si:[ze.
B: [Oh:: boy.

In each of the examples, the co-participant has monitored the content, grammar, and prosody of the current speaker's talk, ***projected possible completion*** of that TCU (at a place where it sounded as if nearing completion) and initiated a new turn, in slight overlap with the just prior turn.

Projecting Possible Completion: New Speaker Yields Turn to Current Speaker Through Continuers

In the case of extended, multi-unit turns, co-participants may signal more minimal involvement in and attention to a current speaker's talk, such that they do not actually take a new turn themselves, but rather indicate to the current speaker that they are simultaneously monitoring the ongoing talk and yielding their own potential turn for the current speaker to continue. These signals are referred to in the literature as **back-channel tokens, response tokens,** and **continuers**. The terms "**continuers**" best underscores the conversational functions of the vocalizations, "displaying recipient[s'] understanding that an extended turn at talk is in progress, but not yet complete, while simultaneously collaborating in the achievement of that multi-unit utterance . . ." (Goodwin, 1986: 207).

The repertoire of tokens used in English to achieve this action include non-lexical vocalizations (e.g., *m hm, uh huh, mmm*), lexical vocalizations (e.g., *yeah, myeah, okay*), and non-verbal signals (e.g., head nods, head shakes, eyebrow raises, shoulder shrugs). Each could be produced from a range of possible prosodic contours (*okay., oka:::y?, Oh kay., yeah, yea:::h?*) or varying degrees of intensity (exaggerated head nod, subtle shoulder shrug) Each signal with its own prosodic or gestural variation, carries a different meaning. Each serves a different interactional purpose, beyond expressing a basic message of "I'm listening and I'm not going to take a turn yet." And each exhibits a different orientation toward the talk just produced. Simple continuer tokens are often produced in overlap (or partial overlap) with a current speaker's talk at transition relevance places or points of possible completion, but not always.

(For detailed discussions and designations of listener response tokens, e.g., "reactive tokens," "backchannel," and so forth, see Clancy et al., 1996; Drummond and Hopper, 1993; Gardner, 2002; Goodwin, 1986; Hayashi, 2003; Heritage, 1984; Iwasaki and Horie, 1998; Jefferson, 1984; Mori, 2006; Norrick, 2012; Sacks, Schegloff and Jefferson, 1974; Schegloff, 2000; Young and Lee, 2004; Zimmerman, 1993.)

This first example illustrates a continuer produced in overlap with a prior turn:

Example 1: [HGH:35]

Hyla: One time I member, •hh 's a girl wrote
          End her, •hh she wz like (.) fifteen er
          Six [teen end] her mother doesn let'er wear,
Nancy: [Uh hu:h]

(Adapted from Goodwin, 1986: 207)

Here, Nancy's continuer token *uh hu:h* spans two TCUs. Its onset is vocalized just prior to the completion of one TCU and it extends into the beginning of another, serving dually to display her attention to the emerging talk while signaling a move to deliberately forfeit a potentially emergent next turn speaker change.

The second example illustrates the use of continuers at an actual transition relevance place. There is no overlap with the prior turn, but the function remains the same—linking TCUs of a prior speaker such that the co-participant forfeits uptake to begin a new turn, and continues to track the ongoing talk:

Example 2: [It's a lot of work]

AA: yeah (1.1) I don't think I- (.) I always wanted to do it (.) earlier,
JA: mhm,
AA in (.) my college career, (0.5) but I'm glad I didn't cuz it's a lot of work.

(Adapted from Young and Lee, 2004: 385)

Note the prosody marked here: AA produces this TCU with a slight rise in her intonation (indicated by a comma at the end of the TCU), a clear signal that she intends to continue, and also a signal that some uptake, however minimal, would be relevant. Note, too, (as do Young and Lee), that JA's continuer is also marked with a slight rise (again, a comma at the end), further bolstering the communicative message of her continuer: "I acknowledge your intonational rise, I am listening, I yield my turn at this point in our conversation, keep going—I do want to hear more." AA is invited, through JA's continuer, complete with interlocutor involving intonation, to continue expressing what she has to say.

Assessments: Evaluations and Judgments in Talk-In-Interaction

Assessments involve the ways in which participants in situated interaction put forward evaluations and judgments, about virtually anything, from appearances and colors and textures of physical objects to abstract ideas and opinions. We are constantly expressing our opinions and judgments and constantly find ourselves in the position of responding to judgments expressed by others. Responses to assessments might be in resonance with the initial assessments, in conflict with them, produced immediately upon hearing the onset of a first assessment, produced after some delay, or withheld entirely.

While talk-in-interaction in general reveals an extraordinary granularity concerning the ways in which participants produce, attend to, and respond to emerging talk, the phenomenon of assessments often reveals even more richly complex insights into the "participant[s]' affect as a socially organized, collaboratively sustained phenomenon" (Goodwin, 1986: 371). (See Goodwin and Goodwin, 1987, 1992; Pomerantz, 1984; Pomerantz and Heritage, 2013; Schegloff, 2007.)

The following classic excerpt from Goodwin and Goodwin (1992) represents one such instance.

Example 1:

Nancy: *Jeff* made en asparagus pie
     ((lowers   ((nod with
     upper   eyebrow flash))
     trunk))

```
              |         |
Nancy:   It was s::[so- goo:d.
Tasha:           [I love   it
                 Nod       Nod
```

(Adapted from Goodwin and Goodwin, 1992: 163)

Assessments make visible, within the course of nanoseconds, the ways in which participants align (or not) with the item or issue being assessed, as well as with co-participants in the talk. In the first example, Nancy proffers a topic, i.e., Jeff's asparagus pie, and foreshadows that some version of an assessment will be forthcoming in a next turn. Nancy's positive assessment then emerges, emphatically intoned through sound stretches on the entire adjective phrase: *so::: goo:d,* followed almost immediately by and in overlap with Tasha's second assessment. What is noteworthy here is that Tasha's assessment-framed response came *before* Nancy's utterance of the adjective "good," yet she was able to predict an ensuing positive evaluation. Tasha produced her own positive comment, though pointing to a different focus of what is being assessed and at a different level of evaluation—one that avoided any claim of past direct experience of having tasted that pie in particular or any asparagus pie at all.

Assessments are inherently jointly produced activities. The utterance of an assessment (or sequences of assessment) makes both relevant and expected a response to it, typically in the form of another assessment.

ASSESSMENTS AND PREFERENCE ORGANIZATION

Pomerantz (1984) provides an extended discussion on assessments and responses to assessments from the perspective of ***preference organization***, as ***preferred* or *dispreferred* responses.** That is, assessments that are designed to elicit some form of agreement are responded to with second assessments that align in quality and polarity with that first assessment—a preferred response. Misaligned assessments, implying or directly stating disagreement, would be dispreferred. Excerpts 2 and 3 provide illustrations of a preferred assessment sequence, whereby a first assessment receives back an assessment that displays implicit agreement.

Preferred responses
assessments seeking agreement, agreement comes, interactional align-ment

Example 2: [JS.II.28]

Positive assessment, agreement preferred
J: T's—tsuh beautiful day out isn't it?
L: Yeh it's just gorgeous . . .

(Adapted from Pomerantz, 1984: 62)

Example 3: [MC:1]

Positive assessment, agreement preferred
A: Isn't he cute
B: O::h he::s a::DORable.

(Adapted from Pomerantz, 1984: 65)

In the examples given, the upgraded second assessments constitute an agreement with the first assessments, both of which are also positive. In each case, a positive descriptor in the first assessment is substituted with a semantically stronger descriptor in the responsive second assessment. "Beautiful," in example 2, becomes "just gorgeous." "Cute," in example 3, becomes "a:::DORable." Upgrading an adjective in a second assessment turn can also be accomplished by adding an intensifier to the second assessment, while recycling the identical descriptor: pretty → very pretty, interesting → very interesting. The foregoing examples are all positive.

The same upgrading move in maintaining agreement where agreement is preferred can also be achieved with negative adjectives: ugly → grotesque, boring → very boring. The pole (i.e., negative or positive) matters little, as long as the move that displays a co-participant's agreement matches the assessment.

Other ways of displaying agreements with positive assessments are through grammatical substitution, ellipsis, or the additive/"likewise" marker, "too." The following two excerpts are also adapted from Pomerantz (1984: 67):

Assessment 1	Assessment 2 (with ellipsis, additive, or substitution)
	No delay in production
He's terrific.	→ He is. [ellipsis—the word "terrific" is left out]
I like it	→ I like it too. [additive "too"]
I think everyone just sitting around talking.	→ I do too. [substitution and "too"]

In contrast, in cases where co-participants are not aligned in their views or opinions, we find distinctions in how second assessments are produced, signaling misalignment between the producer of the first assessment and the speaker who responds. Tell-tale indicators that a dispreferred type of response is about to emerge include no immediate uptake by the responder to the assessment (i.e., no overlapping talk, no latching, no contiguous turns). Instead, a dispreferred response may be foreshadowed by a short gap in time between first assessment completion and onset of the next turn, hedges (*u:hm, well, y'know*), or misstarts (I- we-). Examples 4 and 5 will illustrate:

Dispreferred responses:
assessments seeking agreement →no agreement comes,
agreement hedged or delayed, interactional misalignment

Example 4: [NB:IV:11.-1]

Negative assessment, agreement preferred, disagreement produced

A: God izn' it <u>drea</u>ry?
      (0.6)
A: [Y'know I don't think-
B: [•hh It's <u>warm</u> though.

(Adapted from Pomerantz, 1984: 70)

Example 5: [SBL: 2.2.3.-27]

Negative assessment, disagreement preferred, no assessment produced

B: . . .I wasn't understanding anybody today.
A: Uh huh,

(Adapted from Pomerantz, 1984: 93)

In Example 4, A produces an assessment about the weather. It's clearly negative. It is prefaced by an exclamation (*God*), already foreshadowing a less than favorable viewpoint. Syntactically, A's turn is a negative yes-no question, the preferred response to which would be an affirmation or agreement. A's adjective choice to describe the weather "dreary" conjures up more than simply a lack of sunshine—it encompasses at once a state of mind and an emotion, in addition to the greyness of a day. A's turn is not simply a negative assessment. It is a complaint. It might also be a whiny one, intensifying A's stance.

B's response is delayed. Just over one half second elapses, when A, now realizing that B is not going to agree (signaled by B's lack of immediate uptake), re-shapes her turn, re-focusing her emphasis elsewhere, though the turn is truncated and so we have no idea what actually followed. In perfect overlap with A's new utterance, B does respond, prefacing her turn with audible in-breath, and providing what could be construed as a silver lining—the sun may not be out, but the temperature is warm.

Example 5 is a self-deprecation. As Pomerantz (1984) notes, a *preferred* response to first assessments as self-deprecation is disagreement, e.g., *It was such a dumb thing I did today.* [self-deprecation].—*No it wasn't* [disagreement]. What we have in Example 5 appears to be a hyperbolized self-pitying sort of self-deprecating turn, hyperbolic by virtue of the negative polarity indefinite pronoun *anybody*. "I wasn't understanding anybody today." B places the blame on no one but himself. Moreover, he uses the past progressive, as if communicative mishaps have been continuing over time, and possibly even now in the present, in this very interaction with A. The turn is an assessment, but at the same time, a calling out for empathy, a reaching out for someone (perhaps A) to understand him. In response, rather than a display of compassion or a counter to his "anybody" [surely he must have understood by at least one person], B receives a minimal continuer token "Uh huh," in a place where A would actually rather *not* continue. Canonically, *uh huhs*, and *m hmms*, and *yeahs*, indicate that an interlocutor is both listening and yielding a possible next turn. Sometimes, such continuers make it *sound* as if an interlocutor is listening and yielding a turn. In this case, yielding a turn, when uptake is preferred, establishes an interactional problem.

Assessments and assessment sequences are ripe environments for the analysis of talk-in-interaction in general, and for the study of collaboratively organized displays of affect, emotion, credulity, skepticism, even flirtatiousness. When assessments are produced in interaction, speakers are doing more than simply *assessing*. They are praising, complaining, blaming, belittling, reaching out—explicitly and implicitly, in jointly organized activities of talk.

HEARER'S CHANGE-OF-STATE TOKEN "OH"—CHANGE FROM NOT KNOWING TO KNOWING

"Oh" and the range of prosodic contours with which it is produced in English (e.g., *Oh?, O::::H, oh-*) occupies a special place in the repertoire of listener response tokens. Heritage (1984, 1998, 2002) refers to "oh" as a "change of state token," signaling that the participant who produces "oh" "has undergone some kind of change in his or her locally current state of knowledge, information, orientation, or awareness" (1984: 299).

Excerpts 1 and 2, from Heritage (1984) illustrate the phenomenon:

Example 1: [Rah:II:1]

```
     J:    = Hello there I rang y'earlier b'tchu w'r ou:t.
a→   I:    ↑Oh:: I musta been at Dez's mu:ms =
b→   J:    = ↓aOh::::h =
```

(Adapted from Heritage, 1984: 301)

Example 2: [Goodwin: Family Dinner: 13]

```
     B:    It looks like beef'n bean curd.
           (1.0)
     J:    Well I wan' lots of beef.
     D:    I think it's pork.
→    B:    Oh. Pork.
     D:    Mm hm
```

(Adapted from Heritage, 1984: 312)

In each example, the "oh" producer is vocally signaling that a cognitive change of state has occurred—a realization, a remembering, an immediate grasping of a new piece of information.

Heritage (1984, 1998, 2002) points out a number of interactional patterns that trigger the production of "oh" in conversation. These include a visual trigger in the immediate environment that stimulates a sudden recognition or realization (e.g., *oh, that <u>teeshirt</u> reminded me of . . .* where the speaker has just noticed a photo tee shirt; Heritage, 1984: 299), and a variety of interactional stimuli related to the talk at hand (e.g., informings, as in Example 1, and counterinformings, as in Example 2). "Oh" is also often found in displays of understandings (*Oh, I get it now*), in prefaces to assessments (e.g., *oh good* or *Oh he's ador::able* [from the Pomerantz example]), and as prefaces to responses to questions (see Heritage, 1984, 2002).

As a stand-alone particle (i.e., in a turn of its own as in in 1b), "oh" often closes down a conversational topic, in that it signals simply that an interactant has heard and processed the information as new and as understood, but at the same time invites no further development. Stand-alone "oh" is rare (Heritage, 1984: 325).

"Oh," as an indicator of a cognitive change of state, implying "I did not know this before" (or "I knew it, but I'm acting as if I didn't"), frames information just received by an interactant as both "new" and "newsworthy." As such, it establishes a polar interactional contrast with recipient tokens that signal prior knowledge of something, or a lack of interest in the topic (e.g., *I know that*, *What else is new?*). Depending upon its placement and intonation, "oh" can serve to display alignment with a co-participant or it can effect interactional distance.

And while "oh" marks an individual's cognitive state of mind, as we see in the examples presented here, it is also intricately tied up with emotion and affect. (See Chapter 8, Indexicality, affective and epistemic stance marking).

Collaborative Turn Construction: One Speaker Starts and Another Finishes

Other resources for displaying co-alignment or interactional disjunction include the phenomenon of the collaborative construction of turns (Lerner, 1996, 2003, 2004a, 2004b; Sacks, Schegloff, and Jefferson, 1974; Schegloff, 2007). And, once again, we often (but not always) find such display of collaborative understanding with co-participants producing speaker change at points in the talk where prior turns are not yet complete.

We can observe this interactional practice in Examples 1–3. All three examples illustrate the intricate and keenly coordinated participation in interaction, where each co-participant tracks the talk just produced (not yet complete), and projects appropriate constructions of grammar and resonating stances, in alignment with the talk that has been or will be produced by the current speaker.

Example 1: [GTS]

Ken: insteada my grandmother offering him a drink, of beer she'll say [wouldju-
Louise: [wanna glassa milk?
Ken: [hehh
    [no, wouldju like a little bitta herring*?
*the word *herring* in the original transcript appears to have been pronounced with an accent, such that it emerged as [hɛɣɪŋ]

(Adapted from Lerner, 2004b: 228)

Example 2: [Theodore]

A: If you start watering, it [will get gree-
B: [it will come back
A: y- yes, uh huh

(Adapted from Lerner, 2004b: 230)

In both examples, the first speaker has initiated a turn, providing just enough detail for the second speaker to imagine what might come next (and does) in the first speaker's turn. That is, in Example 1, Ken caricaturizes his grandmother in interaction with another individual in such a way that Louise can immediately display a guess at how Ken will continue. Ken portrays his grandmother in the midst of her offering a drink to another individual—worded by Ken as "wouldju like" and guessed by Louise as "wanna." The object of offer in the actual story by Ken turns out to be pickled fish (herring), while Louise guessed it would be milk, as an appropriate contrast to an offer of "beer." In spite of the fact that it was a wrong guess, as evidenced by Ken's "no"-prefaced correction, the degree of resonance between parties in this interaction is remarkable.

In Example 2, the content of talk (i.e., watering grass that has either burned or turned yellow), coupled with the syntax of the conditional structure, *if* one does x, (then) *y will happen*, makes the projection of up-coming talk more predictable: If you start watering the grass, it will . . . There is a limitation with regard to possible outcomes here: *turn green, grow back, start growing again*, etc. B did, in fact, guess right, as acknowledged by A's doubly marked affirmative response.

Example 3 also illustrates the completion of a turn by a co-participant, except here, the second part of the turn is not produced by two speakers overlapping similar notions. Instead, Kerry first attempted to complete Sparky's turn, backed down and waited, and then completed the second clause.

Example 3: [HIC]

Sparky: It sounds like what you're saying is that (.) [let <u>the:m</u> make the <u>dec</u>:sions =

Kerry: [(if ya)

Kerry: = an let us know what it is.

(Adapted from Lerner, 1996: 245)

Crucially, as Lerner (2003: 249) points out, it is the original speaker, the producer of the initial content, grammar, and stance, who maintains authorship over the turn design and purpose, and, as we observed in Examples 1 and 2, original speakers do acknowledge accurate and inaccurate completions. Collaborative completions shed important light on the mechanism of turn-taking and on the joint orientation of the participants to the ongoing talk.

Adjacency Pairs

As we have just observed, much of turn taking in conversation is built on the sequential ordering and organization of talk. In the excerpts that we have examined in this chapter, we observed speakers in the midst of interactional activity where one speaker produces turns or parts of turns, designed in such a way that some form of interlocutor uptake is both relevant and expected. One of the basic ways that such a dynamic is established in conversation is through the **adjacency pair** framework. An adjacency pair is a two-part, initiatory-responsive construction, where one speaker's utterance of a first pair part makes both relevant and expected the utterance of an appropriately responsive second pair part by another speaker (Drew, 2013; Sacks, Schegloff, and Jefferson, 1974; Schegloff, 1984, 2007). Examples of these include:

First pair part (1pp)	Second pair part (2pp)
Greeting *Hi*	Greeting *Hey*
Question *Whadja do?*	Answer *Stayed home.*
Invitation *Can you come over?*	Acceptance / Rejection *Sure / I wish I could*
Aaachoo!	*Bless you*
Apology *Sorry*	Response *No problem, It's okay, You're fine, No worries*
Thanks *Thanks.*	Response to thanks *You're welcome, My pleasure, Don't mention it*

Thus, when a first pair part (1pp) is produced by a speaker, the production of a second pair part (2pp) is both relevant and expected—and not just at any point in the interaction, but with a minutely keen (and intuitive) sensitivity to timing.

Like assessments, adjacency pairs are also motivated by a system of preference organization. That is, a preferred response to a greeting is the return of a greeting. The preferred response to a question, is an answer, and not, for example, another question. The preferred response to an invitation is the acceptance of an invitation; a dispreferred response would be a rejection. A preferred response to an apology might be an acceptance of the apology or the denial that any wrongdoing was committed by the apologizer in the first place.[7]

Examples 1 and 2, from Sacks, Schegloff, and Jefferson (1974: 716) illustrate the dynamic:

Example 1:   complaint/denial

Ken: Hey yuh took my chair by the way an' I don't think that was
       very nice. [GTS:1   1pp
Al: I didn' take yer chair, it's my chair.   2pp

> **Example 2:   compliment/rejection**
>
> A: I'm glad I have you for a friend.   1pp
> B: That's because you don't have any others.   [FN].   2pp

The speaker of the first pair part in each of the examples sets up an expectation that the interlocutor will provide a relevant and expected second pair part. Ken's complaint in the first pair part in Example 1 is actually two-pronged: It is an accusation ('yuh took my chair') as well as a negative assessment ('I don't think that was very nice.'), the whole of which constitutes the complaint. Al's response, as a second pair part, mirrors the dual act of Ken's utterance. That is, Al responds first to the accusation by denying it ('I didn' take yer chair.'), and then by emphatically contrasting the possessive pronoun *my* in 'it's my chair,' recycling the identical noun phrase as in Ken's first pair part ('yuh took my chair'), and thereby further discounting the accusation—Al said it was his chair in the first place.

In Example 2, A delivers a compliment to B as a first pair part. It, too, is functionally a dual act. It is at once a compliment and an indirect expression of gratitude. B's response, as the second pair part, rejects both the compliment and the indirect thanks, rendering the utterance an insult.

In spite of the fact that the 2pp responses were less than "preferred," note that the uptake by the producer of the 2pp was immediate. There was no delay between turns, no hesitation within the response turn.

Repair: Interrupting the Flow of Conversation to Set It Back on Track

Self-Initiated Repair and Other-Initiated Repair

Repair refers to the conversational phenomenon that occurs involving a snag in the flow of ongoing talk. The unfolding of talk can be snagged or diverted by the speaker or the interlocutor at places in the interaction where a shift in interactional attention is necessary (Schegloff, Jefferson, and Saks, 1977; Kitzinger, 2013).

This can occur where speakers stop mid-turn to correct a word or to qualify a statement. Speakers can also repair their utterances in later turns, when, for example, they sense that interlocutors may not be following the idea. This latter type of repair typically occurs when an interactional sequence has misfired in some way, e.g., when some type of expected response is not produced by an interlocutor. When speakers repair their own turns, it is referred to in the literature as **self-repair** or **self-initiated repair.**

The next examples are from Kitzinger (2013). Excerpt 1 illustrates self-initiated repair by a speaker in the same turn. Excerpt 2 illustrates self-repair by a speaker in a later turn. For Example 2, note the gap—the very brief silence between the turns.

Example 1: Self-repair BC Gray (I)

1   Clr: About **a month** uh (.) about- no about
2   **two weeks** before he made the ca:ll

(From Kitzinger, 2013: 235; emphasis in original)

Example 2: self-repair Holt X(C):1:2:7

1   Mum: What are they then,
2   Les: Shortbreads •hh
3   (.)
4   Mum: No I mean what ma:ke,
5   Les: •hh Oh:: uhm (0.5) hhh well some Scottish make.

(Adapted from Kitzinger, 2013: 247)

In the first example, the speaker calibrates the time frame designation in the narrative from "a month" to "two weeks." In the second example, the self-initiated repair by Mum follows a very brief silence, itself a signal of interactional trouble. Here, Les misinterpreted Mum's question ("What are they, then"), providing an answer that defined the thing in her inquiry ("Shortbreads") rather than naming the brand, which is the information she'd originally sought. The interactional snag occurred as a result of this misreading of Mum's question.

When interlocutors initiate a repair sequence in conversation, it is broadly referred to as **other-initiated repair.** Others in conversation may interrupt the flow of talk by inserting a clarification request (e.g. 'whaddya mean?' or 'who did that?') or a request to repeat some or all of the prior turn ('excuse me?', 'pardon?,' 'what did you just say?') (Bolden, 2011; Kitzinger, 2013; Robinson and Kevoe-Feldman, 2010), as in Example 3 next, from a British Emergency Police call, cited in Kitzinger (2013).

Example 3:

	1	Clr :	Yeah hi: uhm: there's a hedgehog in the middle
	2		of the road on the Wyke road an' 'e's got
	3		'is head stuck in a can 'n 'e can't get it
	4		out (0.2) uhm an' 'e's just wanderin' round an'
	5		I th<u>i</u>nk 'es' gonna get run <u>o</u>ve:r. Uhm what
	6		d'you want me to do just l<u>ea</u>ve it?
→	7	Pol:	It's got a head stuck in wha:t sorry: =
	8	Clr:	In a p<u>o</u>t noodle can.

(Adapted from Kitzinger, 2013: 250)

Here, the caller has reported an emergency involving a hedgehog in trouble. Its head is stuck in a can. The police officer receiving the call got only part of the story and requested clarification. The flow of talk stopped. The caller ended the turn with a question concerning the best way to handle the situation. No answer came. Instead, the officer initiated a repair sequence by posing his own question—a request for clarification of just one bit of the story ("a head stuck in what?"). Based on this turn, it is unclear what parts of the story actually registered. Did the officer know it was a hedgehog? Did he know it was an animal at all? In spite of the odd delivery of the officer's repair initiator ("a head. . ."), the caller responded only to the question segment of it "stuck in wha:t."

Repair emerges in talk-in-interaction to resolve issues that might be unclear or inaccurate, as initiated by a speaker in a same turn or some later turn, based on a speaker's own prediction of a potential inaccuracy or trouble source or on a perceived trouble source in a hearer's understanding (through turns or partial turns of uptake or through delayed uptake), as **self-initiated repair**. Interlocutors can also disrupt ongoing talk by acknowledging some source of in the speaker's prior turns—expressing a mishearing and requesting confirmation, asking for more detail, and so forth, as **other-initiated repair.**

Based on this brief introduction to repair, let's have a quick look at the following excerpt from the Earthquake Stories data that we introduced earlier.

Here, Danny and Bob had been speaking for just a few minutes, getting to know each other and establishing some rapport and common ground between them. At the point in which the following excerpt emerged, they had begun to share details about their respective residences—crucial information in a conversation about earthquakes, to determine how close to the epicenter and most heavily damaged areas that each of them lived. A brief trouble source occurred here—one that may have even escaped notice without the foregoing discussion of repair.

Based on your understanding of CA and the mutual orientation of participants to turn-taking and adjacency pairs, intuitive expectations concerning next-turn content and next-turn timing, analyze the following five lines of transcript:

Earthquake data (excerpt)

1	Danny:	What part a <u>tow::n</u>.	1pp
2	Bob:	uhm (.) <u>I</u> was out in [Sunland.	2pp
3	Danny:	[((sniff))	
4	Bob:	D'you know where <u>that</u> is.	1pp
5	Danny:	<u>Su::nland</u>. uh not <u>exactly</u>. = no.	2pp

What does this short excerpt illustrate with respect to participants' acute orientation to the elements of conversational systematicity that we have presented so far? Explain why and how repair occurs here.

REVIEW AND REFLECTION: CONVERSATION ANALYSIS— TURN TAKING, OVERLAPPING TALK, ADJACENCY PAIRS, CONTINUERS, ASSESSMENTS, AND REPAIR

1. Compare and contrast 1950s and 1960s sitcoms (or police dramas, courtroom dramas, family dramas) to current sitcoms (or dramas). As a an initial basis for comparison, think about: topics of tension or problems to be solved in the program, how the tensions/problems are resolved, and general sources of comedy/drama. Now, look more deeply into the interactional features of the shows. Do the lines sound "natural," i.e., similar to a conversation that might take place in a similar context in the same decade? Do this for the older programs and for the current ones. Does the dialogue sound stilted in any way? If so, is the quality of "stiltedness" related to *register*? Is it related to turn-taking practices, timing, overlapping talk, repair or lack thereof? In what ways have television broadcasts of sitcoms and dramas changed? What factors, do you think, are responsible for

such changes? As you work on this project, be sure to bear in mind topics from other chapters that we have covered, especially *genre, register,* and *participation framework.* Other topics from other chapters (including later ones) may be relevant to your analyses.

2. The following is an excerpt from a face-to-face conversation that took place in the emergency room of a Southern California hospital. The conversation involves a mother (Ann) and her daughter (Steph).

Analyze this excerpt on the basis of "context" from a CA perspective. That is, the methodology must be "context free and capable of extraordinary context-sensitivity." In what ways does "context" become relevant in the excerpt? Is the context relevant to the parties themselves? If so, how do you know? If not, is it acceptable to bring an interpretation of context into the analysis if it is not something that is empirically relevant to the interactants?

Also, analyze the talk on the basis of turn-taking: adjacency pairs, overlapping talk, overall timing of turns, placement and quality of continuers and assessments (and responses to assessments), "newsworthiness" of contributions by interactants (e.g., "oh" / "I know"), and the interactional impact of these features on the conversation. Note how topics are opened, how they develop, and how they close down. Analyze the excerpt in as much detail as possible, pushing yourself to make hypotheses and discoveries related to conversational turns and turn-taking that we have not addressed in detail in this chapter (especially with respect to topic opening and topic closure).

[Hospital Data—Tape 1]

Ann:	= <u>Awaa</u>::. . •hhh aa
Steph:	Aw(h)(h) =
Ann:	= <u>Any</u>way::. =
Steph:	= It's <u>chi</u>lly in here. ((noticing Ann shiver and trying to adjust her sweater))
Ann:	It's <u>FREE</u>zing in he[re. = <u>Absolutely</u> <u>free</u>zing. =
Steph:	[°yeah it was <u>cold</u> out <u>there</u> <u>too</u>.°
Steph:	= °I <u>know</u>°.
Ann:	But <u>I</u> don't wanna <u>bo</u>ther them. = They're <u>all</u> so <u>bu</u>::sy. (("them" / "they" refer to the nurses))
Steph:	I know.

Ann:	So <u>this</u>- (.) <u>hope</u>fully 'll (.) keep me <u>warm</u> fer a while.
	((Ann adjusts her sweater, Steph helps.))
Steph:	Ya <u>want</u> something <u>el</u>se?
Ann:	I don't know <u>wha</u>t right now.
Steph:	Ya <u>want</u> my <u>coat</u>?
Ann:	Oh <u>no no</u>. <u>Not</u>chur coat. Ya know <u>what</u>?
Steph:	W[<u>hat</u>.
Ann:	[uh::;m. The b- <u>blan</u>[ket.
Steph:	[this <u>blan</u>ket.
Ann;	Um <u>hm</u>.
	(2.0)
Ann:	Good <u>idea</u>.
	(3.0)

((Topic of talk shifts to a discussion of other family members))

(Strauss, 1998)

3. Next you will find an excerpt from a transcript of the *Judge Judy* television program. *Judge Judy* is a "reality show" that began airing in 1996 and continues to be aired today. The judge, *Judge Judith Schiendlin* is direct and rough, often insulting the parties who choose to be on the show to settle their small claims disputes in this type of venue (Judge Judy, n.d.). She reads the testimonies prior to the start of the show and is very familiar with each parties' narrative (on the side of the plaintiff and the side of the defendant), as is evident in this transcript as well.

   As you read through the transcript, remember that this is an instance of "institutional talk," and not ordinary conversation. As such, many of the features of turn-taking are very different.

   Read through the transcript and think about the following:

   • What is the genre of discourse? Recall that genre frame boundaries can be permeable. It may be to your advantage to consider this as a hybrid type of discourse. (It would be crucial, here, to identify which elements of which genre you find in the show). Also be sure to think about the concepts of speaker, hearer, audience, and overall participation framework.
   • What features of everyday conversation do you find in this excerpt? What features of everyday conversation are missing from this excerpt? Why do you think this is the case?

- What types of assessments do you see produced in these interactions? How do these differ from assessments in everyday conversation?
- What other features of discourse do you find in the data (whether or not these are linked the foregoing discussion on CA)? (For example, try conducting an alternative analysis of these data using another approach to discourse analysis, e.g., information structure—new, accessible, and given information. What features of each participant's "story" or "narrative" become salient in an information structure approach to discourse that a CA approach might not reveal?)
- What would be a next step toward the development of a more in-depth analysis of this type of media discourse?

Judge Judy Excerpt—The Broken Door Incident

Male announcer:	You: (.) are about to enter the courtroom (.) of Judge Ju^dith Schiendlin. (0.6) the >people< are rea:l (0.4) the ca^ses are real. (0.4) the rulings (.) are final. This: (.) is he^r courtroom. (0.4) Thi^s: (.) is Judge (.) Judy.
Male voice:	Thir^dy-two year old cosmetic surgery o^ffice manager, Joni Ross (0.3) claims fo^rmer boy^friend sports medicine company owner Ma^tthew Sequiera, (.) twenty five (.) kicked her door down (.) in a fit of jealous rage.
Bailiff:	Orde^r. (0.4) All ri^se. (7.2) ((Judge Judy exits her chambers, walks toward her bench and sits down))
Bailiff:	>(Judge this is)< case number twenny nine on the calendar >in the matter< of Ross versus Sequiera. (2.2)

Bailiff:	Parties have been <u>swor</u>n in, you may be sea^ted,
	(1.0)
Bailiff:	((to someone accompanying one of the litigants))
	Have a seat ma'am.
Judge Judy:	Mi^ster Sequiera, this is <u>not</u> a very hard case, (.) sir.
	(3.6)
Judge Judy:	This is yr gi^rlfriend, (0.8) then ya broke u^p (2.2) an'
	ya de<u>ci</u>ded ta go by her h- (.) <u>house</u> one e^vening,
	(1.8) <u>aft</u>ah you broke <u>up</u>. (0.4)
	iz<u>za</u>t ri^ght?
	(1.0)
Sequiera:	Uhh::: (.2) in fact we <u>were</u> still- (0.4) dating.
	(0.6)
Judge Judy:	Bu:^t she wasn'chur gi^rlfriend th[en.
Sequiera:	[Kerrect.
	(0.8)
Judge Judy:	•h So ya went by her <u>hou:se</u>, (0.6) an' didja see
	somebody else's ca^r there?
	(0.4)
Sequiera:	Ye:s I <u>did</u>. =
Judge Judy:	= Yeah.
	(0.4)
Judge Judy:	•hh So: ya got <u>angry</u>.
	(2.4)
Judge Judy:	Ye:s judge. I got <u>angry</u>.
Sequiera:	<u>Ye:s</u>. I got a little up<u>set</u>. = it was my <u>best</u> friend.
Judge Judy:	(xxxx).
	(0.2)
Judge Judy:	•hh So:: ya went ta the <u>doo::^r</u>, (0.3) a:n she
	wouldn't lecha <u>i::^n</u>, an' one two three^ •hh an' (.)
	ya <u>buste</u>d the <u>door</u>.
	(1.0)
Judge Judy:	You <u>kno^w::</u> [(that she bought another) door. =
Sequiera:	[yes yeah
Sequiera:	I <u>do</u>.
	(0.8)
Judge Judy:	She^ wants you ta <u>pay</u> for a new doo^r, (0.8) you <u>say</u>
	(.2) thatchu

	could've gotten it <u>fixed</u> (1.0) fer less <u>mon</u>ey.
	(0.8)
Sequiera:	Kerrect. = I couldda gotten it fixed [(for a lot cheaper)
Judge Judy:	[So <u>that</u>'s yer de<u>fense</u>.
	(0.6)
Judge Judy:	I- k- <u>could</u>da gotten it <u>chea</u>^per.
	(1.8)
Judge Judy:	R[Ight?
Sequiera:	[<u>Cert</u>ainly.
	(0.4)
Sequiera:	Certainly.
	(1.2)
Judge Judy:	<u>She</u> doesn't hafta get it chea^per, (0.4) Mi^ster
	Seeguerra. (0.2) she can get a bra^nd new doo:^r if
	she <u>wants</u> to = R<u>I</u>ght?
Ross:	Yes.

4. Next you'll find a longer stretch of conversation between Danny and Bob. Work with the transcript in the following way:

• Identify the TCUs in the data. For the multi-unit turns, try to determine how each is constructed. That is, determine whether a multi-unit TCU is actually doing more than one thing. The following excerpt is a case in point. Look at Danny's utterance and then Bob's response to it.

   o What is Danny's utterance responding to? What is it actually "doing?" By "doing," we mean to suggest that it is not simply a declarative statement nor is it a simple statement seeking confirmation. So, what could it be? How do you know?

   o What is Bob's utterance "doing?" That is, how does he respond to Danny's prior utterance? There are two parts: "yeah" and "cuz . . . "

   o Bob's response indicates precisely how it is that he has analyzed Danny's prior utterance.

Bob:	•hh uh(h)m <u>looking</u> fer- (.) >y'know< a <u>support</u> beam
	or <u>some</u>thi(h)(h)n'. = and uh (2.2)
→Danny:	So you were <u>able</u> to think that <u>quickly</u>, (0.4) (then.)

> → Bob: YEah. . = cuz <u>we</u> were (0.4) out um (1.2) •mh our ap-
> our apartment (.) <u>ha:ngs</u> over the <u>park</u>ing structure? [so
> it's <u>supported</u> on <u>one end</u> (.) by <u>support beams</u>.
> Danny: [°mhm°

- Analyze the transcript for the features of turn-taking that you have studied in this chapter, with an eye toward how the participants are mutually oriented to the unfolding talk: how are turns begun? How do speakers change? How does the timing between turns change from the earlier segments of the interaction as the conversation progresses? Why do you think this is so?

  o What instances of overlapping talk do you notice?

  o Identify the continuers and the assessments. Do you find any examples that do not appear to belong straightforwardly to one category or the other? Do you find any examples that appear to belong to both categories? What does this tell you?

- Do you find any instances of repair? Identify the sources of trouble for each. Is the trouble "resolved"? How?
- What can we learn about the emergent establishment of "common ground" in conversational talk among strangers? How does a CA-based analysis of these features reveal the subtleties in interactional moves more clearly than other approaches to discourse analysis? What might other approaches to discourse analysis reveal that CA-based analysis would not?

> Danny: <u>Okay::</u>
> (2.2)
> Bob: H[i.
> Danny: [<u>Da::</u>nny,
> Bob: [he he Bo(h)b.
> Danny: [again,
> (0.1)
> Danny: And uh (.) go <u>ahead</u>. = uh (1.0) where were <u>you</u> on the-
> (0.2) >four thirty in the morning<,
> Bob: O(h)(h) I was uh- (1.8) <u>awake</u> actually = he(h)((wheezing sounding laughter)) buhfore the earthquake <u>started</u>.
> (2.0)

Bob: •hh Uhm (2.0) I ws <u>stayin</u> with my <u>girlfriend</u>, (.) at <u>her</u>
        place, (2.0) •h and uh (0.1) I couldn't <u>sleep</u>.
        (2.0)
Bob: >It w's<- (2.0) about four fift<u>ee::n</u> in the morning, (0.4) an'
        (1.0) I was <u>awake</u>, an jus' <u>lyin'</u> there, an I (1.0) <u>felt</u> the first
        <u>tremo</u>rs come <u>i::n</u> an' (1.0) •hh just (.) reached over a(h)
        nd EARTHQUA(h)::K(h)E (1.0) <u>grabbed</u> her an uh (0.4)
        <u>ra:n</u> out inta the <u>hallway</u>. =
Danny: = Oh you <u>di:d,</u> =
Bob: = [yeah
Danny: [°yeah°
        (0.8)
Bob: •hh uh(h)m <u>looking</u> fer- (.) >y'know< a <u>support</u> beam or
        <u>somethi</u>(h)(h)n'. = and uh (2.2)
Danny: So you were <u>able</u> to think that <u>quickly,</u> (0.4) (then.)
Bob: YEah. . = cuz <u>we</u> were (0.4) out um (1.2) •mh our ap- our
        apartment (.) <u>ha:ngs</u> over the <u>parking</u> structure? [so it's
        <u>supported</u> on <u>one</u> end (.) by <u>support beams</u>.
Danny: [°mhm°
        (1.2)
Bob: So: <u>my</u> first thought was well <u>get</u> to the- (1.2) the [<u>solid</u>
        side of the a<u>part</u>ment.
Danny: [<u>solid</u>
        and <u>sa</u>(h)fe p<u>la</u>(h)ce. =
Bob: = <u>Exactly</u>.
Danny: What part a <u>tow::n</u>.
Bob: uhm (.) <u>I</u> was out in [Sunland.
Danny: [((sniff))
Bob: D'you know where <u>that</u> is.
Danny: <u>Su::n</u>land. uh not <u>exactly</u>. = no.
Bob: Yeah, uh let's <u>see::</u>. (.) Out <u>north</u> of <u>Glen</u>dale? near La
        [Ca<u>ñada</u>,
Danny: [Oh right (.) [right
Bob: [yeah right near the- (0.8) the [<u>free</u>ways [out
                                                        there.
Danny: [yeah. [yeah.
Bob: [•hh hu(h)(h) •h °uh:::m°

Danny:	[°hh tha^t's by the ten° (°tha:ts right.°)
Bob:	Well ih- it was clo:se. We got a good ra::ttle. I mean (.) it was uh (.) the stro:ngest earthquake I ever [felt.
Danny:	[m hm
Bob:	But uh (2.0) nothing bro::ke. = Ama::zingly.
	(.)
Bob:	Things fell but no:thing broke.
Danny.	°Yeah you're lu:cky.°
Bob:	yeah.
	(.)
Bob:	•hh uhm (.) we had a bookshelf that almost fell y'kno(h) w (h)but •hh >other than tha::t< it was ju:st uh (1.8) it was just a sca:ry episode. = y'know. it's (.) my first earthquake = well stro:ng one anyway.
	(2.0)
Bob:	And uh (0.2) woh(h)(h) after that I was up all day (.) watchin the news, an' sittin there feeling the a:ftersho(h) cks come through (an') (.) it's quite the experience.
Danny:	[Yeah.
Bob:	[yeah. Where were you?
	(0.1)
Danny:	Well, I- I was in bed, and u:hm (.) my wife and I were aslee:p, (0.2) tsk a:nd I would say the last couple weeks before that, ((sniff)) (.) I was getting a little tense. because I felt the Santa Monica earthquakes. =
Bob:	= Oh. see I was out of town for those.
Danny:	[yeah.
Bob:	[I was in Ohio. =
Danny:	= I [see
Bob:	[so I didn't even know:: (.) that the earthquakes had been [happening until
Danny:	[yeah.
Bob:	(0.1) the day I came ba:ck. And then the next day I think was the earthquake.
	(0.1)
Bob:	So,
Danny:	Yeah there was a little-

PRACTICE WITH CONVERSATION ANALYSIS IN OTHER LANGUAGES: JAPANESE

Review the following transcript in Japanese. The conversation has been transcribed using CA conventions for Japanese. Compare and contrast the turn-taking practices in Japanese with what you have found in English. Specifically note: how turns are constructed, how turns change, continuers (identify the types), assessments (identify the types), overlapping talk, and timing between turns. Do you note any instances of repair? Are they self-initiated or other initiated? What are some implications for cross-linguistic and cross-cultural analysis that might be relevant here?

Write an analysis that compares and contrasts Japanese conversational turn-taking practices with American English turn-taking practices, with a qualification that your analysis is based only on these few samples of discourse data (without access to the actual audio/video materials).

CALPER Japanese Project Transcript

Shokubunka1
((右からアヤ、シン、ノリとする。))

1. アヤ：あの、でも私がねニューヨークいったときは[、＝
2. ノリ：　　　　　　　　　　　　　　　　　　[うん。（うんうん。）
3. アヤ：＝すっごくその、寿司ブーム[だったから、だから：
4. ノリ：　　　　　　　　　　　　[あ：そう、そうなんだ。ほうほうほう（ほうほう
5. 　　　ほう）。
6. アヤ：なんか、あったよね？（　　　　　[　　　　　）巻いて。
7. ノリ：　　　　　　　　　　　　　　　[カリフォルニア巻き。ｈｈ[ｈ
8. アヤ：　　　　　　　　　　　　　　　　　　　　　　　　　　　[そうそう
9. 　　　そうそう。
10. シン：（へ：[：。）
11. アヤ：　　　[で、しかも日本食ってのがすごくヘルシーで：、健康にいいって
12. 　　　いうんで：、その、ヘルシーブームにのっとって、なんていうのかな、
13. 　　　すごくはやった時期があっ、て[ちょうどそのとき：にいったの：[：ね？＝
14. ノリ：　　　　　　　　　　　　　　[本（買った　　。）　　　　　　[（うんうん
15. 　　　うん。）

16. アヤ：＝そのときはね、その、いままでローフィッシュを食べるなんて習慣がないで
17. 　　　［しょ？
18. シン：［あ：：［、はいはいはい。
19. ノリ：　　　　　［う：：ん。
20. アヤ：それなのに：、そういうひ、人たちが、こうこぞって食べるっ［ていうのかなあ
21. ノリ：　　　　　　　　　　　　　　　　　　　　　　　　［へ：：、そう
22. 　　　だったん［（だ）。
23. アヤ：　　　　　［そう。あれはびっくりした。私もびっくりした。で回転寿司屋さんが
24. 　　　けっこうあるのよね？＝
25. ノリ：＝ふんふん［ふん。
26. アヤ：　　　　　［ニューヨークとか探しても。あと、ちゅうかりょ、　中華料理は
27. 　　　どこにでもあるかもしれ［ないけど。
28. ノリ：　　　　　　　　　　　　［うんうんうん。
29. アヤ：ま、スーパーとか行っても：、あの：、売ってるの。（1.0）
30. 　　　［照り焼きサーモンとかって書い、書いて［あるんだけどさ、
31. ノリ：［ふ：：ん。　　　　　　　　　　　　　［hhhhhh
32. アヤ：照り焼きサーモン？
33. ノリ：サーモンって照り焼き、サーモンhh［h
34. アヤ：　　　　　　　　　　　　　　　　［サーモン照り焼きしないで
35. 　　　しょ？とかおも：、思ったんだけど。日本食っていうのは：？（1.0）
36. 　　　［すごくもてはやされてて？うん。それは私もびっくりした。
37. ノリ：［へえ：：：：
38. ノリ：う：ん。
39. 　　　（2.4）
40. ノリ：（あ、そうか。）アメリカ人の味に合うように？照り焼きサーモンに
41. 　　　してあるんだよね？きっと［：。
42. アヤ：　　　　　　　　　　　　［かもね：：、私はおいしくなかった［けど：、それ。
43. ノリ：　　　　　　　　　　　　　　　　　　　　　　　　　　　［hhhhhh
44. アヤ：ものはためしと思って：、みんなが買ってるから：。
45. ノリ：hh
46. アヤ：買ってみよ：：うと思って［買ったけど、

47. ノリ：　　　　　　　　　　　　［hhhh

48. アヤ：［こ、これは食べられない。って私はおもっちゃった。

49. ノリ：［hh、hhhh

50. シン：あ：［：：

51. ノリ：　　　［hh、hh［h

52. アヤ：　　　　　　　　［やっぱり照り焼きはチキンでしょ：［って思って hh

53. ノリ：　　　　　　　　　　　　　　　　　　　　　　［hahaha

54. ノリ：う：：ん。

55. シン：それはあの：、慣れてくればおいしくなるかも？ってことですか？

56. アヤ：う：：ん。［かも：：：、そうかもね、そうだよそうだよ。

57. ノリ：　　　　　　［え、どういうこ- え？どういうこと、どういうこと。

58. シン：え、だ［から：ようはそれを買ってく人がいる。いっぱい［いるってだから＝

59. アヤ：　　　　　［や　　　　　　　　　　　　　　　　　　　　［う：：んだから

60. シン：＝向こうの人はそれが好き。ですよ［ね。

61. アヤ：　　　　　　　　　　　　　　　　　［たぶんね。その照り焼きっていうものが、

62. 　　　　おいしいんだ［ろうね。

63. ノリ：　　　　　　　　［う：：ん。

64. シン：あ：：［：

65. アヤ：　　　　［しょうゆであまからくこう：［：コーティングしてあるわけよね。＝

66. ノリ：　　　　　　　　　　　　　　　　　［ああ、ああ、

67. ノリ：＝だから、おんなじよね、中華も：、日本の中華と：、アメリカの中華と本場の

68. 　　　　中華は違う：わけじゃん。

69. シン：う：：［ん。そう。それはわかる。

70. ノリ：　　　［味が。だから

71. ノリ：う：：ん。その、照り焼きは：：、照り焼きサーモンはきっとアメリカ人の

72. 　　　　味に、にゅ＝ニューヨークの人の味にあわせてあるんだ［よ。

73. アヤ：　　　　　　　　　　　　　　　　　　　　　　　　　　　［う：：ん。

74. ノリ：はは：：：：ん。

SELECTED TRANSCRIPTION CONVENTIONS FOR CA

Adapted from Atkinson and Heritage (1984: ix–xvi) and Jefferson (2004).

TIMING

(.)	micro pause (for pauses less than 0.2 of a second)
(2.6)	timed pause (NOTE: The timing of pauses is based essentially on the saying of the expression "one one thousand" as equivalent to one second.)
[	overlapping speech (note if there is one bracket, there must be another bracket lined up vertically on the following line)

Example: Bob: It was rea:::^lly [great.
Tony: [oh wo::^w.

=	latched speech (immediately contiguous utterance, whether within a turn or between turns)
> <	compressed speech—"rush through" (faster than rest of speech)
< >	drawn out speech (slower than rest of speech)
(cat/calf)	uncertain hearing; transcriptionist cannot tell if it is one word or the other, both words could fit the context.
(candy)	Uncertain hearing; transcriptionist's best guess of what the word sounds like.
(( ))	Description of some background phenomenon, e.g., gestures, grimaces, behaviors of other co-present interactants, telephone ringing, etc.
They-	False start (e.g., y- she-?), truncated speech

Prosody and Other Paralinguistic Features

(h)	aspiration
(hh)	longer aspiration (this could also include laughter)
(hhh)	very long aspiration
and he said	emphasis, stress
a^nd he said	stronger emphasis, more prominent stress
•h	in-breath
•hh	longer in-breath
•hhh	very long in-breath
me:: / yes::	sound stretch (whether on vowels or consonants)
::	longer sound stretch (ditto, re: vowel or consonant)
:::	very long sound stretch (ditto)
~	nasalized speech (e.g., yey~)

WOW	upper case letters—increased volume
°darn°	decreased volume/whisper (word should be within two degree symbols)
.	falling intonation
?	strong rising intonation
,	slight rising intonation, continuing intonation
↑	marked rising intonation
↓	marked falling intonation
!	animated tone, not necessarily exclamation
→	horizontal arrows in the left-hand margin mark turns that are of interest to the analyst.
-x-	isolated single clap (e.g., audience: -x-)
xxXXXxx	string of Xs indicate applause. Lower case x marks quiet and uppercase X marks louder applause

SUGGESTIONS FOR FURTHER READING

Clift, R. and Helani, F. (2010). Inshallah: Religious invocations in Arabic topic transitions. *Language in Society*, 39,3: 357–82.

Golato, A. (2012). German oh, marking an emotional change of state. *Research on Language and Social Interaction*, 45,3: 245–68.

Hayashi, R. (1996). *Cognition, Empathy, and Interaction: Floor Management of English and Japanese Conversation*. Norwood, New Jersey: Ablex.

Heritage, J. and Raymond, G. (2005). The terms of agreement: Indexing epistemic authority and subordination in talk-in-interaction. *Social Psychology Quarterly,* 68: 15–38.

He, A. (2011). The role of repair in modulating modal stances in Chinese discourse. *Chinese Language & Discourse* 2,1: 1–22.

Hopper, R., and Chen, C. H. (1996). Languages, cultures, relationships: Telephone openings in Taiwan. *Research on Language & Social Interaction* 29,4: 291–313.

Katayama, H. (2002). Beyond "Change of State": "Oh" as a facilitator of teacher-student interactions in an ESL conversation class. In *Crossroads of Language, Interaction, and Culture*, vol. 4, pp. 19–32.

Kim, K. (2007). Sequential organization of post-predicate elements in Korean conversation: Pursuing uptake and modulating action. *Pragmatics*, 17, 4: 573–603.

Lazarton, A. (1997). Preference Organization in oral proficiency interviews: The case of language ability assessments. *Research on Language and Social Interaction*, 30,1: 53–72.

Levinson, S. (2005). Living with Manny's Dangerous Idea. *Discourse Studies*, 7(4–5): 431–53.

Luke, K. K. and Zhang, W. (2010). Insertion as a self-repair device and its interactional motivations in Chinese conversation. *Chinese Language & Discourse*, 1,2: 153–82.

Maynard, D. (2013). Everyone and no one to turn to: Intellectual roots and contexts for conversation analysis. In Sidnell, J. and Stivers, T. (Eds.) *The Handbook of Conversation Analysis.* Malden, MA: Wiley-Blackwell. pp. 11–31.

Mondada, L. (2009). The methodical organization of talking and eating: Assessments in dinner conversations. *Food Quality and Preference*, 20,8: 558–71.

Mori, J. and Hayashi, M. (2006). The achievement of intersubjectivity through embodied completions: A study of interactions between first and second language speakers. *Applied Linguistics,* 27,2: 195–219.

Saadeh, E. (2009). The 'How are you?' sequence in telephone openings in Arabic. *Studies in the Linguistic Sciences*: *Illinois Working Papers 2009*, 171–86.

Saft, S. (2007). Exploring *aizuchi* as resources in Japanese social interaction: The case of a political discussion program. *Journal of Pragmatics,* 39,7: 1290–1312.

Schegloff, E. (1996) Turn organization: One intersection of grammar and interaction. In Ochs, E., Schegloff, E., and Thompson, S. *Interaction and Grammar.* Cambridge: Cambridge University Press. pp. 52–133.

Strauss, S. (2005). Cognitive realization markers: A discourse-pragmatic study of the sentence ending particles—*kwun, -ney,* and *-tela. Language Sciences*, 27: 437–80.

Taleghani-Nikazm, C. (2002). A conversation analytical study of telephone conversation openings between native and nonnative speakers. *Journal of Pragmatics*, 34,12: 1807–32.

Wu, R. (2011). A conversation analysis of self-praising in everyday Mandarin interaction. *Journal of Pragmatics* 43,13: 3152–76.

Yoon, K. E. (2010). Questions and responses in Korean conversation. *Journal of Pragmatics*, 42,10: 2782–98.

LINKS

Coon, G. and Crawford, O. (Writers) and Taylor, J. (Director.) (1969, January 10). Let that be your last battlefield [Television series episode]. In G. Roddenberry (Producer), *Star Trek*. United States: CBS Television Distribution. Retrieved from: http://www.youtube.com/watch?v=Zi6iyPto254. Accessed on February 12, 2013.

Judge Judy. (n.d.). In *Wikipedia*. Retrieved from http://en.wikipedia.org/wiki/Judge_Judy. Accessed May 31, 2013.

NOTES

1. For a history and the basic principles of CA, see Sacks (1984) and Maynard (2013).
2. A "quarter" refers to the 10-week period of classwork, in contrast with a 15-week semester. Universities in the United States typically operate on a quarter system (i.e., three 10-week periods in an academic year) or a semester system (i.e., two 15-week periods in an academic year).
3. See Chapter 4 on demonstrative reference and Chapter 5 on reference (especially future-pointing, cataphoric reference) for a discussion on this semantic-pragmatic phenomenon from a different perspective.
4. See Ford, Fox, and Thompson (1996, 2002, 2003) and Fox (2001) for grammatical perspectives on conversation and language-in-interaction.
5. Some questions in English are not produced with rising intonation, most commonly, the so-called "wh-questions," e.g., *What time did you leave the office*? The punctuation required in conventional writing would be a question mark. In CA conventions, however, since the question mark indicates rising intonation, the TCU would end with a period, indicating falling intonation.
6. "Earthquake Stories" were collected in February, 1994 in Japanese (Iwasaki), Thai (Iwasaki; See Iwasaki and Horie, 1988), English (Strauss, 1994), and Korean (Strauss, 1994). Pseudonyms are used here in place of the participants' actual names and towns of residence.
7. See Chapter 7 on speech acts for brief discussion on cross-cultural expectations regarding speech acts and culturally appropriate responses to them. The production, meaning, and appropriate responses to such speech acts as invitations, apologies, expressions of thanks, offers, and compliments are very much culturally shaped.

CHAPTER SEVEN

Pragmatics

Implicature, Speech Act Theory, and Politeness

The domain of PRAGMATICS concerns the process whereby meanings richer than the encoded conventional meanings of signs arise in real contexts. Pragmatic meanings are semiotically accessible and/or logically derivable, but are not semantically encoded. They include contingent aspects of context and common ground (things one knows and things one can see and hear), on the one hand, and derived inferences on the other. Context and common ground constitute input for deriving inferences from encoded meanings . . . The term IMPLICATURE refers to the process or product of such inferences. Implicatures are contingent and context-dependent, arising from given common ground, including speakers' knowledge of the linguistic system and associated expectations of what a speaker 'could have said' but didn't. (Enfield, 2003b: 84; emphasis in original)

PRAGMATICS is the area of linguistic and sociolinguistic study that is concerned with the ways in which speakers/hearers and writers/readers (in any modality of discourse) both create and derive meaning from non-literal interpretations of discourse, while engaged in contextually situated interaction.

Concepts such as common ground[1], common knowledge, mutual orientation, inference, and implicature are key to the mutual creation, communication, and understanding of *meaning* in cases where *meaning is intended well beyond literal or objective meanings of the discursive spates in question*. The study of **conversational implicature, speech act theory,** and **politeness** falls squarely in the domain of PRAGMATICS.

PRAGMATICS is an important field of inquiry for disciplines that study human communication and social interaction, including education, business, communication, intercultural communication, interpersonal communication, linguistics, sociolinguistics, linguistic anthropology, and even phonetics and phonology.

In Chapter 6 on conversation analysis, we observed how participants in ongoing, spontaneous everyday talk orient themselves to emerging discourse on a microsecond-by-microsecond basis. We have examined the precise intricateness underlying turns, the construction and sequencing of turns, and the mutually collaborative coordination of talk, as speakers and their interlocutors exchange ideas, share stories, argue, complain, criticize, and compliment. And they do so in ways that are systematically organized, such that interactants intuitively manage conversational exchange by holding and expanding a turn in progress, responding to immediately prior turns of others, and predicting and projecting the quality and content of talk yet to be uttered by their interlocutors. Interaction is thus both "context free and capable of extraordinary context-sensitivity" (Sacks, Schegloff, and Jefferson 1974: 699), where "context" is built only through the talk as it unfolds, as turns are constructed as actions and then responded to by interlocutors' next actions—in overlap, upon immediate completion, with delay or hesitation, or not responded to at all. Context, then, as viewed from a CA perspective, does not include such issues as the individual identities of the speakers, the relationships between and among them, their interactional histories, configurations of the room in which the talk takes place, ambient lighting or noise, climate or seasons or happenings in the world, unless such issues are made relevant in the ongoing talk.

In sharp contrast, context is key to the field of pragmatics. As we will see in this chapter, central to an understanding of pragmatics are the related notions of interactants' shared common ground and mutual knowledge. In place of "talk as action," as a primary construct in CA, we will examine the pragmatic notion of "discourse as ground for implicit meaning" where interactants in discourse make sense of the world on the basis of inference and implicature. Where CA is context-free, pragmatics is context-dependent.

In this chapter, we will introduce some of the key sub-areas within the field of pragmatics: inference, implicature, speech act theory, and politeness. We will examine the interactional process of sense-making through inference and implicature by focusing on how implicit discursive meaning involves *intended implications* by discourse producers, in conjunction with the discourse recipients' expectations to *infer* those intended meanings, in other words, to "fill in the gaps." This implication-inference exchange between discourse producers and discourse recipients is a natural facet of our daily communication—in speech, in writing, and through digital mediation. For the purpose of this chapter, we will limit the focus of pragmatics to the following areas:

- Inference and conversational implicature
- Speech acts
- Politeness and deference
- Cross-cultural implications (speech acts, face)

We begin with a discussion of inference and implicature and observe the mechanisms by which intended yet unspoken meanings are "filled in" by interlocutors and readers through a look at one of the classic approaches to pragmatics, Grice's maxims. We then introduce speech act theory, examining such speech acts as complaints, compliments, requests, challenges, directives, and invitations, in addition to ways in which such speech acts might be responded to. We interweave Gricean concepts of conversational cooperation and implicature with basic tenets of speech act theory as a foundation to the concept of politeness. We introduce the phenomenon of politeness as viewed through a number of theoretical lenses, and observe the various ways in which politeness is defined and analyzed both theoretically and empirically. We then turn our discussion of pragmatics to humor, jokes, and irony, using a Relevance Theoretical perspective. We conclude the chapter by noting the robust cultural implications surrounding the topic of pragmatics, particularly in connection with concepts of directness and indirectness, face, and politeness.

Inference and Implicature: Grice's Maxims

Key Notions: Inference and Conversational Implicature

INFERENCE refers to the process by which hearers and readers construct meaning beyond what is literally provided in the language. Inference involves making connections between pronouns and their intended referents, between words and ideas, in ways that are more concept-central than language- or structure-central. Inference and inference making crosscuts all modalities of discourse.

CONVERSATIONAL IMPLICATURE refers to the interactional process of meaning-making through implication and inference. Such **inferences** arise from the **content** of the discourse, the **context** of the discourse and the **mutual assumptions** required to be made (or already pre-supposed) between speakers and hearers (and certain readers and writers). Participants in discourse share information, stances, and knowledge in varying degrees. When speakers speak and writers write, they make choices concerning the sufficiency of information required to convey a *particular idea* in such a way that a *particular hearer* or a *particular reader* will be able to *make sense of it* and adequately *fill in the gaps* on his or her own— not providing too much information, not providing too little information, providing relevant connections, and expressing content and ideas clearly.

Meaning has been a core topic within this book. We have looked at meaning from the points of view of literal meaning, grammatical meaning, conceptual meaning, information structure, and meaning as an instance of collaborative construction through conversational turns and social actions.

In this chapter, the focus of discussion shifts from what is *said* in discourse, to what is *unsaid*—in other words, to inference, implicature, and pragmatic meaning.

For starters, let's take some common expressions in English, like the following:

"Last one in is a rotten egg!"
"Can you give me a hand?"
"Look, I didn't just fall off the turnip truck."
"He's up to no good."
"Hit me!"

It should be superficially obvious that none of these expressions would sound natural if taken literally—some would be absurd (e.g., 'What if I **am** last and I morph into a putrefying ovum?') and some could cause physical pain (e.g., 'Hit me!'—ouch!, or 'I fell off of it about six weeks ago, and those purple tubers conked me on the head as I was going down!'). Beyond the literal, though, each expresses a particular kind of speech act: a *challenge to race* toward and jump into a swimming pool, a *request for* a small bit of *physical help*, a *declaration* that a person is *not naïve or gullible*, a *prediction* about the moral character of a designated individual, and a *gambling-based directive* for a player to request one more card from a dealer in the hopes of achieving a "Blackjack" (i.e., a score of 21 points).

Scenarios of various types could be imagined in which each of these expressions might be uttered. In order for them to make sense, a particular *context* would be necessary, as would a particular set of *interactants*, each of whom would be expected to be able to draw certain inferences on the basis of the utterance and its context and to then respond accordingly. Making inferences requires a sharedness of common ground, some degree of mutual knowledge between and among participants that enable them to communicate and interact beyond the literal, beyond what is straightforward and explicit.

In this sense, pragmatics is indeed context-dependent. Speakers and hearers involved in conversation and other socially situated interaction share orientations toward meaning which allow them to interact beyond the literal—to read between the lines, so to speak, to fill in what was not said by making assumptions about intended messages. Seminal work on this phenomenon includes Grice's (1975, 1989) notion of the **cooperative principle,** a core philosophical notion pointing to the maximally efficacious means of using language in conversation and social situations, by saying what should be said at a particular point in time, in a socio-culturally appropriate way, by observing how words and utterances are exchanged in oral interaction and mutual understanding, Grice (1975/1989) identified this principle of cooperation and further categorized its mechanisms into four basic maxims, which, in isolation and in combination with each other, were determined to serve as a basis for efficient and mutually collaborative sharing of information and the expression of personal stance toward people, events, conversation topics, and the like.

The cooperative principle goes like this: "Make your conversational contribution such as is required, at the stage at which it occurs, by the accepted purpose or direction of the talk exchange in which you are engaged" (1989: 26). The maxims are summarized, and adapted, in the following table:

Essentially, the gist of Grice's maxims can be encapsulated as follows: For conversation to be maximally efficient, participants' contributions should be "just right" in terms of amount—not too much and not too little. Contributions

---

The cooperative principle—Grice's maxims (adapted)

A. Maxims of Quantity: *Not too little, not too much.*
   1. Make your contribution as informative as required (for the current purposes of the exchange).
   2. Don't make your contribution more informative than is required.

B. Maxims of Quality: The essential element of quality is TRUTH.
   1. Don't say what you believe to be false.
   2. Don't say what you lack evidence for.

C. Maxim of Relation: Be relevant.

D. Maxims of Manner: Be perspicuous.
   1. Avoid obscurity of expression.
   2. Avoid ambiguity.
   3. Be brief (avoid unnecessary prolixity).
   4. Be orderly.

---

should be truthful. They should make sense in relation to something else in the conversation or context (either explicitly or implicitly), and they should not be obscure nor illogically ordered.

Let's have a look at an example to illustrate the **cooperative principle**:

Think about the maxims of QUANTITY, RELEVANCE, AND MANNER.

Invented scenario 1:

((A history student arrives out of breath to his lecture hall five minutes later than class was supposed to have started. He finds one student sitting in an aisle seat, scribbling some notes. Besides that one student, the classroom is empty.))

| | Entering student A: | What time is it? |
| → | Seated student B: | The prof called in sick. |

A number of context-based inferences can be made in Invented Scenario 1. Student A arrives late and finds only one other student, B, in the lecture hall of a regularly scheduled university class. Student A silently considers a number of possibilities and utters a single statement expressing an assumption that the timekeeping device(s) he was relying on may have been out of order. He was either very, very late and class had already both met *and* adjourned or he was so very early that no one else had shown up as yet. A's question reflects his assumption that it was his *timing* that was off (not that he went to class *on the wrong day* or that he was in the *wrong room*) and poses the question to confirm, implying this very hypothesis. His interlocutor, Student B, the only other individual present, inferred this assumption, responding with a pragmatically appropriate, contextually relevant response—not too detailed, not too scanty, true, and clear. He implied, in turn, that student A should not worry. He is in the right place, but class was cancelled because the instructor was ill.

We find a similar conversational phenomenon in the next example:

Think about the maxims of QUANTITY, RELEVANCE, AND MANNER.

Invented Scenario 2:   (From Levinson, 1983: 102)

                    A. Where's Bill?

→   B. There's a yellow VW outside Sue's house.

In Invented Scenario 2, speaker A asks B about the whereabouts of Bill, a third individual presumably known to both A and B. B responds in a way that might, at first blush, appear cryptic, but which does answer the question by virtue of association (Bill owns a yellow Volkswagen) and inference (what appears to be Bill's car is parked just outside the home of another known individual, Sue) and implicature (You asked where Bill is and I have this bit of evidence that points to the strong possibility that he may be at Sue's house because a car that looks like his is parked in front of it).

In both scenarios, Speaker A poses a question with the intent of receiving a response from Speaker B. In each case, one might consider the contributions by Speaker B as non-conforming to three maxims, if taken literally: quantity, relevance, and manner. That is, "The prof called in sick" and "There's a yellow VW outside Sue's house" are both, in and of themselves, *atypical responses* to questions such as "What time is it?" on the one hand, and "Where's Bill?" on the other. However, given the context and the presumed degree of shared information and mutual knowledge between each pair of speakers, it is not difficult to discern the inferential mechanisms by which the interactional pairs construct meaning in a cooperative fashion, beyond the literal.

In pragmatics, context is key. Mutual knowledge and shared information are crucial. As Enfield (2003b) notes in the opening quotation, pragmatic meanings and conversational implicatures are not *semantically* encoded (emphasis added). That is, the **inferences** arise from the **content** of the talk, the **context** of the talk, and the **mutual assumptions** between the interactants concerning the nature of information required to convey a *particular idea* in such a way that *a particular interlocutor* will be able to *make sense of it* and adequately fill in the gaps on his or her own (see also Levinson, 1983: 104.)

Essentially, if we <u>change the context</u>, we also <u>automatically change the relevance</u>. The category of <u>manner</u> also changes, rendering the response lines obscure at the very least, if not downright absurd, as we illustrate here. The B responses are marked with *, to indicate their pragmatic unacceptability.

Think about the maxims of QUANTITY, RELEVANCE, AND MANNER.

Invented scenario 1 (with changed context):

((Two passengers are seated side by side on an airplane. The landing gear is down and the plane has been descending smoothly, seemingly well ahead of schedule.))

    Passenger A: What time is it?
→ *Passenger B: The prof called in sick.

Invented Scenario 2 (with changed context):

((A couple is at dinner on a Mediterranean cruise ship, en route to Malta. There is one empty seat at their table.))

    Wife: Where's Bill?
→ *Husband: There's a yellow VW outside Sue's house.

So, as we observe, <u>changing the context</u> absolutely changes the *relevance* of an utterance, and it also greatly affects the *manner*. Here, the responses in B make no logical sense, because the *context* provides no logical basis for the establishment of implicatures surrounding quantity, quality, relevance or manner.

Now, let's examine a longer spate of interaction in which speakers purposely violate (or flout) Grice's maxims as they collaboratively build on each other's talk through implicature and the cooperative principle.

Scenario 3 is an excerpt from Season 1, Episode 1 of the BBC television series *Merlin*. This episode, and thus the entire series, opens as Merlin, a young man in his teens or early twenties, enters Camelot for the first time. King Uther Pendragon is denouncing magic and "the evil of sorcery." Within seconds of these words, a commoner, guilty of magic, is publicly executed. Merlin, too, has magic. For him, it is a rare and innate gift, and one that must be kept secret if he wants to live.

The segment that we provide here takes place as Merlin leaves the execution site and enters the castle, in search of Gaius, the court physician. Merlin opens the door to Gaius's room, looks around slowly, and then finds Gaius (an old man with white hair and wrinkled face) in the upper level apothecary loft arranging vials and jars. Gaius is startled by Merlin's sudden and unexpected appearance in his room. Gaius steps backward, snapping the wooden support rails, and he begins to fall, back-first toward the ground. He is saved by Merlin's quick thinking and telekinetic power.

Think about all four maxims: QUANTITY, QUALITY (truthfulness), RELEVANCE, and MANNER.

Scenario 3—*Merlin*, Season 1, Episode 1: "The Dragon's Call"

Merlin: Gaius? ((softly)) achem ((clearing his throat to call gentle attention))

((Gaius turns around and starts to fall in SLOW MOTION, music in background. MERLIN'S EYES CHANGE TO YELLOW as he TELEKINETICALLY slides Gaius's bed to the place just below his downward floating body. NORMAL FILM SPEED resumes. Gaius falls faster and crashes onto his now relocated bed.))

Gaius: What did you just do?
Merlin: Uh::m.
Gaius: Tell me!
Merlin: I uh uh I have no idea what happened.
Gaius: If anyone has seen **that**. . .?
Merlin: No. uhm **That- That- That** was nothing to do with me. **That- That-**

Gaius:	I know what **it** was. I just want to know where you learned how to do **it.**
Merlin:	Nowhere.
Gaius:	So, how is it you know <u>magic</u>?
Merlin:	I don't.
Gaius:	Where did you study?
	((silence))
Gaius:	Answer me!
Merlin:	um- uh- uh I haven't studied magic or been taught.
Gaius:	Are you lying to me, boy?
Merlin:	What do you want me to say?
Gaius:	The truth!
Merlin:	I was born like this.
Gaius:	That's impossible!
	((silence))

(Jones and Hawes, 2008)

The excerpt is rich in conversational implicature. Of the four maxims, the one that is most blatantly flouted by Merlin is that of QUALITY. That is, Merlin cannot be truthful, literally, to save his life.

More broadly, though, we find the interplay in the collaborative and mutual flouting of the maxims of quantity, quality, and manner as a means to protect a young man's secret—one that could be deadly. Both Gaius and Merlin know what just happened. Gaius is shocked at the way in which his bed appeared just below him at just the right time, and he is relieved to have not been injured. Merlin is scared, having done what he had to do, while risking the revelation of a dangerous secret. Both characters consciously and deliberately avoid naming the phenomenon, avoid talking about it perspicuously, explicitly, and succinctly, until such time that they have established the mutual trust to be able to be honest with each other. Gaius' question "What did you just do?" is not a literal one. Instead, as we come to see, the implicature is dually "How (on earth) did you just move my bed and where (on earth) did you learn how?"

Merlin denies not only his power, but the knowledge of his power, thereby absolutely flouting the maxim of quality ('I have no idea what happened'). It is an outright lie. Both Gaius and Merlin continue to build mutual trust through the step-by-step process of what might appear as a flouting of the maxim of manner—using vague and imprecise references with pronouns "that" and "it"

(G: 'If anyone has seen **that**') (M: '**That** has nothing to do with me' and G: 'I know what **it** was . . . where you learned how to do **it**'). However, while potentially "vague," none of the tokens of "that" or "it" is ambiguous. Each speaker knows precisely what the other is referring to. In that sense, the maxim of quantity is upheld and observed with precision. Both characters exhibit an underlying yet unspeakable sharedness of information, a mutual recognition of what just did occur, but neither utters the word, neither labels the phenomenon, until some small degree of trust has been established by these two strangers, assuring that Merlin will remain safe in Camelot, in spite of this mutual secret.

The implicature exchange continues. Gaius puts a name to the happening ("So how is it you know <u>magic</u>?"). Merlin's reply is responsive not to the word "magic" but to the word "know." That is, in upholding all four maxims, Merlin utters but two words—succinctly, truthfully, relevantly, and perspicuously: "I don't." The implicature carried by these two words can be summed up like this: "I don't *know* magic, I just *do* magic." And we learn in the next few lines that such is the case.

Grice's contribution to the disciplines of philosophy, linguistics, pragmatics, and communication contributed much to our understanding of language in context and interaction. See Brown and Levinson (1987), Horn (1984, 2004), Huang (2006), Levinson (2000), Sadock (1974), Searle (1975), Sauerland and Stateva (2007), Sperber and Wilson (1986), Wierzbicka (2003), among others, for discussions and applications of Grice's maxims.

SPEECH ACTS

Speech Acts and Speech Act Theory

SPEECH ACTS are the basic units of communication in which utterances or spates of discourse are viewed as *social acts that fulfill social functions*. Speech acts are produced (and understood) in at least three different ways: as **locutionary act,** expressing propositional content or information *just by virtue of saying something;* as **illocutionary act,** the *interactional function* of the utterance itself (as a speech act, e.g., a request, a demand, a question, a complaint, an invitation, an apology); and as **perlocutionary act,** when change takes place as a result of a speaker having produced a speech act and a hearer having understood it (as in granting the request and causing a related contextual change to occur, ameliorating the situation underlying the complaint and causing a related contextual change to occur, and so forth.

Essentially, **any utterance in discourse is a speech act:** statements of truth, informing, requests, questions (information-seeking, display, rhetorical), apologies, promises, invitations, complaints, criticisms, praise, thanks, congratulations, declarations of war or peace, calls of "out" or "safe" (baseball), designations of a player as "it" in a game of tag, bets, challenges, etc.

As we have observed throughout this book, words and utterances do not simply name or describe objects or events or states. When we utter something, we often are not simply providing informational content or expressing the truth about something or taking a stand that involves our commitment to the truth of a proposition. Philosopher John Langshaw Austin pointed out this very perceptive observation of language (or more precisely, of discourse) in his 1962 book, *How to Do Things With Words*.[2] Austin observed, for example, that words and utterances, when said by the proper person(s) under the proper conditions, can actually change reality. Under certain circumstances, saying can indeed "make it so" (Austin, 1962: 7), as in the following types of institutionally conventionalized expressions:

"I now **pronounce** you man and wife."
"I **christen** this ship *The Beluga*."
"I hereby **appoint** and **ordain** Philip Mazzoris, Esq., Executor of my last will and testament.

Austin refers to the verbs in the previous statements as *performative verbs*, i.e., verbs that name their very actions of speaking. In these cases, the labeling of the action coincides with the reality of that action coming true (pronounce, christen, appoint, ordain). Other performative verbs in English that name the speech act are: *apologize, promise, bet, thank, warn, declare, quit, resign, dub,* and *excommunicate*.

Austin's breakthrough refutation of the commonly held notion in philosophy that "to say something . . . is always and simply to *state* something" (1962: 12), paved the way for newer ways of thinking about language, discourse, and context.[3] Thanks to linguistics and philosophy scholars like

Austin (1962, 1979), Searle (1969, 1975), and Searle and Vanderveken (1985) it became increasingly clear that the speech act category of *assertions*, the category by which a proposition is claimed to be true, is actually far richer as a category for investigation than it seems; an assertion is more than a "speaker's commitment to the truth of a proposition" or a speaker's act of providing propositional content. Assertions of any kind are actually not simply expressions of what we claim or commit to be true. Some categorical assertions, as we saw, are in fact, *performatives*. Some *performatives* uttered under the right circumstances can change reality simply by their having been uttered. The production of any utterance within a context is doing far more than just "uttering" or "stating" or "asserting." See Levinson (1983: 276–277) for a detailed discussion of assertions and speech acts. See also Gazdar (1979, 1981), Garcia-Carpintero (2004), MacFarlane (2005), Pagin (2004), Stalnaker (1978), and Watson (2004) for philosophical discussion of "assertions."

> *"My steak is pink inside."*

To illustrate further, let's look at the foregoing surface level assertion: From the point of view of propositional content, the utterance means what it says: The color of the meat on the inside is pink. The truth of the statement is easily verifiable. One just has to look.

However, the likelihood that an interlocutor would produce such an assertion (*as* an assertion) in a situated context with the intended meaning solely to point out the color of a specific cut of meat is remote.

In context, such a statement could take on a rather wide range of different possible functions, hence different possible speech acts.

- A *complaint* by a restaurant patron who had ordered his meat well-done
- A *compliment* to the chef and/or server
- A *criticism* of the chef and/or server
- An *expression of relief* by a restaurant patron whose meat was cooked exactly to his preference, but who'd worried that it might turn out well-done
- A sideways *request* to have the meat returned to the kitchen

By changing the determiner from **My** steak is pink inside to **This** steak *is pink inside,* even more potential scenarios and intended speech acts are made possible. Try to expand this list of meanings and corresponding speech acts and see how circumstances change.

As Austin (1962: 101) notes: "saying something will often, or even normally, produce certain consequential effects upon the feelings, thoughts, or actions of the audience . . . or other persons." He proposes a three-way hierarchical system of categorizing speech acts, from the meaning-based act of saying or stating propositional content (locutionary act), to the production of the speech act itself (illocutionary act), to the effect or change brought about as a result of that speech act (perlocutionary act). We have summarized these:

Locutionary act:	The act of uttering, stating, saying; the surface level. "This steak is pink inside." (*meaning*)
Illocutionary act:	The speech act of that utterance; what it is intended to do. "This steak is pink inside" as compliment, complaint, criticism, assertion, bribe, or declaration (*force*)
Perlocutionary act:	The consequential effect brought about by virtue of the speech act; the change brought about through the utterance of the speech act. "This steak is pink inside." → Server takes the dish back to the kitchen. (*effect*)

Speech act hierarchy: from meaning to force to effect (adapted from Austin, 1962: 120)

For Austin (1962: 120), the locutionary act is based in *meaning*, the illocutionary act (the speech act) "has a certain *force* in saying something, and the perlocutionary act [involves] the *achieving* of certain *effects* by saying something." Essentially, the system illustrates the progression from <u>*saying words*</u> to *actually* <u>doing things with words</u>.

Let's analyze the hierarchical differences using this utterance:

> *There's smoke coming from Bob's kitchen window.*

- As a **locutionary act** it is an assertion. The speaker is putting into words her observation of an ongoing event, which she claims to be true.
- As an **illocutionary act**, the intended force of the utterance (from among many possibilities—try to extend this list on your own):

  o <u>An exclamation</u> of panic or worry: "I hope he's okay!"
  o <u>A warning</u>: "Stay back! It could be dangerous!"

    o   <u>An appeal for help</u>: "See if he's alright!" "Call 911!" "Get the hose!"

    o   <u>A complaint</u>: "And he thinks we can't smell his cigars from here!"

- As a **perlocutionary act,** a change (or set of changes) takes place because of the speech act—the recipient of the speech act responds in multiple possible ways:

    o   comforting the speaker, expressing empathy

    o   heeding the warning and proceeding with caution

    o   checking on Bob, calling 911, getting the hose or fire extinguisher, putting out the fire

    o   reminding Bob that his cigar smoke is entering others' windows

Searle's Five Categories of Speech Acts

The analytic unit of the speech act is useful in the study of discourse and pragmatics (Cohen and Perrault, 1979; Flowerdew, 1991; Hackman, 1977; Holmes, 1984; Sbisa, 2001; Schegloff, 1988; van Dijk, 1977; van Eemeren and Grootendorst, 1984, 2004). The speech act categories most often appealed to today were first proposed by John Searle in his seminal (1976) article, "A Classification of Illocutionary Acts," outlining five basic categories of speech acts for which he provides clear-cut classificatory criteria: Representatives, Directives, Commissives, Expressives, and Declarations.[4]

Searle's system is actually responsive to Austin's (1962) taxonomy, which is also based on five categories: Verdictives (*acquit, rank, assess*), Exercitives (*veto, dismiss, proclaim*), Commissives (*vow, pledge, promise*), Expositives (*deny, emphasize, concede*), and Behabitives (*apologize, thank, commiserate*).[5] Searle's primary criticism rests on the fact that Austin's taxonomy pinpoints not the illocutionary acts themselves, but "English illocutionary verbs." Recall that Austin's initial observations centered on *performatives*, i.e., the type of verbs that both label the speech act and change reality as a result of carrying it out. Observe the verbal exemplars noted for each of Austin's five categories.

Further, with the exception of Commissives, Searle finds Austin's taxonomy unclear and vague, lacking appropriate criteria for characterizing illocutionary acts as belonging to one category or another (see Austin, 1962; Levinson, 1983; Mey, 2001; Searle, 1975, 1976, 1979; and Searle and Vandereken, 1985, for more discussion).

Next we summarize Searle's (1976) five categories of illocutionary acts. Note that Searle has retained Austin's original category heading of Commissive (though he has altered the definition). The remaining category headings and criteria for each are significantly different.

> **Representatives** (1976: 10) commit the speaker to something being the case, to the truth of a proposition.
>
> > Examples: *asserting, reporting, informing, claiming, fact stating*
>
> **Directives** (1976: 11) involve attempts by a speaker to get a hearer to do something.
>
> > Examples: *requesting, suggesting, commanding, asking, ordering, questioning, seeking confirmation, seeking information, how-to-instructions, rhetorical questions*
>
> **Commissives** (1976: 11–12) commit the speaker to some future course of action.
>
> > Examples: *promising, vowing, swearing, threatening, pledging, offering*
>
> **Expressives** (1976: 12–13) express the speaker's psychological or emotional state.
>
> > Examples: *apologizing, welcoming, congratulating, thanking, cheering*
>
> **Declarations** (1976: 13–14) result in the immediate change of a circumstance or official state of affairs.
>
> > Examples: *resigning, firing, hiring, excommunicating, declaring war, appointing, bequeathing, christening, ordaining, establishing an official role*

We illustrate with a few examples.

UTTERANCE	SPEECH ACT TYPE
I'll call you tomorrow.	**Commissive** *promise, offer*
Shake well. Take with food.	**Directive** *How-to instructions*
—I'm sorry your birthday present is late.	**Expressive** *apology*

—That's okay. I loved it.	**Expressive** *acceptance of apology; thanks*
Tonight's debate comes on the 50th anniversary of the night that President Kennedy told the world that the Soviet Union had installed nuclear missiles in Cuba.	**Representative** *introducing/informing*
How many water molecules does it take to make ice?	**Directive** *information-seeking question*
You're it! (in a game of tag)	**Declaration** *role assignment*

Illustration of Searle's (1976) five types of speech acts

The foregoing discussion on speech acts points to those speech acts in which there is a recognizable form that designates one speech act category or another. That is, an **imperative** is easily associated with the speech act of **directives** (e.g., *Refrigerate after opening, Say hello to your Uncle Patrick*). The use of the **first person singular pronoun,** *I*, with **future-expressing modals** (e.g., *will, shall*) is typically associated with **commissives**, as they have the ring of a promise or a future commitment (*I'll check on that and will get back to you*). Expressions of **thanks or apologies** or **outbursts of joy,** also involving first person singular subject *I* and present tense, typically associate with **expressives** (*I am so sorry, Congratulations on your graduation*). **Performative verbs** like *resign, excommunicate, bequeath,* and *dub,* that change official or relational states of affairs, associate with **declarations**.

Indirect Speech Acts

While some speech acts are identifiable on the surface through lexicon, syntax, and literal interpretation as intending a particular type of social function, many are not. As we have illustrated, some assertions or declarative statements actually serve a different social function. We used these two examples.

> *My steak is pink inside.*
> *There's smoke coming from Bob's kitchen window.*

Each *could* be an instance of the category **representative.** Each is a declarative statement, an assertion. However, the *functions* of each statement, as noted in the earlier section, are clearly not to simply inform or impart information. They could be **expressives** (as criticism, praise, or panic) or they could be **directives,** such that an interlocutor is asked to do something (e.g., take the steak back or call the fire department). Interpretation and meaning construal in cases like these would depend upon such features of **context** as the participants, the activity they are engaged in at the time of the utterance, the location of the activity, qualities of how the speech act was uttered in terms of **prosody** (tone of voice, rate of speech, emphatically intoned words), **gestures**, **facial expressions**, and so forth.

Searle (1975: 60) provides these examples to illustrate—one is a syntactic question and the other is a declarative statement. Both are speech acts of *requests*, falling into the larger category of **directives.**

> *Can you reach the salt?*
> Surface level: question   →   social function: REQUEST
>
> *I would appreciate it if you would get off my foot.*
> Surface level: assertion   →   social function: REQUEST

Here are a few more examples. As you read through them, think about their literal meanings and their surface level forms (e.g., declarative

---

Excerpt 1: Email Advertisement from Sears Department Store

(Email received April 30, 2013; Mother's Day is May 12, 2013)

"We've got the perfect PJs to complement the downtime Mom's been craving: new two-piece sets in the hottest spring trends that were definitely worth the wait. (PHOTOS and PRICING follow)

"Sears" <rewards@rewards.shopyourwayrewards.com>
(Sears, personal communication, April 30, 2013)

statement [assertion], use of modals, register, etc.). Then, try to determine the *functions* of these statements. Why do you think they take the form that they do?

There is a good bit that one could analyze in the partial ad copy provided in Excerpt 1. However, just focusing on speech acts, while the form of the discourse is superficially an assertive (appearing as a declarative sentence) or potentially falling within the **representative** category, the *function* is actually that of a **directive.** Sears wants dads or adult partners and kids to pick a thoughtful gift for the Mom of the house for Mother's Day—Sears's perfect pajamas. It is at once a gift suggestion and an "action" suggestion: "Buy this perfect gift here."

Excerpt 2: Call for Proposals for the 2013 Meeting of the <u>Language and Social Interaction Working Group (LANSI)</u>

(excerpt)

Deadline for electronic submission is May 30, 2013.

Notification of acceptance or non-acceptance will be sent via email by July 15, 2013.

Questions can be sent to: lansi@tc.columbia.edu

In Excerpt 2, we find three sentences, each taking the form of an assertion, but each achieving different speech act functions:

Deadline for electronic submission is May 30, 2013 is a **directive,** functioning as a *command*. This is a hard and fast rule. If submissions are not received by the deadline, they will be automatically rejected.

Notification of acceptance or non-acceptance will be sent via email by July 15, 2013 is actually a **commissive**. It is a statement by the conference organizers committing themselves to the action of notification of review results by or before a specified date.

Questions can be sent to: lansi@tc.columbia.edu is also a **directive,** functioning as a *conditional suggestion* or *invitation* for prospective participants to request additional information or clarification. It expresses *permission* on the part of the conference organizers to submit inquiries. It is a *conditional suggestion* in the sense that it actually means: "*if you have questions, please send them to . . .*" See Levinson (1983) and Gazdar (1981) for discussion of indirect speech acts from the perspective of the **literal force hypothesis** (or LFH).

The So-Called Felicity Conditions

Now, you are probably wondering about some of the following issues as they apply to speech acts:

- Do speech acts always accomplish what their producers hope they accomplish?
- Aren't there certain contextual conditions by which only designated producers of speech acts are entitled to produce them? (e.g., a boss to a subordinate, a subordinate to a boss, an ordained minister to particular members of a congregation or as part of a religious rite, players of specific games—board games, online games, sports).

Our answers to these questions are NO to the first question and YES to the second. Using Austin (1962) and Searle (1975) as foundations, scholars in disciplines such as communication, applied linguistics, philosophy, anthropology, and business have proposed sets of contextually situated conditions that must hold in order for a speech act to be 'felicitous,' in other words, for it to achieve what it is designed to achieve. See Austin (1962); Cook (1989); Levinson (1983); Searle (1969); Searle and Vanderveken (1985).

These conditions are summarized as follows[6]:

- The speech act must follow the conventions of the society for that particular speech act in order for it to be understood as such by the hearer.
- The speaker must be sincere—intends to, is able to, and has the institutional or individual power to carry out the speech act (for commissives and declarations).
- The speaker must be sincere—wants the hearer to carry out the requested action (for directives).
- The speaker must be sincere and truthful concerning the propositional content of the speech acts (for representatives, directives, commissives, expressives, and declarations).
- The hearer must be able to understand the intended meaning of the speech act and be able to carry out the action expected of him or her.
- There must be uptake on the part of the hearer for some speech acts to be felicitous, e.g., a bet. If there is no uptake with a bet, for example, then there is no bet.

Have a look at the following two transcripts from television commercials aired in the United States over the past decade. One is a commercial for the Royal Bank of Scotland (RBS). The second is for FedEx Office. Both are humorous and quite creative. And both are structured on the basis of felicitous and infelicitous speech acts. The dialogues, as written, might actually be a bit more complex than they appear at first glance. Try to conduct a full analysis of each using the basic tenets of speech act theory.

- Note how the questions in the excerpts are posed and how they are answered.
- Try to identify the various types of speech acts (not just the broad categories, e.g., **directives,** but the actual functions that the speech acts fulfill, e.g., *formulaic, institutional question; information-seeking question; rhetorical question*).
- Locate indirect speech acts and categorize them in the same way as previously done.
- Discuss the source of humor as built entirely around speech acts and the basic tenets of speech act theory.

TV Commercial 1: The Royal Bank of Scotland, "Less Talk. Make It Happen."

A man and woman are facing the priest on a pulpit in a church. The camera moves from attendee to attendee, showing their reactions— they are clearly moved by the ceremony.

Priest: **Do you Morgan Ambrose Roberts take this woman** ((eye gaze to the bride)) **to be your lawful wedded wife?**

((There is a pause, and then, the groom speaks))

Morgan: **Of course, that very much depends on what you mean by the question "Do you?"** Forward looking statements involve risk and uncertainties. . . . ((soliloquy continues)) **Who amongst us will ever [know?**

And then, another man in attendance at the wedding rises and states, **"I do,"** even before Morgan has finished the final question in his soliloquy.

This man comes up to the pulpit, and stands where Morgan had been standing, right next to the bride. He takes her hand.

Priest: **I now pronounce you man and wife. =You may kiss the bride**.

(Royal Bank of Scotland, 2004)

As you work on the analysis of this transcript, note the relevant plays on words, and especially the mechanism by which the man's response, "I do," emerges in the discourse. What are the speech acts at work here? What is the source of humor with reference to these plays on words and their connections with speech acts?

Here is another example, taken from an older television commercial for FedEx Office. We have paraphrased the dialogue so that each line describes the content of the dialogue, rather than the lines in the way in which they were delivered. Read through the paraphrased version and transform each line into direct dialogue. For example:

PARAPHRASE:	DIRECT DISCOURSE:
The boss provides a short apology and then tells his subordinate, Stan, that he is fired.	"I'm sorry to tell you this, Stan, but you're fired."
Stan responds that the boss can't fire him:	"You can't fire me."
Boss asks why not?	"_____" . . . and so forth

Now, transform the full text into direct dialogue and then identify each speech act by type and category.

What types of speech acts do you find? How would you categorize them? Do you find both direct and indirect speech acts? What line would represent the indirect speech act? How does the interaction change as the directness of speech act changes? That is, what types of meaning are conveyed by

---

TV Commercial 2: FedEx Office (paraphrased variation)

Two men are in an office by a desk.

- The boss provides a short apology and then tells his subordinate, Stan, that he is fired.
- Stan responds that the boss can't fire him.
- Boss asks why not?
- Stan responds that he has quit.
- The boss tells Stan that he cannot quit.
- Stan asks why not?
- The boss responds that he had already fired him.
- Stan tells the boss that he'd decided to quit the day before that.
- The boss tells Stan that he'd decided to fire him the day before Stan had decided to quit.
- Stan gives the boss some news: He has started using FedEx Office and this could save the company money.
- The boss agrees and asks Stan when he could start.
- Stan says he could start today.
- The boss welcomes Stan aboard.

---

the indirect speech act that might not be possible through a direct speech act? What implications does this text have concerning felicity conditions and speech acts? Explain.

Now, have a look at TV Commercial 3 for Jimmy Dean Skillets, a breakfast product designed to save preparation time for consumers by providing chopped, fresh-frozen omelet ingredients, such as potatoes, peppers, onions, and a variety of breakfast meats. The commercial is structured on the Jimmy Dean trope of the sun. (Its packaging logo is a sunburst, and their slogan is "Great Days Start with Jimmy Dean"; thus, Jimmy Dean = the sun). Many of the Jimmy Dean breakfast foods commercials involve one male actor dressed in a large round sun costume—as if the sun, rising at a particular time, heating the Earth, and attending to other astronomic and meteorological phenomena, e.g., the moon and clouds. Here is a variation of the commercial script:

What types of speech acts do you note here? How would you characterize the speech acts by each character? What is each character actually "doing" with the speech act? That is, what sort of message is the little girl's

TV Commercial 3: Jimmy Dean Skillets

((A little girl is sitting at the edge of the kitchen counter. Her chin is on the counter and she wrinkles her nose as she speaks the first line. She is watching her father as he cooks breakfast. Her father is "The Sun" dressed in a "Sun" costume and preparing an omelet on the stove.))

Little girl: Mommy doesn't make it like that. ((subtle grimace, nose wrinkle))

Dad: This is uh (0.4) the <u>Dad</u>dy way of making it.

Little girl: Yeah, she chops everything up.

Her father then explains that it was the "Jimmy Dean people" who chopped the vegetables for him, because he's busy (after all, he is the Sun); he needs to provide heat and light for the Earth.

(Jimmy Dean Skillets, 2005)

speech act conveying? Is it simply a **representative** (e.g., a simple assertion)? What about the father's response? What sort of speech act is it? Is it, too, just a **representative** (e.g., a simple assertion)?

How do the speech acts in TV Commercials 1 and 2 compare and contrast with those represented in TV Commercial 3? Think about: direct speech acts, indirect speech acts, the *meanings* behind the speech acts, and felicity conditions. Are felicity conditions met in each and every exchange of speech acts represented in the three commercial texts? What sorts of conclusions can you draw from these three commercials about speech acts in general and specific types of speech acts as we use speech acts in everyday life?

Sperber and Wilson's work on Relevance Theory (1986) is an extension of Grice's cooperative principle, and an approach to pragmatics that is applied in a number of discourse analytic studies. Relevance Theory expands Grice's notions of implicature and inference, and emphasizes the crucial feature of relevance as a cognitive phenomenon relating to pragmatic meaning. One area of research where the application of Relevance Theory is particularly well-cited involves humor and irony, where blatant violations of the cooperative principle result in humorous outcomes. Yus (2003, 2008) provides a detailed review of the literature on irony that takes a Relevance Theory approach (e.g., Attardo, 1990, 1994, 2004; Curco, 1998), pointing out that Relevance Theory is "not a theory specifically designed for the analysis of humor, but its theoretical hypotheses are suited to deal with how humorous interpretations are generated" (Yus, 2003: 1327).

We opened this chapter with Grice's notion of implicature and the related ideas that when we communicate, we express and process far more complex messages than the simple words or expressions. The notion of conversational implicature is a particularly important notion in the study of pragmatics.

POLITENESS: FACE, INTERACTION, AND CULTURE

POLITENESS refers to the patterned behaviors through which we routinely interact with others (both linguistically and non-linguistically) to effect a smooth, efficient, non-antagonistic, and mutually cooperative exchange of ideas, feelings, opinions, stances, and so forth—in accordance with the sets of social and cultural norms in which such interaction takes place, and typically taking into account the mutual maintenance of the **face** of the interacting parties. Thus, the central component within politeness theory is **face**—the individual image that one has of oneself and the social value of one's personhood vis à vis others.

In the opening of our chapter, we noted that field of pragmatics involves the "mutual creation, communication, and understanding of meaning in cases where *meaning is intended well beyond the literal or objective meanings of the discursive spates in question*" (emphasis original).

We have examined Grice's maxims and the cooperative principle and have observed spates of interaction in which speakers do exactly that— create, communicate, and understand meaning beyond the literal. We have examined the speech act as *social act fulfilling a social function* whereby speakers commit to doing something, get hearers to do something, present facts, express emotions or stances, or change states of affairs in official and non-official ways.

Politeness is the area in the field of pragmatics that addresses more finely detailed elements of such interaction by addressing the consequences or potential consequences that implicatures and speech acts can have on the interacting parties. In our definition of politeness, we focus on the following elements:

- patterned behaviors of routine interaction
- mutual cooperation (smooth, efficient, unantagonistic)

- social and cultural norms
- maintenance of face of interacting parties (i.e., not just the speaker/writer and not just the hearer/reader/audience)

Social and cultural norms influence much of what we consider politeness to be. Our everyday practices are imbued with preferences for certain types of linguistic and non-linguistic behaviors that often result in tensions between such seemingly polemic issues as directness vs. indirectness, clarity vs. vagueness, interpersonal closeness vs. interpersonal distance, linguistic creativity vs. routinized formula, volubility vs. reserve, self-promotion vs. self-effacement, power and authority vs. subordination. Add to these categories the roles that gender, age, education, profession, social class, and culture might play in situated interaction, all with the goal of maintaining and perpetuating social order.

Research on linguistic politeness has taken into account many of these factors. Lakoff (1973, 1977), Leech (1983), and Brown and Levinson (1987) propose frameworks for the analysis of politeness as a universally human phenomenon—maintaining essentially that smooth, efficient, and non-antagonistic interaction is the optimal goal of interactants. Lakoff's (1973, 1977) politeness rules reflect similar concepts as those in Grice's maxims. They consist of two basic maxims: Be clear (encapsulating the maxims of quantity, quality, relevance, and manner) and Be polite (don't impose, gauge appropriate distance from or closeness to the interlocutor, leave room for interlocutor response, and make the addressee feel good). Essentially, these boil down to three rules to avoid conflict between interlocutors: gauge distance, employ deference, and seek camaraderie.

Brown and Levinson (1987: 59–60) propose a framework based on the Model Person (MP). According to this framework, all MPs are rational in the sense that they exercise practical reasoning (Aristotle, 1969) for means-ends accomplishments. And all MPs are endowed with both positive and negative face. Brown and Levinson (1987: 61) appeal dually to Goffman's (1967) concept of face and to the folk expressions "losing face" and "saving face." See Watts (2003: 124) for one of Goffman's more elegant definitions of "face."

Positive face and negative face are explained on the basis of the distinctions noted in the box on the next page. (adapted from Brown and Levinson, 1987: 61–62):

This politeness model assumes that specific types of actions, often expressed in terms of speech acts, are inherently protective of speakers' and

---

Positive face wants:

> The desire to be liked, accepted, ratified, and agreed with.
>
> The want of every 'competent adult member' that his wants be desirable to at least some others.

Negative face wants:

> The desire to be unimpeded, to have one's territory and/or personal freedom—free from intrusion.
>
> The want of every 'competent adult member' that his actions be unimpeded by others.

---

hearers' dual-poled faces. Others are inherently threatening to them, and these are referred to as face threatening acts (FTAs).

To illustrate, if positive face wants are equated with the desire to be liked and approved of, then the speech act of a *criticism* damages the **hearer's positive face**. And conversely, if negative face wants are equated with the desire to be unimpeded, then the speech act of a *request* damages the **hearer's negative face**.[7]

Other speech act types that **damage the hearer's positive face** include *disagreements, insults,* and *interruptions*. Additionally, speech-based practices such as not using honorifics, deferential language, or inappropriate register choices are also threats to the hearer's positive face.

Additional speech act types that **damage the hearer's negative face** include: *orders, questions, suggestions, threats, and reminders*. Also, *a hyper-expression of emotion* in terms of thanks, congratulations, condolences, appreciation, and so forth, which place the hearer in a position to awkwardly accept or reject such emotional expressions, are also damaging to the hearer's negative face.

The rationality element of the MP comes into play in this way: Before a person commits an FTA s/he will generally think about what is involved. That is, what is the desired outcome of doing the FTA? Is it urgent? Is it expected by the hearer? The socio-cultural factors that are at work in the model are: the **social distance** between the speaker and hearer as equals or in a symmetrical relationship, the **relative power** (as assumed or mutually assumed by speaker and hearer) in an asymmetrical or unequal relationship, and the

weightiness of the FTA (i.e., how serious or how heavy the threat to face will be if the FTA is performed).

Within this model, Brown and Levinson propose a two-step model of options, where **Step 1** involves **doing an FTA**. Built into Step 1 are four options: a) Do the FTA "baldly, on record, and with no redress," i.e., directly, succinctly, and unambiguously, with no mitigation; b) Do the FTA with redress using positive politeness strategies; c) Do the FTA with redress using negative politeness strategies; and d) Do the FTA off record, so that it the FTA is ambiguously delivered, leaving it entirely up to the hearer (or any hearer) to assess what was just heard as a particular type of speech act. **Step 2** is simple. Just **don't do the FTA.**

We provide an encapsulation and adaptation of the model here:

Step 1. Do the FTA
If you do the FTA,

  (a) **do the FTA baldly, with no redress** ("Get out!" "There's a fire!" "I just found out that you cheated on me!")

  (b) **do the FTA with redress** of **POSITIVE POLITENESS strategies**
  Positive politeness: "You did a great job in the introductory paragraph." (a compliment preceding the FTA of suggestion/criticism)
  FTA: "You should use the sample essay to organize the rest of your paragraphs."

  (c) **do the FTA with redress** of **with NEGATIVE POLITENESS strategies**
  Negative politeness: "I'm sorry to bother you, but . . ." (a preparatory apology preceding the FTA of a request)
  FTA: "could I borrow a dollar?"

  (d) **do the FTA off record** so that it is ambiguous in function and the hearer must infer that some action on his or her part may be appropriate as a result of hearing this speech act ("I left my wallet in the car.")

Step 2. Don't do the FTA. Say nothing at all. Do nothing at all.

As evident in the model (albeit a simplified version), the Brown and Levinson approach to politeness involves a focus on the MP speaker. The model is built on the face threatening consequences that arise as a result of interactional behavior, with a focus on the speaker or doer of the face threatening action. Also, the speaker is framed as an MP who may rationally choose to do an FTA or not do one, with an assumed orientation toward consequences of tension, conflict, or antagonism. That is, it is the MP speaker's choice in assessing the degree of conflict that an FTA may have on the hearer's positive or negative face or the speaker's own face, prior to producing the FTA. The model proposes that degrees of threat of some FTAs can be deliberately mitigated or redressed with instances of positive politeness (e.g., agreement, compliment, congratulations) or negative politeness (apology, explicit recognition of intrusion). And, underlying the interaction between speaker (S) and hearer (H) are the socio-cultural elements of power, distance, and weightiness of the FTA. Politeness, as put forward in this model, is presented as a universal phenomenon of human behavior, with **face** as central to its overall structure.

Further, directness (bald, on-record FTAs) is established as maximally face threatening. Indirectness is established as face saving in three ways: using positive and negative politeness to circumvent or redress an FTA, producing an ambiguous "off-record" FTA, or not doing the FTA at all. These mechanisms of indirection are explained as capable of reducing threat to both sides of face for S and H.

Let's apply some of these concepts to actual data. The following excerpt is from the opening monologue of an early broadcast of the *Ellen DeGeneres Show*.[8] It is a talk show broadcast throughout the United States. Ellen is a comedienne and she begins each show with a comedic monologue like the one you find excerpted next, followed by her own brief original dance routine.

As you examine the data, think about these points:

- Ellen's initial discourse is directly responsive to the audience's intense appreciative reaction. She then moves to her monologue, which she introduces using a purported narrative of personal experience. She then shifts to stories and narratives of a more general import, to make a point.
- What types of FTAs do you notice? How do they emerge? That is, who produces them? How are they responded to: by Ellen, by the audience, by the characters in her story narrative? How might the concepts of *genre* and *participation framework* (Chapter 3) enter into an analysis of a larger spate of similar discourse?

- In what ways does Ellen's narrative confirm or disconfirm the principles of politeness as set forth by Brown and Levinson?

Ellen DeGeneres Show Opening Monologue

((Ellen walks out from backstage. The camera pans the audience and we see the crowd on their feet, cheering and applauding. This greeting lasts for nearly a full minute. Ellen is smiling at the audience—camera moves back and forth between Ellen and the audience. Finally, after the minute of applause and cheers, Ellen tries to speak:))

          ((audience standing and cheering))
Ellen: Thank-
          ((audience cheering))
Ellen: Thank-
          ((audience still standing and cheering))
Ellen: Have a seat. Thank you very much. That's really really nice of you. And uh- And uh- w- w- w- KAW KAW KAW KAW
          ((roaring audience laughter))
Ellen: I had a little tiny bit to get out. Sometimes ya just have those- Ya need ta be that happy, ya know ta make it KAW KAW KAW.
          ((roaring audience laughter))
Ellen: So, ah (.) this is- this is- today ah what I'm gonna uhm tell ya about. Uhm, I'm realizing- and I've said it before, I like my age. I'm forty-six. I'm not ashamed of it.
          ((audience cheering and applause))
Ellen: But I still don't think I'm- To me, it's just a number. Like, when I was younger, that was such an old number, that felt like "Oh, that's some lady" and now, I'm forty-six, I don't feel like that at all . . .

((skipped lines))

Ellen: . . . But "lady" can be good or bad . . . depending on how they say it. If something starts with "Look, lady" that never ends well . . .
Ellen: Another one I don't like to be called is "Dear." There should be a rule that you have ta be at least seventy-six ta call me "Dear."
          ((audience laughter))

> Ellen: Ya know, like if you're a waitress in a diner, "Would you like a cookie, dear?" That's sweet. I don't mind that at all . . .
>> ((audience laughter))
>
> Ellen: . . . "Sweetie" I don't like either, unless you're a waitress in a diner, you can say "sweetie," "Hey, sweetie, can I get you some dessert?" That's always fine, but not in a nice restaurant. That's uh—"Sweetie, do you wanna see the wine list?" "Okay, sweetie, I'll call the sommelier."
>> ((audience laughter))
>
> ((skipped lines))
>
> Ellen: "Doll" also. Ya know, when somebody says "doll," get ready ta run an errand.
>> ((audience laughter))
>
> Ellen: "Oh, be a doll and get me some water."
>> ((audience laughter))
>
> Ellen: All those things mean something. You can always tell where it's going.
>
> **(Balian, Anderson, and Patrick, 2004)**

Koziski suggests that stand-up comedians are rather astute anthropologists, commenting on and critiquing "the hidden underpinnings of their culture" (1984: 57). What is your take on how Ellen explains the underpinnings of FTAs according to the Brown and Levinson model?

While Brown and Levinson's groundbreaking model is often cited and appealed to in research from multiple disciplines (Bronstein et al., 2012; Cheng, 2009; Kong and Ladegaard, 2009) it has also received criticism from scholars in more recent politeness research. Notably, Watts proposes a more fluid and dynamic analysis of politeness, deriving from, among other factors, a broader, more "changeable," dynamic, and multifaceted view of face. Watts (2003: 124) re-introduces Goffman's (1955/1967) definition of face, which received a more static and unidimensional treatment in Brown and Levinson:

One's own face and the face of others are constructs of the same order. It is the rules of the group and the definition of the situation which determine how much feeling one is to have for face and how this feeling is to be distributed among the faces involved. (Goffman, 1955/1967: 6)

Watts bases his analytic framework of (im)politeness on *face* along the lines as noted, as well as on Bourdieu's theory of social practice, appealing to such notions as 'habitus,' 'social field,' and 'social capital.' See Bourdieu (1977, 1990) and Bourdieu and Thompson (1991) for more detail.

Matsumoto (1988), and later Ide (1989), Mao (1994), and Yu (2003), claim that Brown and Levinson's dual poles of positive and negative face are not applicable in the same way in East Asia as they might be in Western culture. (See also Bax and Kádár, 2011; Bousfield, 2008; and Bargiela-Chiappini and Kádár, 2011.)

Yu (2011) cites robust research on cross-cultural perspectives on politeness indicating that indirectness and hints are not automatically equated with "politeness" in Israeli society (Blum-Kulka, 1987), in Mexican speech acts of requests (Félix-Brasdefer, 2005), and in Turkish (Marti, 2006). And Lakoff and Ide (2005), in their edited volume entitled *Broadening the Horizon of Linguistic Politeness,* provide new theoretical perspectives on politeness with empirical observations from languages not often represented in the literature, such as Thai, German, Greek, Irish, and Swedish, as does the volume by Bargiela-Ciappini and Kádár (2011), including work on Zimbabwean English (Grainger, 2011), Korean (Brown, 2011), and Georgian medical and academic discourse (Rusieshvili, 2011).

Discussions of politeness in general would also not be complete without reference to the concept of *deference.* Politeness (in the models that we have examined) and deference are not one and the same. Fraser and Nolen (1981) cite Goffman's (1967) definition of deference as a "symbolic means by which appreciation is regularly conveyed." The notions of regularity, formula, and ritual are key to the understanding of deference (Treichler et al., 1984; Scott, 1990), as is the notion of symbolic appreciation, i.e., rendering personal value to the hearer or addressee or creating symbolic and interactional distance through linguistic and kinesic behaviors. See Brown and Gilman (1960), Fragale, Sumanth, Tiedens, and Northcraft (2012); Fraser and Nolen (1981), Hasegawa (2008), Jucker (2011), Ota, McCann, and Honeycutt (2012), Strauss and Eun (2005), Treichler et al. (1984), and others, for extended discussions of deference and its relationship to politeness. Politeness and deference across cultures is a robust area for pragmatics research in interpersonal, intercultural, and organizational communication.

REVIEW AND REFLECTION: CONVERSATIONAL IMPLICATURE, SPEECH ACTS, POLITENESS, AND INTERCULTURAL COMMUNICATION

1A.   Analyze the following utterances from the point of view of Grice's maxims (quantity, quality, relevance, and manner). Some of the utterances are clearly not complete representations of meaning and require "filling in" in order for the intended messages to be communicated. Pay special attention to the italicized lines. What meanings are implied, but not stated? Are any of the maxims actually violated? If so, which ones? If not, why not? (Think about the *Merlin* example from earlier in the chapter.)

A: I finished the potato chips.
B: *Again?*

B.   Now, analyze the same italicized sentences from the point of view of the *speech acts* that they are conveying. Try to identify the types of speech acts performed by each utterance. What is the illocutionary force of each? That is, what is each utterance "doing"? Identify which of the speech acts are direct and which are indirect.

A: Did anyone call while I was out?
B: *Yes, but not who you were hoping for.*

Is it intermission? ((people are getting up and crossing over in front while movie is still going on))

2.   Following is an excerpt from the September, 2002, debut episode of the *Dr. Phil Show*. The episode involves a 10-year-old boy, Vincent, and his abusive mother. In the excerpt provided here, Dr. Phil is speaking with Vincent backstage, asking him questions about his mother and the relationship that he has with her.

Do the utterances in this exchange violate any of Grice's maxims? If so, where and how? If not, why not?

Pay particular attention to the last three lines: Dr. P: *How old are you?* V: *Ten.* Dr. P: *Ten?* What remains unsaid here? How does Dr. Phil's last line relate to previous lines in the interaction? Which previous lines, in particular, does it relate to? Which do you find more interactionally powerful: the unspoken implication by Dr. Phil or an explicitly

articulated one? How would the unspoken utterance compare in illocutionary force to one of the many possible utterances that Dr. Phil could
have produced in explicit terms?

Think about *genre* and *participation framework*. Preston (2012) characterized Dr. Phil's debut show as "part circus, part theater, part soap opera—and
all McGraw" (Dr. Phil's last name is McGraw). Why do you think that *USA
Today* chose those three genres to describe a program such as this one?

> Dr. Phil: What would you do if your mom started ta yell at you,
> (3.0) and she just stopped, (0.4) took a big ole deep breath,
> just came over and gave you a big hug and said, you know
> Vincent, I'm really proud of you and I really love you. (2.0)

> Dr. Phil: What [would you think of that?
> Vincent: [eh ih It would probably tear me up.
> Dr. Phil: yeah?
> Vincent: yeah.
> Dr. Phil: Think that'll ever happen?
> Vincent: Maybe. I think she's done it once.
> Dr. Phil: Done it once?
> Vincent: Yeah.
> Dr. Phil: How old are you?
> Vincent: Ten.
> Dr. Phil: Ten?

(LeVine, 2002)

3. Next you will find two types of "warning" messages. The example
in A, from a university webmail server, is explicitly marked as a
"warning." The example in B is from written warning messages and
orally announced warning messages concerning smoking in airplane bathrooms.

Is each message actually a "warning"? From a speech act perspective, think
about the illocutionary force and consequent perlocutionary effects associated with messages A and B. In addition to "warning," what other types of
speech acts are being expressed here? Is the speech act actually a warning
or is it more specifically something else?

  Think about common speech acts that you encounter regularly
in public discourse. Are they really *one simple* speech act, or are the

messages more functionally complex, like those in A and B? How many speech acts are involved here? What are they? What is the "unsaid" part of the messages?

MESSAGE A
Warning: Some of your folders are approaching their absolute maximum size limit. Any additional mail sent to these folders may be irretrievably lost. More info (click here).

MESSAGE B
Federal law prohibits tampering with, disabling, or destroying any smoke detector in an airplane lavatory; smoking in lavatories; and, when applicable, smoking in passenger compartments.

(Molyneux, 2012).

4   Based on what you have learned about pragmatics, read the following text, and consider these questions:

What is the source of humor in the following excerpt, from the 1950s–1960s family sitcom, *Leave it to Beaver*? *Beaver* is the nickname of the young boy (aged 5 or 6 in the early episodes), Theodore Cleaver, who is the star of the show. The excerpt is from Season 1, Episode 2, called "Captain Jack." Beaver, and his older brother, Wally, had sent away for a live alligator pet—by mail order. They received a tiny live alligator and did not know how to care for it, so they visited a local alligator farm near their home, managed by an alligator expert named Captain Jack.
Leave it to Beaver "Captain Jack"
((Scene changes to Alligator Farm, where Captain Jack works as a guide))
((Alligator growls as it climbs slowly out of alligator pool))

Captain Jack: Now you'll probably notice that some of our scaly friends are minus an arm or a leg or other vulnerable appendages. Now if you was to fall in here among these beasts, you'd probably believe they would bite off your arm, after the fashion of the shark or the barracuda. This is a fallacy. The alligator would not bite off your arm. He would saw it off.

Beaver: Wally, where would he get the saw? ((audience laughter))
Wally: Shhh. Quiet.

(Mosher, Connelly, and Tokar, 1957)

5   Are the following messages FTAs? Do they threaten the reader's positive face wants or negative face wants? There are certain choices
that seem to be "preferred." What sorts of implications does this
have with regard to politeness and FTAs?

MESSAGE A

Message on a cell phone alarm clock tool:

Alarm is off.
Turn on now?
Yes
No

MESSAGE B

This message appears after trying to navigate away from a "gift-
giving" page on a social media site. Instead of following through and
ordering a gift, if one moves from that page (e.g., Starbucks gift), the
following message appears:

Are you sure you want to leave this page?

You haven't finished your gift yet. Do you want to leave without
giving this gift?

LEAVE THIS PAGE   stay on page

Can you correlate the types of selections in both A and B to some
of the issues that we discussed in Chapter 6 regarding *preference
organization?*

Can you apply a politeness-based analysis of *preference organization*
with respect to assessments and adjacency pairs in conversation? See
Chapter 6.

6   Speech Acts

Simon Wiesenthal's book *The Sunflower: On the Possibilities and Limits of Forgiveness* addresses a number of different types of speech acts, including confession, forgiveness, and apology.

Here is an abridged excerpt from Wiesenthal (1976: 52–5). The narrative describes a dilemma that Wiesenthal is facing, between listening to and forgiving a Nazi solider, Karl Seidl, who is dying at Lemberg Concentration Camp hospital, and denying him forgiveness. Wiesenthal has been summoned to Siedl's bedside. Read the excerpt from a speech act perspective. What are the various speech acts that are involved here? Why is each speech act so important to the participants in this context?

Excerpt from The Sunflower

p. 52: . . . Once again he groped for my hand, but I had withdrawn it sometime before and was sitting on it, out of his reach. I did not want to be touched by the hand of death. He sought my pity, but had he any right to pity? . . .

p. 53: . . . He lapsed into silence, seeking for words. He wants something from me, I thought, for I could not imagine that he had brought me here merely as an audience . . .

"I cannot die . . . without coming clean. This must be my confession. But what sort of confession is this? A letter without an answer . . . "

No doubt, he was referring to my silence. But what could I say? Here was a dying man—a murderer who did not want to be a murderer but who had been made into a murderer by a murderous ideology. He was confessing his crime to a man who perhaps tomorrow must die at the hands of these same murderers. In his confession there was true repentance, even though he did not admit it in so many words. Nor was it necessary, for the way he spoke and the fact that he spoke to me was a proof of his repentance . . .

p. 54: . . . "I know that what I am asking is almost too much for you, but without your answer I cannot die in peace." . . .

p. 55: . . . I stood up and looked in his direction, at his folded hands. Between them there seemed to rest a sunflower.

At last I made up my mind and without a word I left the room.

Think about the significance of the various speech acts involved in this excerpt (which is a true life narrative).

Speech acts can be powerful instances of discourse at any level of interaction. What is the significance of the specific speech acts in this interaction? Who, specifically, is involved? (i.e., individual men, representatives of particular groups, representatives of nations) What is the relevance of the "speech act" at the interpersonal level? What other levels of interaction (e.g., morality, religion) are sensitive to the notion the speech act?

How might speech acts be relevant (and significant) at the level of a government and its people? What is the significance of speech acts between governments? That is, can you think of any recent incidents in which the people of a nation were waiting for an apology, for example, by its government? How about when the government of one nation waits for or expects an apology from the government of another nation? What specific historical events do you remember or that you have read about involve the production of a speech act at a level well beyond that of individual participants or small groups? What does this say about the importance of the category of the speech act in discourse?

PRACTICE WITH PRAGMATICS: ENGLISH, JAPANESE, AND KOREAN

1   Have a look at the photograph from a Japanese cigarette vending machine. What sorts of speech acts do you notice? How can you construct an analysis of these messages on the basis of: implicature? politeness? What are the FTAs? Are they mitigated or redressed in any way? How do the messages from this vending machine compare to those that you might have seen on similar vending machines in other languages and in other countries, especially from the perspectives of implicature, politeness (and FTAs), and speech act theory?

2   The following cigarette warnings appear (or appeared) on cigarette packages in Japan, Korea, and the United States. How are these "warnings" articulated discursively? That is, what are the speech acts involved? Is there any redressive actions to mitigate FTAs? What do these instances of

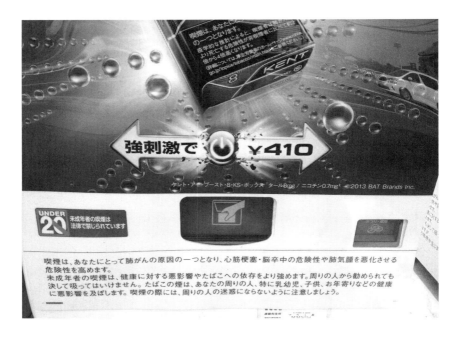

FIGURE 7.1 Photograph by Yumi Matsumoto

discourse tell you about pragmatics, cross-culturally? More specifically, what do they reveal about speech acts, politeness, and face from a cross-cultural and cross-linguistic perspective?

Japan

* 健康のため吸いすぎに注意しましょう (For the good of your health, be careful not to smoke too much) (1972–1989)
* あなたの健康を損なうおそれがありますので吸いすぎに注意しましょう (Be careful not to smoke too much, as there is a risk of damaging your health) (1990–2005)

    On the front of cigarette packages:
* 喫煙は、あなたにとって肺がんの原因の一つとなります。疫学的な推計によると、喫煙者は肺がんにより死亡する危険性が非喫煙者に比べて約2倍から4倍高くなります。 (Smoking is a cause of lung cancer. According to epidemiological estimates, smokers are about two to four times more likely than non-smokers to die of lung cancer.)
* 喫煙は、あなたにとって心筋梗塞の危険性を高めます。疫学的な推計によると、喫煙者は心筋梗塞により死亡する危険性が非

喫煙者に比べて約 1.7倍高くなります。 (Smoking increases risk of myocardial infarction. According to epidemiological estimates, smokers are about 1.7 times more likely than non-smokers to die of a heart attack.)

* 喫煙は、あなたにとって脳卒中の危険性を高めます。疫学的な推計によると、喫煙者は脳卒中により死亡する危険性が非喫煙者に比べて約1.7倍高くなります。 (Smoking increases risk of stroke. According to epidemiological estimates, smokers are about 1.7 times more likely than non-smokers to die of a stroke.)

* 喫煙は、あなたにとって肺気腫を悪化させる危険性を高めます。 (Smoking can aggravate the symptoms of emphysema.)

On the back of cigarette packages:

妊娠中の喫煙は、胎児の発育障害や早産の原因の一つとなります。疫学的な推計によると、たばこを吸う妊婦は、吸わない妊婦に比べ、低出生体重の危険性が約2倍、早産の危険性が約3倍、早産の危険性が約(詳細については、厚生労働省のホーム・ページ www.mhlw.go.jp/topics/tobacco/main.html をご参照ください。) (Smoking during pregnancy is a cause of preterm delivery and impaired fetal growth. According to epidemiological estimates, pregnant women who smoke have almost double the risk of low birth weight and three times the risk of premature birth than pregnant women who do not smoke. (For more information, please visit the Ministry of Health home page at www.mhlw.go.jp/topics/tobacco/main.html.))

* たばこの煙は、あなたの周りの人、特に乳幼児、子供、お年寄りなどの健康に悪影響を及ぼします。喫煙の際には、周りの人の迷惑にならないように注意しましょう。 (Tobacco smoke adversely affects the health of people around you, especially infants, children and the elderly. When smoking, be careful not to inconvenience others.)

* 人により程度は異なりますが、ニコチンにより喫煙への依存が生じます。 (The degree may differ from person to person, but nicotine [in cigarettes] causes addiction to smoking.)

* 未成年者の喫煙は、健康に対する悪影響やたばこへの依存をより強めます。周りの人から勧められても決して吸ってはいけません。 (Smoking while underage heightens the addiction and damage to health caused by cigarettes. Never smoke, even if encouraged to by those around you.)

(Tobacco packaging warning messages, n.d.).

South Korea

* From 1976 to 1989 건강을 위하여 지나친 흡연을 삼갑시다 (For your health, please refrain from smoking too much)
* From December 1989 to 1996 흡연은 폐암 등을 일으킬 수 있으며, 특히 임산부와 청소년의 건강에 해롭습니다 (Smoking may cause lung cancer and it is especially dangerous for teenagers and pregnant women)
* From 1996 to March 2005 Front 흡연은 폐암 등 각종 질병의 원인이 되며, 특히 임신부와 청소년의 건강에 해롭습니다 (Smoking causes lung cancer and other diseases and it is especially dangerous for teenagers and pregnant women) Back 19세 미만 청소년에게 판매할 수 없습니다 (It is illegal to sell cigarettes to people under 19) and additionally, 금연하면 건강해지고 장수할 수 있습니다 (You can be healthy and live longer if you quit), 흡연은 중풍과 심장병도 일으킵니다 (Smoking also causes paralysis and heart diseases), 흡연은 사랑하는 자녀의 건강도 해칩니다 (Smoking also damages your beloved children), 당신이 흡연하면 다른 사람의 건강도 해칩니다 (Smoking damages others)
* From April 2005 to April 2007 Front 건강을 해치는 담배 그래도 피우시겠습니까? (Smoking damages your health. Do you still want to smoke?) Back 19세 미만 청소년에게 판매할 수 없습니다 (It is illegal to sell cigarettes to people under 19) and additionally, 금연하면 건강해지고 장수할 수 있습니다 (You can be healthy and live longer if you quit), 흡연은 중풍과 심장병도 일으킵니다 (Smoking also causes paralysis and heart diseases), 흡연은 사랑하는 자녀의 건강도 해칩니다 (Smoking also damages your beloved children), 당신이 흡연하면 다른 사람의 건강도 해칩니다 (Smoking damages others)
* From April 2007 to April 2009 Front 흡연은 폐암 등 각종 질병의 원인이 되며, 특히 임신부와 청소년의 건강에 해롭습니다 (Smoking causes lung cancer and other diseases and it is especially dangerous for teenagers and pregnant women) Back 19미만 청소년에게 판매 금지! 당신 자녀의 건강을 해칩니다" (It is illegal to sell cigarettes to people under 19! It hurts your children's health)
* From April 2009 to April 2011 (a prospectus) Front 건강에 해로운 담배, 일단 흡연하게 되면 끊기가 매우 어렵습니다 (Smoking damages your health. Once you start smoking, it is very difficult to quit) Back 19세 미만 청소년에게 판매 금지! 당신 자녀의 건강을 해칩니다 (It is illegal to sell cigarettes to people under 19! It hurts your children's health)
  (Tobacco packaging warning messages, n.d.).

United States of America

Cigarettes

* Caution: Cigarette Smoking May be Hazardous to Your Health (1966–1970)
* Warning: The Surgeon General Has Determined that Cigarette Smoking is Dangerous to Your Health (1970–1985)
* SURGEON GENERAL'S WARNING: Smoking Causes Lung Cancer, Heart Disease, Emphysema, And May Complicate Pregnancy. (1985–)
* SURGEON GENERAL'S WARNING: Quitting Smoking Now Greatly Reduces Serious Risks to Your Health. (1985–)
* SURGEON GENERAL'S WARNING: Smoking By Pregnant Women May Result in Fetal Injury, Premature Birth, And Low Birth Weight. (1985–)
* SURGEON GENERAL'S WARNING: Cigarette Smoke Contains Carbon Monoxide. (1985–)

(Tobacco packaging warning messages, n.d.).

SUGGESTIONS FOR FURTHER READING

Aliakbari, M. and Changizi, M. On the realization of refusal strategies by Persian and Kurdish speakers. *International Journal of Intercultural Relations.* 36,5: 659–68.

Bilbow, G. (2002). Commissive speech act use in intercultural business meetings. *IRAL*, 40,4: 287–303.

Chang, W. and Haugh, M. (2011). Strategic embarrassment and face threatening in business interactions. *Journal of Pragmatics*, 43,12: 2948–63.

Chen, Y-S., Chen, C-Y., and Chang, M-H. (2011). American and Chinese complaints: Strategy use from a cross-cultural perspective. *Intercultural Pragmatics*, 8,2: 253–75.

Cook, H.M. (2006). Japanese politeness as an interactional achievement: Academic consultation sessions in Japanese universities. *Multilingua*, 25, 3: 269–91.

Decapua, A. and Dunham, J. (2007). The pragmatics of advice giving: Cross-cultural perspectives. *Intercultural Pragmatics*, 4,3: 319–42.

Dunn, C.D. (2011). Formal forms or verbal strategies? Politeness theory and Japanese business etiquette training. *Journal of Pragmatics*, 43,15: 3643–54.

Economidou-Kogetsidis, M. (2005). aaYes, tell me please, what time is the midday flight from Athens arriving? aa: Telephone Service encounters and politeness. *Intercultural Pragmatics*, 2,3: 253–73.

Holzinger, K. (2004). Bargaining through arguing: An empirical analysis based on speech act theory. *Political Communication*, 21,2: 195–222.

Intachakra, S. (2012). Politeness motivated by the 'heart' and 'binary rationality' in Thai culture. *Journal of Pragmatics*, 44,5: 619–35.

Jiang, X. (2012). Politeness and facework in Chinese language and culture. *Linguistic Insights—Studies in Language and Communication*, 132: 53–88.

Kiesling, S. and Ghosh Johnson (2010). Four forms of interactional indirection. *Journal of Pragmatics*, *42,2*: 292–306.

Kwon, I. (2012). Please confirm what I inferred: On the Korean inferential-evidential marker—napo-. *Journal of Pragmatics*, 44,8: 958–969.

Ladegaard, H. (2009). Politeness, power and control: The use of humor in cross-cultural telecommunications. In W. Cheng and K. Kong (Eds.), *Professional Communication: Collaboration between Academics and Professionals*. Hong Kong: Hong Kong University Press. pp. 191–209.

Lee, H.E., Park, H., Imai, T., and Dolan, D. (2012). Cultural difference between Japan and the U.S. in uses of "apology" and "thank you" in favor asking messages. *Journal of Language and Social Psychology*, 31,3: 263–89.

Mullany, L. (2004). Gender, Politeness, and institutional power roles: Humour as a tactic to gain compliance in workplace business meetings. *Multlingua*, 23,1–2: 13–37.

Schneider, K. (2012). Appropriate behavior across varieties of English. *Journal of Pragmatics*, 44,9: 1022–37.

Tomioka, S. (2009). Why questions, presuppositions, and interventions. *Journal of East Asian Linguistics* 18: 253–71.

Traverso, V. (2001). Syrian service encounters: A case of shifting strategies in verbal exchange. *Pragmatics*, 11,4: 421–44.

Vine, B. (2009). Directives at work: Exploring the contextual complexities of workplace directives. *Journal of Pragmatics*, 41,7: 1395–405.

Wierzbicka, A. (1991). *Cross-Cultural Pragmatics: The Semantics of Human Interaction*. Berlin: Mouton de Gruyter.

Ylanne-McEwen, V. (2004). Shifting alignment and negotiating sociality in travel agent discourse. *Discourse Studies*, 6,4: 517–36.

LINKS

The Royal Bank of Scotland. (2004, September). Do I? [TV Commercial]. Retrieved from http://www.youtube.com/watch?v=cVcZDSlvhgs. Accessed May 20, 2013.

Jimmy Dean Skillets. (2005, September). Why? [TV Commercial]. Retrieved from: http://www.advertolog.com/jimmy-dean/adverts/why-7633405/. Accessed May 23, 2013.

Molyneux, T. (2012, September 22). Federal law prohibits tampering with . . . In *Successful Workplace*. Retrieved from: http://successfulwork-place.com/2012/09/22/federal-law-prohibits-tampering-with/. Accessed May 25, 2013.

Tobacco packaging warning messages. (n.d.). In *Wikipedia*. Retrieved from http://en.wikipedia.org/wiki/Tobacco_packaging_warning_messages. Accessed May 31, 2013.

NOTES

1. As noted by Clark and Brennan (1991: 127), common ground comprises the "mutual knowledge, mutual beliefs, and mutual assumptions" that participants in communication both construct and share through discourse. Common ground emerges from the process of "grounding" (Clark and Schaefer, 1989), which may begin in the domain of the "new," adjusting the discourse to gauge and accommodate varying degrees of mutuality surrounding the knowledge, beliefs, and assumptions of the participants. See also Lee (2001), among others.
2. Austin's (1962) book *How to Do Things with Words* is actually a collection of 12 essays that he delivered at Harvard University in 1955. As indicated by the editor of the book: "The content of [the] lectures is . . . reproduced in print as exactly as possible and with the lightest editing" (Urmson, 1962: v).
3. Wittgenstein's concept of "language games" shares some philosophical assumptions with speech act theory. Although Wittgenstein did not provide an explicit definition for "language games," the concept reflects his "*activity oriented* perspective on language." Wittgenstein emphasizes that utterances

are always a "part of an activity" or a part of a larger "language game" that we are involved in. Thus, the meaning of utterances is interpretable only within the context of the game in which they are used. He lists a number of "regular" language games in which speakers routinely engage, e.g., thanking, speculating, reporting an event, making a joke, asking, making up a story, etc. (See Biletzki and Matar 2011 [Stanford Encyclopedia of Philosophy]; Duranti, 1997).

4. See Derrida (1977), Levinson (1983), Schegloff (1988a, 1992), and Streeck (1980) for additional perspectives and criticisms of Searle's framework.

5. Searle cites Austin's own reservation concerning the "tentativeness" of his proposed categories: "I am not putting any of this forward as in the very least definitive" (Austin, 1962: 151, cited in Searle 1976: 7), and duly credits Austin's contribution as "an excellent basis for discussion" (Searle, 1976: 7).

6. See Austin (1962), Searle (1975, 1976) for complete discussions of 'felicity conditions,' 'essential conditions,' 'sincerity conditions,' 'propositional content conditions,' and 'preparatory conditions.' See also Duranti (1997) and Rosaldo (1973) for culturally-based critiques of speech act theory—particularly, felicity conditions and sincerity conditions.

7. Brown and Levinson's (1987) politeness model also builds in ways in which damage to the speaker's own positive and negative face can occur through FTAs (e.g., self-humiliation [positive face threat] and making excuses [negative face threat]). See Brown and Levinson (1987) for more discussion on this issue.

8. The *Ellen DeGeneres Show* is a syndicated talk show airing on weekday mornings. The show had been on air for less than one year (debuting in September 2003) at the time that these data were collected. The *Ellen DeGeneres Show*, enjoying rave reviews by in-studio and television viewing audiences around the nation, is still popular today.

CHAPTER EIGHT

Indexicality, Stance, Identity, and Agency

> The indexical character of language reaches far beyond pronouns. Communication rests upon a kind of conceptual language-context orchestration that members of communities are capable of imagining, wherein language forms provide just enough meaning to invoke past, present, and irrealis contexts of cultural and/or personal relevance. [Toni] Morrison captured this capacity in her Nobel Lecture: "Language arcs towards the place where meaning may lie" (1994, p. 20). This is a beautiful image of indexicality as not so much an explicit pointing to a context that is outside of language, but rather a gesturing of language towards a potential realm of meanings that are brought into consciousness through the linguistic gesture. Indexicality exquisitely displays how incompleteness systematically and creatively brings together language and context. (Ochs, 2012: 149)

In this chapter, we broaden the scope of pragmatics beyond inference and implicature, speech acts, and linguistic politeness, and examine the concept of *indexicality.* In Chapter 7 (Pragmatics), we observed the extent to which **common ground, common knowledge, mutual orientation, inference, and implicature** are key to the mutual creation, communication, and understanding of meaning, *beyond literal or objective meanings of the discursive spates in question.* We observed some of the interactional processes of meaning making between a speaker (S) and hearer (H) through implication and inference, whereby speakers (and writers) variably uphold and violate **the basic maxims of conversation**—balancing and gauging: how much information or detail might be too much or too little (maxim of **quantity)**, the varying degrees of truthfulness to put forward (maxim of **quality**), connections and relevance

INDEXICALITY refers to a specific type of meaning expressed through linguistic forms that is not semantic or literal and that is entirely dependent upon context.

Indexicality is most clearly understood in the domains of space and time in three very basic areas of language: 1) **personal pronouns** like *I, we, me, you;* 2) **deictic time reference** like *now, today, yesterday, in a few minutes;* and 3) **deictic space reference** like *here, there, five miles away;* where the connections between the words and what they are pointing to require context for meaning to be conveyed and understood. This semiotic function of indexicality involves a closed, finite set of linguistic forms of spatio-temporal and personal deixis.

Beyond such deictic reference of person, time, and space, **indexicality in discourse** involves the patterned, context-dependent connections of linguistic forms to meanings evoking abstract concepts of personal and social identity, gender, agency, power, authority, entitlement, emotion, elitism, resistance, aesthetics, morality, responsibility, imagination, freedom, and so forth—all elements of communication and interaction that pervade our daily lives and existence. This semiotic function of **discursive indexicality** involves an open, infinite set of possible linguistic forms (including words, strings of words, parts of words, and even contours of prosody and phonological variations) that serve as indices of these and other concepts.

of their contributions to the ongoing discourse (maxim of **relevance**), and the varying degrees of clarity and explicitness to best fit their communicative needs (maxim of **manner**). Hearers and readers, in turn, do their part to infer messages and meanings on the basis of the utterances they receive.

We examined speech acts, from the point of view of **locutionary acts**, i.e., the act of a speaker (S) uttering something (e.g., *It looks like that Nor'easter will hit us some time Sunday*) to its **illocutionary force**, the speech act type, or social function that it fulfills (e.g., *warning* ['Hunker down!'], *agreement* ['You were right!'], *excuse* ['So I can't meet you.'], *invitation* ['Do you want to hunker down together?'], *blaming* ['And you said it would be breezy with drizzles.'], and so forth. The **perlocutionary effect** of the utterance would depend upon how the hearer (H) interprets the meaning and acts on it, e.g., staying home and safe alone, canceling a prior appointment with S, spending Sunday with S, and so forth.

We have also examined politeness as a universal phenomenon, with **face** as its central component. In Brown and Levinson's model based on the positive and negative face wants of speaker (S) and hearer (H), face is conceived as the individual image that one has of oneself—in other words, one's self-esteem. **Face** is also viewed as a more fluid, socio-culturally malleable construct and the social value of one's personhood, with (im)politeness conceptualized as social practice (e.g., Bousfield 2008; Ide, 1989; Matsumoto,1988; Watts, 2003).

Pragmatic meaning in implicature, speech acts, and politeness rests on the logical and rational exchange of implication and inference between speaker (S) and hearer (H), ranging from straightforwardly "bald" explicitness to ambiguous "off-record" hints, or even silence, in the case of complete withholding of a speech act or face threatening act. And, as we observed, crucial to the mutual understanding of all of these units and mechanisms of pragmatic discourse is *context*.

In this chapter, we examine pragmatic meaning from the standpoint of indexicality. Indexicality is rooted in semiotics, where meaning derives from the combined elements of signs, symbols, and context. As a discourse analysis lens, indexicality can provide powerful insights into the creation of discursive meaning through patterned, context-dependent connections of linguistic forms as they evoke abstract concepts relating to personhood, society, and culture. We will illustrate how indexical meaning is created discursively, as it relates to:

- stance: affective stance and epistemic stance (with implications concerning speech acts, performance, presentation of self and others, and moral stance)
- identity: ethnicity, race, and gender
- solidarity, agency, power, and control

INDEXICALITY: FROM DEIXIS AND "SHIFTERS" TO STANCE, IDENTITY, AND AGENCY

In Chapter 4, we examined deixis as a category of reference. Deictic reference terms *(deixis*, from Greek *deiktikos* 'to point, to show') involve those word classes for which meaning is empty without additional information that comes from context. Typical examples of deictic linguistic forms are personal pronouns (e.g., *I, me, mine, you, we, us, it,*), adverbs of time (e.g., *now, then, today, in six months*, *four years ago*), and adverbs of space (e.g., *here, there, in twelve miles, on the left, to the right*). We also introduced demonstrative reference markers *this/these* and *that/those*. Without situated or contextual reference points involving person ("who is the 'I' here as speaker/writer?"), time ("when is this utterance taking place?"), place ("where is the speaker/writer right now?"), or gesture ("It hurts me right *here*" ((pointing to top of left knee))), the speaker's or hearer's intended meanings for such linguistic forms could be impossible to discern. Indexicals as deictic reference terms constitute a relatively closed, finite set of linguistic items that function in this way.

For deixis, as for indexicality, context is crucial in order for such *pointing out of meaning* to be realized. The following blog excerpt from Summit-Post.org (Forum)[1] nicely illustrates some of these concepts. The topic for this thread is: "What does 'we' mean to you?" As you read through the post, pay attention to these issues in particular:

- The various "meanings" of the pronouns *we, I,* and *me.*
- The use of *today.*
- Demonstratives *this* and *those.*

---

by lcarreau Mon Jun 07, 2010 12:41

studmuffin451 wrote: (ONE THREAD IN FORUM)
Some people with split personalities might use "**We**" for "**I**", in which case **We**, means **me**. **We** are enjoying the lovely weather which is finally gracing the Colorado Plateau. **Today** is sunny, dry, and a high of 89 is expected at 7000'. Winds, light from 5 to 10 out of the west. **We** love **this**.

(TWO MORE LINES OF COMMENTARY)

I have a question for **you**. Where the hell is Lago, Arizona located ??? Yes, would be really nice if **those winds** died down. **I'm** in the shade right now.

(The Chief et al., 2010)

There are at least two, if not three distinct postings here: the segment by studmuffin451 and two lines of commentary following that. In the first segment, based only on this portion of the thread, we don't know when "today" refers to. We can only be certain that it preceded the 12:41 A.M. posting by lcarreau, on Monday, June 7, 2010. It is unclear whether each line of commentary is an individual post by two different bloggers or whether both lines were produced by one individual. As such, we cannot tell whether the pronoun *I* in both commentary lines designates the same or two different individuals, nor do we know who the *you* refers to. The second line mentions *those winds.* Which winds, exactly? The ones just mentioned? If so, why do they need to 'die down'? (They are only blowing at 5–10 mph). Other winds? Is the comment ironic?

While a pragmatic analysis of all nine posts in this thread (using concepts from Chapter 7 and others) would yield answers to these and other questions, the lack of clarity resulting from the concomitant lack of remaining context illustrates our points exactly. In spite of so many unknowns, the excerpt is wildly interesting from an indexicality-based perspective.

The pronouns *we* and *I* shift from the simple naming of the words merely as lexical items in the first line to an individuated self-designation of the writer, "me," suggesting a humorous self-ascription of a multiple personality disorder, thereby rationalizing how "we" can sometimes mean "I" in English; the plural conceptualization of the pronoun would thus match the reality of the speaker's psyche. The next token of *we,* now first person <u>plural</u>, points ambiguously to EITHER the writer <u>*and someone else*</u> (i.e., at least one other person or the population of an entire geographic location near the Colorado Plateau) OR to the writer <u>*AND him/herself AS at least one additional alter ego*</u> within a "split personality" psyche. Either interpretation makes sense given the full clause "**We** are enjoying lovely weather . . ." That is, it is plausible for a writer to speak for him/herself and to make generalizations concerning other co-experiencers of the same phenomenon, in this case the seemingly long-awaited pleasantness of the weather ('the lovely weather which is *finally* gracing the Colorado Plateau).

And the humor crescendos in the last line of the studmuffin451 post: "**We** love **this**." This humor was created primarily by the pronouns or linguistic shifters (changing in the discourse from *we* and *I* to *we* and *me* and back again to *we,* all surrounding the mention of "personality disorder"). The sentence "**We** love this" contrasts sharply with the clause "We are enjoying . . .," even though both include the identical sentential subject, "We." Here, however, the pronoun "we" no longer includes potentially everyone in the relevant geographic area. It can't. The verb *love* expresses a feeling far deeper and far more personal than *enjoy.* And it is NOT plausible for a writer or speaker to speak for an extended group of others using a verb like "love," since it is unlikely that all members of that group are actually co-experiencers of the same feelings. There would be a pragmatic incongruence between the subject "we" denoting a broad scope of potential referents and the verb "love," on the basis of access to the experiencer's inner feeling. If the writer/speaker has no access (direct or indirect) to such information, the verb denoting that feeling does not fit the discourse. Thus, the discursive scope of reference narrows to EITHER the blogger and another individual (or closely affiliated group of individuals) OR to the blogger and his/her alter ego(s). And herein lies the irony, as the ambiguity concerning the broad and highly inclusive referential scope of "we" fades, leading the reader toward an interpretation of the joke about "multiple personalities." The entry responds to the originally posted Forum question "What does 'we' mean to you?"

As we have seen, both here and in Chapter 4, deictic reference terms as "shifters" or indexicals do require context to determine which entities, persons, or ideas are being designated by this type of linguistic form.

And, as we have also seen in the previous excerpt, indexical reference cannot truly be limited to instances of just the forms themselves. The scope of meaning of "we," for example, in terms of *inclusiveness* is not simply dependent on such contextual elements as the speaker's or writer's identity, the relationship between and among discourse participants, the genre to which the discourse belongs, modality, and the like. As we observed, the scope of meaning expands and contracts as the pronoun interacts with other discursive elements in the immediate context of the discourse—even just the verbs. "**We** are enjoying the lovely weather . . ." and "**We** love this" designate two very different scopes of inclusion for each instance of the sentential subject "we."

Let's examine another Internet-based data sample.

University of Oregon, University Counseling & Testing Center—How to Cope With Homesickness (Excerpts)

Many university students, particularly during their first year, experience distress about being separated from family and community. "Homesickness" is a normal part of college students' development toward adulthood. Such feelings should be acknowledged and accepted, even when uncomfortable. Lonely feelings can tell you to recognize certain needs and to figure out constructive ways to satisfy them.

While you may be tempted to "escape" by moving back home, a certain amount of enduring and working through such feelings helps you grow into maturity. For instance, while a visit home may help you feel more nurtured and connected, if you come home every weekend, then you are probably missing out on opportunities to cultivate a social life and sense of belonging at UO . . .

. . . Try Creative Self-Talk: What we think or tell ourselves (self-talk) influences what we feel. Here are some beneficial things to tell yourself when you feel homesick.

Just because I'm alone now doesn't mean I'll always be alone.

Although I'd rather be with my friends/family at home tonight, being here in Eugene is okay.

(University Counseling and Testing Center, n.d.)

What is the purpose of this webpage? How are the **prospective readers** of this page *referred to*? First, identify the nouns or noun phrases (e.g., *Many university students*) that are used for referring to the reader(s). Next, identify the pronouns used to refer to the reader.

NOUN PHRASES "Many university students," "college students"
PRONOUNS "their first year," "you," "we," "I," "me"

Who is being addressed in this site? That is, who are the prospective readers and/or users? Does this type of shift in personal reference terms work to attract readers and encourage them to take the advice presented here? In what way?

Now, have a look at the noun phrases that signal "homesickness." How are these feelings referred to in the text?

Designation and description of feelings of "homesickness":

- "distress about being separated"
- "Homesickness is a **normal** part of college students' development toward adulthood." (emphasis added)
- "Such feelings should be acknowledged"
- "Lonely feelings can tell you to recognize certain needs . . ."
- "A certain amount of enduring and working through such feelings helps you grow into maturity."

Some of these are also achieved through comparisons and contrasts (e.g., "more nurtured and connected").

Finally, note the expression in the second excerpted line: ". . . if **you** come home every weekend . . ." Does anything strike you here?

Why is the verb "COME" used, and not "GO?" Whose perspective is being represented in this discourse? What effect (albeit subtle) does this help to create in the overall purpose of the website?

SUMMARY: The use of noun phrases "Many university students/college students" shifts to the use of **pronouns.** *You* shifts to *we* and then to *I* and *me*. What other deictic reference terms co-occur with the first person pronoun *I* (e.g., *now, here,* and even *home*)?

- "Just because I'm alone **now** doesn't mean I'll always be alone." (emphasis added)
- . . . being **here** in Eugene is okay. (emphasis added)

Who is being addressed and how?

What or who is being ***pointed out deictically*** through these shifting terms of reference? What sorts of discursive elements serve to try to draw readers in?

The site's primary purpose is to attract readers and encourage them to use the site and the services of the Center—if needed—and to ultimately effect a smoother transition into college life away from home.

Reference terms such as those noted here (and more) combine with other features of discourse (including verbs, adjectives, adverbs, etc.) to construct a sense of security and comfort for those who visit the site and who may benefit from the services provided by the Center.

In the remainder of this chapter, we will explore indexicality more deeply as the patterned, context-dependent connections of linguistic forms to meanings, and we will discuss its power to evoke such abstract concepts as stance, personal and social identity, gender, morality, responsibility, and agency. In contrast with the closed, finite set of forms that constitute indexicals as deictic reference terms, indexicality as viewed from this broader perspective of discourse involves an open, infinite set of possible linguistic forms, from contours of prosody to words and parts of words and strings of words—all of which may potentially serve as indices of many abstract concepts.[2] At the end of this chapter, we will return to the U of Oregon website excerpt and will view it through the lens of indexicality beyond the referential.

Semiotics and Indexicality

Indexicality belongs to the domain of semiotics (see Hanks, 1990, 1992, 2005, 2009; Lyons, 1977a, 1977b; Ochs, 1990, 1996, 2012; Pierce, 1955;

Silverstein, 1976, 1996, 2003, among others). In simple terms, the domain of semiotics involves the connections between signs and their meanings (Lyons, 1977a, 1977b; Pierce, 1931–36, 1955).

Following Lyons, we use the letter **A** to designate the **sign** (as **word, name, idea, image**) and the letter **C** to designate **the meaning that is connected to the sign**.

The connections between sign A and its meaning(s) C, can be ICONIC, SYMBOLIC, or INDEXICAL. In an **iconic relationship**, A **resembles** C. In a **symbolic relationship**, the *connection between the sign and its meaning is arbitrary*. And in an **indexical relationship**, A points to the existence or presence of C. It does not *mean* C (symbolic) and it does not *resemble* C (iconic).

Semiotics simplified

ICONIC relationship: A means C because A **resembles** C. If one is on an airplane and it is too dark to read, one presses a button that looks like this:

Here, the *icon of the light bulb resembles the very thing that will produce light*. Push the button: You get LIGHT.

SYMBOLIC relationship: A means C through arbitrary convention. The English abstract noun "light" bears no resemblance to its meaning of "illumination, absence of darkness." The connection between A (the word "light") and its meaning C is entirely arbitrary. "Light" means "the absence of darkness, or illumination" strictly through convention.

INDEXICAL relationship: A points to the existence or presence of C. A might be the word "light" (used non-literally or metaphorically) or an image depicting light. These instances of "light" as signs might index brilliance, intelligence, sudden realization or understanding, peacefulness, joy, divinity, a state of being awake, a state of being alert, a state of someone being "home" (because the lights are on), etc., by pointing toward these meanings.

Indices in language involve the very "gesturing of language toward a potential realm of meanings that are brought into the consciousness" that Ochs (2012: 149) mentions in the quote that opens this chapter. In the University of Oregon website excerpt, we observed such linguistic gesturing in the systematic shifts of references, and even in the expression ". . . if you **come home** every weekend," where the use of the verb "come" points ambiguously to a reader's perspective as well as to a parent perspective, and not a more distanced writer's perspective that the verb "go" would index. In the sections that follow, we will observe in more detail, with more discourse-based examples, the manifold ways in which "[i]ndexicality displays how incompleteness systematically and creatively brings together language and context" (Ochs, 2012:149).

As we will see, it is not the explicit and overt presence of linguistic structures, lexical items, gestures and prosody that index abstract concepts of identity (e.g., gender, ethnicity, social class, elitism), morality, deference, dominance, and power. Rather, these discursive uses of language and gesture *point to* those concepts, they evoke them through connections with those concepts. "Light," used *indexically* in the previous definition, does not *mean* light in the literal sense of "illumination." It might evoke intellectual sharpness on the abstract and metaphorical level. On the concrete level, it may index that someone is both "at home" and "awake." And on the metaphorically clichéd level, it may index a lack of mental acuity, despite outward appearances of alertness ("The light is on but no one is home."). Similarly, the discourse marker "I know^—:::::" uttered with an extended vowel stretch and a rise-fall-extended level pitch, might index a stance of heightened interlocutor solidarity and involvement, not a literal expression that points to the interlocutor's personal state of knowledge.

Indexicality and Stance

As we noted in Chapter 7, **pragmatics** is the area of linguistic and sociolinguistic study that is concerned with the ways in which speakers and hearers and readers and writers (in any modality of discourse) both create and derive meaning from non-literal interpretations of discourse, while engaged in contextually situated interaction. As such indexicality falls squarely within the domain of pragmatics. The crucial issue here is the notion of "non-literal interpretations of discourse," the filling-in of what is left unsaid, the systematic and creative interweaving of discourse and context through "incompleteness," by expressing more than what the words alone express (e.g., "I know^—:::::").

Indexicality is an indispensable lens for the analysis of discourse. The meaning created by and through such discursive interweaving of what is said with what is not said emerges in **patterns**—patterns which at once create, enact, and reveal how we feel about things, how certain we are about the topics we discuss, and how we morally evaluate them. These patterns index how we construct ourselves, how we construct others, and how others construct us. They index our understandings of agency and of change, and how change takes place—our views of who or what the agents of change are (e.g., ourselves or others, individuals or groups, animate or inanimate entities [like medicines or corporations or weather]). They index our conceptualizations of responsibility and power. And the discursive phenomenon of indexicality all takes place well beyond what speakers and writers explicitly say about these on the surface or literal level.

We have introduced the notion of *stance* using the following definition:

> **STANCE is the speaker's or writer's feeling, attitude, perspective, or position as enacted in discourse.** *Stance taking* is an inevitable consequence of participating in and producing discourse, of putting the world into words. **STANCE** emerges in a speaker's or writer's choice of one linguistic form over another, the coloring of utterances with prosodic contours or punctuation, the sequential ordering of utterances; it emerges in gestures, silences, hesitations, hedges, and in overlapping stretches of talk. In all of these instances of discourse (and others), a speaker's or writer's stance is enacted and created; it is negotiated and re-negotiated.

Stance is inextricably related to *indexicality*—where meaning actually transcends those words and relies on both the bodily and linguistic gestures to fill in the gaps. For research on stance in the fields of linguistics, anthropology, sociolinguistics, and applied linguistics, see Bucholtz, 1999, 2009; Bucholtz and Hall, 2005; Clift, 2006; Du Bois, 2007, 2011a, 2011b; Dubois and Kärkkäinen, 2012; Englebretson, 2007; Jaffe, 2009; Johnstone, 2009; Irvine, 2009; Kiesling, 2005, 2009; Ochs, 1990, 1992, 1996; Jaworski and Thurlow, 2009.

Stance-taking involves the action of evaluating—emotionally, epistemically, morally, and conceptually (see Chapter 2). When we express any point of view about any topic, any person, any deed, we do so from a particular standpoint. We take a perspective. We position ourselves vis à vis what is being evaluated or vis à vis other discursive participants. We express a feeling, an emotive reaction, a moral view of what is right or wrong, of what is normal or aberrant or peculiar, or even just a little odd. We qualify our opinions. We may be cocksure. We may question and doubt. And we may waffle between the extreme. In each case, though, we express a stance—one of feeling or judgment, of alignment or distance.

In this chapter, we will address two main sub-categories of stance[3]:

- Affective stance
- Epistemic stance

Affective stance: reflects "the mood, attitude, feeling, and disposition, as well as degrees of emotional intensity, vis à vis some focus of concern." (from Ochs 1996: 420). See also Besnier, 1990, 1993; Goodwin, C., 2007; Goodwin, M. and Goodwin, C., 2000; Irvine, 1990; Maynard, 1993; Suzuki, 2006, among others.

Indices of affective stance might include: words of disbelief, adverbial intensifiers (so, very, incredibly), adverbial attenuators (just, a little, kind of, kinda), superlatives (the best, worst, greatest, scariest), parts of words like diminutives (doll → dollie or cat → kitty) and words inserted into or between other words (e.g., "un[fill in]believable," or "for like ever"), prosodic features, including such vocal fluctuations as increased volume, frequent exhalation and inhalation, laughter, marked rising intonation, whining intonation, etc. Further, punctuation reflecting such prosodic contours are also potential indicators of affective stance in written discourse.

Here is a classic example from Ochs (1996: 421–422). As you read through the excerpt, pay attention to the following features of the discourse:

- Prosodic contours, especially in Heddi's and Sharon's turns.
- Descriptors (i.e., adjectives)—who uses them and how?

  o What is the predominant descriptor in the excerpt?

- How does the mother respond to the Heddi's and Sharon's assessments?
- What is the primary **speech act** (See Chapter 7) performed by Heddi and Sharon?

```
((Mother, Father, and Grandfather and three children [Heddi, Sharon,
and Kit] are having dinner)):
```

→Heddi: the PEAS are <u>CO:::LD!</u>
Mother: what ((*to Heddi*))
Sharon: ((*while tapping plate with fork*)) [(   )
Kit: [mu mu mu mu mum
→Heddi: [these peas are cold!
Mother: (it won't hurt/okay)—((*to father*)) were- were <u>your</u> peas [cold
              when you ate 'em?
Kit: ((*Kit continues to struggle and whimper*))
Father: I didn't eat 'em—I (haven't had/didn't have) any yet ((*pause*))
Mother: ((*to Kit*)) just a <u>minute</u> I'll get you some mo:re
→Sharon: <u>BU:::[:RR!</u>
?:   (what's a matter Sharon?)
→Sharon: bur[r these peas are cold!
Heddi: [they're f- ((*as she looks into pan for more food*))
Mother: oh =
→Heddi: = they're <u>freezing</u> co::ld!

Heddi's speech act is a complaint, and a strong one. Her position vis à vis the peas are that they are inedible—they are cold, and, to her, not just a little bit cold. She frames them as "freezing." Not only does Heddi's mother see the problem as minor (if she considers it a problem at all), she publicly discounts Heddi's claim by asking her husband whether *his* peas were also cold. Lexically and prosodically, Heddi indexes her dissatisfaction about the peas through the descriptor *cold,* uttered with increased volume and an elongated vowel sound. In fact, both the words *peas* and *cold* are audibly stressed in the discourse through increased volume. Sharon, Heddi's sister, indexes solidarity and alignment with Heddi's position by producing the "I'm freezing" sound of *BRRRRR.* Heddi then upgrades her own assessment, now saying that the peas are not just "cold." They are *freezing cold.* Heddi is not *saying* "I am complaining about the peas." She utters an *indirect speech act* affectively intensified through prosody and lexical choice (and predictably through accompanying bodily gestures as well).

The following excerpt is an extended personal narrative. Here, the speaker, "Katherine" (pseudonym), then a college student, describes an event that took place while she was still in high school—the story involves an added part-time job that "Katherine" took for some extra cash.

- What is the genre of discourse? In what way does genre influence how we organize and produce discourse?
- How would you characterize the various types of affective intensifiers? (e.g., exclamations, prosody, breathiness, lexical items such as descriptors, adverbial intensifiers [e.g., *really, so*]).
- Clearly, there is affect involved. Katherine is emotional. What types of emotions is she indexing? How do you know?
- Is there anything else that you see being indexed here?

Katherine's "Ram" Story

There was these people at my <u>first</u> job ((at a restaurant)), and I was in <u>high school</u>, (0.2) and there was a <u>couple</u>. = They were <u>regulars</u>. = They always came in, (.) and they raised sheep and sheep dogs, (0.2) en they would often take their dogs and maybe a few sheep to competitions. (.) They always needed someone to come watch their animals. = They had ducks and things, = so to make some <u>extra</u> money I would housesit for them.
(0.4)

Well <u>one da:::y</u>, the guy came in. (.) They had a bunch of female sheep and then a <u>ra::m</u>. (1.0) And they always kept the ram in this little hut, (.) just because he got <u>rea::lly</u> terr::<u>ito::</u>ria:l. (.) And even one time the guy came in, and he had- his <u>whole head</u> and face was black and blue and <u>red</u>, and he- What <u>happened</u> was the <u>ra::m corner</u>ed him, (.) and took him <u>do:wn</u>, en <u>attac</u>ked him basically.
(0.8)

Well <u>one</u> of the times that I went there, they're like well, we left the <u>ra:m ou:t</u>, (.) in the field with the sheep. It's okay (.) He's not gonna hurt <u>you</u>, . . . But they're like <u>don't worry</u> about it, just <u>do</u> what you normally <u>do. .</u>
(0.6)

And in the <u>mor:::ni:ng</u>, the first day I went <u>ou:t</u>, I <u>no</u>ticed hi:m, (0.2) you know <u>wa:tching</u> me really <u>clo:sely:</u>, and kinda <u>fo::l</u>lowing me <u>arou:nd</u>, (.) so I was a little bit <u>ne::rv</u>ous about it (.) but I was just like I'm not gonna <u>show</u> him that I'm afrai::d of <u>hi::m</u>, I'm just gonna you know, look him in the <u>eyes</u>, en like try to as<u>se:rt</u> myse:lf, (.) I don't know (.) But I <u>wa:::s</u> scared. (0.4) So that was the <u>mo:r</u>ning, (.) and then when I went out in the afternoo::n, it was a little bit wo:rse, (.). . .you know I was afraid if I ra:n, I mean I would think I could outrun this thi:ng, but I was just literally fro- zen (.) in (.) terror (.) because I kept remembering the guy's hea:d . . . and he was a bi:g ma:n (.) I mean he was bi::g. (0.2) So I just stoo::d there en looked at hi:m, en he bowed his hea:d, and like sta::mped his fee:t, like you see in the mo:vies, (.) en I was oh my go:::sh (.) I couldn't mo::ve. = en he ca:me AT me en bumped me in the stomach. (0.2) and so::, I just like finally I woke up basically:, en I maybe shou::ted en . . . or something. = and took off ru::nning and jumped over the fe::nce en lu::ckily I was oka::y. = >I mean< he didn't really kno:ck me do::wn (.) but it hu::rt and thought I was going to have wre:stling match with this animal. ((laughter)), so . . .

(Feiz and Strauss, 2005)

The excerpt is replete with affect: trust, fear, uncertainty, terror. Make a list of the indices of affect and affective intensifiers that Katherine uses here. Is there a predominant type of "speech act" that you can identify in this excerpt, beyond that expressing fear? If so, what would that be? What else is Katherine expressing? How does she portray the animals in this excerpt? How does she construct the other people involved in the story? Essentially, what emotions, in addition to those explicitly labeled, like "nervous" or "scared," are being indexed in this narrative? What are the underlying messages? How do the concepts of narrative and narrative structure enter into the analysis of this discourse (see Chapter 3)?

EPISTEMIC STANCE

We now move to the category of epistemic stance. We define epistemic stance as follows:

> **EPISTEMIC STANCE:** reflects the belief system of a speaker or writer vis à vis the issues being communicated or discussed, including information source (e.g., *I saw it with my own eyes, Jenna told me yesterday that* . . .), degrees of certainty or shades of doubt in the presentation of facts and opinions, and degrees of personal or institutional commitment to the issue(s) at hand. (See also Biber and Finegan, 1989; Chafe and Nichols, 1986; Hayano, 2011; Heritage, 2012; Kirkham, 2011; Kokelman, 2004; Mushin, 2001.)

Indices of *epistemic stance might include:* expressions of knowing, think-ing, and believing (including these very verbs of cognition); epistemic modals (e.g., should, might, must); adverbials of degrees of certainty (e.g., maybe, perhaps, for sure, certainly, no doubt); adverbials of com-mitment (e.g., in no way, in fact, absolutely); adverbials of mitigation (only, just); unqualified equative expressions with copula *be* (e.g., X is Y: "Home **is** a name, a word, it is a strong one; stronger than magician ever spoke or spirit ever answered to, in the strongest conjuration"[4]).

Next, we illustrate the indexing of epistemic stance using another example from Ochs (1996: 422, originally cited in Goodwin, 1990: 154). As you read through the text, pay attention to the following:

- Note the repetitions of words and phrases in one line and then in the very next line that follows (e.g., fight *yourself* → fight *myself*; Well you *make me* → I can't *make you*; *it's a free world* → I know *it's a free world*).[5]
- Given this type of repetition and the apparent tension between Stacey and Ruby, what type of **speech act** would you say is being expressed throughout this excerpt, including the last line: "I know it's a free world?"
- How does this use of "I know + [assertion]" contrast with the "I know^—:::::" marker of solidarity and co-alignment that we men-tioned earlier in this chapter (and other uses of "I know" with various prosodic contours)?

((Ruby and Stacey are pre-adolescent African-American girls; they are in the midst of an argument.)) [emphasis, i.e., bold and italics, original.]

Stacey: Fight yourself.
Ruby: Well you ***make*** me fight myself.
Stacey: I can't ***make*** you. Cuz it's a free world.
Ruby: I ***know*** it's a free world.

(Goodwin, 1990: 154)

As for the marking of epistemic stance, Ochs (1996: 423) notes that Ruby's use of the verb *know* is doing two things: 1) "constitutively index[ing] her certain knowledge about the proposition 'it's a free world,'" and 2) "con-structing a challenge" to Stacey's just prior utterance.

Further, Goodwin (1990: 151–156) points out that disclaimers such as "I don't care" or "I know ([+assertion])," suggesting that the information just presented is "not newsworthy,[6]" are not uncommon in "oppositional" and confrontational discourse, as in the previous excerpt. Thus, the marking of epistemic stance in discourse functions not simply to index knowledge or certainty about a particular bit of information, but also to index other, more complex, stances of speakers and writers vis à vis an issue, an event, or a set of beliefs. Interestingly, the two words "I know," uttered with different prosodic contours ("I know^—:::::" and "I know."), index diametrically opposite types of stances—one of solidarity, empathy, and co-alignment, and the other of challenge and dismissiveness.

Let's examine epistemic stance marking using another spate of discourse.

The following excerpt, illustrating various aspects of epistemic stance, is taken from an interview with Noam Chomsky, entitled "The Purpose of Education," presented at the Learning Without Frontiers[7] Conference of January 25, 2012, in London. In this excerpt, which is the opening three minutes of talk, Chomsky mentions two distinct views on the topic of education, one which he endorses and the other which he disdains.

As you read through the transcript (and/or watch the video if it is available), pay attention to the following features:

- What is Chomsky's message? Why did he participate in this forum in the first place? In one or two sentences, articulate his main point.
- How would you characterize Chomsky's stance in paragraph 1? How would you characterize Chomsky's stance in paragraph 2? (We assigned "paragraphs" to the spates of talk on the basis of topic: topic opening, topic development, and topic closing).
- Identify indices of epistemic stance in both paragraphs.
- Through what types of linguistic structures (i.e., lexical items and grammar) does Chomsky index his affiliation with the one view?
- Through what types of linguistic structures (i.e., lexical items and grammar) does he index his disdain for the other?

Noam Chomsky: "The Purpose of Education" Excerpt from Learning without Frontiers Interview

Well, we can ask ourselves what the purpose of an educational system is, and of course there are sharp differences on this matter. There's the traditional interpretation that comes from the Enlightenment, which holds that the highest goal in life is to inquire and create, to search the riches of the past, to try to internalize the parts of them that are significant to you, and carry that quest for understanding further in your own way. The purpose of education from that point of view is just to help people determine how to learn on their own. It's you, the learner, who is going to achieve in the course of education. And it's really up to you what you'll master, where you'll go, how you'll use it, how you'll go on to produce something new and exciting for yourself and maybe for others. That's one concept of education.

Now the other concept is essentially indoctrination. People have the idea that from childhood, that young people have to be placed into a framework in which they will follow orders, accept existing frameworks and not challenge, and so on. And this is often quite explicit. And so, for example, after the activism of the 1960s, there was great concern across much of the educated spectrum that young people were just getting too free and independent, that the country was becoming too democratic, and so on. In fact, there's an important study on what's called "The Crisis of Democracy," too much democracy, arguing that there are-, claiming that there are certain institutions responsible for the indoctrination of the young; it's their phrase. And they're not doing their job properly: That's schools, universities, churches. We have to change them so that they carry out the job of indoctrination and control more effectively. And that's actually coming from the liberal internationalists' end of the spectrum of educated opinion. And, in fact, since that time, there have been many measures taken to try to turn the educational system towards more control, more indoctrination, more vocational training, imposing a debt which traps students, young people into a life of conformity and so on . . .

(Chomsky, 2012)

In terms of epistemic stance marking, the entire passage reflects a high degree of certainty throughout. However, Chomsky's position concerning one view of education, as opposed to the other, is discursively constructed in markedly different ways.

In reading through this transcript, think about the types of indices of epistemic stance that Chomsky uses in both paragraphs. How would you characterize Chomsky's shift in stance from the first paragraph to the second? How is this shift in position indicated through linguistic forms?

Compare the content and structure of paragraph 1 to the content and structure of paragraph 2. Paragraph 1 is built around the theme of the Enlightenment and the Kantian goal of intellectual freedom. Note in particular the instances of verbs related to learning and understanding and cognitive growth, with an emphasis on independence, novelty, and creativity, ultimately leading toward the goal of helping oneself and helping others.

Here is a partial list of the verbs relating to cognition and learning from paragraph 1.

> *inquire, create, search* the riches of the past, *internalize* the parts of them . . . , *carry* that quest for understanding further, *help* people *determine* how to *learn* on their own, who is going to *achieve,* what **you** will *master,* where **you** will *go,* how **you'll** *use* it, how **you'll** *go on to produce something new* and *exciting for yourself* and maybe *for others* . . .

Note also the use of the second person pronoun "you." Who do you think that "you" here refers to?

> **it's up to you***, the learner . . . And* **it's really up to you** *what* **you'll master** . . .

The paragraph ends with a six-word sentence (We consider "That's" as two words, since it's contracted). The sentence takes the form of an unqualified equative construction (X is Y) as a sort of coda or concluding remark to tie together the main theme of his talk and his initial arguments—the theme with which Chomsky affiliates more strongly. He sums everything up with the anaphoric pronoun *that,* signaling a sharedness of information among writer and listeners/readers (i.e., "That" = "everything that I have just said"): **That's <u>one concept</u>** *of education*. And by virtue of his use of "one" to qualify the expression, "concept of education," we sense that a contrast, a parallel comparison, will be coming next—essentially, *another* view on the topic.

Paragraph 2 begins with another equative construction (X is Y), and recycles the word *concept,* contrastively linking both the structure and the content to the final sentence of paragraph 1. The word *education* (not mentioned explicitly here) is equated with *indoctrination*: Now **the other concept** *is* *essentially indoctrination.* He has established a binary opposition: *ONE concept* (i.e., education) and *THE OTHER* (i.e., indoctrination).

In paragraph 2, we no longer see any mention of learning or creativity, of mastery or achievement. Instead, we find themes of intellectual restraint and subjugation.

An ideological shift has occurred in Chomsky's talk: from freedom of thought and creativity in learning *in general,* to this becoming a threat in the United States (though he has not explicitly named the nation). There are two themes here in the discourse: 1) the changing state of affairs (particularly in the U.S.), and 2) the consequent reforms in thinking that led the nation to necessitate such intellectual restraint.

Note the thematic indicators of restraint in this paragraph, as well as the indices of change of state, especially through change of state copular forms, like *get, become.* We have underlined those state-change indicators to help them stand out:

> *young people have to be placed into a framework . . ., follow orders, accept existing frameworks, not challenge, young people were just getting too free and independent, the country was becoming too democratic, too much democracy, We have to change them [the institutions] so that they carry out the job of indoctrination and control more effectively, that's actually coming from the liberal internationalists' end of the spectrum, try to turn the educational system towards more control, more indoctrination.*

And, in contrast with **the pronoun *you*** that co-occurred with expressions of freedom of thinking in paragraph 1, we find five tokens of the word ***young*** (4 of which are ***young people***) as the very targets of this intellectual subjugation and indoctrination.

Further, how does Chomsky indicate the nation? Does he name the U.S.? Does he provide other clues? What are they? Who does the pronoun *We* refer to in the clause: "We have to change them. . . ."? Do you note any personal affiliation on Chomsky's part with the nation through any inclusive uses of 1st person plural pronouns *we* or *our?*

Finally, what types of connections can you make that link epistemic stance to the structure of rhetorical argumentation, on the one hand, and discussions of morality on the other? That is, just based this short excerpt, what is Chomsky's underlying purpose in participating in this forum? What ideological beliefs are driving his arguments? Beyond expressing what he knows and what he believes about education in the United States, Chomsky is making moral claims. What are those and how are they framed? For work on moral stance, see Bergmann (1998), Christodoulidou (2010), Drew (1998), Goodwin (2007), Shoaps (2009), and others.

Indexicality and Identity

In Chapter 7, we examined the notion of "face" as it relates to politeness and social interaction. "Face" in English is a common noun. What comes to mind immediately is the visual, outward image of a person—skin color, eye color, eye shape, shape of nose, contour of lips and chin, quality of smile. We examined broader scopes of meaning associated with "face" from a number of theoretical perspectives associated with social interaction, mutual co-alignment, and distance.

The notion of "identity" is similar to "face" in that both terms point to the very essence of our individual personhood—who we are on the inside (our individual make up and personality, our likes, dislikes, beliefs and values) and who we are on the outside (how we want others to perceive us, how others do perceive and recognize us). And both terms are robustly charged with meaning when viewed from theoretical perspectives. Like "face," "identity" is much more than simply one's name, age, date and place of birth, hair and eye color, height, weight, gender, and ethnicity. The construct of identity is seemingly paradoxical in that it points to those very characteristics and traits that distinguish us as uniquely "identifiable" individuals, and, at the same time, it points to commonalities that categorize us as similar to others in systematic ways.

Research on identity in the fields of sociolinguistics, psychology, anthropology, communication, and applied linguistics has been burgeoning—see Agha (2004), Bauman (2001), Bucholtz (2001, 2011), Bucholtz and Hall (2004, 2005, 2008), Buckingham (2008), Butler (1990, 2005), Cameron and Kulick (2003, 2005), Deckert and Vickers (2011), De Fina (2007), Eckert (1989, 2000, 2008), Eckert and McConnel-Ginet (2003), Fishman and Garcia (2010), Hall (2005, 2009), Holmes (2006), Holmes and Myerhoff (2003),Kulick (2003), Nagel (1994), Schilling-Estes (2004), Kiely et al. (2006), and Kiesling (2005, 2009), drawing on foundational work by Giddens (1991), Goffman (1959/1990), and Tajfel (1981, 1982/2010), among others.

For the purpose of discussing identity in relation to indexicality and discourse, we provide the following definition:

> **IDENTITY** refers to the physical and psychological traits and interactional behaviors that characterize who we are as individuals, that distinguish us as unique from others, and that motivate us to think, believe, and act as we do. Identity also refers to those aspects of our outward behaviors and appearances that we portray while interacting with others, in both implicit and explicit ways. Identity, as it relates to the individual (and the private) and as it relates to the social (and the public) is a complex, dynamic construct. Features of our identity can be malleable and permeable on the one hand, and stable and rigid on the other. Alone and in concert with others, we enact our identities in all aspects of our daily lives within any discursive genre and through any modality. In and through discourse, we enact, create, and re-create our identities as thinking and feeling and caring individuals, as gendered and sexual beings, as members of a family, an ethnicity, a race, a social class, a nation, a profession, a religion or a cult, as members of a school or club, as consumers and users and connoisseurs of products, as players in games and sports, as stoic upholders of policy, as workers doing our utmost or just getting by.

Identity is indeed both complex and dynamic. In and through discourse, we index masculinity, femininity, ethnicity, obedience, entitlement, diligence, dominance, and resistance. We index alignment, collaboration, inclusion and group membership, exclusion and disaffiliation. And just as stance bears an inextricable relationship with *indexicality,* so does identity.

And here again, indexical meanings associated with identity actually transcend individual words and rely on Ochs's (2012) notion of bodily and "linguistic gestures" to fill in the gaps.

The following are examples of how identity is indexed in discourse, and how scholars discuss the topic. To illustrate, we focus on:

- Italian cultural and ethnic identity, group affiliation (De Fina, 2007)
- Cool nonchalance and affiliation among college males (Kiesling, 2004)
- Marked and unmarked social categories of race and gender: whiteness, blackness, and maleness (Bucholtz, 1999).

INDEXING ITALIAN ETHNIC IDENTITY, AFFILIATION, GROUP MEMBERSHIP

De Fina (2007) writes about a group of Italian-American men who play cards at a private card club in Washington, DC, called *Circolo della Briscola*. *Briscola* is similar to bridge. *Briscola* decks contain 40 cards: 10 cards in four suits. The suits are *bastoni* 'batons' or 'clubs,' *denari* 'coins' or 'sunbursts,' *spade* 'swords' or 'spades,' and *coppe* 'cups.' Five cards are number cards: 2, 4, 5, 6, and 7. The remaining five cards are picture cards, including *cavallo* 'horseman' and *regina* 'queen,' *donna* 'lady,' and *fante* 'valet' (see Briscola game rules, n.d.; Circolo della Briscola, n.d., for full game rules). The *cavallo* and *regina* are each worth three points. The *donna* and *fante* are worth two points each.

According to De Fina (2007), code-switching from English to Italian in the context of this card game as an important index of ethnic affiliation, especially in the socialization process depicted here, where a newcomer, Carl, is learning the game. Carl speaks no Italian. Two other Italian Americans, Paul and Al, both of whom speak very little Italian, are teaching Carl how to play *briscola*.

As you will note in the excerpt, Carl is not familiar with the picture cards or their values. He shows his frustration at line 5, as he puts his head in his hands, noted by De Fina as "a gesture of desperation." And at line 10, he indexes "disapproval" that they are not using "American cards."

01	Carl:	((pointing at card)) What the hell is this? Is that a queen?
02	Paul:	No that's a horse.
03	Carl:	You don't have a queen in there.
04	Paul:	No.
05	Carl:	((holds his head with his hands))
06	((pointing)) that's three,	
07	Paul:	Three.
08	Carl:	That's two,
09	Paul:	Two.
10	Carl:	((Shakes head)) Why don't you use American cards?
11	Paul:	That's not =
12	Carl:	= What's that thing?
13	Paul:	That's not *tradizionale*! [traditional]@
14	Carl:	@@((annoyed)) What's that thing there?
15	Paul:	That's the ace of spade, *spada*.
16	Carl:	That's ace?

17	Paul:	Now this is (.)
18	Al:	A horse.
19	Paul:	*Cavallo, cavallo di spada.*

(De Fina, 2007: 387)
Note: ((@ indicates laughter))

Paul, in his response to Carl's complaint that they are not using American cards, appeals directly to the concept of Italian tradition. And he does so by code-switching, using the single Italian word, *tradizionale*. He utters his response in an emphatic tone. As De Fina (2007: 387). notes, there is a clear attempt here to "symbolically construct and . . . establish a meaningful past and endow particular cultural forms with value and authority" by "traditional-izing" (Bauman, 1992: 128) the practices and products of the participants' cultural and ethnic heritages and thereby indexing their identity as belonging to and affiliating with that cultural and ethnic heritage. In spite of their limited proficiency in Italian, Paul and Al are teaching Carl how to refer to the cards by suit and picture, using the proper Italian names for each. Through their talk and their behaviors, they are socializing Carl and guiding him into this practice of playing *briscola* as a member of the *Circolo* and as a member of the broader Italian-American community.

Note that Carl, too, begins to code-switch into Italian. The tension between his insistence on "American cards" and the use of Italian cards with Italian names and a different point value system diminishes significantly:

01	Carl:	((addressing Paul)) *Cavallo bastoni* [knight (of) clubs] ah?
02	Paul:	((Nods)) *Cavallo bastoni.*
(.)		
03	Paul:	((addressing researcher)) *Come si dice?* [How do you say?]
04	Res:	*Questo è il* (.) *fante di coppa* [This is the jack of cups]
05	Paul:	*Fante di coppa.*

Through Carl's own use of Italian, as he recognizes and names the cards, he ultimately demonstrates his emergent identity as a member in this community of practice (*briscola* players), as a member of the broader *Circolo*.

Cool Nonchalance and Affiliation Among College Males

Kiesling (2004) points out how the American English slang vocative "Dude" indexes a both a cool nonchalance and solidarity among college males. The excerpted conversation provided here takes place at a bar between two college-aged males, Pete and Dan. Note the contrast in degree of "enthusiasm" indexed in each participant's turns.

This exchange takes place at a bar.

Dan: I love playin' caps.
            That's what did me in the last-   [last week.
Pete: [That's-
            Everybody plays that damn game, DUDE.

(adapted from Kiesling, 2004: 295)

Pete is a fraternity member. Dan, an out-of-town friend, has come to visit another member of the same fraternity. Dan has been making enthusiastic comments in the form of conversational assessments (See Chapter 6) about the drinking game called "caps." His enthusiasm for caps is reflected through the combination of his word choice "love," the reduced -ing ending on the verb "playin'," his attribution of the game's negative effect on some element of his life ("That's what did me in")—because he "loves" it *so much*, and the fact that he plays it regularly ("the last- (time [unsaid]) last week").

As Kiesling (2004: 295) notes, Pete aligns with Dan's general assessment, without echoing the same degree of enthusiasm. Instead, Pete attenuates all levels of enthusiasm about the game by generalizing its popularity ("everybody plays") and by minimizing its allure and importance to him ("that damn game"). Pete has just downgraded Dan's assessment. He then tacks on DUDE, with its particular intonation contour, that both redresses his blatant downgrade and, at the same time, indexes solidarity with Dan, in a "cool and nonchalant" manner.

Unmarked Social Categories, e.g., Maleness and Whiteness

Bucholtz (1999) addresses the indexical construction of identity through contrasts between so-called marked and unmarked social categories. For

Bucholtz, social categories are not fixed and rigid pigeonholes as classificatory terms for members of one ethnic group or another, one racial group or another, and even one gender or another. Instead, social categories are constructed discursively—through language and other semiotic resources. As noted by Bucholtz (1999: 447), "marked" categories typically include women and individuals from non-white, non-English speaking heritage groups, because the former groups are "visible" against the backdrop of the "invisible" white male with ancestors from English speaking nations—in other words, the invisible cultural norm.

Bucholtz (1999) uses Rampton's (1995, 1998) framework of "language crossing" in her analysis of the indexical construction of self and other in the narratives of European American high school boys attending a multi-ethnic, multi-racial high school in California. Different from code-switching[8] (e.g., from English to Italian and back again), as we observed in the previous excerpt from De Fina (2007), "language crossing involves a sense of movement across quite sharply felt social or ethnic boundaries, and it raises issues of legitimacy that participants need to reckon with in the course of their encounter" (Rampton, 1998: 1).

The following excerpt is from a longer narrative produced by a European American male attending the high school noted above, referred to in the article as Brand One. Brand One's story is about an incident that had occurred some two months earlier while he was walking to a bus stop. There are two parties in his story: Brand One, the protagonist, and another person, the "antagonist," as Bucholtz calls him. The narrative is about a conflict. In his story telling, Brand One indexes both race and gender, or more specifically, whiteness, blackness, and masculinity, through his own ideological stance-taking in combination with lexico-grammatical choices and prosody.

Brand One Narrative Excerpt—Part 1

7   . . two months ago this dude [du:d],

2   um(1.5)

3   ((tongue click))

4   I was walking up to uh (.) to (.) the bus stop

5   and he- and he was in my backpack right?

6   This this black dude [du:d] was like six (.) maybe like fi:ve ten he was big,

7   he was a lot bigger than me.

(Bucholtz, 1999: 448)

As you read through the excerpts, note the elements of narrative that are addressed in Chapter 3, especially with respect to structure and "tellability."

Also, note the terms of reference used to designate the identity and the characteristics of Brand One's "antagonist." (See Chapters 2, 4, and 5).

Here is how the narrative opens. In just these few lines of narrative, what indices of race and/or gender, if any, do you note?

Referentially, the slang personal reference term *dude*[9] unambiguously designates gender. The term possibly designates race, but not unambiguously. It is not until line 6 that Brand One qualifies the race of the "dude" in question, i.e., "This this black dude," followed by details relating to the "antagonist's" size. The placement of such qualification in Brand One's narrative is crucial. Up to now, the "antagonist" was simply a "dude," and later referred to as "he" (line 5). But the story is not complete. Because it is not yet accurate. The issue here is that someone, a male, was "in" Brand One's backpack, as if about to steal something from it. Because the narrator reformulated the reference terms for this individual, now specifying a category of race, we learn that the "male someone" is in fact black and tall and big. And not only is he big, he is "a lot bigger than" Brand One. He felt threatened. He felt overpowered.

As Bucholtz (1999) notes, issues of both race and gender were made relevant to the narrative well before the telling even began. That is, as the narrative develops, we observe from Brand One's perspective, that it is actually the "antagonist" who had made both race and gender relevant to the tension and the upcoming conflict in the first place:

Brand One Narrative Excerpt—Part 2

15 And then he walked up beside me right?
16 And there was like a wall {right there kinda you know?} ((high pitch))
17 And then (I pushed him up against it) and he's like,
18 {"What you gonna do you little punk ass whi:te bi:tch."}

(Bucholtz, 1999: 448)

According to Brand One's perspective, it was in fact the "dude" who made salient Brand One's whiteness: "you little punk ass whi::te bi:tch". This justifies Brand One's explicit mention of race ("This this black dude [du:d]") at line 6. And the race/gender combination becomes relevant once again a few lines later in the narrative, where Brand One brings up a group of guys ("dudes") that he knew, who were standing close by, again with a later qualification to indicate that these "dudes" were "all black." Brand One felt some reassurance, albeit temporary, that these guys might come to his aid, if necessary.

Brand One Narrative Excerpt—Part 3

36 Na-1 went back like five feet where there was some dudes [du:?s] I knew?

37 like all black guys right?

38 But he wasn't really intimidated of them because they weren't hard ((('physically intimidating'))) right

(Bucholtz, 1999: 448)

The narrative systematically indexes Brand One's male whiteness in sharp contrast with the "antagonist's" male blackness. This is evident in Brand One's direct quotation of the "antagonist's" own words, re-voiced in the way that Brand One purportedly heard them and designedly repeated them, complete with the grammar and prosodic contours of AAVE. This example and others in the article reflect the clash of ideologies surrounding male whiteness (as unmarked) in contrast with male blackness (as marked). The "antagonist" is black. He is large. He is threatening. His size, his speech patterns, his assumed strength are all indexed through Brand One's narrative stance-taking, including his use of language crossing to re-voice and animate (Goffman, 1974) those particularly salient and marked features of his antagonist's identity—his height, his overall physical size ("big," "a lot bigger than me"), his likely intent to steal ("in my backpack"), and his predisposition to violence as a way to resolve the conflict (through his re-voiced words). Brand One, on the other hand, indexes his unmarked identity as a white male, suspecting imminent foul play by a physically larger member of what he constructed to be a highly marked social category.

As you read through just these few lines of narrative, what strikes you with regard to the social and discursive construction of gender, specifically "maleness"? That is, what are the various "gradations" of gender that are indexed in this narrative? What linguistic forms and construction accomplish this? In what ways do you find gender linked to race in this narrative? What sorts of conceptual contrasts emerge in these few lines of discourse, e.g., male/female, white/black, strength/weakness, predisposition to nonviolence/ predisposition to violence, that reveal Brand One's ideology of whiteness, blackness, and maleness? As you will note in your own analysis of discourse, often the explicit appeal to one conceptual/social category makes relevant the diametrically opposite category in subtle, yet powerful, ways.

INDEXICALITY AND AGENCY

AGENCY refers to the capacity of an individual or group to effect change on some entity, person, experience, state, and so forth. Agency is typically reflected in discourse through grammatical and conceptual meanings of *action, transitivity, voice,* and *causation* (often visible in **verbs**). Agency in discourse is *both fluid and scalar*. Thus, an entity, be it animate or inanimate, may be variably constructed, self-constructed, or evaluated as highly agentive, moderately agentive, slightly agentive, and non-agentive. Agency is enacted in discourse and is thus not discernible only through linguistic forms. It may be indexed through bodily movements and gesture, facial expressions, and eye gaze. Since agency is linked to the potential change of entities, events, and states of affairs, agency is also connected with the notions of power and control.

Agency is another important category of meaning that is created and enacted indexically in discourse. Fasulo, Loyd, and Padiglione, in their work on language socialization of cleaning practices among U.S. and Italian children, suggest a connection between agency, "autonomy," and "free will." Environments filled with freedom and choice are viewed as conducive to helping children become "active social agents that have the power to make decisions" (2007: 25).

Duranti provides the following working definition of agency:

Agency is here understood as the property of those entities (i) that have some degree of control over their own behavior, (ii) whose actions in the world affect other entities' (and sometimes their own), and (iii) whose actions are the object of evaluation (e.g., in terms of their responsibility for a given outcome). (2004: 453)

That agency is not restricted to animate beings is illustrated in Duranti (2004: 464), using examples from the *Los Angeles Times* (May 5, 2001). Note that the symbol [. . .] indicates that portions of the text were omitted:

- A huge falling tree **injured** 20 people at Disneyland's Frontierland on Friday [. . .]
- Rents **jumped** to record highs in Southland [. . .]
- Arbitration claims against brokerage firms **jumped** sharply in April [. . .]
- The decision **dealt another blow** to claims by former senior TRW engineer Nina Schwartz [. . .]

In all four previous examples, the subjects of the sentences are inanimate, yet, as Duranti (2004) points out, human agency was absolutely involved in the second, third, and fourth excerpts, and may have been involved in the first, though we cannot tell based on just this one sentence. "Rents" and "arbitration claims" *jump*. A "decision" *dealt a blow*. A "huge falling tree" *injured* people at a popular Southern California amusement park. However, no *human* agency is visible in the text. Instead, agency, as it relates to inanimate entities, is discursively intensified.

An additional example from Duranti (2004: 465–466) illustrates how agency can also be discursively mitigated through the use of the passive voice. The example is taken from recorded data at a Southern California university. In this excerpt, a Teaching Assistant in charge of a large lecture course is explaining to the students what happened to the textbooks that had been ordered for the course and are currently not available.

UCSB, 11/14/95:

TA: 1 the books came in and **they were sent back.**

2 there was a mistake and **they were sent back** and

3 **they had to be sent again.**

(Duranti, 2004: 465–66)

Line 1: *The books <u>came in</u>* [low agency] vs. *The bookstore **received** the books* [higher agency]

or

*The publisher **shipped** the books.* [high agency]

Line 2: *<u>There was</u> a mistake* [low agency] vs. *The bookstore **misunderstood*** [higher agency]

or

The bookstore made a mistake. [high agency]

As Duranti (2004) notes, this use of the "agentless"[10] passive allows the TA to avoid placing any blame on anyone for the error.

We can examine contrasts of agency in other expressions in this excerpt beyond the passive voice.

Thus, in discourse, agency is often associated with responsibility, action, and cause-effect, in both positive and negative contexts. Agency in discourse can index responsibility and credit for favorable outcomes on the one hand and blame for unfavorable outcomes on the other.

Ahearn (2001: 109) directs "scholars interested in agency to look closely at language and linguistic form." The discursive construction of agency, power, and control is crucial to our understanding of how ideologies, stances, and identities are created and reified in social interaction.

To illustrate, let's have a look at agency in commercials for over-the-counter (OTC) medicines such as Bayer Aspirin and the allergy medication Zyrtec.[11]

Here are a few links to stimulate your thinking about this:

Bayer Aspirin Commercial (Invincible Heart Attack): http://www. youtube.com/watch?v=8mHPgMtjPyo

Zyrtec Commercial (Powerful Allergy Relief): http://www.youtube. com/user/zyrtec?v = wpXmnteG9Xs

Use these two commercials for OTC medications quoted on the following page as starting points for a larger study on the topic. Think about the following as you develop your ideas:

- In what formats are the commercials presented? That is, are they testimonials? Dramas? Non-fiction narratives? Fictionalized narratives?
- How is the audience framed? As addressee? As overhearer?
- Who are the participants? How are they represented?
- How central is the notion of "family" in the commercials that you choose?
- What is the medicine? What can it do? How does it work?
- How is agency constructed in these texts? Be specific. Recall that agency is represented in discourse as having varying degrees of strength (from low to high). Where do you notice the highest degrees of agency? Why do you think this is so?

What observations can you make concerning agency and over-the-counter medicine commercials? Have a look at other advertisements for other medicines (and even other ads for the same medicine). Do you notice similar patterns with respect to *agency*? If so, how? If not, what did you find?

BAYER example

"Man: None of us think bad things are gonna ha^ppen to us. I was here in my house on Thanksgiving Day, and I have a massive heart attack right in my driveway. An artery in your heart is called the "Widow Maker" and mine was 95% blocked. They took me to the hospital and the doctor put me on a Bayer aspirin regimen."

(Bayer, n.d.)

ZYRTEC example

"Try Zyrtec, it gives you powerful allergy relief . . . Zyrtec starts working at hour one on the day you take it . . ."

(Zyrtec, n.d.)

REVIEW AND REFLECTION: INDEXICALITY, STANCE, IDENTITY, AND AGENCY

1. Earlier in the chapter, we introduced the topic of indexicality with a brief discussion of the website excerpt "How to Cope with Homesickness" from the University of Oregon's Counseling & Testing Center website.

    We repeat the excerpt here, for convenience:

    ### How to Cope With Homesickness (Excerpts)

    Many university students, particularly during their first year, experience distress about being separated from family and community. "Homesickness" is a normal part of **college students'** development toward adulthood. Such feelings should be acknowledged and accepted, even when uncomfortable. Lonely feelings can tell **you** to recognize certain needs and to figure out constructive ways to satisfy them.

    While **you** may be tempted to "escape" by moving back home, a certain amount of enduring and working through such feelings helps **you** grow into maturity. For instance, while a visit home may help **you** feel more nurtured and connected, if **you** come home every weekend, then **you** are probably missing out on opportunities to cultivate a social life and sense of belonging at UO . . .

. . . Try Creative Self-Talk: What **we** think or tell ourselves (self-talk) influences what **we** feel. Here are some beneficial things to **tell yourself** when **you** feel homesick.

Just because **I'm** alone **now** doesn't mean **I'll** always be alone.

Although **I'd r**ather be with my friends/family at home tonight, being **here** in Eugene is okay.

(University Counseling and Testing Center, n.d.)

Our initial focus centered on referential indexicality, noting how reference terms shifted from "many university students" to "college students" to "you" and finally to "I," all on the same web page. We also asked you to attend to how "homesickness" was referred to: "distress about being separated," "homesickness [as normal]," "such feelings," and so forth.

Now, with newly gained perspectives concerning stance (affective and epistemic), identity, and agency, try to conduct an analysis of the entire webpage from an indexicality-based perspective (see Links section that follows for the URL).

How are addressees/readers of this text framed? What types of evaluations are expressed in this site? What types of contrasts do you notice (e.g., "adulthood" vs. implications of readers not yet being adults; temporal contrasts of now vs. later; contrasts between newness and novelty and life experience)? How are personal feelings framed in the site?

What characteristics of the readers/addressees are being indexed in the discourse of this site? What characteristics of feelings are indexed by the discourse of this site? How is the process of *adjustment* being indexed here?

Now compare the University of Oregon site on homesickness and adjustment to a similar site for UCLA addressing a similar topic (https://www.orl.ucla.edu/parents/moving). Here is an excerpted version, but again, try to use the entire webpage for your analysis.

UCLA Office of Residential Life—"Moving In and Adjusting" (Excerpted)

Our residence halls are far more than a place to sleep. We firmly believe that a student's living experience can have a positive impact on his/her academic success and overall college experience. Studies indicate that students who live on campus:
((skipped lines))

- report more positive perceptions of the campus social climate
- engage in more frequent interactions with peers and faculty members (Blimling, 1993, as cited in Pascarella and Terenzini, 2005)

((skipped sections))
You have an important role to play in helping your student adjust to living on campus.
((skipped sections))

Adjusting to Residential Living

For many students, attending college marks the first time they have lived away from their friends and family. Homesickness is common among new students. . . . To support your student and reduce their sense of homesickness, encourage him/her to:

- continue to do activities that are familiar, and experience them in a new environment.
- place photos, quotes, posters, and other important items around his/her room to remember home by. . .

((skipped sections))

(UCLA ORL, n.d.)

Using indexicality as an analytic lens, think about how the UCLA site compares to and contrasts with the University of Oregon site, from the following points of view:

- Who are the writers? (Who is "we"?)
- Who are the readers/addressees?

- What are the stances of the producers of these two (i.e., U of O and UCLA) websites? Who are the sponsor(s) of each site?
- What characteristics of readers' identities are indexed here?
- What characteristics of students' identities are indexed here?
- How is agency indexed in the two sites?
- What effect does the notion of *agency* have in the construction of the overall message(s) of each site?

Explain your answers in full detail, noting patterns from each "data" set.

2. Compare and contrast social media postings such as Twitter or Facebook. Choose five individuals who post often to the site and analyze their posts over the past 30 days. Use the lens of indexicality to analyze the discourse (linguistic forms in the individual posts and dialogues with other posters, photographs, videos, other links). Focus on stance (affective, epistemic, moral, and elitist), identity (gender, family, academic), and agency (who is framed as *agentive* and who/what is framed as unagentive?). How does each individual represent him/herself publicly? What is the "public identity" or the "public face" that each individual seeks to create in these online posts? What features of their identities are they indexing through these posts? What features of the identities of others are they indexing? What types of stances are relevant in the posts? How do these five individuals compare and contrast with each other?

For example, are posts designed to portray an individual as:

- An ideal homeschooling mom?
- An intellectual?
- An armchair philosopher?
- An armchair radical?
- A player? A "cool girl?"

What, specifically, is indexing this general "identity" of the social media poster? How consistent are the patterns? Be sure to use *all* instances of discourse—linguistic forms and patterns used by the individual to post to the site, linguistic forms and patterns in the dialogues used by persons responding to and commenting on original posts, emoticons, photos, videos and commentary, etc.

Can you also comment on any area of pragmatics, including politeness, as your analyze the posts?

Write up a full analysis of your findings and support your position with patterns that you find in the "data."

3. Jaworski and Thurlow (2009: 196) define elitism as follows: "a person's orientation or making a claim to exclusivity, superiority, and/or distinctiveness on the grounds of status, knowledge, authenticity, taste, erudition, experience, insight, wealth, or any other quality warranting the speaker/author to take a higher moral, aesthetic, intellectual, material, or any other form of standing in relation to another subject (individual or group). Elitism then is a claim or bid for an enduring identity position that requires constant, momentary, and interactive enactment."

Refer to Jaworski and Thurlow (2009) for an in-depth discussion of elitism and for their analyses of how elitism is a "discursive production of social distinction."

Using the definitions provided in this chapter for both *stance* and *identity*, what elements of each (i.e., stance and identity) do you observe in the following excerpts from Jaworski and Thurlow? How might you extend your observations further to identify elements of elitist stance? That is, try to predict some of Jaworski and Thurlow's arguments based on their definition of elitism and based on what you know about stance, identity, and agency. What types of evaluations are being expressed? How are they constructed lexico-grammatically?

In addition, note the types of *contrasts* that emerged in some of the earlier analyses of data in this chapter. What is being contrasted in these excerpts?

Extract 1 (from *Guardian Travel,* January 31, 2004: 2–3, as cited in Jaworski and Thurlow, 2009: 200)

Barbados is one of those places that doesn't demand but eventually requires that you relax. For men, this tends to mean more undoing that extra button on their short-sleeve shirt *without feeling a sleaze;* for women (though not, *she has asked me to emphasize,* my girlfriend), thinking they *might actually* look *chic* in a batik . . . After three days relaxing, we moved hotel, not because of any problems, but just to see somewhere else. The Colony Club is, *or hopes to be,* a little more *upmarket* than Tamarind Cove. The guests, in other words, may read the same papers (the *Mail* is very popular), but at the Colony *they start from the front, not the back.* (Emphasis by Jaworski and Thurlow)

Extract 2 (from *Sunday Times Travel,* July 16, 2006: 26, as cited in Jaworski and Thurlow, 2009: 200–1)

Mass tourism is horrible. I hate arriving somewhere to find a horde of barbarians who've had that operation to weld a camera to their eyelids: they don't *really* see things, they *just* photograph them and get back on the *coach* . . .Wherever I go, I try to mix with the locals, assimilate myself. That can backfire, of course. My car got broken into in Tunisia, and the policeman was so chatty, he ended up inviting us to supper at his home. What a nice idea I thought: but we arrived to find a really *grim* police barracks, where he was cookin up *vile-looking* goat stew *over a Bunsen burner.* (Emphasis by Jaworski and Thurlow)

4. Read the following "testimonial letter" from Janis B. (a pseudonym), a satisfied (female) customer of a popular U.S.-based diet program. The contents of the letter is a variation on an actual letter from the testimonial section of the Jenny Craig diet website.

Think about indexicality from the multiple perspectives of stance, identity, and agency.

- First, how would you identify the *genre* of this discourse? What is its purpose? Who is the addressee/audience and how is the addressee/audience framed?
- What are the various stances that this author is expressing? What types of evaluations of self and other do you note? (e.g., affective, epistemic, moral)
- How does she explicitly refer to and frame the diet program?
- How does she explicitly refer to and frame herself?
- What features of her identity are being indexed through her lexico-grammatical choices?
- How is agency represented here? Who/what is depicted as highly agentive? Who/what is depicted as non-agentive or with low degrees of agency?

- What kinds of contrasts are established both explicitly and implicitly in this "letter?"
- Analyze the actual "Real Stories" testimonials from the Jenny Craig website (http://www.jennycraig.com/real-stories/) from the points of view of genre, narrative, information structure, cohesion, *indexicality, stance, identity,* and *agency.* Which methodological approach or combination of approaches will serve you in developing an analysis of this genre and related genres of discourse? Why?
- Analyze more diet-related discourse data using perspectives presented in Coupland and Coupland (2009).

Dear Jenny,

That was it. Three weeks ago, the needle on my scale twitched between 220 and 221 pounds. I am 5'6". My all time high was 219, and the scale topped that. That was my wake up call. I panicked. What was I going to do? I never had the will power to diet. I could never count calories or grams. I have a weight scale but not a food scale. My friends diet on points systems. Some count carbs. I can't measure my food out like that. I'd starve to death. When I am hungry, I just eat, and I love food. I was afraid to diet. Afraid I would have to give up my love for food.

I saw your ad on TV and the timing was perfect! It was a sign. I called the number and made an appointment. Your staff was amazing. So encouraging!

The first two weeks of my lifestyle change were terrible: Ups and downs and highs and lows. My Jenny counselor was so helpful at getting me to understand the dysfunctional relationship I had with food. I started to learn how to eat. This was the first time that I began eating right.

I have lost weight. My body has changed. I learned so much about myself and about healthy eating. I feel like a better person now. I am better at my job and with my family as a mom and as a wife.

I learned how to never give up on my goals. My Jenny team never once gave up on me, and I am grateful.

Janis B.

Prepare your responses to these in as much detail as possible, making sure that you note patterns in the discourse that reflect and support your analysis.

PRACTICE WITH INDEXICALITY, STANCE, IDENTITY, AND AGENCY IN ENGLISH AND OTHER LANGUAGES

1. Look at the discourse surrounding over-the-counter medications in English and other languages.

    Here is one example from Korea, for Bayer Aspirin Protect:
    심혈관 질환? 뱃살은 반드시 줄이세요. 음식은 싱겁게 드시구요 . . . (excerpt only—see commercial for full text)

    'Heart disease? Absolutely, reduce stomach fat, eat less salt . . . No matter what, remember, take one aspirin a day . . . Bayer Aspirin Protect.'

    Compare and contrast this Korean commercial (and others for aspirin and other over-the-counter medicines) with the U.S. Bayer Aspirin commercial. Think about *agency*. Who or what is indexed as the *agentive* entity here? That is, in the U.S. commercials and the Korean commercials, think about who or what is framed as the entity in control of and responsible for treating this condition. Is it the consumer? Is it the medicine itself? What types of imperatives and adverbials are used in the Korean commercials? What do these constructions index? (e.g., 반드시 줄이세요, 꼭 기억하세요). How is illness portrayed in U.S. over-the-counter medicine commercials? Through what types of indices? How is it portrayed in Korean over-the-counter medicine commercials? (Bayer Aspirin, 2012)

    Compare and contrast similar medications from other countries in the world.

    Focus on such discursive elements as:

*   Packaging
*   Advertising: print ads, TV commercials, radio commercials

    How are the ads constructed? For print ads, how do the visuals create meaning related to the medicines? For TV ads, what formats are used to present them? How are the audiences of these medicine ads constructed? How are the medicines reflected through lexico-grammatical forms and other semiotic media?

*   As you conduct your analysis on the lexico-grammatical forms, think about stance (affective, epistemic, moral, elitist), evaluation, perspectives,

identities of the individuals portrayed in the ads, and agency. Who/what is framed as highly agentive?

As you work through your analyses, think about the broader picture of culture and society.

What socio-cultural preferences are reflected in these medicines? How do these medicines respond to, reflect, and reify preferences and expectations of health and illness in the cultures you are investigating?

Use your data-based analysis of the discourse to formulate your arguments and support your claims.

2. Compare and contrast social media postings such as Twitter or Facebook—as you did for Question #2, but this time, be sure to focus on entries from other countries and in other languages. Choose five individuals who post often to the site and analyze their posts over the past 30 days.

How does the difference in "linguistic code" (i.e., the various languages that these posts appear in), underscore features of stance, identity, and agency that are not underscored in English? How are socio-cultural preferences reflected in these posts?

Use the lens of indexicality to analyze the discourse (linguistic forms in the individual posts and dialogues with other posters, photographs, videos, other links). Focus on stance (affective, epistemic, moral, and elitist), identity (gender, family, academic), and agency (who is framed as *agentive* and who/what is framed as unagentive?). How does each individual represent him/herself publicly? What is the "public identity" or the "public face" that each individual seeks to create in these online posts? What features of their identities are they indexing through these posts? What features of the identities of others are they indexing? What types of stances are relevant in the posts? For example: Are posts designed to portray an individual as:

- An ideal homeschooling mom?
- An intellectual?
- An armchair philosopher?
- An armchair radical?
- A player? A "cool girl?"

What, specifically, is indexing this general "identity" of the social media poster? How consistent are the patterns? Be sure to use *all* instances of discourse—linguistic forms and patterns used by the individual to post to the site, linguistic forms and patterns in the dialogues used by persons responding to and commenting on original posts, emoticons, photos, videos and commentary, etc.

Can you also comment on any area of pragmatics, including politeness, as your analyze the posts?

Write up a full analysis of your findings and support your position with patterns that you find in the "data."

3. **Polite speech level alternation in Korean (see Strauss and Eun, 2005):** Use the following discourse-based excerpts from a variety of interactional genres in Korean to think about indexicality in polite speech level choice. The so-called polite speech levels are referred to in reference grammars of Korean as the

DEFERENTIAL FORM - ㅂ니다/ - 습니다 and the

POLITE FORM - 요.

Most traditional accounts of Korean grammar indicate that the deferential form— ㅂ니다/–습니다 is the more polite and more formal of the two. The polite form, 요, is the unmarked polite form. Along the same lines, the deferential form is said to be used more in formal settings with individuals of much higher status. The polite form is used in less formal contexts.

Based on this type of account, then, it would be predicted that it is the influence of the *addressee's* identity (i.e., social status, profession, etc.) that determines the use of one form over another by a *speaker*.

However, as you will note, speakers (both in dialogue and monologue) actually *switch* from one form to another and back again. They do so quite systematically. And that system has less to do with *addressee* identity than it does with other factors.

Read the following transcripts and try to come up with a system for the use of these forms—a system centered on an analysis of indexicality.

Excerpt 1:

A RADIO TALK SHOW: 아름다운 세상 'BEAUTIFUL WORLD' (10/04/2000)

FEMALE: 요즘 : 이 중년 남성들의 화제가 'These days the topic among middle-aged males is-'

305

MALE: 음 'Mhm'

FEMALE: 건강이 : 단연 그 일등이라고 **그래요** [: 'People say that health is [POL] the number one (issue).'

MALE: [네 [:: 'Uhhuh'

FEMALE: [화제가 : 'I mean, the issue is-'

MALE: 네 'Uhhuh'

FEMALE: 지난 주 통계청이 발표한 • hh 구십구년 인구동태 조사 결과에**보면은요** ? 'If we look [POL] at the results reported last week by the Bureau of Statistics for 1999,'

MALE: 네 'Uhhuh'

FEMALE: 한 해에 사오십대 남성들의 사망률이 • hh 여성의 세 배라고그럽니다 'It says [DEF] the death rate of male adults in their 40s and 50s is three times that of females.'

Excerpt 2:

English language TV program: Survival English

HOST: 마지막으로 쇼핑해서 물건을 가지고서 집에 가기 전에 해야 될 일이 가격을치러야 **되죠** . 자 ,물건 값을 치를 때 사용할 수 있는 표현을 우리가 중점적으로 오늘공부해 보도록하겠습니다 . 'In the end, when we go shopping, before we take the merchandise home, we have to pay [POL] for it. So, today we will study [DEF] focusing on expressions we can use when paying for merchandise.'

Excerpt 3:

Pastor Cen's Sermon: Theme: "Prayer" part 1
예술의 경지에까지 올라가기 위해서 해야 될 게 뭐냐 첫째는
능숙해야 됩니다. **능숙해야**
돼요.

'What is that we have to do in order to reach the ultimate level in art? First, we must have the ability [DEF]. We must have the ability [POL].'

Excerpt 4:

Pastor Cen's Sermon: Theme: "Prayer" part 2

우리 건물을 지을 때보십시오. 철근이 들어가 있고 기둥만 있을 때 아름답다고 생각하는

사람이 누가있습니까? 그러나 그 철근과 그 기둥의 모양을 보면 이 건물이 몇 층짜리

건물이 될 것인지를 알 수 있습니다. 골격이 좋을수록 높은 빌딩이 올라 갈 수 있다라는
거예요.

So look [DEF] at the time when someone builds a building. When the steel frame is in place and there are only columns, is [DEF] there anyone who would think this is beautiful? But if you look at the shape of the steel frame and columns, we can tell [DEF] how many stories tall this building will be. (In other words), the better the structure, the taller the building can be [POL].'

Copyright 2006 Center for Advanced Language Proficiency Education and Research, The Pennsylvania State University. Data used with permission. (See also Eun and Strauss, 2004, and Strauss and Eun, 2005.) Note: These excerpts are taken from a teaching unit on "Honorific Speech Levels" developed for a project by the Center for Advanced Language Proficiency Education and Research (CALPER).

SUGGESTIONS FOR FURTHER READING

Babel, A. M. (2009). *Dizque,* evidentiality, and stance in Valley Spanish. *Language in Society.* 38: 487–511.

Butler, J. (1997). *Excitable Speech: A Politics of the Performative*. New York: Routledge.

Butler, J. (2005). *Giving an Account of Oneself*. New York: Fordham University Press.

Coupland, N. (2006). *Style: Language Variation, Identity, and Social Meaning.* Cambridge: Cambridge University Press.

Coupland, N. (2007). *Style: Language Variation and Identity*. Cambridge: Cambridge University Press.

Coupland, J. and Coupland, N. (2009). Attributing stance in discourses of body shape and weight loss. In A. Jaffe (Ed.), *Stance: Sociolinguistic Perspectives*. Oxford: Oxford University Press. Pp. 227–50.

Davies, B. and Harre, R. (1990). Positioning: The discursive production of selves. *Journal for the Theory of Social Behavior*. 20,1: 43–63.

Hall, K. (2005). Intertextual sexuality: Parodies of class, identity, and desire in liminal Delhi. *Journal of Linguistic Anthropology*, 15,1: 125–44.

Heritage, J. and Raymond, G. (2005). The terms of agreement: Indexing epistemic authority and subordination in talk-in-interaction. *Social Psychology Quarterly,* 68: 15–38.

Holmes, J. (2006). *Gendered Talk at Work: Constructing Gender Identity through Workplace Discourse*. New York, Oxford: Blackwell.

Holmes, J. and Myerhoff, M. (2003). *The Handbook of Language and Gender.* Oxford.

Kärkkäinen, Elise. (2006). Stance taking in conversation: From subjectivity to intersubjectivity. *Text and Talk*, 26,6: 699–731.

Kiesling, S. (2001). 'Now I gotta watch what I say': Shifting constructions of masculinity in discourse. *Journal of Linguistic Anthropology*, 11: 250–73.

Kramsch, C. (2012). Imposture: A late modern notion in poststructuralist SLA research. *Applied Linguistics*, 33,5: 483–502.

Le Page, R. and Tabouret Kellr, A. (1985). *Acts of Identity: Creole-based Approaches to Language and Ethnicity*. Cambridge: Cambridge University Press.

Lo, A. (2004). Evidentiality and morality in a Korean heritage language school. *Pragmatics*, 14,2–3: 235–56.

Makoni, B. (2011). Multilingual miniskirt discourses in motion: the discursive construction of the female body in public space. *International Journal of Applied Linguistics*, 21,3: 340–59.

McGloin, N. and Konishi, Y. (2010). From connective particle to sentence final particle: A usage-based analysis of *shi* 'and' in Japanese. *Language Sciences*, 32,5: 563–78.

Melander, H. (2012). Knowing how to play the game of jump rope: Participation and stancetaking in a material environment. *Journal of Pragmatics*, 44,11: 1434–56.

Nagel, J. (1994). Constructing ethnicities: Creating and recreating ethnic identity and culture. *Social Problems,* 41,1: 152–76.

Omoniyi, T. and White, G. (Eds.) (2008). *The Sociolinguistics of Identity.* London: Continuum.

Schilling-Estes, N. (2004). Constructing ethnicity in interaction. *Journal of Sociolinguistics,* 8: 163–95.

Thompson, G. and Hunston, S. (2001). Evaluation: An introduction. In S. Hunston and G. Thompson (Eds.), *Evaluation in Text: Authorial*

Stance and the Construction of Discourse. Oxford: Oxford University Press.

Xu, J. (2012). The epistemic stance marker wo juede. *Shijie Hanyu Jiaoxue / Chinese Teaching in the World*, 26,2: 209–19.

Zhang, Q. (2005). A Chinese yuppie in Beijing: Phonological variation and the construction of a new professional identity. *Language in Society,* 34: 431–66.

LINKS

The Chief, Icarreau, Deleted User, Clark_Griswold, and Alpinisto. (2010, June 6). What does "we" mean to you? *SummitPost*. Retrieved from: http://www.summitpost.org/phpBB3/what-does-we-mean-to-you-t53591.html. Accessed May 23, 2013.

University Counseling and Testing Center. (n.d.). How to cope with homesickness. *University of Oregon* website. Retrieved from: http://counseling.uoregon.edu/dnn/SelfhelpResources/Transitions/HowtoCopewithHomesickness/tabid/368/Default.aspx. Accessed May 25, 2013.

Chomsky, N. (2012, November 8). The purpose of education: Learning without frontiers interview. Retrieved from: http://www.youtube.com/watch?v=DdNAUJWJN08. Accessed April 10, 2013.

Bayer Aspirin. (n.d.). Invincible heart attack [TV commercial]. Retrieved from: http://www.youtube.com/watch?v=8mHPgMtjPyo. Accessed September 24, 2013.

Zyrtec. (n.d.). Powerful allergy relief [TV commercial]. Retrieved from: http://www.youtube.com/user/zyrtec?v=wpXmnteG9Xs. Accessed September 24, 2013.

UCLA ORL [Office of Residential Life]. (n.d.). Moving in and adjusting. *UCLA ORL* website. Retrieved from: https://www.orl.ucla.edu/parents/moving. Accessed April 10, 2013.

Bayer Aspirin. (2012). 바이엘 헬스케어 '아스피린 프로텍[Bayer aspirin protect] [TV commercial]. Retrieved from: http://www.youtube.com/watch?v=5Y08gx-eaic. Accessed May 5, 2013.

NOTES

1. SummitPost.org contains information, blogs, and photos about mountains, rocks, and ranges around the world for climbers, hikers, and mountain lovers. The Forum pages include general posts (even "curiosity"-driven musings as in this blog) in addition to the more topic-central posts about climbing, gear, and medical treatment. The exchange represented here is taken from the General section of the Forum. It is one of nine total posts that were exchanged over the 27-hour period between 5:00 P.M. on June 6 and 7:00 P.M. on June 7, 2010.

2. The phenomenon whereby a word, a part of a word, diminutives, or the use of particular registers *index* aspects of stance and identity that are not explicitly named in the text and/or interaction is similar to the notion of *contextualization cues* by Gumperz (1982), Gumperz and Cook-Gumperz (1982), and the notions of *keying* and *frame* by Goffman (1974)

3. Some other sub-categories of stance in the literature include: moral stance (Bergman, 1998, Goodwin, 2007, Shoaps, 2009), authorial stance (Hunston and Thompson, 2000; Hyland, 2002), authoritative stance (Johnstone, 2009), collaborative stance (Kyratzis, 2005).

4. Dickens, 1994: chapter 35.

5. See Goodwin (1990: 177) for her discussion of "format tying," the interactional practice of connecting words and conversational turns through parallelisms in structure and lexical choice, in challenges and arguments.

6. See Chapter 6 (Conversation) and the topic of "Oh" as a change of state marker for discussion on the interrelationships between cognitive state (specifically involving the shift from *not knowing* to *knowing*), affect, and interaction.

7. http://www.learningwithoutfrontiers.com/2012/02/noam-chomsky-the-purpose-of-education/ (accessed on May 22, 2013). "Learning Without Frontiers is a global platform for disruptive thinkers and practitioners from the education, digital media, technology and entertainment sectors who come together to explore how new disruptive technologies can drive radical efficiencies and improvements in learning whilst providing equality of access."

8. For in-depth discussions of "code-switching," "code-mixing," "crossing," and "translanguaging" see Canagarajah, 2011; Goffman, 1974; Gumperz, 1982; Heller, 1988; Hornberger and Link, 2012; Lo, 1999; Myers-Scotton, 1988; Rampton, 1995; and Wei, 2011.

9. Note the contrast in function of the two uses of *dude*: as a vocative in the Kieslang excerpt, indexing affiliation and solidarity (in addition to the nonchalant stance noted by Kiesling), and the 3rd person reference term denoting a male.

10. "Agentless" passive in linguistics refers to the use of the passive voice without the explicit mention of the "agent" through a "by" phrase. That is, the TA in this example does not mention *who* sent the books back: "they were

sent back [**by** the bookstore, by the publisher]" Other examples of agent-less passives are: "We were robbed" "It was mentioned . . .", and "News-paper deliveries were placed on hold." The use of passive voice, in general, to deflect the notion of agency and/or responsibility is a common topic in linguistics literature, from all theoretical orientations.

11. In 2008, Zyrtec was the highest grossing non-food product sold in the United States (Cetirizine, n.d.; Stuart, 2009).

CHAPTER NINE

Critical Discourse Analysis

Calling the approach 'critical' is a recognition that our social practice in general and our use of language in particular are bound up with causes and effects which we may not be at all aware of under normal conditions (Bourdieu, 1977) Specifically, connections between the use of language and the exercise of power are often not clear to people, yet appear on closer examination to be vitally important to the workings of power. For instance, ways in which a conventional consultation between a doctor and a patient is organized, or a conventional interview between a reporter and a politician, take for granted a wide range of ideologically potent assumptions about rights, relationships, knowledge and identities . . . the assumption that the doctor is the sole source of medically legitimate knowledge about illness, or that it is legitimate for the reporter—as one who 'speaks for' the public—to challenge the politician. Such practices are shaped, with their common-sense assumptions, according to prevailing relations of power between groups of people. (Fairclough, 1995a: 54)

CRITICAL DISCOURSE ANALYSIS

CRITICAL DISCOURSE ANALYSIS is the broad, interdisciplinary methodological approach to language and society that centers on *discourse as social practice*: Discursive practices are social in nature and social practices are inherently built on and around discourse. CDA uses micro-level analysis of discourse (words, phrases, conceptual metaphors) to uncover the processes by which ideologies of power abuse, control,

> hegemony, dominance, exclusion, injustice, and inequity are created, re-created, and perpetuated in social life—processes which are often "naturalized" and taken for granted as common-sense notions. The aims of CDA-based work are to uncover those processes and practices, to make them visible and clear, to explain them, and consequently to encourage resistance against them and to effect social change.

In this chapter, we will explore the methodological approach known as Critical Discourse Analysis. Critical Discourse Analysis (henceforth, CDA) centers on the view that all of discourse is *social practice*. That is, our ways of using language and discourse—as producers of discourse and as consumers of discourse—are shaped by society. At the same time, our discursive practices shape and re-shape our ways of seeing, our ways of understanding, and even our ways of being. We understand the world through discourse. Through discourse, we formulate belief systems of class, society, and nation; of right and wrong; of beauty and health and gender; even of how language should be used.[1] Critical Discourse Analysis seeks to uncover the discursive processes through which ideologies are shaped and communicated, normalized, and propagated—ideologies which involve hidden dimensions of power, control, injustice, and inequity, all of which typically go unseen and unnoticed because they are couched in what appear to be common-sense assumptions of social reality and "truth." Ultimately, the goal of CDA research is to encourage resistance against such dominance or ideologies and to effect social change. (See Chilton, 2005, 2011; Fairclough, 1992a, 1992b, 1995a, 1995b, 2001, 2003; Hodge and Kress, 1993; Kress and Van Leeuwen, 2001; Rogers, 2002, 2004; Rogers and Christian, 2007; van Dijk, 1984, 1987, 1988, 1991, 2011; van Leeuwen, 1993, 1995; Wodak, 1989, 1990, 1996, 1997, 2009a, 2011a; Wodak and Meyer, 2009.)

Our everyday experiences are created, expressed, and mediated by discourse, from talking or texting with friends and posting on social media sites; to seeing advertisements and product packaging; to immersing ourselves in the economy, politics, education, health and welfare; to discussing local news, national news, and even the tabloids. Society influences how we interact, personally and privately, socially and publicly—in families, with strangers, and within institutions.

Societal and discursive conventions influence how we understand, interpret, and create genres of discourse, replete with what appear to be genre-specific registers and more general ones, where generic boundaries cross and intermesh and become new, hybrid genres (see Chapter 3). Socio-cultural conventions help us make sense of turn-taking practices in conversation and speech acts: Whose turn is it to speak? How and where does speaker change occur? Does speaker change occur interruptively? Are continuers and other response tokens relevant and expected? If so, what types? If not, why? Is a particular speech act actually an apology or is it an excuse? Is the speaker laying blame or accepting personal responsibility, even liability? Are speech acts of directives actually directives, or are they suggestions, tips, hints, or even insults? (See Chapters 6 [Conversation Analysis] and 7 [Pragmatics].)

Discourse is indeed social practice. It is the process of putting the world into words—and words and how we use and choose them reflect both cognitive conceptualizations and socio-cultural motivations. Even the seemingly simple discursive act of labeling something, of matching a single word to an object, a color, a person, or an activity involves choice. Naming things involves context. And it involves purpose.

As we have shown in Chapter 2 (The Building Blocks of Language), language and words and grammar are, at the very least, conceptual. Words exist in a lexicon in contrast with other words: A newly hatched chick might be labeled a "duckling," or alternatively *a baby duck, our class pet,* or *anas platyrhynchos*. The verb "kill" might be expressed as *mutilate, smother,* or *euthanize*. Mass nouns like "snow" and "water" are used as count nouns like "snows" and "waters," and their meanings change; their conceptual imagery changes. Bullets and shells are *ammunition,* bombers and cargo planes are *aircraft*, forks and spoons are *flatware*. Such conceptual representation creates images in our minds, from amorphous substances (like snow or water or rain) to cyclicity, from individuated bits of concrete materials (like bullets or forks) to circumscribed sets, from actions and who performed them and how and why to the outcomes of the actions, and the how and why of those.

And, beyond the conceptual, our choice to use such lexical items in a spate of discourse like *our class pet* or *anas platyrhynchos* to refer to the same "duckling" or *kill, murder, dismember,* or *euthanize* to denote the action of "taking a life" or "causing to die" (where each denotation itself reflects a distinct position vis à vis the event) is socially driven.

Instances of nominal reference (e.g., *The Duke and Duchess of Cambridge* vs. *The royal couple* vs. *William and Catherine*) depend upon a speaker's or writer's intended message as well as upon how readily identifiable proper nouns and common nouns may be on the part of the reader or listener. The concept of FOCUS as it relates to demonstrative reference (e.g., *This is my wife* vs. *That is my wife* or *These cells from the clone* vs. *The cells from the clone*) takes into account a speaker-hearer or writer-reader relationship whereby the speaker or writer is calling upon the hearer/reader to pay vary-ing degrees of attention to the referents in question (Chapter 4). And as we note in Chapter 5, the framing of entities as given or new or accessible is dependent upon primary assumptions concerning a hearer's or listener's abil-ity to recognize the person or event or idea that is being introduced into the discourse. Speakers and writers choose from numerous referential options (e.g., *You know,* **Mom** *was pretty brave* vs. **Our (my) mom** *was pretty brave* vs. **she** *was pretty brave*) on the basis of focus of consciousness, as a means to "bridge the gap between one mind and the other . . . [as] a way to narrow the chasm between independent minds" (Chafe, 1994: 41).

In Chapter 8, we examined, in-depth, the process of stance taking as an inevitable outcome of "putting the world into words," with a focus on affective stance, epistemic stance, and moral stance. In particular, we observed the interconnectedness between experience and linguistic form, where linguis-tic forms (including prosody) index stances of emotion, certainty, and moral evaluations concerning ideal behaviors of civil empathy and righteousness. Opinions about education and freedom (Chomsky, 2012) are put forward as opinions and observations, but they are also designed to persuade— arguments to elicit agreement or to tug at the unlike-minded and pull them in a new direction. We observed how identities are constructed indexically and how power and agency take shape through linguistic forms.

Research conducted within the area of Critical Discourse Analysis is concerned with discursive phenomena whereby agency, power, and con-trol reach the level of abuse and manipulation, and especially where such abuse is perpetuated under the guise of common-sense assumptions and everyday, routine practices. It relies on a micro-level approach to discourse, an approach that itself reveals cognitive, interactional, stance-driven, and identity-driven motivations underlying linguistic form and its surrounding semiotic elements.

CRITICAL DISCOURSE ANALYSIS—AN OVERVIEW

The discursive construction of power, dominance, and hegemony, and its collaborative and mutual reconstruction by both the dominant and domi-nated groups, finds its roots in works by Althusser (1971), Foucault (1972, 1982), Gramsci (1971), and Habermas (1984), and such early feminist dis-course scholars and work as Key (1975), Lakoff (1975), and Thorne and Henley (1975).

315

Critical Discourse Analysis is a **micro-macro** based analysis of discourse. Discourse from a CDA perspective consists of **linguistic forms**[2] in text and talk in addition to the **relevant surrounding semiotic resources,** e.g., photographs, font size and style, distributions of text and graphics, diagrams and other graphic representations, elements of attire and physical appearance, turn-taking practices, gestures and facial expressions (Charteris-Black, 2004; Fairclough 1993, 1995b, 2003; Graddol, 1996; Hodge and Kress, 1993 Kress, 1993; Kress and van Leeuwen, 1998, 2001; van Dijk, 1993a, 1993b, 2006, 2011; van Leeuwen, 1999).

Micro-level observations of **patterned linguistic features** include such types of **individual lexical items** as adverbs, verbs of knowing and understanding, logical connectors, pronouns of inclusion, pronouns of exclusion, **metaphor and figurative language, euphemisms and dysphemisms,** and other linguistically central stance-marking elements. The i**nterrelationship between such linguistic forms** and the **surrounding semiotic media** may combine to express **macro-level messages** of power, control, racism, hegemony, dominance, and discrimination. This interrelationship of discursive elements creates, reflects, re-creates and reifies underlying ideologies of what is assumed to be "normal" and "natural" and the acceptable ways of doing and being within the dominant perspectives of truth and reality.

Discourse and social practice are interdependent, linked "by 'orders' — orders of discourse and social orders" (Fairclough, 2001: 24). Social order involves the various ways in which society is structured at multiple levels, from the personal to the institutional, each level with its own sets of hierarchies, each with its own sets of members who fulfill roles and functions, and each with its own sets of discursive practices.

As Fairclough (2001: 24) notes,

> [w]e always experience the society and the various social institutions within which we operate as divided up and demarcated, *structured* into different spheres of action, different types of situation, each of which has its associated type of practice . . . '[S]ocial order' . . . refer[s] to such a structuring of a particular social 'space' into various domains associated with various types of practice . . . [A]n order of discourse is really a social order looked at from a specifically discoursal perspective.

The interrelationships between social order and order of discourse are relevant in the discourse of institutions and everyday life, especially when genres, registers, and styles of discourse typically associated with one institution cross-cut the discourse of other institutions: Police discourse becomes both popularized and routinized through TV detective dramas; courtroom discourse of direct and cross-examination seeps into the discourse of political interviews and even everyday personal relationships; music videos become vehicles for social and political commentary; educational textbook discourse becomes prescription for behavior and interpretation; and the discourse of health and beauty sets standards for gender and body image and influences our purchasing habits of food, clothing, diet aids, medicines, cosmetics, and the like.

As noted by Fairclough (1995a), boundaries in media discourse become quite fuzzy where informational purpose blurs with goals of entertainment, as evident in many hybridized forms of discourse in the media. This meshed goal of informing/entertaining is evident in varying degrees in all facets of news reporting, both print and on-air, in local news broadcasts and national news broadcasts. This information/entertainment tension is related to another tension noted by Fairclough (1995a)—that between the public and the private. Public issues and discussions appear to be private conversations and we, the audience, are overhearing the talk unfold, not as addressees, but as overhearers (Bell, 1984, 1991; Bubel, 2008; Clark and Schaefer, 1992; Dynel, 2011; see Chapter 3 for more detail on participation framework.)

And, conversely, private issues become public (Fairclough, 1995a) in daytime TV talk shows where family members seek professional advice about the behaviors and lifestyles of their loved ones; where incendiary legal issues are resolved on "reality-based" court TV programs; and where local residents of disaster-stricken areas are televised crying, in tattered clothing, recounting their narratives of survival and loss, for the world to see. Registers shift from the professional to the colloquial and conversational and back again. Cameras pan and zoom, revealing wide shots and close-ups of destruction of property and despair of victims. We experience the elation and hope and hopelessness of victims and heroes—through their own words and gestures and facial expressions. Probing questions are asked and answered. And media consumers continue to watch and read and comment (online, on air, and in print), and so expands the dialogue between the public and the private, between the news and the human interest factors, between what we used to know and understand as "news" and the current shape it has taken.

This seemingly seamless hybridization of genres of discourse— **interdiscursivity** (Fairclough, 2001)—itself may lead to power creation and the abuse of power, through normalization. As we have seen in media discourse, the traditional structure and content and register of one genre of discourse transforms into a hybridized new genre, as features of other genres, their structures and registers and elements of their content, percolate into it.

A powerful example of this is from Fairclough (2003), where one genre of discourse, an academic job announcement, also contains linguistic and graphic features of promotional and persuasive discourse. The ad designed to recruit highly qualified job applicants simultaneously serves to promote the same university that is conducting the search. "[The] combination of hegemony and **interdiscursivity** in my framework for critical discourse analysis is concomitant with a strong orientation to historical change: to changing discursive practices and their place within wider processes of social and cultural change. Historical change ought, in my view, to be the primary focus and concern of critical discourse analysis if it is to be relevant to the great social issues of our day" Fairclough (2003: 137). Texts and genres become heterogeneous under our very noses. Intertextual relations and interdiscursive practices become powerful vehicles for discourse consumption and for the naturalization of dominant ideologies of power and normalcy.

Following you'll find an excerpt from Fairclough (1995b) that illustrates this very type of interdiscursivity. The excerpt is from a job ad for Sheffield City Polytechnic. It is noteworthy because it exhibits a remarkable mélange of discursive and generic features of a recruitment document and promotional discourse. With regard to the latter, Fairclough points out a number of features of "commodity advertising," prestige or corporate advertising, self-promotional discourse, and narrative evident within the text (1995b: 142).

As you read through the excerpt, pay attention to the following:

- Try to identify the features that are squarely in line with recruitment documents or job ads. (For example, "Application forms and further details are available from the address below.").
- Try to identify features of promotional discourse. (For example, the sidebar message in all caps—"MAKE AN IMPACT ON THE NEXT GENERATION.")
- What types of self-promotional discourse do you find in the ad? How does "narrative" contribute to such self-promotion?
- Identify the pronouns that are used in the first two paragraphs. What types of grammatical parallels are evident in the opening lines of each paragraph? What effect does this parallelism create?

  o Who is being addressed? How? What types of personal qualities are explicitly mentioned in relation to pronoun "you"? What assumptions exist, then, on the part of the institution vis à vis the professional and personal identity of the potential job candidate? How are these expressed discursively—through which linguistic forms and constructions?

o   What types of qualities are explicitly mentioned in relation to the institution and pronoun "we?" Do you note alternations between "we/our" and 3rd person reference? What are the assumptions underlying such shifts?

University Advertisement Excerpt

School of Engineering

With our reputation as one of the UK's leading sources of teaching excellence and research innovation, we're making a lasting impact on the next generation of innovators and business leaders in the field of Engineering—and you can help.

With your ambition, energy and expertise, you will be committed to teaching at both undergraduate and post-graduate level, while enjoying the advantage of our close links with industry and applied research initiatives to add to both your own reputation and ours.

Senior Academic Post
Vehicle Emission Technology

Up to £31,500 p.a. plus substantial enhancement available by negotiation.

The School of Engineering is renowned for its innovative work in the area of Vehicle Emissions Technology and is a leader in the field of Automotive Research. A team leader is now required to join this active team to help build on our success.

This leading post requires an outstanding Engineer who can bring expertise in at least one of the following—Vehicle Pollution, Hybrid Vehicles, Air Quality Systems. You'll also need to be dedicated to progressing research and consultancy whilst lecturing to undergraduate and postgraduate students.

Along with appropriate qualifications, technological expertise and industrial experience, you will need to have energy, enthusiasm and communication skills to motivate your team.

We offer an excellent salary and benefits package, but more importantly the ideal environment and opportunity to really make a contribution to the future of automotive engineering.

You may be awarded the title of Professor if the relevant criteria are met.

For an informal discussion about the post, please ring Professor David Tidmarsh, Director of School of Engineering on (0742) 533389.

Application forms and further details are available from the address below. Ref. 40/92.

MAKE AN

IMPACT ON ((Skipped lines of text))

THE NEXT

GENERATION

((Skipped lines of text))

We are strongly implementing equality of opportunity policies and seek people who share our commitment. Job share applicants welcome. Women are under represented in this area and applications from this group are particularly welcomed.

The University working in Promising Futures with industry and the professions.

Sheffield City Polytechnic

(Adapted from Fairclough, 1995b: 144)

The document establishes a great deal with regard to identity construction — on the part of the applicant and on the part of the institution. The institution is a cohesive team, with a reputation and a story to tell about its current, ongoing accomplishments and its power to transform the future. It is the giant "we" in control of everything, including a sub-team, e.g., The School of Engineering, now in the third-person singular ("is renowned"), in need of a team leader (i.e., "you") to build on "our" success, now including the institution once again.

A close analysis of the pronouns also reveals that "you" as the addressee of the document is intended as a *singular*, individual entity, as if the "right candidate" had already been located. The description of the candidate's requirements is not in the third-person (e.g., "the candidate must. . . ."). It directly addresses this potential candidate as if already on board, teaching and in charge of an existing "team" (". . . you will need to have energy, enthusiasm and communicative skills to motivate **your** team."). Finally, what do you make of the slogan "Promising Futures"? What does this two-word combination mean to you? Fairclough (1995b) provides a full analysis of this data sample. Even with just this abridged segment of the data, issues of institutional power become evident (both on the surface and below), in the university's self-promotion and in the construction of the job candidate's personal and professional identity, all with pre-established fit and potential to add to the School's and the university's success.

Underlying the discourse of power and dominance are the institutional, political, academic, and even personal ideologies whereby inequity, injustice, and abuse are normalized and presented as common-sense assumptions—as given, as natural, as the taken-for-granted norms of society. In this way, dominance is jointly produced; it is condoned, ignored, rationalized; hence, taken for granted. Power and powerlessness are collaboratively perpetuated and institutionalized. It is the goal of research in the various disciplines practicing CDA to uncover those ideologies and the discursive means through with they are formed, and to the extent possible, effect "change through critical understanding" (van Dijk 1993b: 252).

van Dijk (1993b) pinpoints "social cognition as the necessary theoretical (and empirical) 'interface,' if not the 'missing link,' between discourse and dominance" (251). van Dijk appeals to the framework of **triangulation,** taking into account the three crucial elements of **discourse, society, and cognition.** Social power, as typically associated with class, privilege, status, education, and profession, involves control, *not just through action*, *but also, and more subtly, through cognition*. Controlling the minds of others for the purpose of perpetuating such ideologies of power is discursively achieved, through the contextual features of the discourse as well as the linguistic forms. Power is enacted institutionally through such dichotomies as *elite* and *privilege* vs. the *marginalized* and *unprivileged* in terms of production of, access to, and representation by discourse: Who must make appointments to see whom for expert advice? Who may speak when and how? Which voices are validated and which are not? Whose voices are censored, silenced, ignored, or devalued? Whose version of the TRUTH is being advanced and how?

Linguistic means of justifying, rationalizing, legitimizing, and perpetuating inequality, racism, and injustice, and thereby also controlling social cognition, include (see Fairclough, 2003; van Dijk, 1993b, 2006):

- positive representations of US (dominant, elite) and negative representations of THEM (the powerless, the marginalized, the opposition)
- hyperbole
- metaphors and analogies (reflecting positive self-representation and negative other representation—self as "savior," "benefactor," "normal" other as "vermin," "gluttons," "different," and "abnormal")
- creating oppositions and contrasts ("By blacks, I mean those principally of West Indian origin rather than the quieter gentler people from the Indian

sub-continent who are as law-abiding as the rest of the population."—
The Times, 12 October, 1985, in van Dijk 1991: 197)

- granularity of detail (vague or precise, specific or general).
- incorporating others' voices (whose, which quotes, where, and how)
- naming and wording ("person," "human being," "permanent resident,"
  "aliens," "lawful resident")
- euphemisms (military terms such as "friendly fire" or "collateral damage"
  that serve to minimize or even legitimize unintended destruction of property or unintentionally caused injury or death)
- dysphemisms (the opposite of euphemism, using derogatory forms in
  place of more neutral sounding ones; e.g., disparaging racial terms,
  disparaging gender terms, vulgar lexical items: "pissed (off)" in lieu of
  "angry," "crap" in lieu of "stuff," etc.).

Van Dijk—Discourse and Manipulation

van Dijk (2006) builds on the triangulated interplay of discourse, society, and
cognition through his view of manipulation: a form of social power abuse,
cognitive mind control, and discursive interaction. Here, van Dijk introduces
the concepts of Short Term Memory (STM) manipulation and Long Term
Memory manipulation (LTM).

The components involved in STM that enable cognitive manipulation
include: simplified syntax, distinct and slower pronunciation, eye-catching
images, and the use of basic lexical items—discursive features that tend
toward the simple, the more readily comprehensible, the less cognitively tax-
ing. (van Dijk, 2006: 366). LTM is also called "episodic manipulation" and
seeks to establish more stable cognitive results, thus appealing to issues of
knowledge, attitudes, and ideologies (367).

Manipulation, as illegitimate discursive practice, is contrasted with persuasion, as legitimate. The boundaries are both "fuzzy" and "context dependent" as van Dijk (2006: 361) admits. That is, not all recipients of discourse are
susceptible to the manipulative messages in the same ways; some instances
of persuasion (e.g., political, religious, and commercial) may be "ethically legitimate." What constitutes manipulation as manipulation, and not persuasion,
is that "people are being acted upon against their fully conscious will and
interests, and that manipulation is in the best interests of the manipulator"
(2006: 361).

The following excerpt, from van Dijk (2006: 177) is from Tony Blair's
March 18, 2003, speech to the House of Commons (see Blair, 2003, for the
full text of the speech).

As van Dijk notes, Blair was accused first of manipulating Parliament into believing that the decision to go to war was yet to be made and that such a decision rested in Parliament's hands, when the decision to go to war with Iraq had essentially been made in 2002.

As you read through the transcript excerpt, pay attention to the following:

- How Blair opens the speech with respect to the responsibility of the House to *debate* and *pass judgment*.
- Blair's acknowledgment of the "views in opposition," i.e., *I do not disrespect* (through a double negative and not an affirmative statement, "I respect").
- Blair's initial concession of the difficulty of the choice ("This is a tough choice, indeed."), followed immediately by the urgency of it ("but it is a stark one").
- What is that choice that Blair gives? How many options are there? What are they? What is Parliament being asked to consider here?
- What sorts of discursive repetitions do you find in his arguments?

  o "... or to hold firm to the course that we have set ... we must hold firm to that course."
  o "The question most often posed is not 'Why does it matter?' but 'Why does it matter so much?'"
  o "The question most often posed ..." Another issue to question here: Posed by whom? There is no indication whatsoever what Blair intends by this construction. Why do you think Blair used the passive voice here to introduce this discursive device?

- Is there a shift in Blair's stance regarding the opposition? What sort of shift? How is the opposition now framed (at lines 7–12)? How is it first introduced by Blair (lines 7–8), and then clarified (upon request by members in line 10, and then in line 12)?

Extract 1: The opening of Tony Blair's speech at the UK Parliament in March 2003

1 At the outset, I say that it is right that the House debate this issue and pass judgment. That is the
2 democracy that is our right, but that others struggle for in vain. Again, I say that I do not disrespect the

3   views in opposition to mine. This is a tough choice indeed, but it is also a stark one: to stand British

4   troops down now and turn back, or to hold firm to the course that we have set. I believe passionately

5   that we must hold firm to that course. The question most often posed is not "Why does it matter?" but

6   "Why does it matter so much?" Here we are, the Government, with their most serious test, their

7   majority at risk, the first Cabinet resignation over an issue of policy, the main parties internally

8   divided, people who agree on everything else–

9

10   [Hon. Members: "The main parties?"]

11

12   Ah, yes, of course. The Liberal Democrats—unified, as ever, in opportunism and error.

13

14   [Interruption.]

(van Dijk, 2006: 177–78)

Salient in this excerpt, and as pointed out by van Dijk (2006: 177–178) is the polarization of ideologies: democracy on the one hand and dictatorship on the other, creating a clear US vs. THEM opposition. We also find tension between those in favor of Blair's position, and those opposed. Van Dijk also points out the following in his analysis (2006: 178): 1) Blair's positive self-representation through "moral superiority," in that he is, at least on the surface, opening the floor for debate and discussion, expressing "respect" for the opinions of others, and his willingness to fight and "hold firm" in the name of justice and democracy; 2) Blair's standing firm and upholding his authority, in spite of opposing viewpoints; 3) Blair's "discrediting" of the Liberal Democrats as being "unified, as ever, in opportunism and error" (note also the emphatic use of the adverbial "as ever" and the argumentative effect it creates); 4) Blair's strategy of infusing emotion into the speech ("I believe passionately").

van Dijk (2006) develops this analysis further by providing additional excerpts of Blair's speech and additional explications that underscore the very tactics of manipulation—as cognitive mind control—discussed previously.

Discourse Historical Approach (DHA)—Wodak et al.

Other approaches to CDA appeal to a broader range of inquiry as a means of elucidating current texts under investigation, specifically the **discourse historical approach** (commonly abbreviated as DHA). See especially Wodak (2001, 2009b, 2011a, 2011b), Engel and Wodak (2012), Reisigl and Wodak (2009), Wodak, Krzyzanowski, and Forchtner (2012), among others.

A DHA approach to Critical Discourse Analysis rests on the **systematic integration of historical background information and prior related discourse as necessary and essential to the interpretation of specific current texts** (Engel and Wodak, 2012: 77). Such prior related discourse might include policy documents, field notes, transcripts and other documents from official and semi-official meetings, document drafts and the various stages in their revisions, interviews, news reports, and the like. Scholars utilizing DHA analyze power and its (mis)use in institutional contexts—power in/over/of discourse, as reflected in interaction, and as developed discursively over time and through prior, related instances of discourse (Wodak, Krzyzanowski, and Forchtner 2012: 162).

The following excerpt, from Engel and Wodak (2012) illustrates the crucial ties that current texts have to historically preceding events and to the prior discourse that occurred as a result of those events. The data are situated historically in post-World War II discourse in Austria, specifically linked to *Verbotsgesetz,* "prohibition law" related to the Austrian denazification initiative passed in May, 1945, immediately following the end of the war. The law officially bans the "glorification, mystification, or denial" of Nazi crimes (Engel and Wodak, 2012: 76). It was amended in 1992, and it remains in force today. In 2008, there were 17 trials for violating the *Verbotsgesetz,* in 2009, there were 104, and 153 in 2010 (Engel and Wodak, 2012: 77).

The data explicated here are situated within the historical context surrounding issues of Holocaust denial by one political figure in Austria, John Gudenus, then a member of the right-wing Freedom Party of Austria *(Freiheitliche Partei Österreichs,* FPÖ). The segment is an excerpt from the 2005 interview between Gudenus and a reporter, Klaus Dutzler. The topic of this segment concerns Gudenus' position regarding the existence of gas chambers in the Third Reich. Dutzler presses Gudenus through a pointed question that targets Gudenus' earlier claim of 10 years prior. In 1995, Gudenus asserted that he remained clear of discussions about gas chambers, and he also claimed to believe everything "dogmatically prescribed" about the topic. In this segment, ten years later, Gudenus circuitously responds to Dutzler's probing. The interview caused a cascade of negative reactions and Gudenus resigned from his position in the FPÖ the following day.

Have a look at the excerpt in question. The texts of both the English translation (Engel and Wodak's "Text 1") as well as the original German version from the Appendix (Engel and Wodak, 2012: 90) appear next:

As you read through the text, attend to the following (also using the German version, if possible):

- Note the two questions as posed by Dutzler. Are they related to each other or are they sharply different? Did Dutzler receive the response he was looking for in Gudenus's reply to his first question? How did Dutzler re-phrase his question the second time to draw a more direct response from Gudenus? Look carefully at the linguistic constructions and features of language. What is used to preface this question? How is the question itself structured? That is, what type of information is presented in the first clause, and then how is the second clause structured? What is the effect of this type of question, where an interrogative clause is placed first, followed by the coordinating conjunction "or" prefacing a specific qualification to that first question?

- In terms of dialogic responsiveness, what role might adverbials of time play in this excerpt? Note <u>contrasting</u> meanings: D: *Wie sehen Sie diese Debatte **heute*** 'What is your view of this debate **today?**' G: *Ich glaube, ich habe **damals** nicht falsch reagiert* 'I believe I did not react the wrong way (**then, at that time**).

- How would you characterize the epistemic stance of Gudenus? How is this expressed linguistically? That is, what are the specific markers of epistemic stance that you find here (use the original German version, if possible, e.g., *ich glaube* 'I believe,' *ich bin der Meinung* 'I am of the opinion that . . .'/'I think'). Any others? ***ich fordere*** *immer wiederum eine Prüfung.* 'I keep calling for an examination . . .'/'I am urging . . .')

- What discursive effect does Gudenus's citation of Charles Popper (referring to the Austrian-British sociopolitical philosopher, Sir Karl Raimund Popper) create in his response to Dutzler's question?

- What discursive effect is created by Gudenus's appeal to physical and scientific means to determine the existence or non-existence of gas chambers in the Third Reich?

John Gudenus and Klaus Dutzler

DUTZLER: What is your view of this debate today?

GUDENUS: I believe I did not react the wrong way. And I believe Charles Popper once said that one should not set up taboos, but rather study and test using physical and scientific means.

DUTZLER: But the underlying question is: Did gas chambers exist in the Third Reich **or is their existence dogmatically prescribed** . . .

GUDENUS: I believe we should debate this topic in all earnestness and not be forced to answer a question with yes or no. And if we should, then let us test this [assumption]. I am of the opinion . . . I keep calling for an examination*.

Original German text (p. 90)

DUTZLER: Wie sehen Sie diese Debatte heute?

GUDENUS: Ich glaube, ich habe damals nicht falsch reagiert. Und ich glaube Charles Popper hat gesagt man soll nicht Tabus aufstellen, sondern man soll physikalisch und wissenschaftlich prüfen.

DUTZLER: Aber die Grundfrage ist: Hat es Gaskammern im Dritten Reich gegeben, **oder ist es dogmatisch vorgeschrieben diese Existenz zu** . . . .

GUDENUS: Ich glaube man sollte dieses Thema ernsthaft debattieren und nicht auf eine Frage du musst es ja oder nein beantworten. Sollen wir, prüfen wir das. Ich bin der Meinung, ich fordere immer wiederum eine Prüfung.

(Engel and Wodak, 2012: 80)

The excerpt illustrates "calculated ambivalence," the focal theme of Engel and Wodak (2012: 79). "The 'strategy of *calculated ambivalence*' serves to convey at least two contradictory messages in one utterance which addresses different audiences." Through "calculated ambivalence" Gudenus tailors "different claims for different audiences at the same time" (2012: 80), first admitting to the practice of gas chamber exterminations, and then questioning its existence by expressing the need for scientific proof. This is an example of the *topos of legitimate doubt* (2012: 80–81). The logic of his argument goes like this: If we find conclusive evidence of gas chambers in the Third Reich, then they existed. And, if gas chambers existed, we will find evidence of them. Gudenus's reference to Charles Popper is an instance of the *topos of authority* (2012: 81), suggesting that prior findings related to gas chambers are no longer valid, and that only scientific proof will provide a definitive answer. Gudenus did not straightforwardly deny gas chamber exterminations, but he raised sufficient doubt to suggest that they (or perhaps even the Holocaust itself) may or may not have existed.

Dutzler, the interviewer, was adept at drawing out Gudenus's position. Dutzler's rephrasing of his first question, using Gudenus's prior words (from 1995) may have contributed to how Gudenus responded. This is the original quote from ten years earlier: *"Gaskammern? Ich halte mich da raus! Ich glaube alles, was dogmatisch vorgeschrieben ist"* 'Gas chambers? I stay out of such matters. I believe everything that is dogmatically prescribed.' (Engel and Wodak, ibid: 92, fn 18).

Dutzler's now re-structured question represents an instance of **intertextuality,** i.e., the process of using elements of text from prior discourse in a new spate of discourse, resulting in a transformation of meaning (Bakhtin, 1981; Fairclough, 1995b, 2003; Kristeva, 1980, 1986; Plett, 1991; Maˇdronne, 2012; Meinhof and Smith, 2000; Wodak, de Cillia, Reisigl, and Liebhart, 2009).

Dutzler's intertexual reference to Gudenus' earlier claim, not just the two verbatim words recycled in the second part of this question, *dogmatisch vorgeschriben* "dogmatically prescribed," but the entire quote from which they are taken, sets up an important ideological frame. This frame now serves as an invitation to Gudenus to confirm or refute a once-stated qualification to the content of the very question Dutzler posed so directly and so succinctly in the clause just preceding it: *Aber die Grundfrage ist: Hat es Gaskammern im Dritten Reich gegeben*, "But the underlying question is, did gas chambers exist in the Third Reich?"—literally, "Were there gas chambers . . .?"

Two Excerpts for Practice Analysis Using a CDA Lens

Drawing on notions of normalization, legitimization of ideologies, discursive construction of power and control, and the polarization of what is considered to be "normal" and what is considered to be "different" (hence a problematic element in some currently acceptable social structure), analyze the following two excerpts. Also, try to find other historically relevant data connected with the content and positions expressed in either or both excerpts.

Excerpt 1 is from a 1964 textbook called *History of a Free People*, used in 12th grade U.S. History classes in the Los Angeles City School District during the mid-1960s to mid-1970s. Excerpt 2 is a transcript of a television ad for Cymbalta, a prescription antidepressant drug that is currently used in the United States.

As you analyze the discourse here, try to articulate the following:

- What are the underlying assumptions in the texts? How are these assumptions articulated? How are the "people" represented in these spates of discourse?
- Do you find *manipulation* in either or both texts?
- What are the underlying dichotomies or polarizations that are framed in the discourse, both implicitly and explicitly?
    - Note, in particular, the positive representations of one side and the negative representations of the other. How are these representations created through linguistic forms and visual imagery?
- Who or what is constructed as powerful? Who or what is constructed as powerless (or markedly less powerful)? How are these notions discursively created?
- Who is the intended audience of each piece? How does the target audience contribute to the construction of power and the perpetuation of this underlying and unspoken power asymmetry as it relates to each text?
- How would you articulate the intended message of each text? Try to formulate one sentence that captures the message of the text. Then, think of the discursive features that support your analysis. Make a list of them and group them into appropriate categories.

Here is Excerpt 1. Keep these questions in mind as you read through the text.

Excerpt 1: U.S. History Textbook, *History of a Free People* (1964), Los Angeles City Schools

Occupation of Japan—1945–1951

In July, 1945, shortly before atom bombs fell on Hiroshima and Nagasaki, an inter-Allied conference at Potsdam, outside Berlin, drew up plans for postwar treatment of Japan. The essential provisions were as follows: (1) Japanese militarists should be punished and Japan

---

disarmed, (2) Japanese sovereignty should be restricted to the home islands, (3) the Japanese people should be educated in democracy. Troops were to occupy Japan until these aims were accomplished. To carry out this Potsdam Declaration, General Douglas MacArthur was appointed Supreme Commander of the Allied Powers (soon abbreviated to S.C.A.P.).

Although two inter-Allied commissions were appointed to direct or advise him, MacArthur in fact wielded dictatorial power. Under his able direction, Japan underwent a notable period of reform. Japanese armies were disbanded, and war industries destroyed. A few militarists were tried for war crimes; many more were purged from government jobs. Political democracy was advanced by abolition of the secret police, by a new constitution, and by woman suffrage. The Mikado remained as a symbol of national unity but was no longer treated as a god. Economic opportunity was promoted by breaking up great trusts owned by a few families, by encouragement of trade unions, and above all by redivision of the land among the peasants. A reorganized educational system taught democratic ways instead of national myths and blind obedience. At first the intention had been to make Japan pay reparations, but the economic difficulties of the island kingdom proved so great that instead the United States provided nearly two billion dollars as aid. (256 words)

(Bragdon and McCutchen, 1964: 696).

How is the United States represented here? What elements, if any, are symbolic of the U.S.?

What is the relevance of "atom bombs" to this passage? How are the "bombs" depicted? Whose action (". . . shortly before atom bombs *fell. . .*")? Is the verb *transitive* or *intransitive* (see Chapters 2 and 8)? How does the notion of *agency* (or lack thereof) emerge in this excerpt (see Chapter 8)?

List the ways in which the author frames the U.S. involvement in Japan. How are agency and responsibility indexed? How is moral stance indexed?

How is Japan represented? List the ways in which the author frames Japan, the Japanese people, Japanese institutions, and Japanese culture. Is there any sense of agency or control indexed in the discourse?

What is the underlying message? Do you agree with the manner in which each side is depicted here? What elements of bias or superiority or condescension do you find? Through what linguistic means are they communicated?

If you were to re-write this passage, how could you more equitably represent the two nations?

Here is Excerpt 2, one of the current ads for the prescription antidepressant drug Cymbalta. Keep in mind the guiding questions that we provided in the paragraphs that precede both excerpts.

Cymbalta Television Commercial

bold—words that flash on the screen (in white letters)
italics—words read from a script, female voiceover
((constant mood-setting music playing in the background))

sunrise hurts ((Sunrise pouring into a window as a woman is sleeping in bed; it's already broad daylight; the blinds are open and we can see the day through the window; her dresser is messy and her nightstand is piled with books; she is wearing a green, long-sleeved tee shirt.))
With depression, simple pleasures can simply hurt.

wishes hurt ((Women walking toward a dining room table carrying a birthday cake with candles lit; people are laughing and celebrating; one man with a stubbly beard is not smiling; he sighs.))
The sadness, anxiety . . .

hello hurts ((A young woman with long blond hair is sitting on her recliner, her head is propped up on one arm. Her expression is flat. Her white dog comes to her, wags tail slightly, drops a ball, and then realizes she doesn't want to play. The dog sits down at her feet, as if disappointed.))
the loss of interest, the aches, and pains

depression hurts   (The woman who'd been in bed in the first frame gets up; she may be in street clothes—it looks as if she is wearing a long sleeved t-shirt, not pajamas.)
and fatigue . . . depression hurts
Cymbalta can help with many symptoms of depression.

Tell your doctor if you are pregnant or nursing
((warning message discourse omitted))

(Cymbalta, n.d.)

Who is portrayed here? How? What glimpses of everyday lifestyles do you see in this commercial?

Who or what is represented as "powerful?" Through what discursive means?

In what way(s) is *agency* indexed? How are affective and epistemic stances indexed in this excerpt? What overall effect does this create for the viewer, and especially for the viewer who may be in need of the very medication being promoted here?

Who or what is represented as "normal"? What is "not normal"?

What are the so-called simple pleasures that are depicted in the ad, visually and linguistically? What is your reaction as you view this or as you imagine it via the transcript (if there is no access to the video)?

What does "hurt" mean in this leitmotif of "hurt" ("sunrise hurts," "wishes hurt, "hello hurts," "depression hurts")? How are "sunrise," "wishes," and "hello" similar? How are they different? Does "depression" fit within this string? sunrise, wishes, hello, depression?

The clause or sentence "Depression hurts" is ambiguous. Who is the subject of the "hurting"? Who is the object of the "hurting?" That is, who suffers because of depression? Depression hurts the person who has it. But, at the same time, as we observe in the segment "hello hurts" as the dog drops the ball at his owner's feet, *depression hurts others.* One might hear an underlying message here that treatment is not just to help the sufferer, but to help other people (and pets) around that person who might also be suffering. One might hear an underlying suggestion of guilt, because depression just doesn't "hurt" one person, it "hurts" those around us.

With regard to commonplace warning messages that appear with most (if not all) pharmaceutical ads in print and on television, think about these issues: What type of discourse is this? Can you identify its genre(s)? What "speech acts" do the warning messages express? Why do such messages appear in conjunction with these advertisements? What are the assumptions underlying the messages? How are such assumptions discursively created? Who are the "people" represented? What are the medical risks? How are they expressed? How are the risks organized and itemized? Why do you think so?

Based on the previous discussion of van Dijk, do you think that this is an instance of *persuasion*? of *manipulation*? Why or why not? Formulate an argument in which you provide supporting details from the data segment to establish your position. To support your ideas, it might help to locate other similar (or contrasting) instances of public discourse—same genre, other genres, etc.

REVIEW AND REFLECTION: CRITICAL DISCOURSE ANALYSIS

1. For scholars in CDA, discourse is social practice. Discourse creates and is created by social structure and culture. Discourse creates and is created by belief systems and ideologies. And discourse perpetuates them. The goal of CDA is to make visible the invisible injustices and racism and power asymmetries. What are considered to be normal and acceptable behaviors, appearances, and practices are established and maintained through discourse. Access to discourse is afforded to the privileged, the elite. Genres of discourse mesh with other genres, creating hybridized texts that persuade and manipulate. Ideologies of power, abuse, control, hegemony, and exclusion are created, re-created, perpetuated, and reified through our taken-for-granted discursive processes.

   Next we list the areas that are ripe for CDA-based analyses. Think about possible research topics along these lines (or others that may have crossed your mind as you read through the first parts of this chapter) and try to determine some possible data sources for you to conduct a CDA-based analysis.

- Introductory textbooks for children, adolescents, or any newcomer to any field
- Policy documents (educational standards, immigration, workplace practices, plagiarism policies)
- Prison, police, and criminal discourse
- Discourse of the environment, global warming, endangered species, pollution
- Political speeches, debates, fliers
- Documentary films
- Discourse on sexuality and sexual orientation
- Mineral and utility rights among nations with newly drawn borders (e.g., Ukraine and Russia), ownership of islands (Senkaku Islands debate)[3]
- Institutional rationalizations of cruelty, war, or violence
- Food (GMOs, organic produce and meats, fast food, sweeteners and other chemical additives)
- Discourse of illness, health, and health products

- Discursive constructions of youth, beauty, and aging
- Institutional discourse with inherently skewed rights to speak (medical encounters, legal discourse, news interviews, political interviews, parody news shows with celebrity guests)
- Representations of gender, beauty, youth, and aging in children's media and literature (e.g., Disney, children's TV programs and commercials, folk tales, and story books)
- Discourse of intercultural communication

2. The following quotes are from figures who have nothing to do with CDA scholarship, yet the ideas that they express relate to many of the concepts that are noted in CDA literature. Think about the following two excerpts, one from Carl Sagan (U.S. astronomer and scientist), and the other from Cesar Chavez (labor leader and civil rights activist).

    What does each quote mean? What is the relevance to what you've just read concerning CDA and its ideological goals?

Carl Sagan

"One of the saddest lessons of history is this: If we've been bamboozled long enough, we tend to reject any evidence of the bamboozle. We're no longer interested in finding out the truth. The bamboozle has captured us. It's simply too painful to acknowledge, even to ourselves, that we've been taken. Once you give a charlatan power over you, you almost never get it back."

(Sagan, 1995: 230)

César Chavez

"Once social change begins, it cannot be reversed. You cannot uneducate the person who has learned to read. You cannot humiliate the person who feels pride. You cannot oppress the people who are not afraid anymore."

(Chavez, 1984)

3. The history textbook excerpt reports on the "U.S. occupation of Japan." Are there any correlations that you can draw concerning U.S. involvement in other countries of the world more currently? How have situations changed? How have they remained the same? How are the various nations involved depicted in various textbooks and media representations?

4. There are a number of scholars who criticize CDA. Some of these include Hammersley (1997); Widdowson (1995, 1996) and Luke (2002). Read their work and summarize their positions vis à vis CDA scholarship. Do you agree? Why or why not?

5. Analyzing discourse: Two ways (and more) of representing the "TRUTH"—**The Aspartame controversy.**

Aspartame, a common artificial sweetener used worldwide, has been the subject of debate (including at least one Internet hoax).

Wikipedia provides a detailed summary of the debate here (see Asparame controversy, n.d.), including a list of nations who have banned the use of aspartame and/or launched their own studies into its safety:

In the excerpt pair here, we provide two sides to this controversy. As you read through the data, think about the various discursive ways each piece establishes the primary arguments:

- What types of linguistic constructions are used?
- Can you describe the "tones" of each excerpt? What creates that tone?
- Based on your analysis of the discourse, who would you say is the "audience" of each piece? How would you describe the various *registers* of discourse?
- Do you think that the two pieces belong to the same *genre* of discourse? Why or why not?
- Are the arguments intended to be *persuasive* in any way? Are they *manipulative?* Why or why not? Are they convincing? Which side is more convincing to you? Why?
- Try to find other data excerpts about the topic. How are the arguments in those excerpts presented? Do they seem to match the argument style, tone, register, and genre of Excerpt 1 or Excerpt 2? Or, is there an argument style that is altogether different? What discursive

> features create style, tone, and register? What discursive features are characteristic of the particular genres at hand?
> - How does the discourse in these two excerpts compare and contrast with the discourse in the excerpt from the U.S. history textbook (on Japan)? Think about how the linguistic forms are used and organized in the texts in question (aspartame debate, *History of a Free People* excerpt, and any other texts that you consider relevant to this question).

Excerpt 1: "Aspartame: What is aspartame?"

Aspartame

What is aspartame?

Aspartame is one of the most common artificial sweeteners in use today. It is sold under the brand names NutraSweet® and Equal®. Aspartame is composed mainly of 2 amino acids, aspartic acid and phenylalanine. Amino acids are the building blocks of proteins and are found naturally in many foods.

Aspartame is used in many foods and beverages because it is about 200 times sweeter than sugar, so much less of it can be used to give the same level of sweetness. This, in turn, lowers the calories in the food or beverage.

Rumors claiming that aspartame causes a number of health problems, including cancer, have been around for many years. Many of these continue to circulate on the Internet . . .

. . . Does aspartame cause cancer?

Researchers use 2 main types of studies to try to determine if a substance or exposure causes cancer. (A substance that causes cancer or helps cancer grow is called a *carcinogen*.) . . .

. . . In most cases neither type of study provides definitive evidence on its own, so researchers usually look at both lab-based and human studies if they are available.

(American Cancer Society, n.d.)

<u>Excerpt 2</u>: "Aspartame Damages the Brain at Any Dose"

Did you know that Aspartame has been proven to cause brain damage by leaving traces of Methanol in the blood? It makes you wonder why Aspartame has been approved as "safe" and is found in thousands of food products. Currently more than 90 countries have given the artificial sweetener the "OK" to be used in foods . . .

. . . What is this lovely substance (Aspartame) made of?

An Aspartame molecule is essentially made up of 3 different substances. 90% of it is made of two natural amino acids, 1 being aspartic acid and the other being phenylalanine. The other 10% of the molecule is made up of a methyl ester bond (includes Methanol). . . . The big problem with methanol is that it easily passes into your blood-brain barrier and once there, is converted into formaldehyde. Formaldehyde is what is causing the brain damage. While animals are able to detoxify methanol in the body, humans do not have this capability. It doesn't really take a rocket scientist to realize that accumulating formaldehyde in the brain is not a good thing.

(Martino, 2012)

PRACTICE WITH CDA IN ENGLISH AND OTHER LANGUAGES: U.S. AND CHINESE—THE SENKAKU ISLAND CONTROVERSY

In these data, have a look at how the tension over the "ownership" of the Senkaku (Diaoyu) Islands is reflected in U.S. media outlets and Chinese media outlets.

How is the "truth" represented in each data source? How is the background set by each article? Why do you think the background presentation differs in the U.S. data from that in the Chinese data? How is background information presented in other data that you may have found on the topic from the U.S., from Japan, or from Taiwan. It would be revealing to analyze the national perspectives on the issues. What types of metaphors do find in the U.S. data? What types of metaphors to you find in the Chinese data? How does the use of metaphor contribute to the overall power and impact of the particular media reports?

In addition, search for Japanese media outlets to complement these data sources (printed Japanese, English, or both). What types of metaphors do you find there? Specifically, focus on metaphors relating to events, to the various nations involved (China, Japan, and the U.S.).

EXCERPT A: "Understanding the China-Japan Island Conflict" (September 25, 2012)

Sept. 29 will mark 40 years of normalized diplomatic relations between China and Japan, two countries that spent much of the 20th century in mutual enmity if not at outright war. The anniversary comes at a low point in Sino-Japanese relations amid a dispute over an island chain in the East China Sea known as the Senkaku Islands in Japan and Diaoyu Islands in China . . .

. . . These islands, which are little more than uninhabited rocks, are not particularly valuable on their own. However, nationalist factions in both countries have used them to enflame old animosities; in China, the government has even helped organize the protests over Japan's plan to purchase and nationalize the islands from their private owner. . . . Beijing has undertaken a high-profile expansion and improvement of its navy as a way to help safeguard its maritime interests, which Japan—an island nation necessarily dependent on access to sea-lanes—naturally views as a threat. . . .

. . . The United States' underlying interest is maintaining a perpetual balance between Asia's two key powers so neither is able to challenge Washington's own primacy in the Pacific. . . . As China lurches into a new economic cycle, one that will very likely force deep shifts in the country's internal political economy, it is not hard to imagine China and Japan's underlying geopolitical balance shifting again. And when that happens, so too could the role of the United States.

(Stratfor.com Geopolitical Weekly, 2012; article republished with permission from Stratfor.com)

EXCERPT B: CHINA: editorial piece published in the online edition of the well-known newspaper 南方周末 "Southern Weekend".

Note the metaphor of *the body*—the body as lifesource, the body as viewing agent, the body as vulnerable.

扼守海上要道的钓鱼岛,是中国海军命脉的"穴点"? ...

日本一直虎视眈眈,监视着钓鱼岛海面上的风吹草动。早在上世纪90年代,日本就已经开始论证钓鱼岛的地缘战略价值,论证结果一直被列为机密。

. . .

国防大学教授韩旭东说,假如日本在钓鱼岛上设置雷达观测站或者配置P-3C反潜机,观测范围可达600公里以上,福州、宁波以及台湾北部的大部分地区都在监测之下。进出宫古海峡的中国海军舰艇将暴露无遗,"这些瞭望哨正在使中国海军陷入'裸奔'的危险。"

在地缘政治上,日本盘踞着亚洲海岸线第一岛链的北部弧区,从日韩之间的对马海峡延伸到台湾,在这条狭窄的岛弧上,钓鱼岛正处在中间的节点。扼守海上要道的钓鱼岛,正是掐住中国海军命脉的"穴点"?

. . .

Guarding (literally, to choke something tightly with both hands) the sea routes, the Diaoyu Islands is the **pressure point of the lifeline** of the Chinese Navy

. . .

Japan has always been **eyeing** (literally tiger watching its prey, traditional Chinese metaphor), **monitoring** Diaoyu Islands' **sea trouble** (literally, blowing of the wind and movement of the grass, traditional Chinese military metaphor). From as early as the 1990s, Japan had already begun to build its case on the Diaoyu Islands' geostrategic value. The result had been kept confidential.

National Defense University professor, Han Xudong said that if Japan set up radar stations or configured P-3C anti-submarine air-craft on the Diaoyu Islands, their observation range will reach up to 600 km or more. Fuzhou, Ningbo, and large parts of northern Taiwan are under surveillance. The Chinese Navy in and out of the

Miyako Strait will **be exposed completely**. "These lookouts will put the Chinese Navy into the danger of **"streaking ('running while naked,' i.e., in danger of being completely unprotected)."**

(Southern Weekend, 2012)

EXCERPT C: CHINA: "Daioyu Islands are China's inherent territory" Note the metaphor of the *criminal*: thief, power, secrecy, conspiracy, suspicion

二、日本窃取钓鱼岛

　　日本在明治维新以后加快对外侵略扩张。1879年,日本吞并琉球并改称冲绳县。此后不久,日本便密谋侵占钓鱼岛,并于甲午战争末期将钓鱼岛秘密"编入"版图。随后,日本又迫使中国签订不平等的《马关条约》,割让台湾全岛及包括钓鱼岛在内的所有附属各岛屿。

Japan <u>Steals</u> Diaoyu Islands

After the Meiji Restoration, Japan accelerated its foreign aggression and expansion. In 1879, Japan **annexed (literally, swallowed)** Liuqiu and renamed it Ryukyu Okinawa Prefecture. Shortly thereafter, Japan started to **secretly plot** the occupation of the Diaoyu Islands, and near the end of the Sino-Japanese War **secretly "incorporated"** the Diaoyu Islands into Japanese territory. Subsequently, Japan forced China to sign the unequal "Treaty of Shimonoseki," yielding the island of Taiwan and all of its subsidiaries including the Diaoyu islands to Japan.

(一)日本密谋窃取钓鱼岛

　　1884年,有日本人声称首次登上钓鱼岛,发现该岛为"无人岛"。日本政府随即对钓鱼岛开展秘密调查,并试图侵占。日本上述图谋引起中国的警觉。1885年9月6日(清光绪十一年七月二十八日)《申报》登载消息:"台湾东北边之海岛,近有日本人悬日旗于其上,大有占据之势。"由于顾忌中国的反应,日本政府未敢轻举妄动。

　　. . .

(A) Japan conspired to steal the Diaoyu Islands

In 1884, a Japanese person claimed for the first time to have arrived at the Diaoyu Islands, discovering it to be an "uninhabited island." The government of Japan immediately carried out secret investigations and attempted to occupy the islands. Japan's action (lit. 'scheme') aroused China's suspicions. On September 6, 1885 (July 28 Year 11 of Qing Dynasty) the Sheng Newspaper published the headline: "Japanese Flag Found Flying on island northeast of Taiwan—Suspicious of Attempt to Occupy." For fear of Chinese reaction, the Japanese government did not pursue occupation.
. . .

(Xinhuanet News, 2012: section II)

SUGGESTIONS FOR FURTHER READING

Atkin, A. and Richardson, J. (2007). Arguing about Muslims: (Un)Reasonable argumentation in letters to the editor. *Text and Talk*, 27,1: 1–25.

Charlebois, J. (2010). The discursive construction of femininities in the accounts of Japanese women. *Discourse Studies*, 12,6: 699–714.

Fang, J. Y. (2001). Reporting the same events? A critical analysis of Chinese print news media texts. *Discourse and Society*, 12,5: 585–613.

Inoue, M. (2004). The linguistic ideologies of modern Japanese Honorifics and the historic reality of modernity. *Language and Communication*, 24,4: 413–35.

Jones, R. (2000). "Potato seeking rice": Language, culture, and identity in gay personal ads in Hong Kong. *International Journal of the Sociology of Language*, 143: 33–61.

Khosravinik, M. (2009). The representation of refugees, asylum seekers and immigrants in British newspapers during the Balkan conflict (1999) and the British general election (2005). *Discourse and Society*, 20,4: 477–98.

Mǎdronne, I. D. (2012). New times, old ideologies? Recontextualizations of radical right thought in Postcommunist Romania. In R. Wodak and J. Richardson (Eds.), *Analysing Fascist Discourse: European Fascism in Talk and Text*. London: Routledge. Pp. 256–76.

Milonas, Y. (2007). Crisis, conspiracy rights: Imaginaries of terrorism in documentary film. *Critical Approaches to Discourse Analysis*, 1,2: 96–117.

Rogers, R. (2003). A critical discourse analysis of the special education referral process. *Discourse*, 24,2: 139–58.

Schwartz, A. (2006). The teaching and culture of household Spanish: Understanding racist reproduction in 'domestic' discourse. *Critical Discourse Studies*, 3,2: 107–21.

Wang, H. C. (2009). Language and ideology: Gender stereotypes of female and male artists in Taiwanese tabloids. *Discourse and Society*, 20,6: 747–74.

Wohlwend, K. E. (2012). Are you guys girls? Boys, identity, texts, and Disney Princess Play. *Journal of Early Childhood Literacy*, 12: 3–23.

LINKS

Blair, T. (2003, March 18). Full text: Tony Blair's speech. *The Guardian*. Retrieved from: http://www.theguardian.com/politics/2003/mar/18/foreignpolicy.iraq1. Accessed September 24, 2013.

Cymbalta. (n.d.). Simple pleasures. [TV commercial]. Retrieved from *Ad Pharm* website: https://adpharm.net/displayimage.php?album=255&pid=34013. Accessed May, 20, 2013.

Aspartame controversy. (n.d.). In *Wikipedia*. Retrieved from http://en.wikipedia.org/wiki/Aspartame_controversy. Accessed June 8, 2013.

American Cancer Society. (n.d.). *Aspartame: What is aspartame?* Retrieved from: http://www.cancer.org/cancer/cancercauses/othercarcinogens/athome/aspartame. Accessed June 8, 2013.

Martino, J. (2012, October 6). Aspartame damages the brain at any dose. *Collective Evolution*. Retrieved from: http://www.collective-evolution.com/2012/10/06/aspartame-damages-the-brain-at-any-dose/. Accessed June 8, 2013.

Stratfor.com Geopolitical Weekly. (2012, September 25) Understanding the China-Japan island conflict. Retrieved from: http://www.stratfor.com/weekly/understanding-china-japan-island-conflict. Accessed June 20, 2013.

Southern Weekend 南方周末 online newspaper. (2012, September 21). 《南方周末》 http://www.infzm.com/content/81146. Accessed May 23, 2013.

Xinhuanet News (2012, September 25). Diaoyu Islands are China's inherent territory [White paper]. Retrieved from: http://news.xinhuanet.com/2012-09/25/c_113202698_2.htm.

NOTES

1. See List of language regulators (n.d.) for a list of languages and the agencies that regulate them as *standard languages*, from Afrikaans in South Africa (Die Taalkommissie), French in France (L'Académie Française), French in Québec (Office québécois de la langue française), to Yoruba in Nigeria (The Yoruba Academy). The site provides a list of nearly 100 languages of various countries and regions, some with links to their respective language regulating agencies. Also see the language policies (monolingual, bilingual, multilingual) of individual cities, states, public service agencies, places of employment, and so forth.
2. Prosody and other paralinguistic features of talk are included.
3. These topics were addressed as term projects in Strauss' discourse analysis class. Larysa Bobrova wrote on the 2009 Ukrainian Gas Crisis. Siqi Liu wrote on the 2012 Senkaku Islands Dispute.

References

AccuWeather. (2012). http://www.accuweather.com/en/weather-video/breaking-weather-snow-cancels-flights-in-denver/1670024770. Accessed June 8, 2012.

Agar, M. (1985). Institutional discourse. *Text,* 5,3*:* 147–68

Agha, A. (2004). Registers of language. In A. Duranti (Ed.), *A Companion to Linguistic Anthropology*. New York and Oxford: Blackwell.

Agha, A. (2005). Voice, footing, enregisterment. *Journal of Linguistic Anthropology,* 15,1: 38–59.

Agha, A. (2007). Recombinant selves in mass mediated space-time. *Language and Communication,* 27: 320–35.

Ahearn, L. (2001). Language and agency. *Annual Review of Anthropology*, 30: 109–37.

Ainsworth-Vaughn, N. (1998). *Claiming Power in Doctor-Patient Talk*. Oxford: Oxford University Press.

Althusser, L. (1971). Ideology and ideological state apparatuses. In L. Althusser (Ed.), *Lenin and Philosophy and other Essays*. New York: Monthly Review Press. Pp. 127–88.

American Cancer Society. (n.d.). *Aspartame: What is aspartame?* Retrieved from: http://www.cancer.org/cancer/cancercauses/othercarcinogens/athome/aspartame. Accessed June 8, 2013.

Antaki, C. (2011). *Applied Conversation analysis: Intervention and Change in Institutional Talk.* New York: Palgrave Macmillan.

Antaki, C. (2012). Affiliative and disaffiliative candidate understandings. *Discourse Studies*, 14,5: 531–47.

Antaki, C and Jahoda, A. (2010). Psychotherapists' practices in keeping a session "on-track" in the face of clients' "off-track" talk. *Communication and Medicine*, 7: 11–21.

Aristotle. (1969). *Nicomachean Ethics*. Translated by David Ross. London: Oxford University Press.

Aspartame controversy. (n.d.). In *Wikipedia*. Retrieved from: http://en.wikipedia.org/wiki/Aspartame_controversy. Accessed June 8, 2013.

Atkinson, J. M. and Heritage, J. (Eds.). (1984). *Structures of Social Action: Studies in Conversation Analysis*. Cambridge: Cambridge University Press.

Attardo, S. (1990). The violation of Grices Maxims in jokes. *Proceedings of the Berkeley Linguistics Society*. Pp. 355–62.

Attardo, S. (1994). Non-literalness and non-bona-fide in language: An approach to formal and computational treatments of humor. *Pragmatics and Cognition*. 2,1: 31–69.

Attardo, S. (2004). *Linguistic Theories of Humor.* Berlin, New York: Mouton de Gruyter.

Auer, P. (2005). Projection in interaction and projection in grammar. *Text*, 25,1: 7–36.

Austin, J. (1962). *How to Do Things with Words.* J. Urmson and M. Sbisá (Eds.). Cambridge, MA: Harvard University Press.

Austin, J. (1979). *Collected Papers* (3rd ed.). J. Urmson and G. Warnock (Eds.). Oxford: Oxford University Press.

Bailey, B. (1997). Communication of respect in interethnic service encounters. *Language in Society*, 26,3: 327–356.

Bakhtin, M. (1981). *The Dialogical Imagination.* Austin: University of Texas Press.

Bakhtin, M. (1986). *Speech Genres and Other Late Essays.* C. Emerson and M. Holquist (Eds.) and V. McGee (Translator). Austin, TX: University of Texas Press.

Balian, A. and Anderson, K. (Writers) and Patrick, L. (Director). (2004). Opening monologue of show dated August 2, 2004 [Television series episode]. In V. A. Ernst, J. Gabel, and B. Brillowski (Producers), *The Ellen DeGeneres Show*. Los Angeles, CA: NBC.

Bamberg, M. (2010). Blank check for biography? Openness and ingenuity in the management of "Who-am-I question" and what life stories actually may not be good for. In D. Schiffrin and A. Nylund (Eds.), *Telling Stories: Language, Narrative, and Social Life*. Washington DC: Georgetown University Press. Pp. 109–21.

Baquedano-Lopez, P. (2001). Creating identities through doctrina narratives. In A. Duranti (Ed.), *Linguistic Anthropology: A Reader.* Malden, MA: Blackwell. Pp. 364–77.

Baquedano-López, P. (2008). The pragmatics of reading prayers: Learning the Act of Contrition in Spanish-based religious education classes (doctrina). *Text & Talk 28*, 5: 582–602.

Bargiela-Chiapini, F. (2009). *The Handbook of Business Discourse.* Edinburgh, UK: Edinburgh University Press.

Bargiela-Chiapini, F. and Harris, S. (1997). *Managing Language: The Discourse of Corporate Meetings.* Philadelphia: John Benjamins Publishing.

Bargiela-Chiappini, F. and Kádár, D. (Eds.). (2011). *Politeness Across Cultures.* New York: Palgrave Macmillian.

Baum, L. F. (writer) and Fleming, V. (director). (August, 1939). *The Wizard of Oz* [Motion picture]. United States: Metro Goldwyn-Mayer.

Bauman, R. (1986). *Story, Performance, and Event: Contextual Studies of Oral Narratives.* Cambridge: Cambridge University Press.

Bauman, R. (1992). Contextualization, tradition, and the dialogue of genres: Icelandic legends of the Kraftaskáld. In C. Goodwin and A. Duranti (Eds.), *Rethinking context: Language as an interactive phenomenon.* Cambridge: Cambridge University Press. Pp. 127–43.

Bauman, Z. (2001). Identity in the globalizing world. *Social Anthropology*, 9,2: 121–129.

Bax, M. and Kádár, D. (2011). The historical understanding of historical (im)politeness: Introductory notes. *Journal of Historical Pragmatics*, 12,1: 1–24.

Bayer Aspirin. (n.d.). Invincible heart attack [TV commercial]. Retrieved from: http://www.youtube.com/watch?v=8mHPgMtjPyo. Accessed September 24, 2013.

Bayer Aspirin. (2012). 바이엘 헬스케어 '아스피린 프로텍[Bayer aspirin protect] [TV commercial]. Retrieved from: http://www.youtube.com/watch?v=5Y08gx-eaic. Accessed May 5, 2013.

Bazerman, C. (1997). The concept of concepts. *Readerly/Writerly Texts*, 4,2: 9–20.

BBC News. (2012, July 1). *Euro 2012 final: Spain v Italy as it happened.* Retrieved from: http://www.bbc.co.uk/sport/0/football/17875873. Accessed December 24, 2012.

BBC News. (2012, November 24). *UKIP couple have foster children removed from care.* Retrieved from: http://www.bbc.co.uk/news/uk-20474120. Accessed December 20, 2012.

Bell, A. (1984). Language style as audience design. *Language in Society,* 13,2: 145–204.

Bell, A. (1991). *The Language of News Media*. Oxford: Blackwell.

Bell, A. (2001). Back in style: Reworking audience design. In P. Eckert and J. Rickford (Eds.), *Style and Sociolinguistics Variation.* Cambridge: Cambridge University Press.

Bell, A. and Garrett P. (1998). *Approaches to Media Discourse*. Oxford: Blackwell.

Benor, S. B. (2012). *Becoming Frum: How Newcomers Learn the Language and Culture of Orthodox Judaism*. Rutgers: Rutgers University Press.

Bergmann, J. (1998). Introduction: Morality in discourse. *Research on Language and Social Interaction* (special issue), 31: 279–94.

Besnier, N. (1990). Language and affect. *Annual Review of Anthropology*, 19: 419–51.

Besnier, N. (1993). Reported Speech and affect on Nukulaelae Atoll. In J. Hill and J. Irvine, (Eds.), *Responsibility and Evidence in Oral Discourse.* Cambridge: Cambridge University Press. Pp. 161–81.

Bhatia, V. (2004). *Worlds of Written Discourse: A Genre-Based View*. London: Continuum.

Bhatia, V., Candlin, C., Gotti, M. (2012). *Discourse and Practice in the International Commercial Arbitration*. Farnham, UK: Ashagte Publishing.

Biber, D. (1994). An analytic framework for register studies. In D. Biber and E. Finegan (Eds.), *Sociolinguistic Perspectives on Register*. New York: Oxford University Press.

Biber, D. and Finegan, E. (1988). Adverbial stance types in English. *Discourse Processes*, 11: 1–34.

Biber, D. and Finegan, E. (1989). Styles of stance in English: Lexical and grammatical marking of evidentiality and affect. *Text,* 9: 93–124.

Biber, D. and Conrad S. (2009). *Register, Genre, and Style.* Cambridge: Cambridge University Press.

Biletzki, A. and Matar, A., (2011). Ludwig Wittgenstein. In E. N. Zalta (Ed.), *The Stanford Encyclopedia of Philosophy* (Summer 2011 Edition). http://plato.stanford.edu/archives/sum2011/entries/wittgenstein/

Birner, B. (1994). Information structure and word order. *Language*, 33: 233–59.

Birner, B. and Ward, G. (1998). *Information Status and Noncanonical Word Order in English*. Amsterdam and Philadelphia: John Benjamins.

Birner, B. and Ward, G. (2006). Information structure. In B. Aarts and A. McMahon (Eds.), *Handbook of English Linguistics*. Oxford: Basil Blackwell. Pp. 291–317.

Birner, B. and Ward, G. (2009). Information structure and syntactic structure. *Language and Linguistics Compass*, 3: 1167–87.

Blair, Tony. (2003, March 18). Full text: Tony Blair's speech. *The Guardian*. Retrieved from: http://www.theguardian.com/politics/2003/mar/18/foreign policy.iraq1. Accessed September 24, 2013.

Blommaert, J. (2005). *Discourse: A Critical Introduction*. Cambridge: Cambridge University Press.

Blum-Kulka, S. (1987). Indirectness and politeness in requests: Same or different? *Journal of Pragmatics*, 11: 131–46.

Bolden, G. B. (2011). On the organization of repair in multiperson conversation: The case of other-selection in other-initiated repair sequences. *Research on Language and Social Interaction*, 44,3: 237–62.

Bolinger, D. (1961). Contrastive accent and contrastive stress. *Language*, 37: 83–96.

Bolinger, D. (1972). Accent is predictable (if you're a mind-reader). *Language,* 48: 633–44.

Bolinger, D. (1989*). Intonation and Its Uses*. Redwood City, CA: Stanford University Press.

Bourdieu, P. (1977). *Outline of a Theory of Practice*. R. Nice (Trans.). Cambridge: Cambridge University Press.

Bourdieu, P. (1990). *The Logic of Practice*. Stanford: Stanford University.

Bourdieu, P. and Thompson, J. (1991). *Language and Symbolic Power*. Cambridge, MA: Harvard University Press.

Bousfield, D. (2008). *Impoliteness in Interaction.* Amsterdam: John Benjamins Publishing Company.

Bragdon, H. W. and McCutchen, S. P. (1964). *History of a Free People.* New York: Macmillan.

Breeze, R. (2012). Legitimation in corporate discourse: Oil corporations after Deepwater Horizon. *Discourse and Society*, 23,1: 3–18.

Briscola game rules. (n.d.). In *Wikipedia.* http://en.wikipedia.org/wiki/Briscola. Accessed May 24, 2013.

Bronstein, I., Nelson, N., Linat, Z., and Ben-Ari, R. (2012). Rapport in negotiation: The contribution of the verbal channel. *The Journal of Conflict Resolution*, 56,6: 1089–115.

Brown, G. and Yule, G. (1983). *Discourse Analysis*. Cambridge: Cambridge University Press.

Brown, L. (2011). Korean honorifics and 'revealed,' 'ignored,' and 'suppressed' aspects of Korean culture and politeness. In F. Bargiela-Chiappini and D. Kádár (Eds.), *Politeness Across Cultures*. New York: Palgrave Macmillian. Pp. 106–27.

Brown, P. and Gilman, A. (1960). The pronouns of power and solidarity. In T. A. Sebeok (Ed.), *Style in Language*. Cambridge: MIT Press. Pp. 253–76.

Brown, P. and Levinson, L. (1987). *Politeness: Some Universals in Language Use*. Cambridge: Cambridge University Press.

Bruner, J. (1986). *Actual Minds, Possible Worlds.* Cambridge, MA: Harvard University Press.

Bruner, J. (1990). *Acts of Meaning.* Boston: Harvard University Press.

Bruner, J. (2010). Narrative, culture, and mind. In D. Schiffrin and A. Nylund (Eds.), *Telling Stories: Language, Narrative, and Social Life.* Washington, DC: Georgetown University Press. Pp. 45–50.

Bubel, C. M. (2008). Film audiences as overhearers. *Journal of pragmatics*, 40: 55–71.

Bucholtz, M. (1999). You da man: Narrating the racial other in the production of white masculinity. *Journal of Sociolinguistics*, 3,4: 443–60.

Bucholtz, M. (2001). The whiteness of nerds: Superstandard English and racial markedness. *Journal of Linguistic Anthropology,* 11,1: 84–100.

Bucholtz, M. (2009). From stance to style: Gender, interaction, and indexicality in Mexican immigrant youth slang. In A. Jaffe (Ed.), *Stance: Sociolinguistic Perspectives*. Oxford: Oxford University Press. Pp.146–70.

Bucholtz, M. (2011). *White Kids: Language, Race, and Styles of Youth Identity.* Cambridge: Cambridge University Press.

Bucholtz, M. and Hall, K. (2004). Language and identity. In S. Duranti (Ed.), *A Companion to Linguistics Anthropology.* Oxford: Basil Blackwell. Pp. 369–94.

Bucholtz, M. and Hall, K. (2005). Identity and interaction: A sociocultural linguistic approach. *Discourse Studies*, 7,4–5: 585–614.

Bucholtz, M. and Hall, K. (2008). Finding identity: Theory and data. *Multilingua,* 27,1–2: 151–63.

Buckingham, D. (2008). Introducing identity. In D. Buckingham (Ed.), *Youth, Identity and Digital Media*. The John D. and Catherine McArthur Foundation Series on Digital Media and Learning. Cambridge: The MIT Press. Pp. 1–24.

Butler, J. (1990). *Gender Trouble: Feminism and the Subversion of Identity.* New York: Routledge Classic Series.

Butler, J. (1994). Gender as performance: An interview with Judith Butler. *Radical Philosophy: A Journal of Socialist and Feminist Philosophy*, 67(Summer): 32–9.

Cameron, D. and Kulick, D. (2003). *Language and Sexuality.* Cambridge: Cambridge University Press.

Cameron, D. and Kulick, D. (2005). Identity crisis? *Language & Communication* 25: 107–25.

Canagarajah, S. (2011). Translanguaging in the classroom: Emerging issues for research and pedagogy. *Applied Linguistics Review*, 2: 1–28.

Capps, L., Ochs, E., and Bruner, J. (1996). *Constructing Panic: The Discourse of Agoraphobia.* Boston, MA: Harvard University Press.

Cazden, C. (2001). *Classroom Discourse: The Language of Teaching and Learning.* Portsmouth, NH: Heinemenn.

Center for Advanced Language Proficiency and Research (CALPER) at the Pennsylvania State University. (n.d.). Discourse, genre, and the National Standards: The Korean Wave. In *CALPER.* Retrieved from: http://calper.la.psu. edu. Accessed February 12, 2013.

Center for Advanced Language Proficiency and Research (CALPER) at the Pennsylvania State University. (n.d.). Learning through listening towards advanced Japanese. In *CALPER.* Retrieved from: http://calper.la.psu.edu/japanese. php. Accessed February 12, 2013.

Cetirizine. (n.d.). In *Wikipedia.* Retrieved from: http://en.wikipedia.org/wiki/Cetirizine. Accessed September 24, 2013.

Chafe, W. (1970). New and old information. In H. Harris (Ed.), *Papers from the 4th Annual Kansas Linguistics Conference*, 36–65. Lawrence, Kansas.

Chafe, W. (1972). Discourse structure and human knowledge. In R. Freedle and J. Carroll (Eds.), *Language Comprehension and the Acquisition of Knowledge.* Washington: V. H.Winston. Pp. 41–69.

Chafe, W. (1974). Language and consciousness. *Language,* 50: 111–33.

Chafe, W. (1976). Givenness, contrastiveness, definiteness, subjects, topics, and point of view. In C. Li (Ed.), *Subject and Topic.* New York: Academic Press. Pp. 25–55.

Chafe, W. (1987). Cognitive constraints on information flow. In R. Tomlin (Ed.), *Coherence and Grounding in Discourse.* Amsterdam: John Benjamins. Pp. 21–51.

Chafe, W. (1992). Information Flow in Speaking and Writing. In P. Downing, S. Lima, and M. Noonan (Eds.), *The Linguistics of Literacy*. Amsterdam: John Benjamins.

Chafe, W. (1994). *Discourse, Consciousness, and Time: The Flow and Displacement of Conscious Experience in Speaking and Writing*. Chicago: The University of Chicago Press.

Chafe, W. (1998). Language and the flow of thought. In M. Tomasello (Ed.), *The New Psychology of Language: Cognitive and Functional Approaches to Language Structure*. Mahwah, NJ: Lawrence Erlbaum. Pp. 93–111.

Chafe, W. and Nichols, J. (1986). *Evidentiality: The Linguistic Coding of Epistomology*. Westport, CT: Praeger.

Chapman, G., Cleese, J., Gillam, T., Idle, E., Jones, T., and Palin, M. (Writers) and MacNaughton, I. (Director). (1969, November 23). It's the arts (or: The BBC entry to the zinc stoat of Budapest) [Television series episode.] In I. MacNaughton and I. C. Saltzberg (Producers), *Monty Python's Flying Circus*. United Kingdom: BBC1.

Charteris-Black, J. (2004). *Corpus Approaches to Critical Metaphor Analysis*. Palgrave-MacMillan.

Chavez, C. (1984). Address by César Chavez to The Commonwealth Club of San Francisco. November 9, 1984.

The Chief, Icarreau, Deleted User, Clark_Griswold, and Alpinisto. (2010, June 6). What does "we" mean to you? *SummitPost*. Retrieved from: http://www.summitpost.org/phpBB3/what-does-we-mean-to-you-t53591.html. Accessed May 23, 2013.

Chilton, P. (2005). Missing links in the mainstream CDA. In R. Wodak and P. Chilton (Eds.), *A New Agenda in (Critical) Discourse Analysis*. Amsterdam: John Benjamins. Pp. 19–51.

Chilton, P. (2011). Still something missing in the CDA. *Discourse Studies*, 3,6: 769–783.

Chomsky, N. (1957). *Syntactic Structures*. The Hague: Mouton & Co.

Chomsky, N. (2011). *Power and Terror: Conflict, Hegemony, and the Rule of Force*. Boulder, CO: Paradigm Publishers.

Chomsky, N. (2012, November 8). The purpose of education: Learning without frontiers interview. Retrieved from: http://www.youtube.com/watch?v=DdNAUJWJN08. Accessed April 10, 2013.

Christodoulidou, M. (2010). Complaints about misbehavior. *Journal of Greek Linguistics,* 10,2: 295–316.

Circolo della briscola. (n.d.). Retrieved from: http://www.briscolausa.com/circolo dellabriscola/default.htm. Accessed May 24, 2013.

Clancy, P., Thompson, S., Suzuki, R., and Tao, H. (1996). The conversational use of reactive tokens in English, Japanese, and Mandarin. *Journal of Pragmatics*, 26,3: 355–87.

Clark, H. H. and Carlson, T. (1982). Hearers and speech acts. *Language,* 58: 332–72.

Clark, H. H. and Haviland, S. (1977). Comprehension and the given-new contract. In R. O. Freedle (Ed.), *Discourse Production and Comprehension*. Hillsdale, NJ: Erlbaum. Pp. 1–40.

Clark, H. H. and Brennan, S. (1991). Grounding in Communication. In L. B. Resnick, J. M. Levine, and S. D. Teasley (Eds.), *Perspectives on Socially Shared Cognition.* Washington, DC: American Psychological Association. Pp. 127–49.

Clark, H. H. and Schaefer, F. (1992). Dealing with overhearers. In H. H. Clark (Ed.), *Arenas of Language Use*. Chicago: University of Chicago Press. Pp. 248–73.

Clayman, S. (2010). Address terms in the service of other actions: The case of news interview discourse. *Discourse and Communication* 4,2: 161–83.

Clayman, S. (2013a). Conversation analysis in the news interview context. In T. Stivers and J. Sidnell (Eds.), *Handbook of Conversation Analysis*. Oxford: Wiley-Blackwell. Pp. 630–56.

Clayman, S. (2013b). Turn constructional units and transition relevance place in conversation. In T. Stivers and J. Sidnell (Eds.), *Handbook of Conversation Analysis*. Oxford: Wiley-Blackwell. Pp. 150–66.

Clayman, S. and Heritage, J. (2002). *The News Interview: Journalists and Public Figures on the Air: Studies in Interactional Sociolinguistics.* Cambridge: Cambridge University Press.

Clift, R. (2006). Indexing stance: Reported speech as an interactional evidential. *Journal of Sociolinguistics,* 10,5: 569–95.

CNN News. (2011, July 4). *Prince William crash-lands—on purpose—on Prince Edward Island*. Retrieved from: http://www.cnn.com/2011/WORLD/ameri cas/07/04/canada.royal.visit/index.html. Accessed July 23, 2012.

Codo, E. (2011). Regimenting discourse, controlling bodies: Disinformation, evaluation and moral categorization in a state bureaucratic agency. *Discourse & Society*, 22,6: 723–42.

Cohen, L. (2010). A tripartite self-construction model of identity. In D. Schiffrin and A. Nylund (Eds.), *Telling Stories: Language, Narrative, and Social Life.* Washington, DC: Georgetown University Press. Pp. 69–82.

Cohen, P. and Perrault, C. (1979). Elements of a plan-based theory of speech acts. *Cognitive Science,* 3,3: 177–212.

Cohen, T., Reich, A., and Calhoun, W. (Writers) and Burrows, J. (Director). (1998, February 26). The one with all the rugby [Television series episode]. In K. S. Bright, M. Kauffman, and D. Crane (Producers), *Friends.* Warner Bros. Studios: Burbank, CA.

Collot, N. and Belmore, M. (1996). Electronic language: A new variety of English. In S. Herring (Ed.), *Computer Mediated Communication: A Linguistic, Social, and Cross-Cultural Perspective.* Philadelphia: John Benjamins. Pp. 13–28.

Conrad, S. and Biber, D. (2000). Adverbial marking of stance in speech and writing. In S. Hunston and G. Thompson (Eds.), *Evaluation in Text: Authorial Stance and the Construction of Discourse*. Oxford: Oxford University Press. Pp. 56–73.

Cook, G. (1989). *Discourse.* Oxford: Oxford University Press.

Cooke, M. (1996). A different story: Narrative versus 'question and answer' in Aboriginal evidence. *Forensic Linguistics*, 3,2: 273–88.

Coon, G. and Crawford, O. (Writers) and Taylor, J. (Director.) (1969, January 10). Let that be your last battlefield [Television series episode]. In G. Roddenberry (Producer), *Star Trek.* United States: CBS Television Distribution. Retrieved from: http://www.youtube.com/watch?v=Zi6iyPto254. Accessed on February 12, 2013.

Cordella, M. (2004). *The Dynamic Consultation: A Discourse Analytical Study of Doctor-Patient Communication*. Amsterdam: John Benjamins.

Coulthard, M. (1985). *An Introduction to Discourse Analysis*. London: Longman.

Couper-Kuhlen, E. (2008). Intonation and Discourse: current views from within. In D. Schiffrin, D. Tannen, and H. Hamilton, H. *The Handbook of Discourse Analysis.* Malden, MA: Blackwell. Pp. 34–54.

Couper-Kuhlen, E. and Thompson, S. (2008). On assessing situations and events in conversation: 'Extraposition' and its relatives. *Discourse Studies,* 10,4: 443–67.

Coupland, N. (1983). Patterns of encounter management: Further arguments for discourse variables. *Language in Society,* 12,4: 459–76.

Coupland, J. and Coupland, N. (2009). Attributing stance in discourses of body shape and weight loss. In A. Jaffe (Ed.), *Stance: Sociolinguistic Perspectives*. Oxford: Oxford University Press. Pp. 227–50.

Craig, J. (n.d.). Riddles. In *Jack Craig's Home Page.* Retrieved from: http://www. angelfire.com/fl/JackCraig/HUMOR-RIDDLES.html. Accessed May 23, 2013.

Crystal, D. (2009). *Txtng: The gr8 db8.* Oxford: Oxford University Press.

Crystal, D. (2011). *Internet Linguistics.* London: Routledge.

Curco, C. (1998). Indirect echoes and verbal humor. In V. Rouchota and A. Jucker (Eds.) *Current Issues in Relevance Theory.* Amsterdam: John Benjamins. Pp. 305–25.

Cymbalta. (n.d.). Simple pleasures. [TV commercial]. Retrieved from: https://adpharm. net/displayimage.php?album=255&pid=34013. Accessed May, 20, 2013.

Deckert, S. and Vickers, C. (2011). *An Introduction to Sociolinguistics: Society and Identity.* London: Continuum.

De Fina, A. (2007). Code switching and the construction of ethnic identity in a community of practice. *Language in Society,* 36: 371–92.

De Rosnay (2007). *Sarah's Key.* New York: St. Martin's Press.

Denvir, P. and Pomerantz, A. (2009). A qualitative analysis of a significant barrier to organ donation: Receiving less-than-optimal medical care. *Health Communication,* 24: 597–607.

Derrida, J. (1977). *Limited Inc.* Chicago: Northwestern University Press.

Devitt, A. (2004). *Writing Genres.* Carbondale: Southern Illinois University Press.

Dickens, C. (1994). *Martin Chuzzlewit.* London: Wordsworth.

Di Stasio, J. (n.d.). *Épinards à la vapeur.* In *à la di Stasio.* Retrieved from: http:// aladistasio.telequebec.tv/recettes/recette.aspx?id=134. Accessed May 23, 2013.

Drew, P. (1984). Speakers' reportings in invitation sequences. In M. Atkinson and J. Heritage (Eds.), *Structures of Social Action: Studies in Conversation Analysis.* Cambridge: Cambridge University Press. Pp. 129–51.

Drew, P. (1998). Complaints about transgression and misconduct. *Research on Language and Social Interaction,* 31: 295–325

Drew, P. (2013). Turn design. In J. Sidnell, and T. Stivers (Eds.), *The Handbook of Conversation Analysis.* Malden, MA: Blackwell-Wiley. Pp. 131–49.

Drew, P. and Heritage, J. (1992). *Talk at Work: Studies in Interactional Sociolinguistics.* Cambridge: Cambridge University Press.

Drummond, K. and Hopper, R. (1993). Back channels revisited: Acknowledgment tokens and speakership incipiency. *Research on Language and Social Interaction,* 26,2: 157–77.

Du Bois, J. (2007). The stance triangle. In E. Englebretson (Ed.), *Stancetaking in Discourse: Subjectivity, Evaluation, Interaction.* Amsterdam: John Benjamins. Pp. 139–82.

Du Bois, J. (2011a). Co-opting intersubjectivity: Dialogic rhetoric of the self. In C. Meyer and F. Girke (Eds.), *The rhetorical emergence of culture*. Oxford: Berghahn. Pp. 52–83.

Du Bois, J. (2011b). *Take a Stance in the Stance Field; Get a Life in the Life World*. Center for Language Acquisition Lecture, Penn State University, State College, PA. April 21, 2011.

Du Bois, J. and Kärkkäinen, E. (2012). Taking a stance on emotion: Affect, sequence, and intersubjectivity in dialogic interaction. *Text and Talk,* 32, 4: 433–51.

Duchan, J., Bruder, G., and Hewitt, L. (1995). *Deixis in Narrative: A Cognitive Science Perspective*. Hillsdale, NJ: Lawrance Erlbaum.

Duranti, A. (1986). The audience as co-author: An introduction. *Text,* 6: 239–47.

Duranti, A. (1997). *Linguistic Anthropology*. Cambridge: Cambridge University Press.

Duranti, A. (2004). Agency in language. In A. Duranti (Ed.), *A Companion to Linguistic Anthropology*. Malden, MA: Blackwell. Pp. 451–73.

Duranti, A. (2011). Linguistic anthropology: Language as a non-neutral medium. In R. Mesthrie (Ed.), *The Cambridge Handbook of Sociolinguistics.* Cambridge: Cambridge University Press.

Dynel, M. (2011). "You talking to me?" The viewer as a ratified listener to film discourse. *Journal of Pragmatics*, 46,6: 1628–44.

Eckert, P. (1989). *Jocks and Burnouts: Social Categories and Identity in the High School*. New York: Teacher's College Press.

Eckert, P. (2000). *Linguistic Variation as Social Practice*: The Linguistic Construction of Identity in Belten High. Oxford: Blackwell.

Eckert, P. (2008). Variation and the indexical field. *Journal of Sociolinguistics,* 12: 453–76.

Eckert, P. and McConnel-Ginet, S. (2003). *Language and Gender*. New York: Cambridge University Press.

Edmunds. (n.d.). 2011 *Mitsubishi Endeavor review*. Retrieved from: http://www.edmunds.com/mitsubishi/endeavor/2011/?sub=suv&ps=used#fullreview. Accessed May 21, 2013.

El Confidencial (2013, June 1). Mitalipov: "No debemos clonar humanos porque sabemos que no es seguro." *Teknautas*. Retrieved from: http://www.elconfidencial.com/tecnologia/2013/05/20/mitalipov-no-debemos-clonar-humanos-porque-sabemos-que-no-es-seguro-4926/. Accessed May 31, 2013.

Eggins, S. and Martin, J. R. (1997). Genres and registers of discourse. In T. van Dijk (Ed.), *Discourse as Structure and Process*, V. I. London: Sage Publications. Pp. 230–256.

El-Sharif, A. (2012). Metaphors we believe by: Islamic doctrine as evoked by the Prophet Muhammad's metaphors. *Critical Discourse Studies*, 9,3: 231–45.

Enfield, N. (2003a). The definition of WHAT-d'you call it: Semantics and pragmatics of "recognitional deixis." *Journal of Pragmatics*, 35: 101–17.

Enfield, N. (2003b). Demonstratives in space and interaction: Data from Lao speakers and implications for semantic analysis. *Language*, 79,1: 82–117

Enfield, N. and Stivers, T. (2007). *Person Reference in Interaction: Linguistic, Cultural and Social Perspectives.* Cambridge: Cambridge University Press.

Enfield, N. J., Stivers, T., and Levinson, S. C. (2010). Question-response sequences in conversation across ten languages: An introduction. *Journal of Pragmatics*, 42,10: 2615–19.

Engel, J. and Wodak, R. (2012). "Calculated ambivalence" and Holocaust denial in Austria. In R. Wodak and J. E. Richardson (Eds.), *Analysing Fascist Discourse: European Fascism in Talk and Text.* London: Routledge. Pp. 73–96.

Englebretson, R. (2007). Stancetaking in discourse: An introduction. In R. Englebretson (Ed.), *Stancetaking in Discourse.* Amsterdam: John Benjamins.

Epicurious. (2012, April 27). *Japanese ohitashi spinach salad*. Retrieved from: http://www.epicurious.com/recipes/member/views/JAPANESE-OHITASHI-SPINACH-SALAD-50181150#ixzz2UOxIdnG6. Accessed May 25, 2013.

Eun, J. and Strauss, S. (2004). The primacy of information status in the alternation between the deferential and polite forms in Korean. *Language Sciences* 26. Pp. 251–72.

Evans, G. (1982). *The Varieties of Reference*. Oxford: Oxford University Press.

Fackler, M. (2011, March 11). Powerful quake and tsunami devastate northern Japan. *The New York Times*. Retrieved from: http://www.nytimes.com/2011/03/12/world/asia/12japan.html. Accessed May 23, 2013.

Fairclough, N. (1992a). *Discourse and Social Change*. Cambridge: Polity.

Fairclough, N. (1992b). Discourse and text: Linguistics and intertextual analysis within discourse analysis. *Discourse and Society*, 3,2: 1893–217.

Fairclough, N. (1993). Critical discourse analysis and the marketization of public discourse: The universities. *Discourse and Society*, 4,2: 133–68.

Fairclough, N. (1995a). *Media Discourse.* London: Edward Arnold.

Fairclough, N. (1995b). *Critical Discourse Analysis*. London: Longman.

Fairclough, N. (2001). *Language and Power*. London: Longman.

Fairclough, N. (2003). *Analyzing Discourse: Textual Analysis for Social Research.* London: Routledge.

Fasulo A., Loyd, H., and Padiglione, V. (2007). Children's socialization into cleaning practices: A cross-cultural perspective. *Discourse and Society*, 18: 11–33.

FedEx. (n.d.). Retrieved from: http://www.fedex.com/us/. Accessed December 30, 2012.

Feiz, P. and Strauss, S. (2005). Narratives of personal experience. Unpublished narratives and conversation in English and Persian.

Félix-Brasdefer, J. (2005). Indirectness and politeness in Mexican requests. In D. Eddington (Ed.), *Selected Proceedings of the 7th Hispanic Linguistic Symposium.* Somerville, MA: Cascadilla Press. Pp. 66–78.

Ferguson, C. (1982). Simplified registers and linguistic theory. In L. K. Obler and L. Menn (Eds.), *Exceptional Language and Linguistics*. New York: Academic Press. Pp. 49–68.

Ferguson, C. (1994). Dialect, register, and genre: Working assumptions about conventionalization. In D. Biber and A. Finegan (Eds.), *Sociolinguistic Perspectives on Register.* New York: Oxford University Press. Pp. 15–30.

Fillmore, C. (1982). Towards a descriptive framework for spatial deixis. In R. Jarvella and W. Klein (Eds.), *Speech, Place, and Action Studies in Deixis and Related Topics*. New York: John Wiley and Sons. Pp. 31–59.

Fillmore, C. (1971/1997). *Lectures on Deixis*. CSLI Publications. Stanford, CA.

Finch, G. (2005). *Key Concepts in Language and Linguistics*. Basingstoke, UK: Palgrave Macmillan.

Fishman, G. and Garcia, O. (Eds.), (2010). *Handbook of Language and Ethnic Identity*. Oxford; Oxford University Press.

Flowerdew, J. (1991). Pragmatic modifications on the 'representative' speech act of defining. *Journal of Pragmatics*, 15,3: 253–64.

Ford, C. (2004). Contingency and units in interaction. *Discourse Studies*, 6,1: 27–52.

Ford, C., Fox, B., and Thompson, S. (1996). Practices in the construction of turns: The 'TCU' revisited. *Pragmatics* 6,3: 427–54.

Ford, C., Fox, B., and Thompson, S. (2002). *The Language of Turns and Sequences*. New York: Oxford University Press.

Ford, C., Fox, B., and Thompson, S. (2003). Social interaction and grammar. In M. Tomasello (Ed.), *The New Psychology of Language,* Volume 2. Englewood, NJ: Lawrence Erlbaum. Pp. 1489–522.

Ford, C. and Thompson, S. (1996). Interactional units in conversation: syntactic, intonational, and pragmatic resources for turn management. In E. Ochs, M. Schegloff, and S. Thompson (Eds.), *Interaction and Grammar*, Cambridge: Cambridge University Press. Pp. 134–84.

Foucault, M. (1972). *The Archeology of Knowledge*. New York: Pantheon.

Foucault. M. (1982). The subject and power. *Critical Inquiry*, 8,4: 777–95.

Fox on Stocks. (2012, November 8). *Hurricane Sandy or post-tropical storm Sandy?* Retrieved from: http://foxonstocks.com/how-does-hurricane-sandy-or-post-tropical-storm-pts-sandy-affect-the-stock-market/. Accessed June 2, 2013.

Fox, B. (2001). An exploration of prosody and turn projection in English conversation. In E. Couper–Kuhlen and M. Selting (Eds.), *Studies in International Linguistics.* Amsterdam: John Benjamins. Pp. 287–316.

Fox, B. and Thompson, S. (2007). Relative clauses in English conversation: Relativizers, frequency, and the notion of 'construction.' *Studies in Language,* 31,2: 293–326.

Fragale, A. R., Sumanth, J. H., Tiedens, L. Z., and Northcraft, G. B. (2012). Appeasing equals: Lateral deference in organizational communication. *Administrative Science Quarterly,* 57,3: 373–406.

Fraser, B. and Nolen, W. (1981). The association of deference with linguistic form. *International Journal of the Sociology of Language*, 27: 93–111.

Gallagher, E. J. (n.d.). The Enola Gay controversy. *Lehigh University Digital Library.* Retrieved from: http://digital.lib.lehigh.edu/trial/enola/about/. Accessed May 20, 2013.

Gammill, T. and Pross, M. (Writers) and Cherones, T. (Director). (1993, December 9). The cigar store Indian [Television series episode]. In B. Scott, H. West, G. Shapiro, and A. Scheinman (Producers), *Seinfeld*. New York: NBC.

Garcia-Carpintero, M. (2004). Assertion and the semantics of force-markers. In C. Bianchi (Ed.), *The Semantics/Pragmatics Distinction*. Stanford, CA: CSLI Publications. Pp. 133–66.

Gardner, R. (2002). *When Listeners Talk: Response Tokens and Listener Stance.* Amsterdam: Benjamins.

Gazdar, G. (1981). Speech act assignment. In A. Joshi, I. Sag, and B. Webber (Eds.), *Elements of Discourse Understanding*. New York: Cambridge University Press.

Gazdar, G. (1979). *Pragmatics: Implicature, Presupposition, and Logical Form*, New York: Academic Press.

359

Gee, J. (2005). *An Introduction to Discourse Analysis*. New York: Routledge.

Gee, J. (2010). *How To Do Discourse Analysis: A Toolkit.* New York: Routledge.

Georgakopoulou, A. (2011). Computer-mediated communication. In J. Ostman and J. Verchueren (Eds*.), Pragmatics in Practice (Handbook of Pragmatics Highlights)*. Amsterdam, The Netherlands: John Benjamins. Pp. 93–108.

Gerofsky, S. (2004). *A Man Left Albuquerque Heading East: Word Problems as Genre in Mathematics Education.* New York: Peter Lang Publishing Co.

Giddens, A. (1991). *Modernity and Self-Identity: Self and Society in the Late Modern Age.* Stanford University Press.

Gill, V. T., Pomerantz, A., and Denvir, P. (2010). Preemptive resistance: Patients' participation in diagnostic sense-making activities. *Sociology of Health and Illness*, 32,1: 1–20.

Gissiner, B. (2012, December 3). Any time Cleveland wins it is a favorite NFL moment. In *Yahoo Voices*. Retrieved from: http://voices.yahoo.com/any time-cleveland-wins-favorite-nfl-moment-11919530.html?cat=14. Accessed December 29, 2012.

Glenwright, P. (2012). The discourse of amateur cricket: A linguistic examination of pre-match bulletins. *Hong Kong Journal of Applied Linguistics*, 13,2: 50–69.

Goffman, I. (1967). *Interaction Ritual: Essays on Face-to-Face Behavior.* New York: Anchor Books.

Goffman, E. (1974). *Frame Analysis: An Essay on the Organization of Experience.* New York: Harper and Row.

Goffman, E. (1979/1981). *Forms of Talk.* Philadelphia: University of Pennsylvania Press.

Goffman, E. (1959/1990). *The Presentation of Self in Everyday Life.* New York: Penguin.

Good Housekeeping Illustrated Cookbook (1989). New York: Hearst Books.

Goodwin, C. (1981). *Conversational Organization: Interaction Between Hearers and Speakers*. New York: Academic Press.

Goodwin, C. (1986). Between and within: Alternative sequential treatments of continuers and assessments. *Human Studies*, 9,2–3: 205–217.

Goodwin, C. (1995a). Co-constructing meaning in conversations with an aphasic man. *Research on Language in Social Interaction*, 28,3: 233–260.

Goodwin, C. (1995b). The negotiation of coherence within conversation. In M. Gernsbacher and T. Givon (Eds.). *Coherence in Spontaneous Text.* Philadelphia and Amsterdam: John Benjamins. Pp. 117–38.

Goodwin, C. (1996). Transparent vision. In E. Ochs, M. Schegloff, and S. Thompson (Eds.), *Interaction and Grammar.* Cambridge: Cambridge University Press. Pp. 370–404.

Goodwin, C. (Ed.). (2003). *Conversation and Brain Damage*. Oxford: Oxford University Press.

Goodwin, C. (2007). Participation, stance, and affect in the organization of activities. *Discourse and Society*, 13,1: 53–73.

Goodwin, C. and Goodwin, M. (1987). Concurrent operations on talk: Notes on the interactive organization of assessments. *Ipra Papers in Pragmatics*, 1,1: 1–55.

Goodwin, C. and Goodwin, M. (1992). Assessments and the construction of context. In A. Duranti and C. Goodwin (Eds.), *Rethinking Context: Language as an Interactive Phenomenon*. Cambridge: Cambridge University Press. Pp. 147–89.

Goodwin, C. and Heritage, J. (1990). Conversation analysis. *Annual Review of Anthropology*, 19: 238–307.

Goodwin, M. (1990). *He Said, She Said: Talk as Social Organization Among Black Children.* Bloomington: Indiana University Press.

Goodwin, M. and Goodwin, C. (2000). Emotion within situated activity. In N. Budwig, I. C. Uzgiris, and J. V. Wertsch (Eds.), *Communication: An Arena of Development*, Stamford CT: Ablex. Pp. 33–54.

Gore, A. (2012, September 2). First World War ammunition frozen in time for nearly a century has been found as glacier melts. *The Daily Mail.* Retrieved from: http://www.dailymail.co.uk/news/article-2197174/First-World-War-ammunition-frozen-time-nearly-century-glacier-melts.html#ixzz2GdOt5Y2B. Accessed December 31, 2012.

Graddol, D. (1996). The semiotic construction of a wine label. In S. Goodman and D. Graddol (Eds.), *Redesigning English: New Texts, New Identities.* London: Routledge and Open University. Pp. 73–81.

Grainger, K. (2011). Indirectness in Zimbabwean English: A study of intercultural communication in the UK. In F. Bargiela-Chiappini and D. Kádár (Eds.), *Politeness Across Cultures*. New York: Palgrave Macmillian. Pp. 171–93.

Gramsci, A. (1971). *Selections From the Prison Notebooks*. London: Lawrence and Wishart.

Greatbatch, D. (1986). Aspects of topical organisation in news interviews: The use of agenda shifting procedures by interviewees. *Media, Culture and Society,* 8: 441–55.

Greatbatch, D. (1988). A turn-taking system for British news interviews. *Language in Society,* 17,3: 401–30.

Grice, P. (1975). Logic and conversation. In P. Cole and J. Morgan (Eds.), *Syntax and Semantics* (Volume 3). New York: Academic Press. Pp. 41–58.

Grice, P. (1989). *Study in the Way of Words*. Cambridge: Harvard University Press.

Gringberg, E. (2012, December 29). Families 'in limbo' after Russian adoption ban. In *CNN*. Retrieved from: http://www.cnn.com/2012/12/28/living/russian-adoptions-limbo/index.html. Accessed December 20, 2012.

The Guardian. (2012, December 30). Winter blast causes outages, traffic restrictions on P.E.I. Retrieved from: http://www.theguardian.pe.ca/News/Local/2012-12-30/article-3148620/Winter-blast-causes-outages,-traffic-restrictions-on-P.E.I./1. Accessed December 31, 2012.

The Guardian. (2013, February 13). Mexican 'ape woman' buried 150 years after her death. Retrieved from: http://www.guardian.co.uk/world/2013/feb/13/mexican-ape-woman-buried. Accessed February 14, 2013.

Gumperz, J. J. (1982). *Discourse Strategies*. Cambridge: Cambridge University Press.

Gumperz, J. J. and Cook-Gumperz (1982). Introduction: Language and the construction of social identity. In J. Gumperz (Ed.), *Language and Social Identity*. Cambridge: Cambridge University Press. Pp. 2–22.

Gundel, J. (1985). Shared knowledge and topicality. *Journal of Pragmatics*, 9: 83–107.

Gundel, J. (1988). Universals of topic-comment structure. In M. Hammond, E. Moravczik, and J. Wirth (Eds.) *Studies in syntactic typology.* Amsterdam: John Benjamins. Pp. 209–39.

Habermas, J. (1981/1984). *Reason and the Rationalization of Society*, Volume 1 of *The Theory of Communicative Action*. Translated by T. McCarthy. Boston: Beacon Press (originally published in German in 1981).

Hackman, D. (1977). Patterns in purported speech acts. *Journal of Pragmatics*, 1,2: 143–54.

Hall, K. (2005). Intertextual sexuality: Parodies of class, identity, and desire in liminal Delhi. *Journal of Linguistic Anthropology*, 15,1: 125–44.

Hall, K. (2009). Boys' talk: Hindi, moustaches and masculinity in New Delhi. In P. Pichler and E. Eppler (Eds.), *Gender and Spoken Interaction*. Houndmills, Basingstoke: Palgrave Macmillan. Pp. 139–162.

Halliday, M. (1967). Notes on transitivity and theme in English, part 2. *Journal of Linguistics*, 3, 199–244.

Halliday, M. (1970). *A Course in Spoken English: Intonation*. Oxford: Oxford University Press.

Halliday, M. (1978). *Language as Social Semiotic*. London: Arnold.

Halliday, M. (1994). *An Introduction to Functional Grammar,* 2nd ed. London: Edward Arnold.

Halliday, M. (1977/2002). Linguistic studies of text and discourse. In J. Webster (Ed.), *Collected Works of M.A.K. Halliday.* Continuum International Publishing Group.

Halliday, M. and Hasan, R. (1976). *Cohesion in English.* London: Longman.

Halliday, M. and Matthiessen, C. (2004). *An Introduction to Functional Grammar*. Oxford: Oxford University Press.

Halone, K. K. and Meân, L. (2010). Situating sport, language, and culture as a site for intellectual discussion. *Journal of Language and Social Psychology,* 29, 3: 386–96.

Hammersley, M. (1997). On the foundations of critical discourse analysis. *Language and Communication,* 17, 3: 237–48.

Hanks, W. (1990). *Referential Practice, Language and Lived Space Among the Maya.* Chicago: The University of Chicago Press.

Hanks, W. (1992). The indexical ground of deictic reference. In A. Duarnti and C. Goodwin (Eds.), *Rethinking Context: Language as an Interactive Phenomenon.* Cambridge: Cambridge University Press. Pp. 43–76.

Hanks, W. (2005). Explorations in the deictic field. *Current Anthropology*, 46: 191–220.

Hanks, W. (2009). Fieldwork on deixis. *Journal of Pragmatics*, 41,1: 10–24.

Harris, R. (1983). Translator's introduction. In C. Bally and A. Sechehaye (Eds.), R. Harris (Trans.), *Course in General Linguistics. Ferdinand de Saussure*. Chicago and La Salle, IL: Open Court. Pp. ix–xvi.

Harris, R. (1993). *The Linguistics Wars*. Oxford: Oxford University Press.

Harris, S. (1995). Pragmatics and power. *Journal of Pragmatics,* 23, 2: 117–35.

Harris, S. (2001). Fragmented narratives and multiple tellers: Witness and defendants accounts in trials. *Discourse Studies,* 3,1: 53–74.

Hasegawa, Y. (2008). Simultaneous application of negative and positive politeness. *Papers from the Regional Meetings, Chicago Linguistic Society*, 44,1: 125–40.

Hashim, A. and Hassan, N. (2011). Language of the legal process: An analysis of interactions in the *Syariah* court. *Multilingua,* 30, 3–4: 333–56.

Haviland, S. and Clark, H. (1974). What's new? Acquiring new information as a process in comprehension. *Journal of Verbal Learning and Verbal Behavior*, 13: 512–21.

Hayano, K. (2011). Claiming epistemic primacy: yo–marked assessments in Japanese. In T. Stivers, L. Mondada, and J. Steensig (Eds.), *The Morality of Knowledge in Conversation*. Cambridge, England: Cambridge University Press. Pp. 58–81.

Hayashi, M. (2003). *Joint Utterance Construction in Japanese*. Amsterdam: John Benjamins.

Heath, C. and Luff, P. (2013). Embodied action and organizational activity. In J. Sidnell and T. Stivers (Eds.), *The Handbook of Conversation Analysis*. Malden, MA: Blackwell-Wiley. Pp. 283–307.

Heller, M. (Ed.). (1988). *Codeswitching: Anthropological and Sociolinguistic Perspectives*. Berlin: Walter de Gruyter.

Heritage, J. (1984). A change-of-state token and aspects of its sequential placement. In J. M. Atkinson and J. Heritage (Ed.). *Structures of Social Action*. Cambridge, UK: Cambridge University Press. Pp. 299–345.

Heritage, J. (1985). Analyzing news interviews: Aspects of the production of talk for an overhearing audience. In T. van Dijk (Ed.), *Handbook of Discourse Analysis, Volume 3*. New York: Academic Press. Pp. 95–117.

Heritage, J. (1998). Oh-prefaced responses to inquiry. *Language in Society,* 27,3: 291–334.

Heritage, J. (2002). Oh-prefaced responses to assessments: A method of modifying agreement/disagreement. In C. Ford, B. Fox, and S. Thompson (Eds.), *The Language of Turn and Sequence*. Oxford, Oxford University Press. Pp. 196–224.

Heritage, J. (2009). Conversation analysis as an approach to medical encounter. In J. B. McKinlay and L. Marceau (Eds.), *Behavioral and Social Science Research Interactive Textbook*. Office of Behavioral and Social Science Research. http://www.esourceresearch.org

Heritage, J. (2012). Epistemics in action. *Research on Language and Social Interaction*, 45,1: 1–29.

Heritage, J. and Clayman, S. (2002). *The News Interview: Journalists and Public Figures on the Air*. Cambridge: Cambridge University Press.

Heritage, J. and Lindstrom, A. (2012). Advice-giving: Terminable and interminable. In H. Limberg and M. Locher (Eds.), *Discourse of Advice*. Amsterdam: Benjamins: 169–94.

Heritage, J. and Maynard, D. (2006). *Communication in Medical Care: Interaction Between Primary Care Physicians and Patients: Studies in Interactional Sociolinguistics.* Cambridge: Cambridge University Press.

Heritage, J. and Robinson, J. D. (2011). Applying conversation analysis to the primary-care visit: Reflections on a study of unmet patient concerns. In C. Antaki (Ed.), *Applied Conversation Analysis: Intervention and Change in Institutional Talk*. Basingstoke, New York: Palgrave Macmillan.

Herring, S. (1996). *Computer Mediated Communication: A Linguistic, Social, and Cross-Cultural Perspective*. London: Philadelphia: John Benjamins.

Herring, S. (2012). Grammar and electronic communication. In C. Chapelle (Ed.), *Encyclopedia of Applied Linguistics.* Hoboken, NJ: Wiley-Blackwell.

Herring, S. C. (2013). Relevance in computer-mediated conversation. In S. C. Herring, D. Stein, and T. Virtanen (Eds.), *Handbook of pragmatics of computer-mediated communication*. Berlin: Mouton. Pp. 245–68.

Herring, S. C., Stein, D., and Virtanen, T. (2013). Introduction to the pragmatics of computer-mediated communication. *Handbook of Pragmatics of Computer-Mediated Communication*. Berlin: Mouton.

Hodge, R. I. V. and Kress, G. R. (1988). *Social Semiotics*. Cornell University Press.

Hodge, R. I. V. and Kress, G. R. (1993). *Language and Ideology*. London: Routledge.

Holmes, J. (1984). Modifying illocutionary force. *Journal of Pragmatics*, 8,3: 345–65.

Horn, L. (1984). Towards a new taxonomy for pragmatic inference: Q-based and R-based implicature, in D. Schiffrin (Ed.), *Georgetown University Round Table on Languages and Linguistics.* Washington, DC: Georgetown University Press. Pp. 11–42.

Horn, L. (2004). Implicature. In Horn, L. and Ward, G. (Eds.), *The Handbook of Pragmatics.* Oxford: Oxford University Press. Pp. 3–28.

Hornberger, N. and Link, H. (2012). Translanguaging and transnational literacies in multilingual classes: A biliteracy lens. *International Journal of Bilingual Education and Bilingualism*, 5,3: 261–278.

Huang, Y. (2006). Neo-Gricean pragmatics. In K. Brown (Ed.), *The Encyclopedia of Language and Linguistics* (2nd ed.). New York: Elsevier. Pp. 231–8.

Hundt, M., Denson, D., and Schneider, G. (2012). Relative complexity in scientific discourse. *English Language and Linguistics*, 12,2: 209–40.

Hunston, S. and Thompson, G. (Eds.). (2000). *Evaluation in Text: Authorial Stance and the Construction of Discourse.* Oxford: Oxford University Press.

Hutchby, I. (2001). *Conversation and Technology: From Telephone to the Internet.* Cambridge: Polity.

Hutchby, I. and Tanna, V. (2008). Aspects of sequential organization in text message exchange. *Discourse and Communication,* 2,2: 143–64.

Hyland, K. (2002). Authority and invisibility: Authorial identity in academic writing. *Journal of Pragmatics*, 34: 1091–112.

Hymes, D. (1974). Ways of speaking. In R. Bauman and J. Sherzer (Eds.), *Explorations in the Ethnography of Speaking.* Cambridge: Cambridge University Press.

Hyon, S. (1996). Genre in three traditions: Implications for ESL. *TESOL Quarterly*, 30,4: 693–722.

Ide, S. (1989). Formal forms and discernment: Two neglected aspects of universals of linguistic politeness. *Multilingua*, 8,2/3: 223–48.

Irvine, J. (1979). Formality and informality in communicative events. *American Anthropologist*, 40, 8: 773–90.

Irvine, J. (1990). Registering affect: Heteroglossia in the linguistic expression of emotion. In C. A. Lutz and L. Abu-Lughod (Eds.), *Language and the Politics of Emotion.* Cambridge University Press. Pp. 126–85.

Irvine, J. (2009). Stance in a colonial encounter: How Mr. Taylor lost his footing. In A. Jaffe (Ed.), *Stance: Sociolinguistic Perspectives*. Oxford: Oxford University Press. Pp. 53–71.

Iwasaki, S. and Horie, P. I. (1998). The "Northridge Earthquake" conversations: conversational patterns in Japanese and Thai and their cultural significance. *Discourse and Society*, 9,4: 501–29.

Jaffe, A. (2009). Introduction: The sociolinguistics of stance. In A. Jaffe (Ed.), *Stance: Sociolinguistic Perspectives*. Oxford: Oxford University Press. Pp. 3–28.

Jakobson, R. (1957). Shifters, verbal categories, and the Russian verbs. *Russian Language Project,* Department of Slavic Languages, Harvard University.

Jakobson, R. (Author), Waugh, L., and Monville-Burston, M. (Eds.). (1995). *On Language*. Boston: Harvard University Press.

Jaworski, A. and Coupland, N. (2006). *The Discourse Reader.* New York: Routledge.

Jaworski, A. and Thurlow, K. (2009). Taking an elitist stance: Ideology and the discursive production of social distinction. In A. Jaffe (Ed.), *Stance: Sociolinguistic Perspectives*. Oxford: Oxford University Press. Pp. 195–226.

Jefferson, G. (1984). Notes on a systematic deployment of the acknowledgment tokens "Yeah" and "Mm hm." *Papers in Linguistics*, 17,1: 197–206.

Jefferson, G. (2004). Glossary of transcript symbols with an introduction. In G. Lerner (Ed.)., *Conversation Analysis: Studies from the First Generation*. Amsterdam: John Benjamins. Pp. 13–30.

Jimmy Dean Skillets. (2005, September). Why? [TV Commercial]. Retrieved from: http://www.advertolog.com/jimmy-dean/adverts/why-7633405/. Accessed May 23, 2013.

Johnstone, B. (2008). *Discourse Analysis*. (2nd ed.). Oxford: Blackwell.

Johnstone, B. (2009). Stance, style, and the linguistic individual. In A. Jaffe (Ed.), *Stance: Sociolinguistic Perspectives*. Oxford: Oxford University Press. Pp. 29–52.

Jones, J. (Writers) and Hawes, J. (Director). (2008). The dragon's call [Television series episode]. In S. de Beauvoir (Producer), *Merlin*. Wales: BBC.

Jucker, A. (2011). Positive and negative face as descriptive categories in the history of English. *Journal of Historical Pragmatics*, 12,1–2: 178–97.

Judge Judy. (n.d.). In *Wikipedia*. Retrieved from: http://en.wikipedia.org/wiki/Judge_Judy. Accessed May 31, 2013.

Kamio, A. (1997). *Territory of Information*. Amsterdam: John Benjamins Publications.

Katayama, H. (2009). *A Cross-Cultural Analysis of Humor in Stand-up Comedy in The United States and Japan*. Diss. The Pennsylvania State University.

Keillor, G. (2009). *A Prairie Home Companion Pretty Good Joke Book* (New 5th ed.). Minneapolis, MN: HighBridge Company.

Kelly, G., Crawford, T., and Green, J. (2001). Common Task and uncommon knowledge: Dissenting voices in the discursive construction of physics across small laboratory groups. *Linguistics and Education*, 12,2: 135–74.

Kevoe-Feldman, H. and Robinson, J. D. (2012). Exploring essentially three-turn courses of action: An institutional case study with implications for ordinary talk. *Discourse Studies*, 14,2: 217–41.

Key, M. R. (1975). *Male/Female Language: With a Comprehensive Bibliography*. Metuchen, NJ: Scarecrow Press.

Kiely, R., Rea-Dickins, P., Woodfield, H., and Clibbon, G. (2006). *Language, Culture, and Identity in Applied Linguistics. Selected papers from the Annual Meeting of the British Association for Applied Linguistics*. University of Bristol, September 2005. London: Equinox.

Kiesling, S. (2004). Dude. *American Speech*, 79,3: 281–305.

Kiesling, S. (2005). Variation, stance, and style: Word-final. *English World-Wide*, 26,1: 1–42.

Kiesling, S. (2009). Style as stance: Stance as the explanation for patterns of sociolinguistic variation. In A. Jaffe (Ed.), *Stance: Sociolinguistic Perspectives*. Oxford: Oxford University Press. Pp. 171–94.

Kikkoman. (n.d.). **ほうれん草のおひたし**. Retrieved from: http://www.kikkoman. co.jp/homecook/college/sub/ohitashi.html. Accessed May 25, 2013.

Kirkham, S. (2011). Personal style and epistemic stance in classroom discussion. *Language and Literature*, 20,1; 201–17.

Kitzinger, C. (2013). Repair. In T. Stivers and J. Sidnell (Eds.), *The Handbook of Conversation Analysis*. Malden, MA: Wiley-Blackwell. Pp. 229–56.

Kokelman, P. (2004). Stance and subjectivity. *Journal of Linguistic Anthropology*, 14,2: 127–50.

한류 (문화). (n.d.). In *Wikipedia*. Retrieved from: http://ko.wikipedia.org/ wiki/%ED%95%9C%EB%A5%98_(%EB%AC%B8%ED%99%94). Accessed September 24, 2013.

Korean website: http://www.benhur.kr/board/cl_viewbody.php?code=bbs_work& number=95&viewmode=clipcopy고정민 외

Koziski, S. (1984). The standup comedian as anthropologist. *The Journal of Popular Culture*, 18,2: 57–76.

Kozloff, S. (2000). *Overhearing Film Dialogue*. Berkeley: University of California Press.

Krauthammer, C. (2002, June 24). The fatal promise of cloning. *Time*, 159: 54.

Kress, G. (1993). Against arbitrariness: The social production of the sign as a foundational issue in critical discourse analysis. *Discourse and Society*, 4,2: 169–91.

Kress, G. and van Leeuwen, T. (1998). Front pages: (The critical) analysis of newspaper layout. In A. Bell and P. Garret (Eds.), *Approaches to Media Discourse*. Oxford: Blackwell Publishers. Pp. 186–218.

Kress, G. and van Leeuwen, T. (2001). *Multimodal Discourse.* London: Arnold.

Kress, G. and van Leeuwen, T. (2006). *Reading Images: The Grammar of Social Visual Design.* New York: Routledge.

Kress, G. (2010). *Multimodality: A social semiotic approach to contemporary communication*. London: Routledge.

Kristeva, J. (1980). *Desire in Language: A Semiotic Approach to Literature and Art*. New York: Columbia University Press.

Kristeva, J. (1986). Word, dialogue, and novel. In T. Moi (Ed.), *The Kristeva Reader*. Oxford: Blackwell. Pp. 34–61.

Kulick, D. (2003). Language and desire. In J. Holmes and M. Myerhoff (Eds.), *The Handbook of Language and Gender* Oxford: Blackwell. Pp. 119–41.

Kuno, S. (1972). Functional sentence perspective: A case study from Japanese and English. *Linguistic Inquiry,* 3,3: 269–320.

Kuno, S . (1978). Generative discourse analysis in America. In W. Dressler (Ed.), *Current Trends in Texilinguistics*. Berlin and New York: de Gruyter. Pp. 275–94.

Kyratzis, A. (2005). "Because" as a marker of collaborative stance in preschool children's peer interactions. In A. Tyler (Ed.), *Language in Use: Cognitive and Discourse Perspectives on Language and Language Learning*. Washington D.C.: Georgetown University Press. Pp. 50–61.

Kwukmin Ilbo (online news) 국민일보. (2002, December 28). [사설] 인간복제, 보고만 있을 건가 Retrieved from: http://cafe426.daum.net/_c21_/bbs_search_read?grpid=4yxQ&fldid=Gn8k&contentval=0004qzzzzzzzzzzzzzzzzzzzzzzzzzz&nenc=&fenc=&q=&nil_profile=cafetop&nil_menu=sch_updw. Accessed May 31, 2013.

Labov, W. (1972a). *Language in the Inner City.* Philadelphia: University of Pennsylvania Press.

Labov, W. (1972b). *Sociolinguistic Patterns.* Philadelphia: University of Pennsylvania Press.

Labov, W. (1997). Some further steps in narrative analysis. *Journal of Narrative and Life History*, 7: 395–415.

Labov, W. (2010). Where should I begin? In D. Schiffrin and A. Nylund (Eds.), *Telling Stories: Language, Narrative, and Social Life.* Washington DC: Georgetown University Press. Pp. 7–22.

Labov, W. and Fanshell, D. (1977). *Therapeutic Discourse*. New York: Academic Press.

Labov, W. and Waletzky, J. (1968). Narrative analysis. In W. Labov, P. Cohen, C. Robins, and J. Lewis, (Eds.), *A Study of the Nonstandard English of Negro and Puerto Rican Speakers in New York City*. Pp. 286–338. New York: Columbia University.

Lakoff, R. (1973). *The logic of politeness: Or minding your P's and Q's.* In C. Corum, T.C. Smith-Stark, and A. Weieser (Eds.), *Papers from the Ninth Regional Meeting of the Chicago Linguistic Society.* Chicago: Chicago Linguistic Society. Pp. 292–305.

Lakoff, R. (1975). *Language and Women's Place*. New York: Harper and Row.

Lakoff, R. (1977). What you can do with words: Politeness, pragmatics, and performatives. In R. Rogers, R. Wall, and J. Murphy (Eds.), *Proceedings of the Texas Conference on Performatives, Presuppositions, and Implicature.* Arlington, VA: Center for Applied Linguistics.

Lakoff, R. (1989). The limits of politeness: Therapeutic and courtroom discourse. *Multilingua,* 8,2–3: 101–29.

Lakoff, R. and Ide, S. (Eds.). (2005). *Broadening the Horizon of Linguistic Politeness*. Amsterdam: John Benjamins.

Langacker, R. (1998), Conceptualization, symbolization, and grammar. In M. Tomasello (Ed.), *The New Psychology of Language.* Englewood, NJ: Lawrence Erlbaum. Pp. 1–33.

Langacker, R. (2008). *Cognitive Grammar: A Basic Introduction*. New York: Oxford University Press.

Larrain, A. and Haye, A. (2012). The discursive nature of inner speech. *Theory and Psychology*, 12: 3–22.

Larson, J. (1997). Indexing instruction: The social construction of the participation framework in Kindergarten journal-writing activity. *Discourse and Society,* 8,4: 501–21.

Lee, B. P. H. (2001). Mutual knowledge, background knowledge and shared beliefs: Their roles in establishing common ground. *Journal of Pragmatics* 33: 21–44.

Lee, D. Y. (2006). Patterns of temporal adverbials and their modification of verbs in complex sentences of Korean weather news. *Language Research*, 42,1: 99–123.

Leech, G. (1983). *Principles of Pragmatics*. London: Longman.

Le Parisien. (2011, March 3). Le 11 Mars 2011, 14h46: Un séisme et un tsunami dévastateurs frappent le Japon. Retrieved from: http://www.leparisien.fr/tsunami-pacifique/le-11-mars-2011-14h46-un-seisme-et-un-tsunami-devastateurs-frappent-le-japon-11-03-2011-1352998.php. Accessed May 21, 2013.

Lerner, G. (1996). On the "semi-permeable" character of grammatical units in conversation: Conditional entry into the turn space of another speaker. In E. Ochs, E. A. Schegloff, and S. A. Thompson (Eds.), *Interaction and Grammar*. Cambridge: Cambridge University Press. Pp. 238–76.

Lerner, G. (2003). Selecting next speaker: The context-sensitive operation of a context-free organization. *Language in Society*, 32: 177–201.

Lerner, G. (2004a). On the place of linguistic resources in the organization of talk-in-interaction: Grammar as action in prompting a speaker to elaborate. *Research on Language and Social Interaction,* 37,2: 151–84.

Lerner, G. (2004b). Collaborative turn sequences. In G. Lerner (Ed.), *Conversation Analysis: Studies from the First Generation*. Amsterdam: John Benjamins. Pp. 225–56.

Lerner, G. (2004c.). Introductory remarks. In G. Lerner (Ed.), *Conversation Analysis: Studies from the First Generation*. Amsterdam: John Benjamins. Pp. 1–11.

LeVine, A. (Director). (2002, September 16). Dr. Phil's first show [Television series episode]. In M. E. Glynn and C. Patrick (Producers), *Dr. Phil Show*. United States: CBS.

Levinson, S. (1983). *Pragmatics.* Cambridge: Cambridge University Press.

Levinson, S.(1988). Putting linguistics on a proper footing: Explorations in Goffman's participation framework. In P. Drew and A. Wootton (Eds.), *Goffman: Exploring the Interaction Order*. Oxford: Polity Press. Pp. 161–227.

Levinson, S. (1992). Activity types and language. In P. Drew and J. Heritage (Eds.), *Talk at Work: Interaction in Institutional Settings*. Cambridge University Press. Pp. 66–100.

Levinson, S. (2000). *Presumptive Meanings: The Theory of Generalized Conversational Implicature*. Cambridge, MA: MIT Press

Levinson, S. (2013). Action formation and ascription. In T. Stivers and J. Sidnell (Eds.), *The Handbook of Conversation Analysis*. Malden, MA: Wiley-Blackwell. Pp. 103–30.

Linde, C. (1993). *Life Stories: The Creation of Coherence*. Oxford: Oxford University Press.

Ling, R. and Baron, N. (2007). Text messaging and IM: Linguistic comparison of American college data. *Journal of Language and Social Psychology*, 26, 3: 291–98.

List of language regulators. (n.d.). In *Wikipedia*. Retrieved from: http://en.wikipedia.org/wiki/List_of_language_regulators. Accessed May 23, 2013.

Lo, A. (1999). Code-switching, speech community membership, and the construction of ethnic identity. *Journal of Sociolinguistics*, 3(4), 461–79.

Luke, A. (2002). Beyond science and ideology critique: Developments in critical discourse analysis. *Annual Review of Applied Linguistics*, 22: 96–110.

Lyons, J. (1977a). Deixis, space and time. *Semantics*, 2: 636–724.

Lyons, J. (1977b). *Semantics. Volume I.* Cambridge: Cambridge University Press.

Lyons, J. (1995). Grammar and meaning. In J. Palmer (Ed.), *Grammar and Meaning*. Cambridge: Cambridge University Press. Pp. 221–46.

MacFarlane, J. (2005). Making sense of relative truth. *Proceedings of the Aristotelian Society*, 105: 321–39.

Mao, L. (1994). Beyond politeness theory: "Face" revisited and renewed. *Journal of Pragmatics*, 21: 451–86.

Marcoccia, M. (2004). Online polylogues: Conversation structure and participation framework in internet news groups. *Journal of Pragmatics,* 36,1: 115–45.

Matosean, G. (1999). Intertexuality, affect, and ideology in legal discourse. *Text,* 19,1: 73–109.

Marti, L. (2006). Indirectness and politeness in Turkish-German bilingual and Turkish monolingual requests. *Journal of Pragmatics*, 38: 1836–69.

Martin, J. (2008a). *Genre Relations: Mapping Culture*. London: Equinox.

Martin, J. (2008b). Cohesion and texture. In D. Schiffrin, D. Tannen, and H. Hamilton (Eds.), *The Handbook of Discourse Analysis*. Malden, MA: Blackwell Publishing. Pp. 35–53.

Martino, J. (2012, October 6). Aspartame damages the brain at any dose. *Collective Evolution.* Retrieved from: http://www.collective-evolution.com/2012/10/06/aspartame-damages-the-brain-at-any-dose/. Accessed June 8, 2013.

Math Stories. (n.d.). House of math word problems for children. Retrieved from: *MathStories.com* website: http://www.mathstories.com/. Accessed May 23, 2013.

Matsumoto, Y. (1988). Reexamination of the universality of Face: Politeness phenomena in Japanese. *Journal of Pragmatics,* 12: 403–26.

Matsumoto, K. (2000). Japanese intonation units and syntactic structure. *Studies in Language*, 24, 3: 515–64.

Maynard, K. (2013). *Discourse Modality: Subjectivity, Emotion and Voice in the Japanese Language.* Amsterdam: John Benjamins.

Maynard, D. (2013)

Mayr, A. (2006). *Language and Power: An Introduction to Institutional Discourse*. London: Sage Publications.

Mayr, A. (2012). *The Language of Crime and Deviance: An Introduction to Critical Linguistics Analysis in Media and Popular Culture*. London: Sage Publications.

Mcgovern, A. (1993). *The Pilgrims' First Thanksgiving*. New York: Scholastic.

Meân, L. J. and Halone, K. K. (2010). Sport, language, and culture: Issues and intersections. *Journal of Language and Social Psychology*, 29,3: 253–60.

Mears, B. (2009). Obama re-takes oath of office at the White House. In *CNN Politics*. Retrieved from: http://politicalticker.blogs.cnn.com/2009/01/21/obama-re-takes-oath-of-office-at-the-white-house/. Accessed September 8, 2013.

Mehan, H. (1979). *Learning Lessons: Social Organization in the Classroom*. Cambridge, MA: Harvard University Press.

Mehan, H. (1985). The structure of classroom discourse. In T. van Dijk (Ed.), *Handbook of Discourse Analysis, Volume 3*. New York: Academic Press. Pp. 120–31.

Meinhof, U. H. and Smith, J. (Eds.). (2000). *Intertextuality and the Media: From Genre to Everyday Life.* Manchester: Manchester University Press.

Mey, J. (2001). *Pragmatics: An Introduction (Second Edition).* Malden, MA: Blackwell Publishers.

Merritt, M. (1976). On questions following questions. *Language in Society,* 5,3: 315–57.

Miller, C. R. (1984). Genre as social action. *Quarterly Journal of Speech,* 70: 151–67.

Molyneux, T. (2012, September 22). Federal law prohibits tampering with . . . In *Successful Workplace.* Retrieved from: http://successfulworkplace.com/2012/09/22/federal-law-prohibits-tampering-with/. Accessed May 25, 2013.

Mondada, L. (2006). Participants' online analysis and multimodal practices: Projecting the end of the turn and the closing of the sequence. *Discourse Studies*, 8,1: 117–29.

Mori, J. (2006). The workings of the Japanese token *hee* in informing sequences: An analysis of sequential context, turn shape, and prosody. *Journal of Pragmatics*, 38,8: 1178–205.

Mosher, B. and Connelly, J. (Writers) and Tokar, N. (Director). (1957). Captain Jack [Television series episode]. In J. Connelly and B. Mosher (Producers), *Leave it to Beaver.* Los Angeles, CA: Universal Studios.

Mushin, I. (2001). *Evidentiality and Epistemological Stance: Narrative Retelling.* Amsterdam: John Benjamins.

Myers-Scotton, C. (1988). Codeswitching as indexical of social negotatiation. In M. Heller (Ed.), *Codeswitching: Anthropological and Sociolinguistic Perspectives.* Berlin: Walter de Gruyter. Pp. 151–86.

National Geographic Kids. (2013). Real or fake? Tree octopus discovered. Issue 430: p. 27.

NBC Universal Media. (2012, June 7). Weather. In *NBC New York* website. Retrieved from: http://www.nbcnewyork.com/video/#!/weather/stories/Evening-Weather-for-Thursday--June-7/157929735. Accessed June 30, 2012.

Norrick, N. (2000). *Conversational narrative: Storytelling in everyday talk.* Amsterdam and Philadelphia: John Benjamins.

Norrick, N. (2012). Listening practices in English conversation: The responses responses elicit. *Journal of Pragmatics*, 44,5: 566–76.

Ochs, E. (1990). Indexicality and socialization. In J. Stigler, G. Herdt, and R. Shweder (Eds.), *Cultural Psychology: The Chicago Symposia*. Cambridge: Cambridge University Press. Pp. 287–308.

Ochs, E. (1992). Indexing gender. In A. Duranti and C. Goodwin (Eds.), *Rethinking Context: Language as an Interactive Phenomenon*. Cambridge: Cambridge University Press. Pp. 335–58.

Ochs, E. (1996). Linguistic resources for socializing humanity. In J. Gumperz and S. Levinson (Eds.), *Rethinking Linguistic Relativity*. Pp. 407–35.

Ochs, E. (2012). Experiencing language. *Anthropological Theory*, 12,2: 142–60.

Ochs, E. and Capps, L. (1996). Narrating the self. *Annual Review of Anthropology*, 25: 19–43.

Ochs, E. and Capps, L. (1999). Narrating lives in balance. *SALSA V: Proceedings of Symposium about Language and Society*. Austin, TX, 1997.

Ochs, E. and Capps, L. (2002). *Living Narrative: Creating Lives in Everyday Story-telling*. Boston: Harvard University Press.

Ochs, E., Schegloff, E., and Thompson, S. (Eds.). (1996). *Interaction and Grammar*. Cambridge: Cambridge University Press.

O'Keefe, A. (2006). *Investigating Media Discourse*. London: Routledge.

O'Keefe, B. (n.d.). Abercrombie & Fitch CEO Mike Jeffries: Stop telling teens they aren't beautiful; make clothes for teens of all sizes. In *Change.org* website. Retrieved from: http://www.change.org/petitions/abercrombie-fitch-ceo-mike-jeffries-stop-telling-teens-they-aren-t-beautiful-make-clothes-for-teens-of-all-sizes. Accessed May 12, 2013.

Ota, H., McCann, R., and Honeycutt, J. M. (2012). Inter-Asian variability in intergenerational communication. *Human Communication Research*, 38,2: 172–98.

Pagin, P. (2004). Is assertion social? *Journal of Pragmatics*, 36: 833–59.

Peräkylä, A. (1995). *AIDS Counseling: Institutional Interaction and Clinical Practice*. Cambridge: Cambridge University Press.

Philips, S. (1984). The social organization of questions and answers in courtroom discourse: The study of the changes of plea in an Arizona court. *Text*, 4,1–3: 225–48.

Pierce, C. (1931–36). *The Collected Papers*. Volumes 1–6. C. Hartshorne and P. Weiss (Eds.). Cambridge, M.A.: Harvard University Press.

Pierce, C. (1955). *Philosophical Writings of Pierce*. J. Buchler (Ed.). New York: Dover Publications.

Pinker, S. (1994). *The Language Instinct*. New York: Harper Perennial Modern Classics.

Plesser, R. and Heffernan, J. (n.d.). The spinning earth: Your world is tilted. In *Learn NC*. Retrieved from: http://www.learnnc.org/lp/editions/earth-sun/6572. Accessed February 3, 2013.

Plett, H. F. (1991). *Intertextuality.* Berlin, New York: W. de Gruyter.

Pomerantz, A. (1984). Agreeing and disagreeing with assessments: Some features of preferred/dispreferred turn shapes. In J. M. Atkinson and J. Heritage (Eds.), *Structures of Social Action*. Cambridge: Cambridge University Press. Pp. 57–101.

Pomerantz, A. and Denvir, P. (2007). Enacting the institutional role of chairperson in upper management meetings: The interactional realization of provisional authority. In F. Cooren (Ed.), *Interacting and Organizing: Analyses of a Management Meeting*. Mahwah, NJ: Lawrence Erlbaum Associates. Pp. 31–51.

Pomerantz, A., Gill, V. T., and Denvir, P. (2007). When patients present serious health conditions as unlikely: Managing potentially conflicting issues and constraints. In A. Hepburn and S. Wiggins (Eds.), *Discursive Research in Practice: New Approaches to Psychology and Interaction*. Cambridge: Cambridge University Press. Pp. 127–46.

Pomerantz, P. and Heritage, J. (2013). Preference. In J. Sidnell and T. Stivers (Eds.), *Handbook of Conversation Analysis*. Boston: Wiley–Blackwell. Pp. 210–28.

Preston, K. S. (2012, October 14). Dr. Phil dishes out advice right in your face. *USA Today*. Retrieved from: http://usatoday30.usatoday.com/life/2002-10-14-dr-phil-1acover_x.htm. Accessed May 22, 2013.

Prince, E. (1981). Toward a taxonomy of given/new information. In P. Cole (Ed.), *Radical Pragmatics*. New York: Academic Press. Pp. 223–54.

Prince, E. (1992). The ZPG letter: Subjects, definiteness, and information status. In S. Thompson and W. Mann (Eds.), *Discourse Description Diverse Analyses of a Fundraising Text*. Amsterdam and Philadelphia: John Benjamins. Pp. 295–325.

Puck, W. (n.d.). Recipes. In *Wolfgang Puck* website. Retrieved from: http://www.wolfgangpuck.com/recipes/search/results/Pizza. Accessed December 31, 2012.

Radden, G. and Dirven, R. (2007). *Cognitive English Grammar*. Amsterdam: John Benjamins Publishing Company.

Rae, J. (2001). Organizing participation in interaction: Doing participation framework. *Research on Language and Social Interaction,* 34,2: 253–78.

Rampton, B. (1995). *Crossing: Language and Ethnicity Among Adolescents*. London: Longman.

Rampton, B. (1998). Language crossing and the redefinition of reality: Expanding the agenda of research on code-switching.. In P. Auer (Ed.), *Code-switching in Conversation: Language, Interaction, and Identity.* London; Routledge. Pp. 290–317.

Reisigl, M. and Wodak, R. (2009). The discourse-historical approach. In R. Wodak and M. Meyer (Eds.), *Methods for Critical Discourse Analysis*. London: Sage. Pp. 87–121.

Revlon. (n.d.). *Jean Naté*. Retrieved from: http://www.revlon.com/Revlon-Home/Products/Fragrance/Jean-Nate/Jean-Nat%C3%A9-After-Bath-Splash-Mist-15-flpt-ozpt-443-mL.aspx. Accessed May 30, 2013.

Reuters. (2011, March 3). Un terremoto de magnitud 8.9 arrasa Japón y deja miles de muertos. In *El Mundo.* Retrieved from: http://www.elmundo.es/elmundo/2011/03/11/internacional/1299824643.html. Accessed May 22, 2013.

Rivière, V. (July 30, 2010). Ma liste des courses: épcerie, fruits et legumes. In *Journal des Femmes* (Women's Journal) website. Retrieved from: http://sante.journaldesfemmes.com/forme/regime/regime-citron/epicerie-fruits-et-legumes.shtml. Accessed May 23, 2013.

Roach, H. (Producer) and Parrott, J. (Director). (1932). *Helpmates* [Motion picture]. United States: Metro Goldwyn Mayer.

Robbins, B., Lowry, H., and Tollin, M. (Producers) and Gatins, J. (Director). (2005). *Dreamer: Inspired by a true story* [Motion picture]. United States: Dreamworks.

Robinson, J. (2008). Physician-Patient Interaction. In W. Donsbach (Ed.), *The International Encyclopedia of Communication*. Wiley Blackwell. Pp. 1396–400.

Robinson, J. (2011). Conversation analysis and health communication. In T. Thompson, A. Dorsey, K. Miller, and R. Parrott (Eds.), *Handbook of Health Communication* (2nd ed.). Mahwah, NJ: Lawrence Erlbaum. Pp. 501–518.

Robinson, J. and Kevoe-Feldman, H. (2010). Using full repeats to initiate repair on others' questions. *Research on Language and Social Interaction*, 43: 232–59.

Robinson, T. (2001). *The Everything Kids' Science Experiments Book.* Avon, MA: Adams Media Corporation.

Rogers, R. (2002). A critical discourse analysis of the special education process. *Anthropology and Education Quarterly*, 33,2: 213–37.

Rogers, R. (2004). Discursive alignment and conflict in social transformation. In R. Rogers (Ed.), *New Directions in Critical Discourse Analysis*. Mahwah, NJ: Lawrance Erlbaum Associates. Pp. 51–78.

Rogers, R. and Christian, J. (2007). "What could I say?" A critical discourse analysis of the construction of race in children's narratives. *Race, Ethnicity, and Education*, 10,1: 21–46.

Rombauer, I. S. and Becker, M. R. (1931/1997). *The Joy of Cooking*. New York: Penguin Putnam, Inc.

Rosaldo, M. Z. (1973). I have nothing to hide: The language of the Ilongot Oratory. *Language in Society*, 2: 193–224.

The Royal Bank of Scotland. (2004, September). Do I? [TV Commercial]. Retrieved from: http://www.youtube.com/watch?v=cVcZDSlvhgs. Accessed May 20, 2013.

Rusieshvili, M. (2011). Modes of address between female staff in Georgian professional discourse: Medical and academic contexts. In F. Bargiela-Chiappini and D. Kádár (Eds.), *Politeness Across Cultures*. New York: Palgrave Macmillian. Pp. 149–80.

Sacks, H. (1984). On doing "being ordinary." In J. Atkinson and J. Heritage (Eds.), *Structures of Social Action: Studies on Conversation Analysis*. Cambridge: Cambridge University Press. Pp. 413–29.

Sacks, H. (1987). Conversation analysis as discipline. In G. Lerner (Ed.), *Conversation Analysis: Studies From the First Generation*. Amsterdam: John Benjamins.

Sacks, H., Schegloff, E., and Jefferson, G. (1974). A simplest systematics for the organization of turn-taking for conversation. *Language* 50,4: 696–735.

Sadock, J. (1974). *Toward a Linguistic Theory of Speech Acts*. New York: Academic Press.

Sagan, C. (1995). *The Demon-Haunted World: Science as a Candle in the Dark*. New York: Random House.

Sapir, E. (1921/2011). *Language: An Introduction to the Study of Speech*. Charleston, SC: Nabu Press.

Sauerland, U. and Stateva, P. (Eds.). (2007). *Presupposition and Implicature in Compositional Semantics*. Houndsmills, Basingstoke, Hampshire: Palgrave Macmillan.

Sbisa, M. (2001). Illocutionary force and degrees of strength in language use. *Journal of Pragmatics*, 33,12: 1791–814.

Schegloff, E. (1980). Preliminaries to preliminaries: "Can I ask you a question?" ' *Sociological Inquiry,* 50: 104–52.

Schegloff, E. (1984). On some questions and ambiguities in conversation. In J. M. Atkinson and J. Heritage (Eds.), *Structures of Social Action*. Cambridge, Cambridge University Press. Pp. 28–52.

Schegloff, E. (1988a). Presequences and indirection: Applying speech act theory to ordinary conversation. *Journal of Pragmatics*, 12: 55–62.

Schegloff, E. (1992). To Searle on conversation. A note in return. In H. Parret & J. Verschueren (Eds.), *(On) Searle on Conversation*. Amsterdam: John Benjamins. Pp. 113–28.

Schegloff, E. (2000). Overlapping talk and the organization of turn-making for conversation. *Language in Society,* 29,1: 1–63.

Schegloff, E. (2007). *Sequence Organization in Interaction: A Primer in Conversation Analysis I*. Cambridge, England: Cambridge University Press.

Schegloff, E. A., Jefferson, G., and Sacks, H. (1977). The preference for self-correction in the organisation of repair in conversation. *Language*, 53: 361–82.

Schiffrin, D. (1994). Making a list. *Discourse Processes*, 17: 377–408.

Schiffrin, D. (1996). Narrative as self portrait: The sociolinguistic construction of identity. *Language in Society*, 25,2: 167–203.

Schiffrin, D. (2006). From linguistic reference to social reality. In A. de Fina, D. Schiffrin, and M. Bamberg (Eds.), *Discourse and Identity.* Cambridge, UK: Cambridge University Press.

Scott, J.C. (1990). *Domination and the Arts of Resistance.* New Haven, CT: Yale University Press.

Searle, J. (1969). *Speech Acts*. Cambridge: Cambridge University Press.

Searle, J. (1975). Indirect speech acts. In P. Cole and J. Morgan (Eds.), *Syntax and Semantics, 3: Speech Acts*. New York: Academic Press. Pp. 59–82.

Searle, J. (1976). A classification of illocutionary acts. *Language in Society*, 5: 1023. Pp. 10–23.

Searle, J. (1979). *Expression and Meaning*. Cambridge: Cambridge University Press.

Searle, J. and Vanderveken, D. (1985). *Foundations of Illocutionary Logic*. Cambridge: Cambridge University Press.

Sephora. (n.d.). *Coach Signature*. Retrieved from: http://www.sephora.com/signature-P259929. Accessed May 23, 2013.

Shoaps, R. (2009). Moral irony and moral personhood in Sakapultek discourse and culture. In A. Jaffe (Ed.), *Stance: Sociolinguistic Perspectives*. Oxford: Oxford University Press. Pp. 92–118.

Sidnell, J. (2008). Alternate and complementary perspectives on language and social life: The organization of repair in two Caribbean communities. *Journal of Sociolinguistics*, 12,4: 477–503.

Sidnell, J. (2010a). The design and positioning of questions in inquiry testimony. In A. Freed and S. Erlich (Eds.), *Why do you ask?: The Function of Questions in Institutional Discourse.* Oxford: Oxford University Press. Pp. 17–41.

Sidnell, J. (2010b). *Conversation Analysis: An Introduction*. Malden, MA: Blackwell-Wiley.

Sidnell, J. and Stivers, T. (Eds.). (2013). *The Handbook of Conversation Analysis*. Malden, MA: Blackwell-Wiley.

Silverstein, M. (1976). Shifters, linguistic categories, and cultural description. In K. Basso and H. Selby (Eds.), *Meaning in Anthropology*. University of New Mexico Press. Pp. 11–55.

Silverstein, M. (1996). Indexical order and the dialectics of sociolinguistic life: In R. Ide, R. Parker, and Y. Sunaoshi (Eds.), *Third Annual Symposium About Language and Society, Austin*. Austin: University of Texas, Department of Linguistics. Pp. 266–95.

Silverstein, M. (2003). Indexical Order and the Dialectics of Sociolinguistic Life. *Language and Communication*, 23,3–4: 193–229.

Sina. (n.d.). 《仙台沉没.》 Retrieved from: http://news.sina.com.cn/c/2011-03-12/053222099634.shtml. Accessed May 23, 2013.

Sinclair, J. (1987). Classroom discourse: Progress and prospects. *RELC Journal*, 18,2: 1–14.

Singh, H., Kaur, P., and Thavamalar, T. (2011). Language for reconciliation in religious discourse: A critical discourse analysis of contradictions in sermons explored through the activity theory framework. *Multilingua,* 30,3–4: 391–404.

Soffer, O. (2012). Liquid language? On the personalization of discourse in the digital era. *Media and Society,* 14,7: 1092–110.

Southern Weekend 南方周末 online newspaper. (2012, September 21). «钓鱼岛对中国意味着什么?»http://www.infzm.com/content/81146. Accessed May 23, 2013.

Sperber, D. and Wilson, D. (1986). *Relevance: Communication and Cognition*. Cambridge, MA: Harvard University Press.

Spillner, B. (1997). The weather report in daily newspapers. *Fachsprache* 19,1–2: 2–8.

Stalnaker, R. (1978). Assertion. In P. Cole (Ed.), *Syntax and Semantics 9*, New York: Academic Press. Pp. 315–32.

Staples. (n.d.). Just shake it [TV commercial]. Retrieved from: http://www.you tube.com/watch?v=8qCthZz9sj0. Accessed September 23, 2013.

Stivers, T. (2012). Physician-child interaction: When children answer physicians' questions in routine medical encounters. *Patient, Education and Counseling*, 87: 3–9.

Stratfor.com Geopolitical Weekly. (2012, September 25). Understanding the China-Japan island conflict. Retrieved from: http://www.stratfor.com/weekly/ understanding-china-japan-island-conflict. Accessed June 20, 2013.

Strauss, S. (1993). Why "this" and "that" are not complete without "it". In K. Beals et al. (Eds.), *Proceedings from the 29th Meeting of the Chicago Linguistic Society, CLS 29, volume 1: The Main Session.* CSLI, Stanford. Pp. 403–17.

Strauss, S. (1994). Earthquake data. Unpublished English and Korean oral narrative and conversation data on the topic of the 1994 Northridge, CA Earthquake.

Strauss, S. (1998). Hospital data. Unpublished English oral narrative and conversation between mother and daughter in intensive care unit.

Strauss, S. (2002). *This*, *that*, and *it* in Spoken American English: A demonstrative system of gradient focus. *Language Sciences,* 24: 131–52.

Strauss, S. (2013). Discourse Analysis. In Nussbaum, J. (Ed.), *Readings in Communication Research Methods, From Theory to Practice*. Pp. 121–35.

Strauss, S. and Eun, J. (2005). Indexicality and honorific speech level choice in Korean. *Linguistics,* 43: 611–651.

Strauss, S. and Feiz, P. (2012). Beyond alef , be, pe: The socialisation of incipient ideology through literacy practices in an Iranian first-grade classroom. *Language Awareness*: 1–23.

Streeck, J. (1980). Speech acts in interaction: A critique of Searle. *Discourse Processes*, 3: 133–54.

Stuart, Elliot. (2009, March 24). A strategy when times are tough: "It's new!" *The New York Times,* p. B3. Retrieved from: http://www.nytimes.com/2009/03/25/ business/media/25adco.html. Accessed September 24, 2013.

Suzuki, S. (Ed.). (2006). *Emotive Communication in Japanese*. Amsterdam: John Benjamins.

Swales, J. M. (1990). *Genre Analysis: English in Academic and Research Settings.* Cambridge: Cambridge University Press.

Swales, J. M. (2004). *Research Genres: Explorations and Applications*. Cambridge: Cambridge University Press.

Tajfel, H. (1981). *Human Groups and Social Categories: Studies in Social Psychology*. Cambridge: Cambridge University Press.

Tajfel, H. (1982/2010). *Social Identity and Intergroup Relations*. Cambridge: Cambridge University Press. Reissue edition.

Tannen, D. (2009). The dynamics of closeness/distance and sameness/difference in discourse about sisters. In B. Fraser and K. Turner (Eds.), *Language in life and a life in language: Jocob Mey—A Festschrift*. Bingley, UK: Emerald Group.

Tavakoli, M. and Ghadiri, M. (2011). An investigation into the argumentation in dialogic media genres: The case of sport talk show interviews. *Discourse and Communication*, 5,3: 273–88.

Think Quest. (n.d.). *Dolphins*. Retrieved from: http://library.thinkquest.org/3935/DOLPHINS.HTM. Accessed February 18, 2013.

Thorne, B. and Henley, N. (Eds.). (1975). *Language and Sex: Difference and Dominance*. Rowley, MA: Newbury House.

Tic-tac-toe. (n.d.). In *Wikipedia*. Retrieved from: http://en.wikipedia.org/wiki/Tic-tac-toe. Accessed February 23, 2013.

Tobacco packaging warning messages. (n.d.). In *Wikipedia*. Retrieved from: http://en.wikipedia.org/wiki/Tobacco_packaging_warning_messages. Accessed May 31, 2013.

Tomasello, M. (1998). Introduction. In M. Tomasello (Ed.), *The New Psychology of Language*: *Cognitive and Functional Approaches To Language Structure, Volume I*. Mahwah, New Jersey: Lawrence Erlbaum Associates. Pp. vii–xxiii.

Tovares, A. (2010). Managing the voices: Athlete self-talk as a dialogic process. *Journal of Language and Social Psychology*, 29,3: 261–77.

Treichler, P. A. Frankel, R. M., Kramarae, C., Zoppi, K., and Beckman, H. B. (1984). Problems and problems: power relationships in a medical encounter. In C. Kramarae, M. Schulz, W. O'Barr (Eds.), *Language and Power*. Beverly Hills, CA: Sage. Pp. 62–88.

Tseng, M. Y. (2010). Analyzing the discourse of job-application videos: Performance and relevance. *Text & Talk*, 30,5: 571–89.

UCLA ORL [Office of Residential Life]. (n.d.). Moving in and adjusting. *UCLA ORL* website. Retrieved from: https://www.orl.ucla.edu/parents/moving. Accessed April 10, 2013.

University Counseling and Testing Center. (n.d.). How to cope with homesickness. *University of Oregon* website. Retrieved from: http://counseling.uoregon.

edu/dnn/SelfhelpResources/Transitions/HowtoCopewithHomesiIckness/ tabid/368/Default.aspx. Accessed May 25, 2013.

United States District Court—Middle District of Pennsylvania. (n.d.). *Jury FAQs: Most frequently asked jury questions.* Retrieved from: http://www.pamd. uscourts.gov/?q=jury-faqs. Accessed September 24, 2013.

U.S. Marine Corps. (n.d. a). *Physical prep.* Retrieved from: http://www.marines. com/becoming-a-marine/ocs-physical-prep. Accessed December 31, 2012.

U.S. Marine Corps. (n.d. b). *First to fight.* Retrieved from: http://www.marines. com/operating-forces/first-to-fight/. Accessed May, 21, 2012.

Van Buren, A. (2013, May 20). GED hopefuls should get diploma before costs go up. In *Yahoo News.* Retrieved from: http://news.yahoo.com/g-e-d-hopefuls-diploma-costs-050115801.html. Accessed May 20, 2013.

van Dijk, T. (1977). Context and cognition: Knowledge frames and speech act comprehension. *Journal of Pragmatics*, 1,3: 211–33.

van Dijk, T. (1984). *Prejudice in Discourse*. Amsterdam: John Benjamins.

van Dijk, T. (1987). *Communicating Racism: Ethnic Prejudice in Thought and Talk*. Beverly Hills, CA: Sage Publications.

van Dijk, T. (1988). *News as Discourse.* Hillsdale, NJ: Erlbaum.

van Dijk, T. (1991). *Racism and the Press*. London: Routledge.

van Dijk, T. (1993a). *Elite Discourse and Racism*. Newbury Park, CA: Sage Publications..

van Dijk, T. (1993b). Principles of critical discourse analysis. *Discourse and Society,* 4,2: 249–83.

van Dijk, T. (2006). Discourse and manipulation. *Discourse Studies,* 17,3: 359–83.

van Dijk, T. (2011). Introduction: Discourse as interaction in society. In T. van Dijk (Ed.), *Discourse Studies: A Multidisciplinary Approach*. London: Sage Publications. Pp. 1–37.

van Dijk, T. (Ed.). (2011). *Discourse Studies: A Multidisciplinary Approach*. London: SAGE.

van Eemeren, F. and Grootendorst, R. (1984). *Speech Acts in argumentative discussions: A theoretical model for the analysis of discussions directed towards Solving Conflicts of Opinion*. Dordrecht: Floris Publications.

van Eemeren, F. and Grootendorst, R. (2004). *A Systematic Theory of argumentation: The pragma-Dialectical approach*. Cambridge: Cambridge University Press.

van Leeuwen, T. (1993). Genre and field in critical discourse analysis. *Discourse and Society*, 4,2: 193–223.

van Leeuwen, T. (1995). Representing social action. *Discourse and Society*, 6,1: 81–106.

van Leeuwen, T. (1999). *Speech, Music, and Sound*. Basingstoke: Macmillan.

van Lier, L. (1996). *Interaction in the Language Curriculum*. London: Longman.

Vannini, P. and McCright, A. (2007). Technologies of the sky: A socio-semiotic and critical analysis of televised weather discourse. *Critical Discourse Studies*, 4,1: 49–73.

Vigouroux, C. (2010). Double-mouthed discourse: Interpreting, framing, and participant roles. *Journal of Sociolinguistics*, 14,3: 341–69.

Vygotsky, L. (1968). *Mind in Society.* Cambridge, MA: Harvard University Press.

Vygotsky, L. S. (1986). *Thought and Language.* Translated by A. Kozulin. Cambridge, MA: The MIT Press.

Xinhuanet News (2012, September 25). Diaoyu Islands are China's inherent territory [White paper]. Retrieved from: http://news.xinhuanet.com/2012-09/25/c_113202698_2.htm.

wa Thiong'o, N. (2004). Recovering the original. In W. Lesser (Ed.), *The Genius of Language.* New York: Anchor Books. Pp. 102–10.

Walnut Valley Water District. (n.d.). *How to turn off your water*. Retrieved from: http://www.wvwd.com/index.php?option=com_content&view=article&id=33&Itemid=28. Accessed February 20, 2013.

Walters, G. (Producer) and Stanton, A. and Unkrich, L. (Directors). (2003). *Finding Nemo* [Motion picture]. United States: Walt Disney Pictures, Pixar Animation.

Ward, G. and Birner, B. (1994). A unified account of English fronting constructions. *Penn Working Papers in Linguistics,* Vol. 1, Department of Linguistics, University of Pennsylvania. Pp. 159–165.

Ward, G. and Birner, B. (2011). Discourse effects of word order variation. In K. von Heusinger, C. Maienborn, and P. Portner (Eds.), *Semantics: An International Handbook of Natural Language Meaning*. Berlin/Boston: Mouton de Gruyter. Pp. 1934–63.

Watson, G. (2004). Asserting and Promising. *Philosophical Studies*, 117: 57–77.

Watts, R. (2003). *Politeness.* Cambridge: Cambridge University Press.

Wei, L. (2011). Moment Analysis and translanguaging space: Discursive construction of identities by multilingual Chinese youth in Britain. *Journal of Pragmatics*, 43,5: 1222–35.

Wharry, C. (2003). Amen and hallelujah preaching: Discourse functions in African American sermons. *Language in Society*, 32,2: 203–25.

Widdowson, H. (1995). Discourse analysis: A critical view. *Language and Literature*, 4,3: 157–72.

Widdowson, H. (1996). Reply to Fairclough: Discourse and interpretation: Conjectures and refutations. *Language and Literature*, 5,1: 57–69.

Widdowson, H. (2004). *Text, Context, Pretext: Critical Issues in Discourse*. Oxford: Blackwell Publishing.

Wierzbicka, A. (2003). *Cross-Cultural Pragmatics: The Semantics of Human Interaction*. Berlin: Mouton de Gruyter.

Wiesenthal, S. (1976). *The Sunflower: On the Possibilites and Limits of Forgiveness*. New York: Schocken Books.

Williams, M. (2012). Reimagining NASA: A cultural and visual analysis of the U.S. space program. *Journal of Business and Technical Communication*, 26,3: 368–89.

Wilson, C. (2013, February 13). An artist finds a dignified ending for an ugly story. *The New York Times,* p. C1. Retrieved from: http://www.nytimes.com/2013/02/12/arts/design/julia-pastrana-who-died-in-1860-to-be-buried-in-mexico.html?pagewanted=all&_r=0. Accessed February 14, 2013.
Wodak, R. (Ed.). (1989). *Language, Power, and Ideology: Studies in Political Discourse*. Amsterdam: John Benjamins.

Wodak, R. (1990). Discourse analysis: Problems, findings, perspectives. *Text,* 1–2: 125–32.

Wodak, R. (1996). *Disorders of Discourse*. London: Longman.

Wodak, R. (1997). *Gender and Discourse*. London: Sage.

Wodak, R. (2001). The discourse historical approach. In R. Wodak, and M. Meyer (Eds.), *Methods of Critical Discourse Analysis.* London: Sage. Pp. 63–95.

Wodak, R. (2009a). *The Discourse of Politics in Action*. Basingstoke, UK: Palgrave Macmillan.

Wodak, R. (2009b). The semiotics of racism: A critical discourse-historical analysis. In J. Renkema (Ed.), *Discourse, of course: an overview of research in discourse studies.* Amsterdam: Benjamins. Pp. 311–26.

Wodak, R. (2011a). Critical discourse analysis. In K. Hyland and B. Paltridge (Eds.), *Continuum Companion to Discourse Analysis.* London: Continuum. Pp. 38–53.

Wodak, R. (2011b). Suppression of the Nazi past, coded languages and discourses of silence: Applying the discourse historical approach to post-war anti-Semitism in Austria. In W. Steinmetz (Ed.), *Political Languages in the Age of the Extremes*. Oxford: Oxford University Press.

Wodak, R., De Cillia, R., Reisigl, M., and Liebhart, M. (2009). *The Discursive Construction of National Identity* (2nd ed.). Edinburgh: Edinburgh University Press.

Wodak, R., Kryzanowski, M., and Forchtner, B. (2012). The interplay of language ideologies and contextual cues in multilingual interactions: Language choice and code-switching in European Union institutions. *Language in Society*, 41,2: 157–86.

Wodak, R. and Meyer, M. (2009). *Methods for Critical Discourse Analysis*. London: Sage.

Waring, H.Z. (2008). Using explicit positive assessment in the language classroom: IRF, feedback, and learning opportunities. *Modern Language Journal*, 92: 577–94.

Young, R. and Lee, G. (2004). Identifying units in interaction: Reactive tokens in Korean and English conversations. *Journal of Sociolinguists,* 8,3: 380–407.

Yu, M. (2003). On the universality of face: Evidence from Chinese compliment response behavior. *Journal of Pragmatics*, 35: 1679–710.

Yu, M. (2011). Learning how to read situations and know what is the right thing to say or do in an L2: A study of socio-cultural competence and language transfer. *Journal of Pragmatics*, 43,4: 1127–47.

Yus, F. (2003). Humor and the search for relevance. *Journal of Pragmatics*, 35,9: 1295–331.

Yus, F. (2008). A Relevance-Theoretic classification of jokes. *Lodz Papers in Pragmatics*, 4,1: 131–57.

Zimmerman, D. (1993). Acknowledgment Tokens and Speakership Incipiency Revisited. *Research on Language and Social Interaction,* 26,2: 179–94.

Zyrtec. (n.d.). Powerful allergy relief [TV commercial]. Retrieved from: http://www.youtube.com/user/zyrtec?v=wpXmnteG9Xs. Accessed September 24, 2013.

Appendix

Basic Grammatical Categories

Here we provide an overview of some of the basic categories of grammar that will be useful in the analysis of English discourse.[1] These categories are:

nouns and noun phrases
pronouns
adjectives
verbs (verb types)
modals
tense and aspect
adverbs

I. NOUNS AND NOUN PHRASES

Nouns are words that designate things, people, ideas, concepts, and places. Nouns are typically divided into two basic categories:

Proper Nouns and Common Nouns

Proper Nouns are specific names of people, places, eras, businesses, schools, places of worship, sports complexes, companies, planets, months of the year, days of the week, and titles (of books, movies, articles, chapters). Proper nouns are graphically represented in English with an upper-case letter at the beginning of that name: Japan, MacDonald's, Xerox, Harvard, California, Jupiter, Saturday, King Tut, George Washington, Buffalo, Kalamazoo,

August, Lord of the Rings, Temple Aliyah, Our Lady of Victory, Wikipedia, The Ice Age, Apple, Independence Day, Wednesday, Beyoncé.

Common Nouns are nouns that are not specific names. If a noun is not a proper noun, it is common. Examples include: buffalo, apple, place, person, boy, female, desk, hat, chair, furniture, mahogany, heat, light, coffee, blunder, deed, purpose, pleasure, garden, freedom, battle, peace, computer, contractor, architect, blueprint, umbrella, gloom, brightness, daylight, itch, desire.

Common nouns are further broken down into two more basic categories, **count nouns** and **non-count (or mass) nouns.**[2]

The category **count noun** pertains to common nouns that can be "counted" or made plural. Most nouns in English are of this type. Most can be made plural by simply adding the regular plural marker –s.

misdeed	a misdeed	several misdeed**s** ← plural –s
award	an award	five award**s**
boat	one boat	a few boat**s**
door	a door	door**s**

Other examples of count nouns are: boy, girl, sled, airplane, pebble, brick, hormone, atom, meteor, transaction, club, banana, letter, world, place, planet, chair, screen, palette, color, hue.

Count nouns with irregular plural markers include: tooth (teeth), child (children), man (men), goose (geese), spectrum (spectra), datum (data), criterion (criteria), mouse (mice), knife (knives), ox (oxen), locus (loci).

The category **non-count noun** pertains to common nouns that are typically not counted or made plural in English. We provide example sets here, in three categories.

A. Rarely, if Ever, Made Plural in English

singular form	plural form (not grammatical)
luggage	*luggages
advice	*advices
information	*informations
furniture	*furnitures
transportation	*transportations
stuff	*stuffs
garbage	*garbages
evidence	*evidences

B. Nouns Used as Mass Nouns or Count Nouns

Mass, as *substance* or *abstract concept*	Count, *bounded in containers* or referring to *distinct types of things*
water	two waters
coffee	three coffees
pudding	two puddings
meat	meats of the world
freedom	First Amendment freedoms
death	pollution contributed to nearly 12,700 deaths . . .
honor	graduated with honors
hope	high hopes

C. Mass Nouns Designated With Partitives

bread	a <u>loaf</u>, a <u>slice</u> of bread
sand	a <u>grain</u> of sand
flour	a <u>cup</u> of flour
advice, information	a <u>piece</u> of advice, a <u>piece</u> of information
luggage	a <u>piece</u> of luggage
transportation	a <u>vehicle</u> of transportation
oil	How many <u>barrels</u> of oil are consumed in a day?

Noun Phrases

Basically, a noun phrase in English refers to the main noun (or head noun) and all other words that precede that noun to modify it. A very simple one-word noun modifier is a determiner. Examples include *a, the, my, his, such, this, that, these, many, much, some* (See Chapter 4 on Reference for a more complete discussion on the conceptual meanings expressed by the wide array of possible determiners in noun phrases).

Determiner	Noun
the	dean
a	rhinoceros
this	pit bull
some	reports

| that | research |
| Ø | bullying (e.g., Stop Ø bullying cf. Stop the bullying) |

Now, having just introduced some distinctions between count nouns and mass nouns, we can also see that the choice of certain determiners is often influenced conceptually by the type of noun that it co-occurs with.

One such example involves the determiners *many* and *much*.

Many **with plural count nouns:**	*Much* **with singular mass nouns:**
many lives	much life
many suitcases	much luggage
many utensils	much flatware
many innovative ideas	much despair
many ways to win	much uranium
many children with high IQ	much influence

II. PRONOUNS

Pronouns are words that take the place of nouns. In the case of *I, we*, and *you*, the pronouns designate the speaking/writing entity (I) or the recipient or addressee of the message (you), and don't necessarily replace other full nouns, as is the case with third person referents (*he, she, it, they, them, his, hers*, and so forth). The general lists of subject, object, and possessive pronouns for English are as follows:

English Subject Pronouns

I	first-person singular	we	1st person plural
you	second-person singular	you, you all	2nd person plural
he, she, it	third-person singular	they	3rd person plural

English Object Pronouns

me	first-person singular	us	1st person plural
you	second-person singular	you, you all	2nd person plural
him, her, it	third-person singular	them	3rd person plural

English Possessives

Determiner	Pronoun
my	mine
your	your

his, her, its	his, hers
our	ours
your	yours
their	theirs

Examples

subject:	<u>She</u> went to Paris.
object:	We saw <u>her</u> at the conference last year.
possessive determiner:	<u>Her</u> son is an engineer.
possessive pronoun:	The fingerprint on the weapon was not <u>hers</u>.

III. VERBS (LEXICAL VERBS AND AUXILIARY VERBS)

A lexical verb is the category of grammar or part of speech that provides three different, but related types of information concerning the subject of the sentence: 1) the subject performs an action, 2) the subject is in a particular state of being, 3) the subject is simply linked to something else—typically, another noun or an adjective. These three functions of verbs are often described as:

action verbs:　designate dynamicity or movement
　run, study, examine, observe, analyze, conclude, participate, jump, compete

stative verbs:　designate stativity, lack of movement, automaticity
　remain, contain, persist, love, involve, include, know, believe, understand

copular verbs:　links a subject noun or pronoun to another noun or adjective
　be, appear, seem, become, taste, smell, grow

<u>**Examples:**</u>	A tulip **is** a bulbous plant.	[copula: be]
	If the gravy **tastes** salty. Add potato.	[copula: taste]
	Does your basement **smell** musty?	[copula: smell]
	Marvin **grew** bored of her antics.	[copula: grow]

Verbs can also be divided into three other basic categories: **transitive verbs, ditransitive verbs**, and **intransitive verbs**.

Transitive verbs	Ditransitive verbs	Intransitive verbs
take a direct object	take direct AND indirect objects	cannot take a direct object
eat	*give*	*contain*
drink	*send*	*happen*
read	*offer*	*sleep*
write	*donate*	*arrive*
explore		*sit*
devour		
hunt		*lie*
strike		*emerge*
understand		*appear*
hit		*seem*
tap		*laugh*
paint		*daydream*
draw		*rise*
trust		*fall*

Some verbs can be either transitive or intransitive, depending upon the conceptualization of the event.

divide, freeze, explode, cook, bake, smoke, float, move, run, walk, twirl, spin, taste, grow, smell

Examples:

Transitive:	Her son **found** <u>a five dollar bill</u> at the grocery store.
	verb <u>direct object</u>
Ditransitive:	The kids **mailed** <u>their package to Grandma</u> on Saturday.
	verb <u>direct object indirect object</u>
Intransitive:	And then a deer suddenly **appears** out of nowhere.
	verb

Verbs that can be either transitive or intransitive:

Should married couples **divide** <u>their money</u>?	Transitive
(direct object)	
Why do cells **divide**? (no direct object possible)	Intransitive
Jason only **smokes** <u>cigars and pipes</u>.	Transitive
(direct object)	

Why does my lawn mower **smoke**? (no direct object possible)   Intransitive

Can anyone learn to **taste** <u>wine</u>?   Transitive

(direct object)

Do all red wines **taste** the same? (no direct object possible)   Intransitive

An **auxiliary verb** is a small set of verbs that co-occur with lexical verbs to express aspect (see IV) and modality. The most common auxiliary verbs in English are *be* and *have*. Modals (see VI) are a separate class of auxiliary verbs that express other meanings beyond aspect (e.g., obligation, permission, degrees of certainty, etc.)

Subject-verb agreement

In English, subjects and verbs agree in terms of person (i.e., First, Second, Third) and number (singular or plural).

Subject-verb agreement is only grammatically visible in four general cases:

1. Irregular verb *be* in both present and past tenses:

    Present tense forms: *am, is, are*

I am	we are
you are	you are
he, she, it is	they are

    Past tense forms: *was, were*

I was	we were
you were	you were
he, she, it was	they were

2. Irregular verb *have* in present tense only:

    Present tense forms: *have, has*

I have	we have
you have	you have
he, she, it has	they have

3. Irregular verb ***do*** in present tense only:

    Present tense forms: *do, does*

I do	we do
you do	you do
he, she, it does	they do

4. Verbs with third-person singular subjects in the present tense, visible through the final –s. Most regular verbs pattern this way:

read, write, tell, invest, withdraw, divide, pretend, animate, populate, compute, ride, sell, prepare, understand, perpetuate, draw, create, report

Examples: (the verbs are marked in boldface, the final –s is underlined for emphasis)

My 10-year old is one of those people who **reads** dictionaries for fun.

Oxygen **combines** with nearly all other elements in the periodic table.

Colorado **Elects** First Gay House Speaker

Jupiter **travels** at a rate of about 29,000 miles per hour.

Voice: Active Voice and Passive Voice

Active voice: The subject in the sentence is the *agent* or *doer* of the action.

Charles Darwin [subject] **discovered** [transitive verb] new species of finches [object] on the Galapagos Islands.

Passive voice: What used to be the **object of that transitive verb** now becomes the SUBJECT of the sentence, in passive voice. What used to be the subject of the sentence **with a transitive verb** in the active voice is now mentioned as the "agent" with a by-phrase—or not mentioned at all in the sentence.

New species of finches **were discovered**   **[by Charles Darwin]** on the Galapagos Islands.

[SUBJECT]   [passivized transitive verb]   [AGENT—optional]

IV. TENSE AND ASPECT

TENSE refers to how users of language indicate time of events or states or activities. English has two simple tenses: present tense and past tense. Future tense is expressed in English by the modal *will* or through other grammatical means, e.g., simple present, present progressive aspect, etc.

Present tense denotes an action or state that is current, regular, time-less, a synopsis of events, or set to occur in the future.

Examples:

Every fall, some trees **lose** their leaves.	[timelessly true]
The fur of a polar bear **looks** white because each hair is hollow.	[timelessly true]
We **eat** at Bobby's almost every Saturday night.	[regular occurrence]
Marilyn: The Exhibit is now at the Hollywood Museum.	[current]
"Sixty Years Later: Sarah's story **intertwines** with that of Julia Jarmond, an American journalist investigating the roundup [and arrest of Jewish people by the French police]. In her research, Julia **stumbles** onto a trail of secrets that link her to Sarah and to questions about her own romantic future." (Excerpted from the back cover of de Rosnay, 2007)	[event synopsis]
We **have** a test in Environmental Education tomorrow.	[set to occur in future]

Past tense denotes an action or state that is over and done with, that occurred regularly in the past and no longer holds, or that is an event that no longer has connection to or import with the present time. Past tense can also be used to express hypothetical or counterfactual situations when used with conditional "if."

Examples:

Jascha Heifitz **began** playing violin at age three.	[event is complete]
My string of good luck **started** after I **lost** my wallet.	[events are complete]
They **said** it **was** an old Dutch sailor who **saved** the town.	[events are complete]
"He **lay** on his tummy on a high table in the assembly hall with all the students and staff present. Two teachers **held** his head and legs and **pinned** him to the table and called him monkey, as the third whip **lashed** his buttocks." (wa Thiong'o, 2004: 102)	[events are complete]

How much would you weigh on the moon if you
weighed 100 pounds on Earth?   [hypothetical]

    Future tense points to an event or state that has not yet taken place. Future tense can also express predictions, especially with conditionals.

South Korea **will** host the 2018 Winter Olympic Games.   [not yet occurred]

If you make that noise, someone **will** think you are sick.   [not yet occurred]

What **will** you do during the break?   [not yet occurred]

    Aspect provides details about the unfolding of the event. Is the event or state currently underway, right as we speak? Was it taking place simultaneously with something else that was happening? Did the event happen prior to another event? Is there any connection between an event that has already happened and a later period in time? Could something have happened in the past and still be relevant now?

    Progressive aspect designates an event or state that is unfolding, as if right now, in front of our very eyes. Progressive aspect can be expressed with present, past, and future tense marking on its auxiliary verb **be.** Progressive aspect is formed with the auxiliary verb *be* plus the *present participle verb ending, -ing.*

Present Progressive: The cats **are fighting** on the front lawn!   [underway]

    Jason **is pretending** to be sick.   [underway]

    The kids **are watching** *Life of Pi*.   [underway]

    Locations nearby **are reporting** rain.   [underway]

Present Progressive can also express future time:

    What time **are** you **leaving**?   [future]

    They**'re predicting** rain for tonight.   [future]

and regular or habitual occurrences of a state or event, depicted as if currently ongoing and now underway:

    They**'re arguing** daily now.   [regularity]

Past Progressive: He **was explaining** the difference between apes and monkeys when the lights went out.   [underway in the past]

Future Progressive: We **will be stopping** in Rome to refuel.   [future]

Perfect aspect designates that an action that happened in the past is relevant to a later time. Perfect aspect can be expressed with present, past, and future tense markers on its auxiliary verb **have**. Perfect aspect is formed with the auxiliary verb *have* and the *past participle verb ending –ed* or *–en* (or irregular participles like *seen, gone, done, written*).

Present Perfect: I **have** finally **found** that health and happiness are more important than anything else.   [later relevance]

Guns **have** now **become** the topic of talk throughout the nation.   [later relevance]

Past Perfect is used to designate that an event in the past happened prior to the occurrence of a second event.

I heard about it [September 11] from a guy who is a local workman, works in the area. He **had** just **passed** by and **told** me he had seen it on television. So that's the first I heard.

(Chomsky, 2011: 13).   [prior past occurrence]

Future Perfect designates the prediction of the end of an event to the conclusion of a state by the time another event happens.

These faculty members **will have been teaching** at our university for 30 years when they receive their awards.   [future completion by the time another event takes place]

V. MODALS

Modals are auxiliary verbs that co-occur with lexical verbs to express permission, expectation, obligation, certainty, doubt, possibility, likelihood, and ability. Modals are not inflected for present tense (e.g., third-person singular –s) or past tense (typically –ed). They keep the identical form in every case of usage, regardless of the sentential subject or the tense.

Following is a common list of modals:

can, could, should, would, may, might, must, will

Can and *may* are often associated with permission.
Can is typically also associated with ability.
Would often designates a hypothetical or counterfactual situation.
May and *might* express diminished certainty.
Must expresses degrees of certainty and obligation.
Should expresses degrees of moral or behavioral expectations.
Will expresses future occurrences and states, predictions, or intentions.

Example:

Juror Information U.S. District Court For the Middle District of Pennsylvania Most Frequently Asked Questions

Can I postpone my jury service or be excused from serving?

If you want to postpone your service to a later date or be excused, you **must** make a request in writing to the jury office of the courthouse to which you have been summoned. You **must** describe the reasons you believe you **should** be postponed or excused and provide as much information as possible, including supporting documentation. The request **should** be received by the jury department at least five (5) business days before your term of service begins. You **may** also request a postponement or excuse via the court's website after you have completed your questionnaire.

(United States District Court—Middle District of Pennsylvania, n.d.)

VI. CONDITIONALS

Conditionals are similar to modals, in that they can, among other functions, express hypothetical situations. The most common conditional marker in English is "if."

The beginning words in each sentence all indicate "conditionality."

If you have any questions, please don't hesitate to contact me.
Should you have any questions, please don't hesitate to contact me.

Whenever you have any questions, please don't hesitate to contact me.
In the event that you have any questions, please don't hesitate to contact me.

VII. ADJECTIVES

Adjectives Describe Nouns

They can occur as one word: a <u>red</u> coat, that <u>scarlet</u> oak, her <u>serendipitous</u> finding, the <u>overwhelming</u> majority, a <u>small</u> amount.

They can also occur as strings of words: "The <u>Little Red</u> Hen," a <u>tall skinny iced sugar-free</u> mochaccino, The <u>round silver metallic color-coded</u> labels, a <u>spacious white three-story Tudor</u> mansion.

Placement of Adjectives

Adjectives can come **before the noun**, as in all of the previous examples, and in the following: a <u>tender, juicy</u> steak; <u>genetic</u> traits; <u>safe</u> sex; preventive medicine; five <u>golden</u> rings. This type of adjective is called an *attributive adjective*.

Adjectives can also be placed **following the copular verbs** *is, become, get, appear, seem, look, sound*, as in: the answer **is** <u>simple</u>, the results **are** <u>inconclusive</u>, I **got** <u>nervous</u> during the interview, your alibi **sounds** <u>watertight</u>. This type of adjective is called a *predicative adjective*.

Nouns can also function as adjectives when they precede other nouns:

Examples:

silver necklace	aircraft carrier	wedding dress
gene therapy	paper plate	coffee cup
lunch hour	bubble gum	school board
sea creature	cotton plantation	air conditioner
hand sanitizer	nerve ending	country bumpkin

Adjectives also appear in **comparative** forms (to compare two nouns to each other) and **superlative** forms (to compare three or more nouns or to designate an ultimate one from among an infinite number).

Regular comparatives and superlatives are formed by adding regular endings to the adjective (note spelling irregularities, e.g., final "e" is deleted, final "y" changes to "i," or the final consonant may double):

<u>base</u>	<u>comparative –er</u>	<u>superlative –est</u>
green	greener	greenest

small	smaller	smallest
large	larger	largest
simple	simpler	simplest
juicy	juicier	juiciest
thin	thinner	thinnest

For the case of *good*, the comparative form is *better* and the superlative form is *best*.

For the case of *bad,* the comparative form is *worse*, and the superlative form is *worst.*

VIII. ADVERBS

Adverbs are probably the part of speech that is the least easy to recognize. The most obvious sign of an adverb is the *–ly* at the end. We can make adjectives like *shy* into an adverb: *shyly. Furious* becomes *furiously. Realistic* becomes *realistically,* and so forth.

Forming adverbs from adjectives, then, using the *–ly* suffix is rather productive (note spelling irregularities):

happy	happily
fortunate	fortunately
eerie	eerily
factual	factually
obvious	obviously
blatant	blatantly
regular	regularly

BUT, there are so many other words that function as adverbs.

Some of these constructions *add* to the meaning of an adjective that they precede, like *very, extremely, exceedingly, really, horribly, awfully, quite, so.*

Some *diminish* the meanings of words that they describe, and are phrases (i.e., more than just one word), like *a little, a tad, a tiny bit, to some degree, to a limited degree, in some sense, just, only.*

Other adverbs describe: frequency: *often, every day, twice a week, bimonthly*; time: *today, yesterday, at 6:00 P.M ., before her husband returned, in May, until Dec. 31*; manner: *with sadness, gladly, with open arms, without looking, by himself*; direction: *to the North, upward, sideways, to the left, toward Palestine, into the clouds*; location: *outside the box, inside the Petri dish, behind closed doors, underneath, in Rome.*

IX. NOMINALIZATION

Nominalization refers to the process of creating nouns or noun phrases from other parts of speech, such as verbs and adjectives.

For example:

verbs can be nominalized:

Scientists **created** artificial blood (VERB)
The creation of artificial blood led to. . . .
(NOMINALIZATION from verb)

adjectives can be nominalized:
K2 is one of **the steepest** mountains to climb. (ADJECTIVE)
K2's **steepness** makes it one of the most difficult mountains to climb.
(NOMINALIZATION from adjective)

X. NON-DEMONSTRATIVE USES OF "THAT"

"That" can serve as a demonstrative determiner ("**that** sort of result") or demonstrative pronoun ("He is always negatively affected by **that**").

The word "that" is also used in English as a relative pronoun:

Dean Knott is the most heartless administrator **that** the College of
Engineering has seen.

"That" is also used as a complementizing element in reporting information:

Some experts claim **that** aspartame has no adverse effects on humans.
The New York Times reported this morning **that** a special meeting of the
shareholders will take place on Tuesday morning. . . .

NOTES

1. The grammatical categories provided here are basic and foundational. An understanding of grammar at this level is minimally required for a deep understanding of discourse.
2. Each language has its own system for accounting for count and non-count sorts of distinctions. Some languages do not pattern in this way (e.g., Korean, Chinese, Japanese, Persian).

Index

231, 232, 234, 236; subject-verb
agreement 393–4; tense 27–9,
394–6; transitive 25–7, 37–9,
391–3; voice 394
vergictives 234
viewpoint 62–3
vision 154–5
vocalic alterations 47n1
vocalizations: lexical 189; non-lexical
189
voice 394
volume 47n1

warning messages 253–4, 332
Watts, R. 250–1

weather reports 78–84, 86
wh-questions 219n5
Wittgenstein, L. 263n3
Wodak, R. 325, 327–8
words: choice of 3, 17, 124; as
conceptual 314; in discourse 10;
meaning of 14–15, 75
written discourse 47n1, 50, 65,
67–72
written modalities 63–5, 70–2
written register 66

you 112–13

zero article 140